ANCIENT EMPIRES: *From Mesopotamia to the Rise of Islam*

Ancient Empires is a relatively brief yet comprehensive and evenhanded overview of the ancient Near East, the Mediterranean, and Europe, including the Greco-Roman world, Late Antiquity, and the early Muslim period. Taking a focused and thematic approach, it aims to provoke a discussion of an explicit set of themes supplemented by the reading of ancient sources. By focusing on empires and imperialism as well as on modes of response and resistance, it is relevant to current discussions about order, justice, and freedom. The book concludes that some of the ancient world's most enduring ideas, value systems, and institutions were formulated by peoples who were resisting the great empires. It analyzes the central, if problematic, connection between political and ideological power in both empire formation and resistance. The intricate inter-relations among ideological, economic, military, and political power are explored for every empire and resisting group.

Eric H. Cline is Associate Professor and the Chair of the Department of Classical and Near Eastern Languages and Civilizations at George Washington University. The author of more than eighty articles, his most recent books include *Biblical Archaeology: A Very Short Introduction* (2009) and *From Eden to Exile: Unraveling Mysteries of the Bible* (2008).

Mark W. Graham is Associate Professor in the Department of History at Grove City College, Pennsylvania. He has published numerous articles in scholarly journals and contributed chapters to several books, including *Encyclopedia of Greece and the Hellenic Tradition* (2000) and *Encyclopedia of the Empires of the World* (2011). Most recently, he authored *News and Frontier Consciousness in the Late Roman Empire* (2006).

ANCIENT EMPIRES

From Mesopotamia to the Rise of Islam

Eric H. Cline
George Washington University

Mark W. Graham
Grove City College

CAMBRIDGE
UNIVERSITY PRESS

CAMBRIDGE
UNIVERSITY PRESS

University Printing House, Cambridge CB2 8BS, United Kingdom

One Liberty Plaza, 20th Floor, New York, NY 10006, USA

477 Williamstown Road, Port Melbourne, VIC 3207, Australia

4843/24, 2nd Floor, Ansari Road, Daryaganj, Delhi - 110002, India

79 Anson Road, #06-04/06, Singapore 079906

Cambridge University Press is part of the University of Cambridge.

It furthers the University's mission by disseminating knowledge in the pursuit of education, learning and research at the highest international levels of excellence.

www.cambridge.org
Information on this title: www.cambridge.org/9780521717809

© Cambridge University Press 2011

First published 2011
Reprinted 2016

A catalogue record for this publication is available from the British Library

Library of Congress Cataloging in Publication data
Cline, Eric H.
Ancient empires : from Mesopotamia to the rise of Islam / Eric H. Cline, Mark W. Graham.
    p. cm.
Includes bibliographical references and index.
ISBN 978-0-521-88911-7 (hardback) – ISBN 978-0-521-71780-9 (paperback)
1. Civilization, Ancient.   2. Civilization, Classical.   3. Islamic civilization.
4. Imperialism.   I. Graham, Mark W., 1970–   II. Title.
CB311.C697   2011
930–dc22   2010048092

ISBN 978-0-521-88911-7 Hardback
ISBN 978-0-521-71780-9 Paperback

Dedicated to our families; to our students, past, present, and future; and to the whole IHUM gang.

CONTENTS

ILLUSTRATIONS

ACKNOWLEDGMENTS

The idea for this book emerged in the dynamic and innovative Introduction to the Humanities (IHUM) program at Stanford University in which both authors taught. Any similarities between this text and a certain team-taught Ancient Empires course in that program – originally designed by Ian Morris and Jennifer Trimble – are not "purely coincidental" at all, especially given that Ian Morris has kindly supported and encouraged this project from its inception. Other former IHUM colleagues on the Ancient Empires teaching team, particularly Emma Blake, Maura Heyn, and Cindy Nimchuk, will also note their influence on, respectively, portions of the early western Mediterranean, Palmyrene, and Achaemenid sections of the present text. A National Endowment for the Humanities Summer Seminar at the University of Chicago entitled "Culture and Communication in the Pre-Modern Islamic World" inspired Chapter Fourteen.

Chuck Dunn was the first to suggest that the Ancient World course at Grove City College, based roughly on Ancient Empires, should be turned into a textbook, and many others have since helped to develop the basic idea into this textbook. Beatrice Rehl's solid editorial guidance throughout has been indispensible, as have the critiques made by two rounds of excellent anonymous reviewers. Several friends and colleagues also read and commented insightfully on drafts of chapters, including Fred Donner, Iain Duguid, Steven L. Jones, and David Michelson.

Both authors helped envision and shape the layout of the book from its inception. The initial research for, and writing of, each chapter was then done by Graham, with Cline subsequently editing and fine-tuning the text. Stephen Morrison and Andrew Welton provided first-rate research assistance at Grove City College, Andrew as the framework of the project was unfolding and Stephen as the project neared completion, including the preparation of the index. An additional group of Grove City College students agreed to test-drive a draft of the manuscript, and their feedback as undergraduate readers proved very useful: Pierce Babirak, Christina Corrin, Emma Finney, Jordan Mihalik, and Abigail Morrison. Another group of students assisted with illustrations and copyrights, while also providing editorial assistance: Carolyn Augspurger, John Hayward, Matthew Koval, Elizabeth Mubarek, and Jonathan Riddle. The Calderwood Fund at Grove City College helped support the work of these students, for which the authors are most grateful.

INTRODUCTION

WHAT IS AN (ANCIENT) EMPIRE?

If historians eschew theory of how societies operate, they imprison themselves in the commonsense notions of their own society.

— Michael Mann, *Sources of Social Power*[1]

SOMETIME BETWEEN 520 AND 510 B.C., during the reign of King Darius I, the "Great King, King of Kings, King of Persia, King of Countries," a native Egyptian noble named Udjahorresne erected a statue of himself (Fig. I.1). Formerly a naval commander under the Egyptian kings Amasis and Psamtik III, he had fought against the encroaching Persian Empire. Udjahorresne had witnessed the Persian invasion and seizure of Egypt under Cambyses, the direct predecessor to Darius I, in 525 B.C. In the aftermath of the invasion, Udjahorresne had cooperated with the Persians so effectively that he was given an important honorific position in the administration of Persian Egypt. In the long self-glorifying inscription carved directly onto his statue, Udjahorresne waxed eloquent on the wonderful acts he had performed for the Persians. He praised the Persian ruler for taking his advice and thereby making the transition to Persian rule over Egypt smooth and efficient.

Udjahorresne could easily be dismissed as a nasty traitor and a hide-saving collaborator – a sycophant to his new Persian masters. Yet his self-congratulatory story offers some valuable glimpses into the workings of ancient empires:

> When the great King of all lands, Cambyses, came to Egypt, the people of all (foreign) lands were with him. He exercised sovereignty in the land in its entire extent; they settled down in it, he being the great King of Egypt, the mighty Sovereign of this country. His majesty conferred upon me the dignity of Chief San, and granted that I should be by

I.1. Udjahorresne statue.

him as Smer and Provost of the temple. He assumed the official title of
Mestu-Ra. I made known to His majesty the grandeur of Sais, as being
the abode of Neith, the Great Mother, who gave birth to the Sun-god
Ra, the First-born, when as yet no birth had been, together with the
doctrine of the grandeur of the house of Neith, as being a Heaven in its
whole plan. . . . I made supplication to the King Cambyses against the
people who had taken up their abode in this temple of Neith, that they
should be dislodged from it in order that the temple of Neith should be
restored to all its splendours as formerly. . . . His Majesty did this because
I had instructed him as to the grandeur of Sais, as being the city of all the
gods who dwell upon their thrones within it forevermore. . . . I was pious
towards my father and did the will of my mother; kindhearted towards
my brethren. I established for them what His Majesty had ordered,
giving to them splendid lands for an everlasting duration. . . . I shielded
the weak against the strong, I protected him who honoured me, and
was to him his best portion. I did all good things for them when time

came to do them. . . . I was devoted to all the masters that I had, and they bestowed upon me decorations of gold and gave me all glory. . . . A royal table of offerings grant Osiris Hemaka, abundance of bread, beer, beeves, geese, and all good and pure things to the image of Chief San, Ut'a-Horesnet, pious toward the gods of Sais.[2]

Most ancient inscriptions are more or less self-glorifying, and thousands of them survive – often the only written material we have – that proclaim the formation and strengthening of empires. One of the central problems confronting the ancient historian is how to analyze such documents to construct a general picture (i.e., the "story" in the history). What can this inscription and others like it tell us about the formation and maintenance of ancient empires? Note that the specific acts of the Persians and Udjahorresne fall into some basic categories: some are political, some ideological or, more specifically, religious, and a few are economic. The political message is right up front: Cambyses the Persian "exercised sovereignty in the land in its entire extent." He is now clearly the ruler of Egypt. However, the ideological message is probably the most pronounced: Egyptian temples have been restored, and the traditional religious system has been reinstated. The weak are protected from the strong; justice is maintained. Finally, it is clear that material goods are part of the motivation and reward for those who uphold the new order in the land. Udjahorresne and his family are publicly and richly rewarded for their efforts and for their loyalty to the foreign masters as elite collaborators. A combination of political, ideological, and economic factors helps keep the new empire in place. The fortunate survival of this statue and inscription provides a few of the pieces we need to put together the story of the Persian Empire.

DEFINITION OF EMPIRE

The most interesting aspects of history often are not the issues about which everyone agrees (those are rather rare and not very exciting anyway) but those about which historians differ. Let us start with our central term – "empire." The word itself is ultimately derived from the Latin term *imperium*, which denotes command, order, mastery, power, and sovereignty. It originally described the powers of rule and conquest granted to a Roman consul. Gradually, it came to denote a territory, closer to what we now would think of when we speak, for example, of the sun never setting on the British Empire. We often think of empire as an expanding or expansive territory that can be traced on a map. The Romans were usually more inclined, at least early in their history, to see a sphere of command or control, something like the modern terms "hegemony" or "sovereignty." When we employ the term empire in studies of the distant past, then, we often invoke more modern sensibilities. For these and other reasons, some scholars agree with historian Sir Keith Hancock that "imperialism is no word for scholars."[3] Others are not sure it can be so easily disposed of:

> To suggest, for example, that we should abandon "empire" as a category in Greek history and speak only of "hegemony" does not seem to me helpful or useful. It would have been small consolation to the Melians, as the Athenian soldiers and sailors fell upon them, to be informed that they were about to become the victims of a hegemonial, not an imperial, measure.[4]

One of the most helpful current definitions of the term *empire* comes from Columbia University's International Relations scholar M. W. Doyle:

> A system of interaction between two political entities, one of which, the dominant metropole, exerts political control over the internal and external policy – the effective sovereignty – of the other, the subordinate periphery.[5]

As with most technical definitions, that might seem be a bit heavy at first, so let us take it apart a bit, "unpack" it, as academics like to say. It is important for us to do this, because Doyle's definition of empire is our basis throughout this text.

Note first that empire assumes a relationship, an interaction between a dominant group and a subordinate and necessarily foreign group. One group rules over another, incorporating their people, land, temples, and so on into its own holdings. What goes without saying in Doyle's definition is that an empire is territorially extensive. Persia in the late sixth century B.C., for example, would be the "dominant metropole," and Egypt would be the "subordinate periphery." Yet the story of the Persian takeover of Egypt is not a simple matter of making a wasteland out of the conquered, killing and/or enslaving their inhabitants, and dashing their infants' heads against the stones. There is a foreign entity, the Persian Empire, now ruling Egypt, and yet Udjahorresne, a subordinate Egyptian, maintains a high social position within it; he is part of the "system of interaction" Doyle mentions. Udjahorresne takes great pride in the fact that, at his supposed suggestion, many things continue in Egypt "as they had been before." There is much continuity in terms of social power from the days before Persia's arrival. Yet the Persians are now calling the shots. Much of Udjahorresne's inscription reveals the means through which the Persians initially maintained their dominant position.

How, exactly, did the Persian – or any other ancient – empire manage to hold that dominant position? How did it lose its power? One of the ways that historians can balance broad surveys and meaningful analyses of such huge questions involving long periods of time is to keep focused on a central theme. Here we use a theoretical model, borrowed from the discipline of sociology, to help define our central theme. Such theoretical models aid in the challenging task of turning material from fragmentary sources, never intended for the critical eye of the modern historian, into a comprehensible story.

Michael Mann, a sociologist at the University of California–Los Angeles, proposed an influential model of power that many historians find useful. Mann's model will help us focus on a manageable problem – the question of how ancient humans exercised power over social and geographic space. Many other approaches to ancient history are possible and productive, but this approach is intriguing because it raises questions that are on the minds of many people today. According to Mann's model, societies are organized as power networks with four overlapping sources of social power: ideology, economics, military, and politics (hereafter abbreviated as IEMP). We have already encountered almost all of these in Udjahorresne's inscription. Empires are built on these "sources of social power," as Mann terms them; strong empires are evidence of all four sources working together effectively. The discussions raised by the IEMP model, as we call it from now on, are relevant to any period of history.

These four sources of social power must work together; generally speaking, none of them can be demonstrated as primary or more important than the others. Take the example that Michael Mann uses from a much later historical context: the Swiss pikemen of late medieval Europe. It is a basic military fact of history that, in the fourteenth century A.D., the famous armored mounted knights were defeated by armies of infantry pikemen. Much flowed from this defeat, including the decline of what is sometimes called classical feudalism and the rise of modern centralized states. The historical question of "why?" *seems* easily answered here: "changes in the technology of military relations lead to changes in political and economic power relations. With this model, we have an apparent case of military determinism." On the surface, then, military power was the ultimate cause of this important shift in human history. Such an explanation would be attractive and concise, but many relevant and significant factors would be ignored if we stopped there (as some history professors and History Channel specials tend to do). Central to the victors

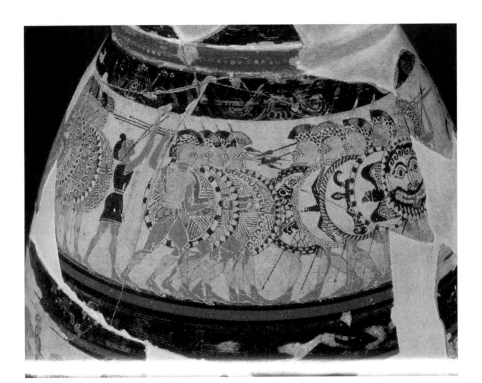

I.2. Chigi vase. Detail of hoplites, oenochoe (wine pitcher) from Corinth.

was a "form of morale" a "confidence in the pikemen to the right and to the left and at one's back." This, in turn, was shaped by the "relatively egalitarian, communal life of Flemish burghers, Swiss burghers, and yeomen farmers."[6] Thus, the answer to the historical "why?" question actually lies deeper and is more complicated than it first appears, involving all four of our sources (IEMP).

We could apply this same type of analysis to the Greek phalanx, a highly effective form of military organization about which we will learn in Chapter Five (Fig. I.2). Did the Greeks defeat the Persian Empire simply because of their tight military formations? What made that military technology so appealing to the Greeks as well as so effective in their famous wars against Persia? The phalanx itself arose within a certain type of social arrangement among some Greek city-states, one built on ideals of wide political participation and visions of equality, and therefore came about because of other social forces – some ideological, some political, and some, no doubt, economic. Military power "requires morale and economic surpluses – that is, ideological and economic supports – as well as drawing upon more narrowly military traditions and development. *All* are necessary factors to the exercise of military power."[7] The bottom line is that all of these sources of social power, working together, are important and necessary for the expression of dominance and the formation of empire (as well as for the resistance to it). With these sources of social power working together in the ancient world, empires were not only formed but could also be effectively resisted or overthrown.

We also argue throughout this text that religious ideology is much more than just a crass cover for materialist or military agendas (contrary to what many recent surveys and studies assume). For example, Udjahorresne emphasizes his religious acts far more than the tangible rewards he and his family receive. How do we read this? Are the material rewards, barely mentioned in the inscription, his real motivation here, even if not explicitly stated as such? Many people today would certainly think so, but what do we do with the ancient source that seems to emphasize religion above all else? Analysis and interpretation force us to ask such questions of our sources as we put together the "big picture."

Some parts of our text might seem to overemphasize the ideological dimensions of empire, of which religion was a significant part. Think of this as a corrective rather than as an attempt to present ideology or religion as the most important or ultimate source of social power. One of many useful aspects of making theory explicit in historical study is that it invites the reader to discuss it, debate it, affirm it, challenge it. We aim to communicate a vision of the ancient world that prompts a nuanced and historically informed understanding of social power, especially as it relates to discussions of cosmos (order), justice, and freedom. Our discussions of empire begin with the third millennium B.C., although the book itself focuses most on the period between the eighth century B.C. and the eighth century A.D., a period that witnessed an unbroken succession of empires, which we call the Age of Ancient Empires.

EMPIRE, RESPONSE, AND RESISTANCE

A key feature of this IEMP approach is that it allows us to explore both the formation and bases of ancient empires as well as the significant responses to them. Sometimes people seem to appreciate being folded into a growing empire, even if that inclusion challenges or even undermines age-old ways of life. The importance of such people was long ago appreciated by a Roman consul and conqueror, who claimed that "an empire remains powerful so long as its subjects rejoice in it."[8]

At other times, not surprisingly, groups at the "subordinate periphery" do not always appreciate being dominated by a foreign power, even if that foreign power claims to or actually does benefit them in some basic ways. As will be seen, some of the world's most enduring and still-influential ideas, value systems, and institutions, interestingly, were formulated, not by the great empires of the ancient world but rather by the peoples resisting them. The theme of resistance is, therefore, a major focus here alongside the more traditional study of "the rise and fall of empires."

Even a brief study of the Age of Ancient Empires reveals that many of the peoples who respond to empires will, in time, build (or aspire to build) empires themselves: Urartians, Greeks, Indians, "barbarians," Arabs. The variety of ways through which they do so is one of the avenues of exploration here. Resistance also utilizes IEMP, for a coherent system of resistance often integrates these sources of social power into an empire in its own right. And so the cycle continues.

EMPIRES, ANCIENT AND MODERN

Although ancient historians explore the distant past, they, like all historians, usually have at least one eye on the present and the not-so-distant past. It might surprise some students to learn that, up until World War I, the majority of the world's population still lived in self-described empires. The Ancient

After World War I, itself caused in part by the nineteenth-century Age of High Imperialism, calling your own political entity an empire became passé and even dangerous. "Imperialism," a handy term meaning the drive to build and maintain an empire, fell on hard times. Historians such as Niall Ferguson continue to debate whether age-old dynamics of empire actually disappeared at that time. Exploring the foundations of empire during the Age of Ancient Empires can allow us to think about the larger and arguably enduring issues involved in this power dynamic. The terms used throughout this study are therefore also relevant to discuss the current world political situation, and the theoretical model employed in this text can just as easily be applied to the discussions of World Wars I and II, the Cold War, the First Gulf War, and so on.

Is imperialism just a basic instinct built into human societies? The famous Austrian economist Joseph Schumpeter explored the "purely instinctual incli-nation towards war and conquest" that he claimed characterized the premod-ern world.[9] Is it forever true that, as ancient Athenians once argued, "the strong do what they can, and the weak suffer what they must"?[10] Scholars continue to debate this age-old question. Many claim that we, in the mod-ern world, have moved beyond the desire or need for empire. Such scholars say that liberal and democratic institutions have taken the place of empires. Others are not so sure, pointing out that the dynamics of empire continue to flourish in our contemporary world, whether we use the term empire or not.

We raise such questions as we analyze the great Age of Ancient Empires in this book.

QUESTIONS, QUESTIONS, QUESTIONS

We begin here with a set of large questions, not all of which will be answerable yet. Each subsequent chapter begins with a correlated set of specific questions. Keeping both sets of questions in mind as one reads the individual chapters will help focus and sharpen one's analysis and critical thinking about what we have written, as well as about any additional sources, ancient and modern, which may be relevant. These questions do not necessarily have straightforward "right" answers, as will be seen. Scholars often disagree strongly on exactly how to answer them. However, these questions should also help to organize thoughts about global social and political issues through time, right up to the current day, as well as to provoke discussions and help the reader gain a better understanding of the fascinating complexity of the human past.

* How can one define "**ancient**"?
* How do **theories** shape the telling of ancient history?
* How do ancient historians define and use **evidence**?
* What is an **empire**? Why did ancient humans consistently create them? How did they maintain them?
* How do the four sources – **IEMP** – interact to produce an empire? How do these sources of social power, individually and collectively, fuel resistance to empires?
* To what extent did ancient groups define and maintain **cosmos/order** and **justice** in similar ways? To what extent in different ways?

CHAPTER ONE

PRELUDE TO THE AGE OF
ANCIENT EMPIRES

With axes of bronze I conquered.

"The Legend of Sargon of Akkad"

* How were ideology, economics, military, and politics (what we will refer

~~to in this text as IEMP) related to the emergence of urbanism and city~~

states?
* What trade, diplomatic, and political relationships among the various types and stages of integration and consolidation existed beyond the level of the city-state?
* How did history's first empires emerge?

THE AGE OF ANCIENT EMPIRES, that largely unbroken succession of empires stretching from the eighth century B.C. into the eighth century A.D., did not emerge ex nihilo, out of nothing. By the time the age began, a long history of city-states, kingdoms, and even a few empires had already run its course – a rich history about twice as long as the Age of Ancient Empires itself. Before that was an indefinite and many times longer span of "prehistoric" human settlement. The Age of Ancient Empires was built on very old foundations.

A series of significant changes, beginning around 4000 B.C., ushered in a new era in human history. Settlement patterns changed, as city-states – politically independent cities and their surrounding hinterlands – became important centers of dense populations and unprecedented creative accomplishments. By approximately 3000 B.C., those changes produced what scholars call the Bronze Age, stretching to just after 1200 B.C. Trade and diplomatic connections began to emerge over distances, forming fairly stable networks and empires but also precipitating battles and wars. The first armies came together, led into battle by divine-right kings.

In between eras of growth, consolidation, and integration were approximately century-long periods of fragmentation, retraction, and collapse known as dark ages because they produced few written records or monuments. This was no inexorable march of progress, but it was cumulative. With each period of recovery, some city-states reached a larger scale in terms of the size of their consolidated areas, populations, and monuments. The final period of retraction that began in the twelfth century B.C., a period of more than three hundred years often known as the Dark Age, signaled the end of the Bronze Age. The political and cultural recovery that began in the Dark Age marked the true beginning of the Age of Ancient Empires.

THE DAWN OF EMPIRE

Our story begins in the Near East, a large ancient region stretching between the eastern Aegean coast and central Persia, and between northern central Anatolia and southern Egypt (Fig. 1.1). Nearly all ancient empires would begin here; many would expand well beyond the region. The few that did not actually originate in the Near East would come to include significant portions of it. Several millennia later, our story will end in the center of the region, in almost exactly the same spot where it started.

Four broad sections or arenas made up the Near East. Mesopotamia, the "Land between the Rivers" – the Tigris and Euphrates – might be called its epicenter. Urbanism began there, and in time, more ancient empires would arise from this particular region than from any other. To the northwest was Anatolia, part of modern-day Turkey, which, although it produced only one empire, would remain an important crossroads and battleground arena throughout the ancient world. To the southwest was Egypt, the most unified and stable of the regions, established along the Nile River. Its long and rich history would include several phases of empire. To the west of Mesopotamia was the Levant, the eastern shores of the Mediterranean Sea and adjoining regions. This area produced no major empires but rather many smaller kingdoms that often found themselves in the direct path of expanding empires. For the first millennium of the Bronze Age, these four regions developed in relative isolation. After that, they were integrated more closely together through trade, diplomacy, and conquest.

Two other regions would be integrated temporarily into Near Eastern developments and patterns, one fairly early in our story, the other much later. The western Aegean, the Mycenaean Kingdom of mainland Greece

in particular, moved with the rhythms of the Near East for the last three
hundred years of the Bronze Age. With the demise of this kingdom, the
western Aegean would go its own way for centuries. Arabia, actually located
in the middle of the Near Eastern arena, would play an important role only
briefly, at our study's end.

In the Near East, humans settled into three climatic zones. The densest
population was located in the coastal and riverine plains, the predominant
setting of ancient history. The rivers were often inhospitable and unpredictable, necessitating large-scale engineering work before extensive human
settlement was possible. Older descriptions of parts of the Near East as the
"Fertile Crescent" tend to obscure this fact. The second zone, the foothills,
contained some of the oldest human settlements in the region and had abundant scrub and animal life but less potential for agriculture. Population shifts
from the foothills to the plains were pivotal in early stages of human history, as we will see. Mountains and deserts represent the most marginal of
the climate zones, with extremely sparse human populations. The mountains,
for their part, housed the gods, according to the ancient peoples of these

We begin with the Urban Revolution, a fundamental demographic shift
that occurred in Mesopotamia between 4000 and 3000 B.C. In one sense, the
term "revolution" is a bit strong, because the changes took place over the
course of a millennium. As a basic reordering of human settlement, however,
the term fits. This was the era of the birth and growth of the city-state as the
basic political form. A prime example is Uruk, the population of which has
been estimated to be approximately 1,500 people soon after 4000 B.C. and
20,000 by 3000 B.C. The city-states had clear social hierarchies from their
inception: nobility (in several levels), commoners, slaves, and so on.

Helping support the growing population were new techniques and technologies that increased agricultural productivity by as much as ten times.
Irrigation and river dikes, the invention of the plow, and the use of animal
power were among the chief innovations in food production. A "chicken-
and-egg" question for scholars has long been whether these technological
developments produced, or rather were produced by, the political developments seen in the city-states. That is, did the challenges of food production
along the harsh and often unpredictable rivers demand political systems and
hierarchies to make dwelling possible, or did increasingly coherent political
hierarchies provide the oversight and leadership that made the technological
developments feasible? The latter has seen greater consensus among scholars over the past several decades, although many now suspect this conundrum might well be a false dichotomy. What the changes undoubtedly did

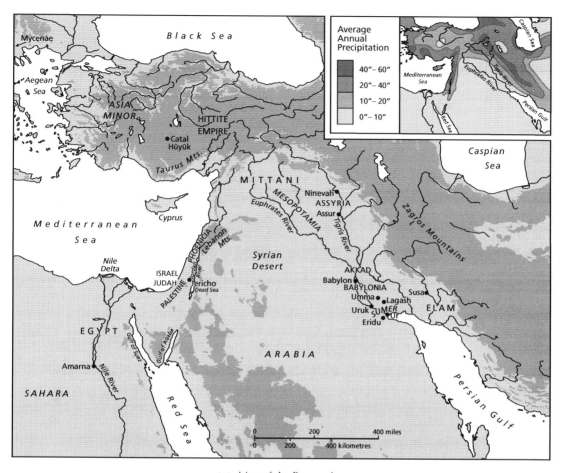

1.1. Map of the Bronze Age.

represent, at all events, was a series of successful and creative human responses to the challenges of a temperamental environment.

These political and technological shifts produced the Bronze Age, which came with a whole cluster of social changes. Ideology, economics, military, and politics were knit together in the fabric of the city-state, as can be seen in its major characteristics: monumental architecture, writing, permanent class hierarchy, armies, and large-scale wars. Although useful, lists such as these are not exhaustive, and few see them anymore as the collective sine qua non for "civilization." Traditionally, the development of writing has been taken as the starting point for human history (as opposed to "prehistory"). This is as good a measure as any, as long as we note its limitations. There was, after all, at least one empire in history without a writing system (the Incas of South America).

Religious ideology and politics were inextricably intertwined from the earliest time that either can be traced in the sources. As one famous anthropologist once put it, "Kingship everywhere and at all times has been in some degree a sacred office."[1] The most obvious example of this was sacral monarchy, which characterized all Near Eastern political entities. The king was a mediator between humans and the gods, whether he was seen as a god himself or, more usually, as the priest-king or representative of the gods. The king ruled the city-state, performed many vital religious functions, and personally led forth his army into battle against neighboring city-states. A whole body of priests were the functionaries of the city-state's religious system.

Whether religious systems first emerged as a means of social or political control (or both) — as many scholars contend — is a question of deepest controversy; how one answers it probably says as much about the interpretation of evidence as it does about one's own presuppositions. Temples and ziggurats dominated the skyline of Mesopotamian city-states. Along with a plethora of lesser deities, each city-state revered a single high god who was said to reside at the apex of the ziggurat. The ziggurat was probably shaped like a mountain to make the gods feel at home in their new dwellings in riverine plains (Fig. 1.2).

The dominant source of wealth was tax or tribute on agricultural goods

center of the city-state. The process is probably captured in the famous Near Eastern adventure tale *The Epic of Gilgamesh*, although it was written centuries later. At one point, the goddess Ishtar promises Gilgamesh, the leader of Uruk, that "the *yield* of hills and plain they [i.e., his subjects] shall bring thee as tribute."[2] The economic surplus generally went into the religious and political monuments, which became more elaborate with increased wealth — economics and politics, like politics and ideology, were deeply integrated. The temples were often the key centers of economic distribution.

The question of who actually owned the land is complicated. Recent research shows that there was not a single system throughout Mesopotamia and throughout time, but a diverse mixture in which temples, palaces, and even private individuals owned the land. In time, the kings would come to own or control most, if not all, of the land and would parcel it out as land grants to encourage and ensure loyalty.

Patterns of trade emerged fairly early on, most importantly for bronze production. Bronze was used for sculpture, domestic objects, and weapons. An alloy, it consisted of copper mixed with other materials, usually tin, in a 7:1 to 10:1 ratio (i.e., seven to ten times as much copper as tin). The production of bronze absolutely depended on long-distance trade because the materials were relatively scarce in the Near East and had to be gathered together from various disparate sources. The end of such trade networks would thus effectively spell the end of the Bronze Age.

1.2. Temple ziggurat, Agargouf, Iraq. DeA Picture Library/Art Resource, NY.

Small but decisive moves toward economic and political consolidation beyond the city-state level probably predate the beginning of the Bronze Age. These at first worked within larger territorial and cultural units: southern Mesopotamia, collectively known as Sumer, saw them first; northern Mesopotamia followed soon thereafter. Consolidation came initially through trade and alliance and then through conquest, producing the world's first, albeit brief, empires.

The first general consolidation can be traced to Uruk, in southern Mesopotamia, between 3500 and 3000 B.C. Through vigorous trade alliances, Uruk came to establish and command a large trading network. Uruk never actually came to control the internal political affairs of the city-states in its circuit, however, and it never followed up with conquest, although it seems to have established far-flung colonies. It appears that the elites of other city-states benefited greatly from their incorporation into Uruk's trading network. Although not an imperialist arrangement, it did set the stage for other types of consolidation to follow.

Soon thereafter, according to some Near Eastern scholars, the Kengir or Sumer League (2900–2300 B.C.) brought further unification. The evidence is shadowy and indirect, but it probably began as a broad trade association and evolved into a political and religious league, as well as a formal military and defensive league. The center of the League was at Nippur, an important religious center in the north of Sumer. There might well have been a series of such ephemeral unions and leagues, although the evidence is slight.

Military conquest and political consolidation followed from such centralization. There was a major barrier to be overcome, however, before real empire could emerge. As much as religious ideology would eventually be a fundamental ingredient in ancient empires, we will see over and over again that at first it was actually a hindrance. The city-states of Mesopotamia each claimed to be founded by a different deity, who continued as the main god. Expansion and unification alike were thus a challenge to the divine mandate of the conquered and conquering city-states. In time, traditions favoring broad expansion in the name of a specific deity would arise, bringing religious ideology and conquest firmly together.

The first known major military and political consolidation was carried out by Lugalzagesi (r. c. 2400 B.C.), a leader of the city-state of Umma. He conquered and subordinated the nearby city-states of Ur, Uruk, and Lagash

Near Eastern kings who conquered thereafter, someone probably stretched the truth a bit in an inscription that declared his conquests:

> When to Lugal-zagesi, King of Uruk, King of the Land, priest of An, "prophet" of Nisaba . . . [the gods] Enlil, King of countries had given the kingship of the Land, made the Land obedient to him, thrown all countries at his feet, and subjected them to him from sunrise to sunset, − at that time he made his way from the Lower Sea [Persian Gulf], via the Tigris and Euphrates, to the Upper Sea [Mediterranean], and Enlil had allowed none to oppose him from sunrise to sunset.[3]

Note how Enlil gives him his conquests − a hint at ideological traditions of empire building to come. Yet he obviously offends another god in the process; a consequent curse was pronounced against him:

> The man of Umma [Lugalzagesi], because he has destroyed Lagash, has sinned against Ningirsu! May the hand he has used against him [i.e., the god Ningirsu] be cut off![4]

Like most of these early conquests, the empire probably barely outlasted the founder.

Northern Mesopotamia would soon follow the Sumerian pattern of consolidation, and even go beyond it. Like Uruk in the south, the city-state of

Kish first began to establish influence and a primary place through trade networks. A conqueror named Sargon usurped the throne of Kish and expanded throughout both northern and southern Mesopotamia from his new capital at Akkad, overcoming Lugalzagesi himself. Because Sargon united most of Mesopotamia and even extended his rule into parts of the Levant, he usually gets pride of place as history's first empire builder. From his inscriptions and those of his grandson, Naram-Sin, who brought the empire to its territorial height, we can see a new type of rulership emerging: heroic kingship, which would characterize most ancient empires to come. Naram-Sin in particular epitomized early heroic kingship:

> Naram-Sin, the strong one, king of Akkad: when the four corners (of the universe) together were hostile to him, he remained victorious in nine battles in a single year because of the love Ishtar bore for him, and he took captive those kings who had risen against him. Because he had been able to preserve his city in the time of crisis, [the inhabitants of] his city asked from Ishtar in Eanna, from Enlil in Nippur, from Dagan in Tuttul, from Ninhursaga in Kesh, from Enki in Eridu, from Sin in Ur, from Shamash in Sippar, and from Nergal in Kutha, that he be the god of their city Akkad, and they built a temple for him in the midst of Akkad.[5]

Older Mesopotamian kings had usually described themselves as "shepherd kings." They looked on their people in a paternalistic way, and their authority was guaranteed by their upholding of traditional patterns of justice. The heroic king, in contrast, received and maintained his position on the basis of personal merits and accomplishments, conquests often foremost among them. A "King of the Land" or "King of the Four Quarters" dominated through a warrior aristocracy. With Sargon and Naram-Sin, we see an obvious trend toward greater power, wealth, and sophistication. This dominance was proclaimed in architecture, relief, and sculpture, the creation of which reached impressive levels of expertise with Sargon and Naram-Sin (Fig. 1.3). However, after Naram-Sin, the empire declined, and, once more, an era of disconnected city-states descended across Mesopotamia.

A few centuries later, c. 2100 B.C., the next major moment of consolidation, again short-lived, began at the city-state of Ur. The leader of Ur, Ur-Nammu, seized control of both Sumer and Akkad, directly invoking a distant past of unification. This is a pattern we will see often in this study: to build legitimacy, would-be emperors often presented themselves or their kingdoms (or both) as the restorers of glorious days of old. More than a millennium later, the Neo-Assyrian and Neo-Babylonian Empires would model themselves on Bronze Age kingdoms, even intentionally erecting temples and

1.3. Stele of the Victory of Naram-Sin. Erich Lessing/Art Resource, NY.

palaces directly on the sites of ruined Bronze Age structures. Approximately 1,600 years after Sargon, one of the greatest of the Neo-Assyrian kings would even take on his name. Not long after the death of Ur-Nammu's son, however, his empire folded as its local governors declared their autonomy.

A little more than a century later, two contemporary kings politically reconstituted the two regions of Mesopotamia. Shamshi-Adad (r. 1814–1781 B.C.), claiming descent from Sargon's Akkadian dynasty, conquered northern Mesopotamia. Hammurabi (r. 1792–1750 B.C.), descended from a line of western nomads known as Amorites, united a loose confederation of central and southern Mesopotamian city-states and ruled from Babylon, once a province of Ur-Nammu's empire. The empires these two kings carved out hardly outlived the founders, however; Hammurabi's name happens to live on because he promulgated a famous law code – most of it derived from previous examples. Another century-long dark age followed. From it emerged an unprecedented and important era of integration and consolidation, about three hundred years long, known as the Late Bronze Age.

As city-states, leagues, and empires rose and fell in Mesopotamia, Egypt was building a powerful kingdom to the southwest. Clinging to the Nile, a generally more predictable and hospitable river than the Tigris or Euphrates, Egypt similarly benefited from technological innovations that brought greater agricultural efficiency and productivity. From its inception, Egypt emerged in a more unified fashion than Mesopotamia. In Egypt there were no city-states but rather two initial kingdoms that, early on, united into one to form the kingdom of Egypt. Later, during periods of stress, Egypt would divide and fragment, but here, disunity remained the exception rather than the rule.

Sometime around 3000 B.C., as the Bronze Age dawned in Mesopotamia, a semilegendary leader named Narmer (or Menes) forcibly united the two kingdoms, Upper and Lower Egypt (think in reverse, as the Nile flows – Upper Egypt is in the south and Lower Egypt in the north). The union held strongly from the beginning, centered around the capital at Memphis (Fig. 1.4). Egypt's history is traditionally told through dynasties; this early period is known as the Early Dynastic Period. It is likely that some important changes during this period – in architecture and decorative elements, for example – were modeled directly on the pattern of Uruk, diffused through trade links during the fourth millennium B.C.

A long period of prosperity, peace, and near complete political isolation followed with the formation of the Old Kingdom (2715–2134 B.C.). This period is often called the Pyramid Age because it was during this time that those famous monuments of the ancient world were produced. The king, or pharaoh, was at the center of the unified kingdom – a god, a political ruler, a divine mediator, he embodied the standard of justice and cosmos that the Egyptians knew as *ma'at*.

The pyramids present a clear example of the power of the image and the place of monumental architecture in strong kingdoms: ideology, economics, and politics come together clearly in them. The royal imagery that adhered to these monuments enhanced the mythology of the divine king and the myth of the unified state. The first pyramid was built around 2700 B.C. and represents the first monumental use of stone in the history of the world. Egyptian leaders and architects continued to experiment with pyramid styles for the next century or so, always striving for perfection in form (Figs. 1.5–1.7).

The Great Pyramids, the most famous symbols of Egypt to this day, were built in Giza around 2600 B.C. Requiring enormous planning and organization, they are still, after 4,600 years, a vivid testimony of the power of a centralized state that marshaled the human intelligence and power to create such monuments. Royal tomb complexes constructed around the pyramids

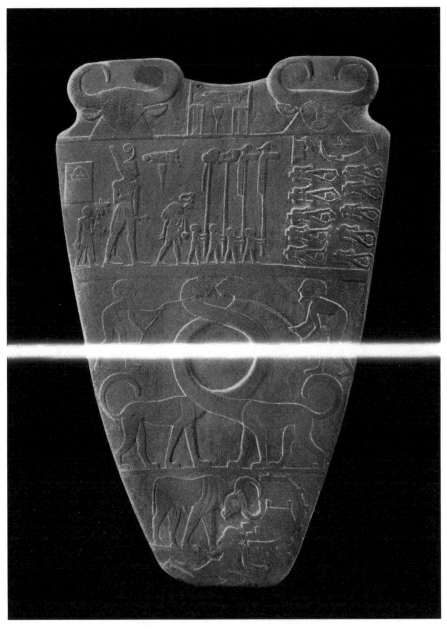

1.4. Narmer Palette. Werner Forman/Art Resource, NY.

also clearly show the integration of politics and ideology. Each pyramid had
two associated temples. In one of these temples, the last rites were performed
for the king; here, the priests would continue to perpetuate the king's memory.
The other temple was probably the site of the mummification ritual. A series
of smaller buildings show the close connection of the king to his officials and
proclaim the beginnings of a bureaucracy.

1.5. Step pyramid of Djoser/Zoser. James Morris/Art Resource, NY.

1.6. Bent pyramid of Sneferu at Dahshur. Werner Forman/Art Resource, NY.

1.7. Giza pyramids. Photo by Lynette Miller.

Old Kingdom Egypt collapsed in 2134 B.C. amid dynastic strife and
the assertive rise of local nobles. Some of these began building tombs even
larger than those of the pharaohs, suggesting a growing local autonomy
that ultimately undermined central authority (or that perhaps arose with its
weakening). Some have pointed as well to a series of disastrously low Nile
seasons, which also might have challenged central authority.

A period of relative fragmentation, known as the First Intermediate Period,
immediately followed the collapse of the Old Kingdom. There was some
consolidation soon thereafter with the rise of the Middle Kingdom (2025–
1550 B.C.). Overall, the Middle Kingdom was a period of internal divisions and
mediocre, if not forgettable, accomplishments, from a political and economic
point of view. The final years of the Middle Kingdom, between 1720 and
1550 B.C., were dominated by the mysterious "rulers of foreign lands," the
Hyksos. The origins of these invaders have long been disputed, but there
is now a consensus that they were Semites, probably from the region of
Canaan, located to the north of Egypt. The removal of them by a native

Egyptian family from Thebes would mark the beginning of New Kingdom Egypt, a period of vast expansion and empire.

Elsewhere in the Near East, the historical record is more difficult to follow, but clues point to some familiar patterns. In Anatolia, a conglomeration of city-states emerged by the twentieth century B.C. During the nineteenth century, it appears that city-states with similar culture were briefly united into a single state, before they descended into civil war and division. By the eighteenth century, there was a degree of unity again, but the next few centuries are opaque. Not much is known until the fifteenth century, when a true Hittite Empire materialized about the same time as New Kingdom Egypt and other powerful, long-lived kingdoms throughout the Near East.

In third- and early-second-millennium Levant, a few thriving city-states, such as Ebla, appeared. Scholars debate the extent to which these city-states arose through their internal development or in reaction to outside factors, such as long-distance trade or the expansion of rule from Mesopotamia's earliest empires, prompting local response and city-state formation. (The latter dynamic, known as secondary-state formation, is explored in several later chapters.) The initiative to consolidate above the city-state level, however, rarely came from within the Levant, during this period or in later centuries.

BETWEEN AMARNA AND QADESH: REALPOLITIK BRONZE AGE STYLE

Beginning around 1500 B.C., if not slightly before, the Bronze Age story can no longer be told simply in isolated parts. From this point until just after 1200 B.C., all regions of the Near East and even areas beyond were integrated into history's first international system, an age of Realpolitik and great powers. In this period, often called the Late Bronze Age, several impressive empires, kingdoms, and large territorial states – in Mesopotamia, Egypt, Anatolia, and Egypt, east of the Tigris, and the Aegean – arose, allied, fought, and then fell around the same time. In the Levant, city-states such as Jerusalem, Aleppo, and Damascus often found themselves caught between the push and pull of great power politics. A fortunate survival of an archive at Tell el-Amarna in Egypt gives unrivaled insight into the international relations and power politics.

The interactions among six particular major players – in terms of trade, diplomacy, and war – defined the age. Some background on each power will help situate the extent of integration among them, starting with the two greatest empires the Bronze Age produced. New Kingdom Egypt, begun with the Hyksos expulsion in 1550 B.C., carved out an empire stretching from the Sudan in the south well into the Levant in the north. A highly visible signal of the ideological impetus behind this expansion was extensive temple building focused on its chief god of conquest and empire, Amon-Re. In Egypt's central regions as well as far-flung and expanding peripheries, temples of Amon-Re proclaimed a world empire. The New Kingdom ruler almost always appears in art and literature as a warrior, conquering in the name of Amon-Re.

One of the most important conquerors of the age was Thutmose III (r. 1479–1425 B.C.), who carried the Egyptian expansion into Southwest Asia, expanded Egyptian borders well into the Levant, and pressed deep into Nubia, the only major gold-producing region of the Bronze Age. He fought a coalition of Levantine city-states at the Battle of Megiddo (1479 B.C.), which is considered one of the turning points in world history, confirming Egypt as the dominant power in Africa and the Near East. The account of the battle highlights the vital role of Amon-Re:

> His majesty [Thutmose III] commanded that [the victories which his
>
> in the temple which his majesty had made for [his father Amon, in order to set down] each individual campaign, together with the booty which [his majesty] carried [off from it, *and the dues of*] every [*foreign country*] which his father Re had given to him . . . departure from this place, in valor, [in victory,] in power, and in justification, in order to overthrow that wretched enemy, and to extend the frontiers of Egypt, according to the command of his father Amon-Re, the [*valiant*] and victorious, that he should capture.[6]

The Hittite Empire arose about a century after New Kingdom Egypt. In the latter half of the fifteenth century B.C., the Hittites began expanding from their capital Hattusa into the Euphrates and Levant, where they were met by a coalition of Egypt and the Syrian kingdom of Mitanni. They initiated a lengthy proxy war in which the Great Powers engaged in warfare via vassals and satellites. During the reign of Suppiluliuma I (r. 1344–1322 B.C.), the empire stretched from the Aegean coast in the west to Lebanon and the Euphrates' headwaters in the east. Suppiluliuma would successfully campaign against the powerful kingdom of Mitanni, even sacking their capital. In true Realpolitik form, he then established friendly relations with his erstwhile foe, New Kingdom Egypt, during the reign of either Akhenaten (r. 1350–1333 B.C.) or Tutankhamun (r. 1333–1323 B.C.). The friendly relations did not hold out long, however, as both sides again used Levantine city-states in their

1.8. Funerary temple of Ramses II at Abu Simbel. Photo by Lynette Miller.

competition, leading eventually to the Battle of Qadesh, on the Orontes River in Syria, in 1274 B.C.

This battle stands out as the world's first "superpower" engagement, pitting two powerful and growing empires against each other, New Kingdom Egypt versus the Hittite Empire. It is also the first battle in history for which accounts from both sides survive – and both sides claim victory. Most scholars agree that the Hittites actually won, but this was not a war of annihilation; the equilibrium and balance of powers returned in a few short years, with the frontier of both empires now more or less defined at the site of Qadesh.

The Egyptians were led by Pharaoh Ramses II, an important warrior and noteworthy builder who constructed multiple temples to Amon-Re at Egypt's peripheries, such as the famous Abu Simbel in Nubia (Fig. 1.8). This temple also commemorated his supposed victory at the Battle of Qadesh.

The Hittite king at Hattusa, known as the Great King, was the central religious, military, and political figure. The main priest of all the gods, he traveled throughout his realm both to campaign and to preside at the major religious festivals throughout the year. Additional titles such as "My Sun" and "The Hero" underscore his centrality to the ideological system. He was seen not actually as divine but as very close to the gods, joining their ranks at death. In fact, the Hittite term used to describe a king's death literally meant "become a god." His success in war not only guaranteed a steady supply of tribute and warriors but also demonstrated the gods' favor on his rule and realm.

The Hittite Empire was held together through a set of oaths and treaties, many of which survive in extensive archives. Under the Great King was a whole series of lesser local kings, his vassals. Their oaths were sworn before the imperial court at Hattusa and before military leaders in the name of the Hittite gods, demonstrating the ideological, military, and political facets of their dependence on the Great King. The vassals supplied troops and fought for him, provided items for the celebration of the Hittite cults, and brought annual tribute. The Great King, in response, granted estates to the leading families. The system held together as tightly as these oaths, or

Warfare involving one of the Hittite vassals has been memorialized and mythologized in the famous ancient tales of the Trojan War, one of the myriad battles and skirmishes of the Late Bronze Age. Probably just a few decades after the Battle of Qadesh, the Mycenaean kingdom of the western Aegean moved mightily against the smaller city-state of Troy, a vassal or "servant" of the Hittites on the western coast of Anatolia. The rest is history — and a whole lot more.

From northern Syria, the kingdom of Mitanni began an expansion that would eventually take it beyond the Tigris and into Anatolia. When Mitanni actually began is unclear; it appears first in Egyptian archives and developed between the eighteenth and fifteenth centuries B.C. Their first major king, Parrattarna (r. early fifteenth century), had an array of vassal kings under him. Mitanni dominated northern Syria into the mid-fourteenth century, when it became a major rival of Egypt, primarily fighting a proxy war through respective Levantine vassals. By the end of that century, they had allied with Egypt but soon after came under the dominance of the Hittite Empire. The realm was then essentially divided between the Hittites in the west and the Assyrians in the east.

In Babylon, Kassites, probably from east of Mesopotamia, seized the throne after a period of fragmentation there dating back almost to Hammurabi. They were able to control Babylon politically, but the Babylonian culture was too strong for Kassites to register much culturally here. We will

1.9. Elamite complex. Bryn Mawr College (MJM-03757). Photographed by Machteld Johanna Mellink.

see this trend later with Babylon, as it comes under the sway of various foreign empires yet refuses to yield much culturally to rulers from the outside. Coming up against growing Assyrian might, their influence weakened by the thirteenth century.

Assyria was at first a region of small city-states that became a larger territorial state by the fourteenth century. They were masters of both campaigning and diplomacy, particularly the latter, although their artwork consistently proclaims only the former. Their power would eclipse that of Mitanni and Kassite Babylon. Their first significant ruler, Assur-Uballit (r. 1363–1328 B.C.), pulled together a large region connected to the capital of Assur.

On the eastern extreme of the Near East, beyond Mesopotamia, the kingdom of Elam emerged as a major player, although probably the weakest of the six major players in this age of Realpolitik. By the fourteenth century, it had reversed a long period of fragmentation to function as a centralized kingdom, although not nearly as much is known of this kingdom as the others. The Elamites were known, however, for a durable building technique; in fact, to this day, the best-preserved ziggurat is Elamite, located at Chogha Zanbil in the Khuzestan province of Iran (Fig. 1.9).

One of the central characteristics of the Late Bronze Age – and a fortunate one for modern scholars – was the frequent interchange and communication among major players and between major players and the smaller city-states, their vassals. The letters, inscribed on durable clay tablets, were preserved in various archives throughout the Near East. Relative power status is always clear in the letters, once established; the major powers addressed one another as "brothers" and the lesser powers and city-states as "servants."

The archive discovered at Tell el-Amarna, Egypt, has been particularly helpful in elucidating this age. The pharaoh Akhenaten/Amenhotep IV (r. 1350–1333 B.C.) built a new imperial capital at Akhetaten or Tell el-Amarna, based in part on a bizarre religious conversion. Claiming Aten, the sun-disk, as the high god – if not the only god – he constructed Akhetaten as an isolated capital and outdoor temple to his god. The site (like his religious reform) was abandoned soon after his death and remained deserted, preserving a rich collection of diplomatic interchanges from the middle of the fourteenth century. Approximately 350 clay tablets document Egypt's political relations, mostly with the various subordinate city-states of the Levant.

letters are fairly formulaic, with a glaring pattern of obsequiousness standing out:

> To the king, my lord, the Sun-god from heaven: Thus Zatatna, prince of Accho [Acre], thy servant, the servant of the king, and the dirt (under) his two feet, the ground which he treads. At the two feet of the king, my lord, the Sun-god from heaven, seven times, seven times I fall, both prone and supine. Let the king, my lord, hear the word of his servant! [Zir]damyashda has withdrawn from Biryawaza.[7]

Approximately forty of the tablets are from "Great Kings" and show the other major powers relating to Egypt. The language of these letters is that of brothers and peers. In a letter from the king of Mittani to the pharaoh of Egypt:

> Tell Nimmureya, king of Egypt, my brother, my son-in-law, whom I love and who loves me; Tushratta, king of Mittani, who loves you, your father-in-law, says: "All is well with me. May all be well with you. May all be well with your house."[8]

The letter then goes on to make a polite request.

The language of most of the letters presents the Great Kings as collective heads of a single larger international community (some describe it as the language of an "extended household"). Marriage alliances, gift exchanges,

1.10. Akhenaten, Nefertiti, and their children blessed by the Aten. Werner Forman/Art Resource, NY.

and requests for gold and other precious materials dominate the letters from equals. The letters from the vassals are usually either fawning requests for aid or tattling reports on other small city-states and kingdoms.

COLLAPSE OF THE INTERNATIONAL SYSTEM

For reasons that scholars have long debated, this remarkable period of integration, expansion, and Realpolitik came to a rather abrupt halt. Just as the whole system suddenly emerged in the fifteenth century B.C., it unraveled almost completely in the early twelfth. The political and trade integration assured that great powers stood and fell more or less together. Monumental architecture, long-distance trade, political alliances, population expansion, and literacy declined or ceased fairly abruptly in most areas. Wealth declined drastically, as seen in tombs and burial goods. A by now ancient pattern of small-scale city-states returned to the Near East during what some scholars call the Dark Age.

Scholars have proposed three major types of explanations: external invasions, internal social unrest, and natural or environmental catastrophes. All three of these appear in available sources, and so the recent consensus among scholars has been to acknowledge multicausal explanations, as opposed to looking for a single cause. The most famous invaders – although not the only ones – were the mysterious Sea Peoples, who invaded the eastern Mediterranean, Egypt, and the Aegean. We get a glimpse of them in Egyptian Pharaoh Ramses III's (r. 1184–1153 B.C.) record of his successful, if short-lived, effort to stem their tide:

> The foreign countries made a *conspiracy* in their islands. All at once the lands were removed and scattered in the fray. No land could stand before their arms, from Hatti [Hittites], Kode, Carchemish, Arzawa, and Alashiya [Cyprus?] on, being cut off *at* [*one time*]. A camp [was set up] in one place in Amor. They desolated its people, and its land was like that which has never come into being. They were coming toward Egypt, while the flame was prepared before them. Their confederation was the
>
> They laid their hands upon the lands as far as the circuit of the earth, their hearts confident and trusting: "Our plans will succeed!"[9]

The denouement of Ramses III's reign provides a perfect example of the intersection of the three types of causes. After he successfully repelled a group of Sea Peoples, ("they were dragged in, enclosed, and prostrated on the beach, killed, and made into heaps from tail to head"[10]), he came home to face famine in Egypt and was finally assassinated in a palace conspiracy. The priests of Amon then established a weak theocratic state at Thebes during the ensuing Dark Age.

The Hittite Empire would decline over the course of a few decades after 1200 B.C., probably under invasion from the Sea Peoples as well as internal division – peripheral areas calved off from the realm, breaking their oaths, thereby decreasing the wealth flow to the center as well as taking away significant military presence (Fig. 1.11). At the same time, Assyrians and Babylonians were fighting Aramaeans from the desert.

Not all was gloom and doom, however. Recent archaeological research shows that some areas actually thrived during the Dark Age. Smaller city-states, for example, could enjoy a new sense of autonomy and freedom from the larger kingdoms that perennially subordinated them as vassals. A few places, such as parts of Cyprus, actually experienced some growth at this time. A series of smaller kingdoms, known as Neo-Hittite, carried on Hittite

1.11. Warriors fighting onboard ships: naval battle against the Sea Peoples. Erich Lessing/Art Resource, NY.

culture in Anatolia and northern Syria. In the Near East, the decline was comparatively less as one moved east from the Euphrates.

In a few famous cases, the relative deprivations of the Dark Age forced humans to innovate in some far-reaching and influential ways, forcing them out of comfortable routines. Iron became widespread during this period for a very practical reason. Known during the Bronze Age, by the Hittites as well as others, it had been used only for ornamental purposes. No one had yet developed technology to craft useful tools and weapons. Bronze, of course, was the metal of choice, although it was softer, more costly, and more difficult to produce. Iron, in contrast, was readily available throughout the Near East, and unlike bronze, its production did not depend on large-scale trade networks. Requisite technologies for iron smelting were developed in the twelfth and eleventh centuries, even producing steel. The product was much harder than bronze and could be produced entirely locally and cheaply; it is no wonder that the period after the collapse of the Bronze Age is often called the "Iron Age."

The disappearance or extreme retraction of writing systems during the Dark Age also encouraged the development of one of history's most significant inventions – the alphabet. Like iron, the idea of the alphabet existed in the earlier period, but it was not widely used. Its first meaningful and extensive use was by the Phoenicians (as discussed in Chapter Three), a people from the Levant. The alphabet was a simpler system than the cuneiform of Mesopotamia and the hieroglyphic of Egypt and could be learned with much less training and educational infrastructure, making it appropriate to a period of small-scale settlements. Its use soon spread well beyond the Phoenicians, particularly to the West. As at the beginning of our story, a basic challenge called forth profound creativity.

After the Dark Age hiatus, subsequent ancient empires would continue to grow larger – much larger – than anything the Bronze Age ever saw. The synthesis of ideology, economics, military, and politics will become far more explicit and clear via a comparative abundance of visual and written sources as well as archaeological material. Modes of resistance and response to imperialism and expansion will become far more extensively documented and, presumably, more nuanced. Yet the basic patterns of control and dominance by one group over others appear remarkably similar. Whether this was primarily because of deliberate modeling on past empires – as most subsequent empires would explicitly do – or because imperialism is an inevitable

entire study.

CHAPTER TWO

THE RISE OF THE AGE OF
ANCIENT EMPIRES

May Ashur, who gave you the scepter, lengthen your days and years! Spread your land wide at your feet! . . . May the lesser speak, and the greater listen! May the greater speak, and the lesser listen! May concord and peace be established in Assyria!

– "Coronation Hymn of Ashurbanipal II"[1]

* What brought the Near East and Mediterranean out of the Dark Age?
* Why were the Neo-Assyrians so brutal?
* How did their imperial system hold together?

THE RECOVERY FROM THE DARK AGE marked the real beginning of the Age of Ancient Empires. The more or less continuous succession of empires stretching from the eighth century B.C. to the eighth century A.D. saw the rise and fall of some of the most profound complex societies known. Across the Near East as well as in the Eastern and Western Mediterranean, major changes in the late ninth and eighth centuries B.C. heralded some important new beginnings.

In the Near East, the Neo-Assyrians consolidated their rule with a brutality that animates their own records as well as nineteenth-century English Romantic poetry. To the west, the Mediterranean began to emerge as a unit distinct from a "barbarian hinterland," with profound implications for later centuries and for the spread of empire westward. Phoenician sailors increasingly reconnected the western Mediterranean and the Near East through their far-flung commercial networks that diffused goods as well as culture. One group of Phoenician settlers established Carthage, which would become a major North African kingdom.

In the Aegean, Greek populations expanded markedly, encouraging the spread of Greek colonists throughout the Western and Eastern Mediterranean. The Greeks also began experimenting in architecture and art under strong influence from models diffused from the recovering Near East. In central and northern Italy, the Etruscans began the construction of some long-lasting city-states and a highly influential culture. In one small Tiber-washed town in the shadow of Etruscan power, another group, known as the Latins, began to make a mark on the archaeological record at this time, and their much-later legends trace the Roman rise back to the middle of the eighth century B.C.

The size and scale of these changes set this era apart from even the high points of the Bronze Age. How can the historian explain all of these important new beginnings going on at roughly the same time? Our analysis of this question will demonstrate the usefulness of the IEMP (ideology, economics, military, and politics) model. It will also suggest the importance of considering, when possible, some even larger forces, such as changing weather patterns, which take us across space and time. To answer fully the question of why so many new developments are afoot, we must look well beyond the

the time. Therefore, this chapter briefly sets forth the larger context, while focusing specifically on the rise of the Neo-Assyrian Empire, the first empire in the Age of Ancient Empires. We return in later chapters to concurrent developments westward.

THE LEVELS OF HISTORICAL TIME AND
THE RISE OF THE AGE OF ANCIENT EMPIRES

History often seems the simple story of famous people (usually men) carrying out major events (usually battles). The Neo-Assyrian rise to Near Eastern dominance is famously portrayed in Assyrian Royal Annals as well as other ancient texts in vivid terms: battles, conquests, sieges, raids, and construction projects. Such details are vital to understanding the Neo-Assyrian rise and must be taken into account by historians, not least because they are often the only written evidence we have. However, there are obvious limitations to reconstructing the past solely from written texts composed by the victors and centered on the doings of kings. Many historians have come to recognize that history, of any era, unfolds in interrelated time levels, in different ways and at different speeds. There is much below and beyond the surface-level events, which the historian can use to reconstruct the past. History is, in one sense, the story of both change and continuity. To appreciate both fully, we must look at immediate personal action in the context of longer-term trends.

To make sense of the various levels of time, an analogy of three different-sized interlocking gears – one small, one medium, and one large – might help. A top layer, that of actual events, would be the smallest of the three gears. It moves the fastest, its position changes the quickest, and its motions are the most noticeable. At this level are the doings of the kings, queens, and nobles, usually recounted in glowing inscriptions such as those that survive in the Neo-Assyrian archives:

> At that time I seized the entire extent of the Lebanon Mountain and reached the Great Sea of the Amurru country. I cleaned my weapons in the deep sea and performed sheep-offerings to (all) the gods. . . . I (had) made a sculpted stela (commemorating) my heroic achievements and erected (it) there.[2]

People and events are central in this layer, as will be seen, but the scholar of the ancient world should not stop with them in analyzing the past.

Beneath this top "gear" is a mid-sized one, turning at a somewhat slower rate, but with movements still discernible to the careful observer. At this level are the social structures of human societies and groups. Sociologists who have analyzed this level have been of much help to historians, showing them how economic, ideological, and other patterns unfold and change over time, but almost always more slowly than the turnover of kings on a king's list, for example. Usually (although not necessarily always), these patterns and trends last much longer than a single person's lifetime and thus must be analyzed from more than just the accounts that fortunately survive from a given time period. At this level, some historians analyze *mentalités*, mental structures that characterize a people or group over a long period of time – *le longue durée*, as it is usually called. Michael Mann and his fellow historical sociologists generally work at this middle level, exploring longer sociological trends such as the development of social hierarchies and power, demographic patterns, and family structures.

To most observers, the largest "gear" actually may seem not to move at all; yet its hardly perceptible movements can drastically affect what happens at the other two levels. This level, the longest extreme of *longue durée*, is the ecological time layer. Climate change and the long-term relationship of people to the land are the most obvious factors here. At critical junctures in history, the scholar can explicitly see the connections between this layer and both the top layer of events and the middle level of broader social structures.

The rise of the Age of Ancient Empires is one of those full moments in which all three gears may be seen turning together. For example, as we shall soon see, many scholars see a major climate change as one important

trigger for the Age of Ancient Empires. Along with other factors, this may
have helped propel new developments in the western Mediterranean as well
as in the eastern Mediterranean and Near East. The climate change allowed
for population and agricultural changes that created enticing opportunities
for someone with the wherewithal to seize them. The results were profound.
The Neo-Assyrians had the IEMP necessary for the task at a critical era in the
Near East, and they executed it brilliantly. The interaction of all three "gears"
helps us to understand what happened and why in the eighth century, the
period of the real rise of the Age of Ancient Empires.

CLIMATE CHANGE AND THE BIRTH
OF A NEW AGE

Over the course of the ninth century B.C., the climate throughout the Near
East and the Mediterranean became decidedly cooler and wetter than it had
been in the previous centuries. Scholars have traced this shift through data
derived from studies of bogs in northern Europe that register a rise in the water

ice caps from this period. Climatologists have posited that more consistent
"Westerlies" resulted in more consistent rain across a large section of the
world. One significant and noticeable result of this change was a relatively
sharp rise in population numbers, as food production markedly increased.
Increased food production helped encourage more births as well as larger
sustainable populations. In some areas, the population went up 100 percent
or more over the course of the eighth century B.C. in response to the climate
shifts of the previous century, showing the ability of certain groups to take
advantage of the new opportunities.

Climate change did not act alone in prompting the new developments,
but it certainly altered the setting and opened the door for new possibilities,
as we will see. The repopulation and recovery of some areas that had been
devastated by the Bronze Age collapse, especially in the Aegean and the Near
East, are clear to current scholars. The resulting population "explosion," if
a movement that lasted longer than any one person's lifetime can be called
such, carried with it significant historical implications for both the short- and
longer-term reckoning of history. In effect, the changing climate led both
directly and indirectly to changes in demographics and in the configuration of
power relationships throughout the Near Eastern and Mediterranean worlds.

Increased agricultural potential and growing populations brought with
them new opportunities for local elites. By the early eighth century, many
such local elites had become as wealthy and powerful as some of the kings

of a previous era. Commerce beyond the local level was also reemerging on a larger scale, both a cause and effect of some newly developing power dynamics. Ambitious kings and would-be consolidators, such as the Assyrians of the ninth century B.C., found it challenging to extract booty from these increasingly powerful local elites. With the rise in population, wealth, and trade, the stakes were set increasingly higher across the Near East by the late ninth century. The stage was set for a new type of power to incorporate these smaller groups forcibly into larger configurations, the first real empires in history.

THE NEO-ASSYRIAN REVIVAL

The restoration of order to the Near East after the Dark Age was a task that could be accomplished only with a great deal of unifying force and power. The first major player "out of the gates" – the Neo-Assyrians – employed some of the most graphic examples of aggression that the ancient world would see. By the middle of the eighth century B.C., the Neo-Assyrian Empire had rapidly and brutally expanded into the largest kingdom the Near East had yet seen. With its rise, we see the small and medium "gears" of historical time working together, responding to the shifts at the environmental level.

During their earlier history as a player in Bronze Age Realpolitik, the Assyrians had originally occupied the heavily fortified commercial city-state of Ashur on the middle Tigris. Their earliest history shows them as a periphery to the stronger Bronze Age centers of southern Mesopotamia. As a group, they were primarily a collection of agricultural villages, but cities were always at their center. By the twelfth and eleventh centuries B.C., they had embarked on an expansion that brought them some impressive relative power for a time in northern Mesopotamia with centers in Ashur, Nineveh, Arbela, and Kilizi, all traditionally part of the old Assyrian heartland. Troubled constantly by raiders, such as the Aramaeans, they were on par with the smaller kingdoms of the Dark Age era. With borders never more than 75 miles across, they were smaller than the state of Connecticut.

By the ninth century, however, they had reemerged from some initial setbacks and begun a definite consolidation, connecting themselves politically and ideologically with the Assyrian kingdoms of the past. Although the connections to earlier phases were clear, innovation and change were also central to the Assyrian rise. Their language of Akkadian, their central ideas of kingship, and their all-important cult of Ashur were some of the key continuities across the stages of Assyrian history. In all three of these areas, however, there was change. One important thing that they took from their enemies the Arameans was a language, Aramaic, which they would help spread throughout the Near East as a lingua franca. The Assyrian Empire became bilingual, with significant groups of Aramaic speakers alongside the speakers of native Akkadian. Their ideas of kingship, as will be seen, also changed and developed; the king became the high priest of Ashur in a way not seen before.

Their initial, if comparably unspectacular, phase of expansion began in the tenth century under Adad-nirari II (r. 911–891 B.C.) and his son Tukulti-Ninurta II (r. 890–884 B.C.). Their campaigns united upper Mesopotamia under Assyrian rule and began a process of economic exploitation and tribute collection that began to fill the Assyrian coffers. A real move toward empire, however, began under Ashurnasirpal II (r. 883–859 B.C.), who campaigned and conquered in all directions from the Assyrian heartland, eventually bringing his rule to the shores of the Mediterranean. Assyrian kings were finally living up to the longstanding boast among Mesopotamian royalty of washing their weapons in the sea. In areas that they conquered, the Neo-Assyrians generally removed the upper-level elites, replacing them with

in place to ensure continuity and stability. With Ashurnasirpal II in particular, we see the rise of the strong language of universal dominion that will characterize the rest of the Assyrian Empire and most others which came after it:

> Ashurnasirpal, vice-regent of Ashur, chosen of the gods Enlil and Ninurta, beloved of the gods Anu and Dagan, destructive weapon of the great gods, strong king, king of the universe, king of Assyria . . . valiant man who acts with the support of Ashur, his lord, and has no rival among princes of the four quarters . . . the king who subdues those insubordinate to him, he who rules all peoples . . . he who is victorious over all countries.[3]

Establishing his capital at Caleh, Ashurnasirpal revamped the Assyrian palace style, giving it a distinctive decorative program that featured primarily royal campaigns, regal hunts, and imperial rituals. At the dedication of his palace at Caleh, he bragged that 47,074 "men and women were invited from every part of my land," plus various dignitaries and locals, for a grand total of 69,574 guests. These he wined and dined, bathed and anointed "for ten days" before sending them back to the farthest reaches of his kingdom to declare the beauties of his palace and the wonders of his dedication ceremony.[4] He was clearly declaring his sovereignty at both the center of his kingdom and its peripheries through this act.

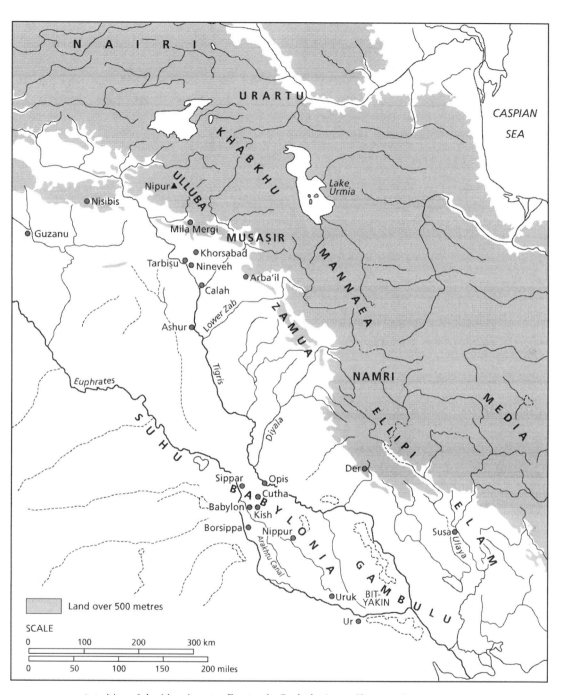

2.1. Map of the Neo-Assyrian Empire. In *Cambridge Ancient History*, vol. 3, pt. 2, p. 72.

Ashurnasirpal's son, Shalmaneser III (r. 858–824 B.C.), struggled to maintain Assyrian hegemony against a variety of rebelling or resisting groups and
frontier raiders. In 853, at the Battle of Qarqar, a coalition of Phoenician and
Syrian polities came together with Ahab of Israel and fought the Assyrians
to a halt. In the aftermath of Shalmaneser's reign, Assyrian power diminished

2.2. Tiglath-pileser III attacking a city with a battering ram. Werner Forman/Art Resource, NY.

further. Throughout this period and after, the Assyrians were challenged by Babylonian revolts. The Babylonians, with a rich history and influential cul-

subdued. The Assyrians, therefore, treated the Babylonians and their culture with a bit of ambivalence. Although they maintained a great deal of respect for the older Babylonian culture, even employing Babylonian as their literary dialect, the Assyrians also insisted on their dominance over the Babylonians.

The Assyrian heartland, however, remained essentially intact during this temporary phase of decline. There was some loss of territory as some local governors proclaimed their autonomy, and a lack of expansion caused a decided loss of prestige in the international context. Local powers were hard to control in a time when local wealth was on the rise, as discussed earlier. However, this early phase of expansion set the stage for the more pronounced empire to come.

The real moment of Assyrian dominance over the Near East began with Tiglath-pileser III (r. 744–727 B.C.), who began a successful and unprecedented expansion against the surrounding kingdoms in Mesopotamia, Syria, Anatolia, and Egypt (Fig. 2.2). Along with some crucial administrative changes within the provincial government (such as dividing military and economic tasks), he created a permanent standing army, the *kitsir sharruti*. His sons, Shalmaneser V (r. 726–722 B.C.) and Sargon II (r. 721–705 B.C.), continued the conquests, solidifying Assyrian rule in Anatolia and the Levant. They both followed their father in having themselves crowned king of Babylon as well as of Assyria. Resistance to Sargon II's rule, in particular, was fairly firm, due in part to questions about his legitimacy as heir to the throne. His entire reign was spent subduing internal revolts and repelling groups such as the Urartians,

2.3. Tower with defenders. Assyrians attack the Jewish-fortified town of Lachish. Erich Lessing/Art Resource, NY.

Chaldeans, Israelites, and even Greeks from Cyprus. His own official annals claim, somewhat misleadingly, that he conducted a major campaign every single year of his reign.

The Assyrian kings who followed Sargon II – Sennacherib (r. 704–681 B.C.), Esarhaddon (r. 680–669 B.C.), and Ashurbanipal II (668–631/627? B.C.) – further stabilized Assyrian rule, especially along the frontier zones, and expanded Assyrian gains in Egypt and Elam. Sennacherib established his own capital at Nineveh and spent his reign subduing rebellions, including one in Judah, which resulted in a siege of Jerusalem and the destruction of Lachish by the Assyrian army, graphically depicted in a series of reliefs in Sennacherib's "Palace without a Rival" at Nineveh (Fig. 2.3). Tired of the rumblings from Babylon, he simply destroyed the city. Esarhaddon, his son, rebuilt Babylon and continued to work out imperial strategies for keeping down the revolts in Babylon and elsewhere. Officially, he divided the kingship of Assyria and Babylon between his sons, a measure that had some success for a time.

Under Ashurbanipal II, the Assyrian Empire reached its territorial height. Ashurbanipal is noteworthy as well for his extensive rebuilding of temples

throughout his reign, showing, as is explored later, the connection in the
Assyrian mind between piety and warfare. From temple rededications and
other inscriptions, the number of written texts from his reign is unparalleled
among Assyrian rulers. As a result, historians have remarkable insight into the
workings of the Assyrian system at its height.

Overall, and despite the frequent revolts, some scholars have called the
period between the late eighth and the late seventh centuries in the Near
East the Pax Assyriaca ("Assyrian Peace"). This was a time during which
Assyrian order was established far and wide, and a large Assyrian realm was
both expanded and maintained. (Note, for example, the emphasis on establishing concord and peace in the "wide land" in the "Coronation Hymn of
Ashurbanipal II," the opening quotation for this chapter.)

THE LOGIC OF ASSYRIAN DOMINATION

With their power solidified, and with relatively abundant visual and verbal
examples of their methods, the techniques of Assyrian expansion and rule

then seize the booty. The fortuitously surviving Assyrian Royal Annals, as
well as many modern surveys, provide a canonical litany of acts such as
tongues torn out, lips cut off, massive flayings of live prisoners whose skins
were then plastered on walls of watchtowers as "wallpaper," vivid scenes
of hundreds of conquered rebels pierced with stakes and hung around the
conquered cities, and so on (Fig. 2.4). One poignant scene pictures banqueting
Assyrian notables in a beautiful garden, with musicians setting the mood.
One tree has a human head dangling from it, like fruit, above the musicians
(Fig. 2.5). The long list of their self-professed atrocities is unparalleled in
human history. Their own inscriptions and visual arts openly declared such
exploits. The Assyrians, then, did not acquire their reputation at the hands
of bitter enemies. It would be hard for any enemy to make them look more
brutal than they made themselves look. But were they really just fearsome
pirates on a grand scale?

Scholars have explained the extreme Assyrian measures in several ways.
One angle points to their brutality as the price tag for harnessing the Near East
at this time. Desperate times, simply put, called for desperate measures. The
Dark Age and its late-rising local nobles made consolidation a difficult and
formidable task – and formidable the Assyrian solution was, by any estimation.

A related angle points out that the Assyrian cruelty was intended to create
a "wall of fear" necessitated by a lack of natural frontiers. They could not rely
on rivers or mountains to help them hold their empire, and so they defended

2.4. Assyrian warriors impaling Jewish prisoners after conquering the Jewish fortress of Lachish. Erich Lessing/Art Resource, NY.

themselves simply by inspiring formidable fear in everyone around them – an effective form of propaganda. Theirs was an empire built primarily on a type of "defensive imperialism," just as some have claimed for the Roman Empire. Their heartland indeed lay wide open, throughout their history, with Babylonia to their south, the Levant and Anatolia to their west, and invaders from the Zagros mountains to their north and east.

Frequently, the Assyrian imperial drive is seen simply as ambition fueled chiefly by the desire for glory and profit on the part of its leaders. However, although there is certainly some legitimacy to all of these angles and explanations, none of them alone accounts for why it was the Assyrians, as opposed to any other Dark Age kingdom, who came out on top for more than a century.

More recent nuanced analysis of the Assyrian social system by scholars has revealed a complex interchange of IEMP. Theirs was not simply an empire built with inhuman brutality and unbridled conquest (contrary to what was claimed by them as well as by some historians). In fact, their actual military

2.5. A harpist in Sennacherib's gardens. Erich Lessing/Art Resource, NY.

action, as with most empires, was usually the last resort in building and maintaining an empire. Scholars now suggest that despite the strident bellicose rhetoric to the contrary, the Assyrians much preferred coercive diplomacy to military campaigns, because the latter came with a high cost in human life and disruption of production and trade. To be sure, a show of conquest and brutality was built right into their system, but they dramatically magnified their claims of brutality to avoid martial action. As a result, military action was more often used as a persuasive threat than actually carried out in reality. However, there is also much more to the story.

Recent research has also focused on their religious ideology as an impetus for expansion as well as a mode of legitimation of their rule over subject populations. Whereas earlier scholars tended to downplay this aspect and see religious ideology as simply a cover for more concrete motivations, political or material, many recent scholars do not see such proclamations as smokescreens and instead see them as an expression of very real motivations for the Assyrians. For the Assyrians, "war was presented as a divine commandment, never as an act of pure military aggression."[5] War was, in essence, an act of piety. Their chief god, Ashur, commanded them to carry order (or cosmos) from the divine realms to earth. In texts, Ashur calls the world his "hunting ground." The Assyrians were given the divine commandment to conquer and subdue it, thus making the earthly hierarchy fit with the heavenly. Their conquest and then subsequent establishment of imperial order simply aimed to "bring heaven to earth." They were to bring a divine order (cosmos) to the fragmentary chaos that had characterized the previous centuries. Their inscriptions are fairly clear and explicit on this. For example, Esharhaddon explains his treatment of rebels in a mountainous region:

> You began fighting and battle against me and disturbed the grim weapons of Ashur from their resting-place. I did not listen to his [a king who initially refused to surrender] pleas, I did not accept his imploring, I did not allow his pleading. I did not turn my averted face towards him, my enraged senses were not calmed against him. My turbulent heart did not find rest, I felt no pity for him and did not speak "Mercy (ahulap)!" to him.[6]

The conclusion is expected – this stubborn ruler, who "disturbed the grim weapons of Ashur" would soon, and deservedly, be mercilessly destroyed.

At the visible apex of the Assyrian ideological system was the king – "the great King, mighty King, King of the universe, King of the country of Ashur," as many texts call him. In Neo-Assyrian texts, he is also known as the Šangû (Priest or Divine Administrator) of Ashur. The famous "Coronation Hymn of Ashurbanipal II" praises the king as "blessed," "just," and "circumspect." He embodied a moral force by virtue of his position as the administrator of Ashur, commanded to extend the divine order by expanding and consolidating Assyrian military gains (Fig. 2.6).

We should also note that in the "Coronation Hymn," a key result flowing from a righteous reign is that the "lesser" will speak and the "greater" will listen. The prayer was that social justice at all levels would flow from his rule. For the king, then, conquest and punishment were, quite literally, freeing the world of evildoers and upholding divine justice. His frequent presentation as a warrior of "righteousness" thus reveals part of the Assyrian ideological system: anyone who defied Assyrian rule (i.e., refused to submit to Ashur's mandate) was, in fact, an "evildoer" and thus had to be dealt with. Even worse was anyone who betrayed his loyalty to Ashur. Justice, peace, and order would, to the Assyrians, only follow from submission to Ashur, by way of his representative on earth, the great king of the universe.

2.6. Triumphal march of Ashurnasirpal, with Ashur above. Line drawing by Andrew Welton.

A formidable military system was needed to back up and support the Assyrian claims. Fortunately, several techniques and innovations made their army an effective defender of the divine order that the Assyrians strove to maintain. The army consisted of charioteers armed with bows, backed up by a powerful cavalry (history's first real, organized cavalry); infantry armed with a helmet, shield, spear, and dagger; and, finally, skilled slingers (Fig. 2.7). The chariots and cavalry utilized heavier, faster horses than had ever been

2.7. Assyrian soldiers. Line drawing by Andrew Welton.

2.8. Siege weapons. Line drawing by Andrew Welton.

consistently used before in military maneuvers. The Assyrians were also one
of the first groups to use iron on a large scale throughout their ranks. Finally,
to aid in breaking down the walls of their opponents' fortified cities, they
developed and improved on siege weapons such as the battering ram, for
smashing gates, and the turtle, used to house and protect soldiers as they
undermined walls (Fig. 2.8). In return, knowing their own similar vulnerability,
the Assyrians also defended themselves by constructing heavily fortified walls
around their cities, as they had done throughout their earlier history.

Part of their success came from a more widely armed populace, right down
to the level of the free peasants fighting in the armies. This was something
new; bronze weapons of an earlier era, in addition to being softer than iron,
were usually expensive and were carried only by a small number of soldiers.
Their army was initially and strictly made up of Assyrians, but the demands
of such a quickly growing empire soon forced them to use conquered subjects
and employ mercenaries. One crucial group of foreigners was the Ituaeans, an
Aramaic tribe that, once conquered by Tiglath-pileser III, became "a highly
mobile and versatile branch of the standing army."[7] One recent estimate sees
an army in excess of one hundred thousand members by the eighth century
B.C., including a significant number of professional soldiers.[8] The numbers
are widely contested, however, with other estimates as low as forty thousand.
Regardless of the numbers involved, the Neo-Assyrians' impressive military
organization would often be copied, each time with modifications, by later
aspiring lords of the Near East.

On the ground, so to speak, the Assyrian method of conquest was fairly
formulaic and repetitive, at least as presented in their own sources. The king
and his army would show up at the walls of a foreign or rebellious city,

asking that its inhabitants submit to his rule. All foreigners who submitted immediately were spared but were required to swear an oath of loyalty to the god Ashur. This was by no means an exclusive oath (the Assyrians were as radically polytheistic as virtually all Near Eastern societies), but it did mean that they would submit to Ashur's will, as mediated by his representative on earth. As a reminder, sometimes the Assyrians would capture local god statues from rebellious cities and then return them with "Ashur" stamped on them. The submitters then became vassals of the Assyrians and were required to pay an annual tribute, as the price of maintaining order and as an offering to Ashur. The inhuman brutality for which the Assyrians have become famous usually was reserved for those who stiffly resisted conquest or, worse, broke the oath of loyalty to Ashur – skinning people alive or impaling them on stakes was the least the Assyrians could do to those who had so defied the very moral order of the universe. The extreme actions simply demonstrated that the king himself embodied a moral force that distinguished right from wrong. It also shows that their definition of the "necessity" of a military action was of a different nature than ours.

These elite administrators held office for thirty years. They were granted large estates that would supply troops, which in turn carried out conquests for which they were then granted larger estates. An upward spiral gave the system strength and expansive power, for a time. The more successful the noble, the more possibility of rich rewards, both in land and in the future service of the soldiers. The Mâr Banûti, then, had strong economic incentives to remain loyal and to continue the conquests in the name of their king and the god Ashur.

Assyrian elites replaced the foreign elites in most instances. In what has become known as the Elite Replacement Model, the conquerors would remove the highest social strata of a conquered people, placing Assyrian top elites in their place. The majority of the population, more than 90 percent, was largely left alone. This pattern was a general one throughout the premodern world and speaks to the long-term continuity of such social rearrangement patterns. Ernest Gellner sees the general pattern in these terms:

> The ruling class forms a small minority of the population, rigidly sep-
> arate from the great majority of direct agricultural producers, or peas-
> ants. . . . Below the horizontally stratified minority at the top there is
> another world, that of the laterally separated petty communities of the
> lay members of society. The state is interested in extracting taxes, main-
> taining the peace, and not much else."[9]

Life was fairly consistent across the board for the commoners, no matter who was ruling. As noted earlier, lower-level administrators were often kept in their place, however, to ensure continuity of rule at the local level. As long as the tribute continued, the local structure remained largely intact. This type of system characterizes virtually every Near Eastern empire that we will study in this book. (Recall from the Introduction that Udjahorresne was granted a social position and was instrumental in helping ensure smooth continuity between empires; the highest-level political power was reserved for Persians.) The big exception to this ancient model of conquest and governance was the Roman Empire, which used a system of elite co-option instead of elite replacement in which key non-Roman elites were "won over" by the Romans and used for key and powerful leadership positions.

To what extent were the common people affected by the Assyrian imperial system? Or, to borrow the words from the "Coronation Hymn" of Ashurbanipal II, to what extent did the "lesser" speak and the "greater" actually listen? It is always difficult in the ancient world (and most historical periods) to reconstruct the lives of the nonelites, and it is usually impossible to be firm on their feelings about the empire within which they found themselves due to a basic absence of sources. There are two ways that historians have attempted to reconstruct their lives. The first is a broad approach, using nonspecific theory to fit the nonelites into a general picture of the premodern world. The parallels of common lives across the millennia in the Near East and Mediterranean are fairly striking here. Gellner's model of continuity across the premodern world of the large groups of producers is one such influential attempt. The second approach, usually integrated with the first, uses painstaking efforts to connect stray shreds of information to construct a general picture.

A fairly specific picture of the nonelites is thus beginning to emerge. Although we really do not even know the size of the population of what Kuhrt calls the "semi-free" persons of the Assyrian Empire, recent research has revealed information about a significant number of common people working for hire, such as "weavers, victuallers, leatherworkers, oil-pressers, ironsmiths, shepherds, farmers, gardeners."[10] All of these people contributed, in their own way, to this vast and diverse empire. One recent study combed 177 legal and administrative texts to reconstruct the family life of "lower stratum families."[11] We will probably never know what most of these people thought about being conquered and ruled by a foreign master, but internal revolt occurred frequently enough that it is certain some did not appreciate the Assyrian hegemony (although the leaders of such revolts were generally of fairly high social standing).

The Assyrian Empire, like nearly all those that came after it, was divided into provinces for ease of organization and rule. Each province was ruled by a governor (*šaknu*), who was responsible for upholding the imperial system. The *šaknu* helped maintain the imperial infrastructure such as roads, buildings, and communication systems at the local level. At his governor's palace, he would host the traveling king and support him with soldiers and other resources as needed. One of his most important roles was ensuring the collection and passage of tribute to the imperial centers. Later, the Persian Empire would famously employ a sophisticated provincial system; it is often forgotten how much the Persians owed to the earlier Assyrians.

One innovative and famous Assyrian administrative tool had long-term demographic repercussions. This was the process of deportation, or reportation, in which the Assyrians would either take a conquered population and settle it far from its original home or simply switch two subjugated populations. The practice, which began with Tiglath-pileser III, displaced a sizable number of people. One historian has estimated that between 745 and 612 B.C., in 157 documented deportations and reportations, as many as 4.5 million

displaced 470,000 people. Traditionally, this has been seen simply as a measure to discourage revolt, because it broke down local loyalties and identities associated with place – that is, people are less likely to revolt if they are not living on, and defending, their own traditional lands. Recent scholarship has pointed out that deportation and reportation were probably also intended to replenish depopulated areas to keep the land under cultivation, thereby keeping the imperial food supply as steady and consistent as possible amid war, sieges, and revolts.

The Assyrians declared their conquests and maintenance of empire through an artistic and cultural program, the scale and detail of which was unprecedented in the Near East. Called by some the Assyrian Renaissance, this program saw the construction of new cities, palaces, and temples, accompanied by incredible architectural and interior and exterior artistic expression (Fig. 2.9). The Assyrians are widely given credit, in fact, for provoking the real (re-)urbanization of Mesopotamia, both by building up areas they conquered and setting a far-reaching example of urban beautification. Their impressive, if macabre, palaces were adorned with both frescoes and reliefs of scenes of war, conquest, hunting, and banqueting. From the Assyrians onward, the connection between empire and monumental art and architecture was quite clear. All subsequent empires would follow them in employing massive artistic programs to declare their empire and, with it, proclaim the restoration of the divine order on earth. The modern mind sometimes struggles with how

2.9. Relief panels. The Metropolitan Museum of Art/Art Resource, NY. Gift of John D. Rockefeller, Jr., 1932.

such beauty and cruelty could work together so seamlessly. Yet trying to understand the Assyrians necessitates seeing the world in the same way that they did.

The Assyrian kings also built extensive canals and gardens next to their palaces, a practice followed most famously by the Babylonians. This, along with conquest, made the earthly realm replicate the heavenly. Sennacherib describes his "great park, like unto Mount Amanus, wherein were set out all kinds of herbs and fruit trees, such as grow on the mountains and in Chaldea."[13] The extensive imperial gardens recently have been interpreted as "botanical and zoological maps of the empire, in which the Assyrian kings made clear their control of the periphery by bringing it to the center."[14] Their urban beautification thus served two clear purposes. On one hand, it sent a strong message of empire and order out from the civic centers to the imperial peripheries. On the other hand, the gardens, in particular, brought the periphery back to the center to show firm imperial control.

In addition to the archaeological excavations of their cities and gardens, much of what we know about Assyrian civic programs has been gleaned from their extensive texts and records, for literature was a key aspect of the Assyrian Renaissance. In the Great Library of Ashurbanipal at Nineveh, more than twenty thousand tablets were found, including the official annals (Royal Annals), King's Lists, and the like. The conquerors boasted frequently in their imperial inscriptions and relief panels of the silver, gold, garments, cattle, and so forth that they extracted by the conquest and taxation, all of which made such a "renaissance" possible. Literary, religious, and medical texts survive in relative abundance. Their myths and legends have been of much interest to historians and literature specialists. The famous *Epic of Gilgamesh* survives today largely in Assyrian copies. The *Enuma Elish* records their mythical origins in terms that parallel other creation stories from the Near East and Levant.

A close inspection, then, of the Assyrian social system shows IEMP working together firmly to expand, declare, and maintain a vast empire. Environmental changes provided opportunities, and IEMP provided the means through which the Assyrians built an empire, constructed and beautified cities, and crushed resistance. A difficult question with which scholars continue to struggle is which came first – the material drive or the ideology? Were the Assyrians initially driven by material consideration, and was it only later that they exploited the story of Ashur's demands as a sort of justification?

Neo-Assyrian period. Was their hoary religious ideology recast at this time to justify their desire for political power over others or to accumulate wealth (or both)? Or was the initial drive toward empire really the perceived command of Ashur and the material benefits necessary to create heaven on earth simply followed? Such thorny questions are difficult to answer decisively, yet they must be raised, for they point to the complexity of imperialism (and human motivation in general). It is certain, in any event, that IEMP are all present and contributing to the expansion and consolidation of the Assyrian Empire.

THE DEMISE OF ASSYRIAN DOMINATION

Despite its unprecedented size and apparent stranglehold on the Near East, the Assyrian Empire collapsed with remarkable and somewhat mysterious speed after the reign of Ashurbanipal II. At its demise, the empire was near its territorial height, and there is little or no evidence of decline over time. Shortly after 612 B.C., the empire vanished completely as invading Medes and Babylonians razed the strong cities of Nineveh, Ashur, and Nimrud. The transition to the subsequent empires – Babylonian and then Persian – was remarkably smooth. Some historians have suggested that the Assyrians had been so effective at eliminating rivals that a space was cleared, more or less, for the new invaders, who apparently had an easy time taking over.

It is certain that, as an empire, the Assyrians had never been able to integrate peoples fully, and revolt – even though responded to with such widely proclaimed brutality – challenged the empire throughout, especially from areas with long-established cultures such as Egypt and Babylonia. Although no empire has managed to prevent all revolts, subsequent empires worked out strategies for reducing their number. For the vast majority of the people, there was simply no loyalty to, or love lost on, the empire. This became a problem as the Assyrians were forced, more and more, to rely on non-Assyrians who did not necessarily share the imperial ideology or program. Responding to endemic problems of ruling over foreigners with identities of their own, later empires, such as the Persian, cultivated, through its artistic programs and governmental policies, a sense of subject people belonging to a much larger imperial whole. Subjects were presented as a necessary component of imperial order, not simply as its subordinates. The Romans, by far the most effective ancient empire on this score, would later work with a variety of methods, such as the extension of the concept of citizenship as a way of including conquered outsiders.

Approximately two hundred years after the fall of the Assyrians, the Greek historian Xenophon participated in the famous "March of Ten Thousand," which passed through the ruins of two major Assyrian cities, one of which was Nineveh. The local villagers could give him no information about the previous inhabitants of these deserted sites. They simply assumed that the cities had been built and occupied at one time by the Medes. Yet although the specific details of the Assyrian Empire had faded in the minds of the local populace, the story of the Neo-Assyrian rise and fall helps elucidate the entire age of ancient empires. By utilizing a rigorous program, which we now can say combined all aspects of IEMP, the Assyrians began a spiral of empire that would continue until the end of the ancient world (and beyond). The opportunities were afforded, at least in part, by a change at the most basic level of history, that of climate change.

Subsequent empires would continue to work within what Paul-Alain Beaulieu calls one of their greatest legacies – a new sort of "imperial idea." Empire was here to stay; "there was no serious attempt at returning to the previous state of political fragmentation." With the new age, the "irreversible fact" of empire emerged, which was inculcated "so deeply in the political culture of the Near East that no alternative model could successfully challenge it, in fact almost up to the modern era."[15]

Several other themes have emerged in this chapter that we will see again and again in our study. The empires to come will be consistently larger in scale than anything seen before. Massive urban programs, complete with large-scale monumental political and religious art and architecture and road and communication systems, will be the rule in subsequent empires. Along with this show of massive force and impressive urban renewal, however, there will also be a consistent emphasis on protecting the weak and securing order and the safety of those inside the empire. A general sense of social justice was seen as flowing from the imperial system, however harsh it appears to us. The terms of this order and justice were (and are) highly contested, of course. The rhetoric of reprisal against "evildoers," inside and outside the empire, remained strong. The threat of bald force was always present – all subsequent empires would be brutal, in many cases comparable to the Assyrians. Although all empires exercised hegemony, most actually seem, on close examination, reluctant to use physical force, employing it as a last resort. The brutality, then, aimed to make a memorable example in one or a few cases at most to avoid force in the other instances. Yet the Assyrians, like many other empires, also show us that what constituted a necessity and what constituted an extreme or last resort was strongly bound to their religious ideology. We cannot ignore the fact that they conquered in the name of a deity who demanded that they

A final and important note about the Assyrian Empire is that, like all subsequent empires, it changed and developed even as its rulers looked back to a long past for identity and direction. The Assyrians adjusted and experimented as they faced the challenges of their world. Too often, their realm (along with all other Near Eastern empires) is seen as static and unchanging, a timeless abode of so-called Oriental despots and submissive, servile populations. The truth is far richer and more interesting. Their adjustments and responses to change resulted in some profoundly influential structures and innovations. Subsequent empires would continue to both borrow and experiment. The Assyrian powerhouse had paved the way by both revealing the potential for wide-scale and dynamic empire and demonstrating some of the serious challenges and problems in maintaining such an empire for any substantial length of time. It is specifically to such challenges that we turn in the next chapter.

CHAPTER THREE

DEALING WITH EMPIRES: VARIETIES
OF RESPONSES

*For from Jerusalem a remnant shall go out, and from Mount Zion a band of survivors.
The zeal of the LORD [Yahweh] of hosts will do this.*

— Isaiah the Prophet, as recorded in II Kings 19:31 (New Revised
Standard Version [NRSV])

* How did resistance to the Neo-Assyrian Empire use ideology, economics,
  military, and politics (IEMP), together or in part?
* Why were some methods of resistance more effective than others?
* What relationships were there between resistance and identity?

THE RISE OF THE NEO-ASSYRIANS changed the rules of the Near
Eastern political game. The small surrounding kingdoms had to
respond to these changes if they wished to survive. However, not
all encounters with the Assyrians resulted in conquest, destruction, forced
tribute, or deportations; the outcome could vary widely, depending on the
response of the smaller kingdom.

This chapter explores a few case studies of how surrounding peoples
responded to or resisted the Neo-Assyrian Empire. Most small kingdoms
joined temporary coalitions to survive. A few kingdoms were actually created or re-created in response to the new threat. Some threatened kingdoms
intensified deeply seated cultural habits and traditions, whereas others borrowed or invented them. Some people survived by clinging strongly to a
dynamic religious identity. Far-reaching and significant results flowed from
these various reactions. As we will see throughout this book, the responses to
empire often are even more significant than the actions of the great empires
themselves.

SECONDARY STATE FORMATION: URARTU

A little more than a century ago, archaeologists began exploring and
unearthing remains of a powerful kingdom on Assyria's northern frontier. Its
impressive mountain fortresses, palaces, temples, cult centers, and storehouses
once dominated an area of nearly 200,000 square kilometers in what is today
eastern Turkey, northwestern Iran, and Armenia (Fig. 3.1). Scholars continue
to piece together the history of this large and powerful kingdom, known as
Urartu, from its physical structures, its few inscriptions, and references in the
Assyrian Royal Annals.

From its rugged mountainous heartland, essentially inaccessible to the
outside world for much of the year, Urartu resisted Neo-Assyrian advances
and launched an impressive expansion of its own. The similarities between
Urartian and Assyrian political and ideological systems are striking. So is the
fact that Urartu does not even predate the Neo-Assyrian rise. It seems simply
to have emerged suddenly, right after and in response to the initial rise of the
Neo-Assyrians.

have given it a name: secondary state formation. The basic pattern is that a
"primary state," consisting of a strong and central state, provokes the formation – or sometimes reformation – of a "secondary state," that is, a neighboring
polity. The secondary state emerges through a process of either outright imitation of the powerful neighbor or concerted resistance to it but usually a
combination of both. The growing Assyrian Empire was the primary state
for a few secondary states that emerged at its peripheries, such as Urartu,
Persia, and perhaps Media. In the case of Urartu, several small groups of
Hurrian-speaking pastoralists were pulled together rather suddenly against
the threatening Neo-Assyrians. They formed a kingdom that would thrive for
nearly 250 years, even outlasting the Neo-Assyrian Empire itself.

The rise and growth of this kingdom closely paralleled the major stages
of the Neo-Assyrian Empire. In the mid-ninth century, Urartu emerged under
the leadership of a king named Aramu (r. 860?–840 B.C.) and his successor
Sarduri I (r. 840–825 B.C.), probably in direct response to the initial phase of
Neo-Assyrian aggression that began with Ashurnasirpal II (r. 883–859 B.C.).
Almost immediately upon the emergence of Urartu, Assyria's Shalmaneser III
(r. 858–824 B.C.) and his army campaigned against the fledgling kingdom,
and it is largely from his written accounts and carved reliefs that we can
reconstruct early Urartian history.

Shalmaneser depicted his campaign in a typical Neo-Assyrian manner
on the great bronze temple gates at Balawat (Fig. 3.2). The main message

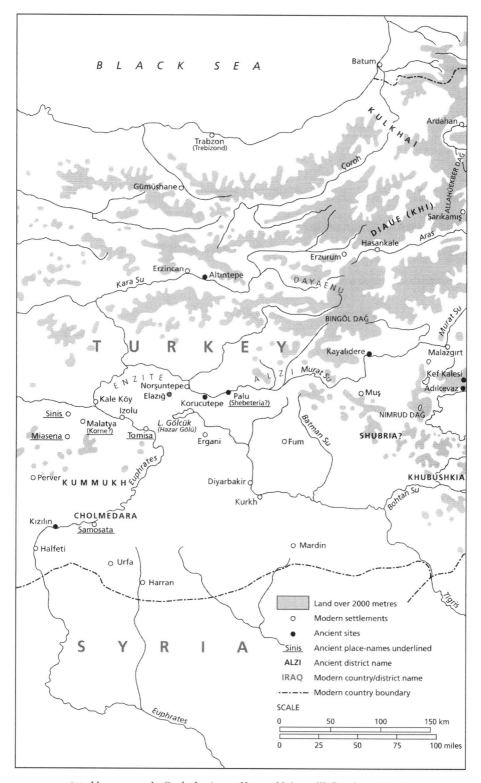

3.1. Urartu map. In *Cambridge Ancient History*, Volume III, Part I, pp. 324–5.

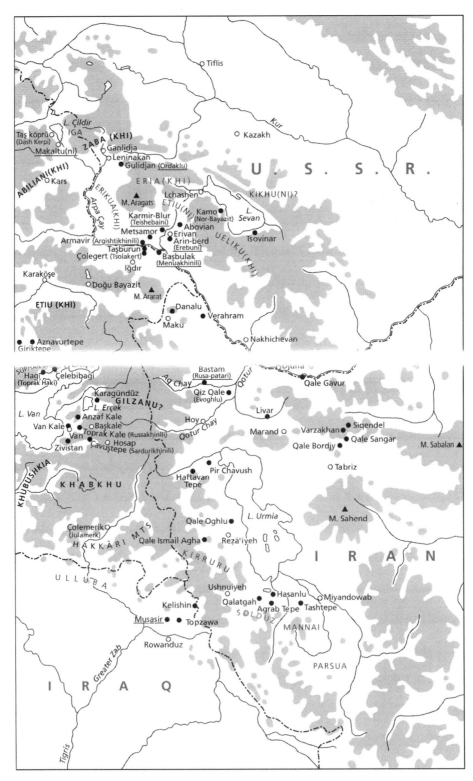

3.1 (*continued*)

3.2. Bronze band from the gates of the palace of Shalmaneser III. The Trustees of the British Museum/Art Resource, NY.

is that he prevailed against Urartu despite the rugged terrain through which he had to fight. On the gates' panels, "fortresses set on mountain peaks are shown being burnt by the Assyrian army; Assyrian soldiers cut down fruit trees and wheel away gigantic storage jars. At the same time, the horrendous physical obstacles that the soldiers had to overcome are illustrated, with Assyrian soldiers heaving their horses up and down the sheer mountains."[1] Shalmaneser, in fact, did not even come close to eliminating the Urartian threat. This secondary state continued to expand at Neo-Assyrian expense, for Urartu's heyday was yet to come.

The initial period of Neo-Assyria's relative weakness in the late ninth and first half of the eighth century B.C. provided a golden opportunity for Urartu to expand and consolidate. It did so by utilizing an emerging network of urban centers that became the focal points of Urartian identity and helped it claim a wide economic base, all while challenging the Assyrian kings' bold universalist claims. The Urartians strengthened their resistance by conquering neighbors and cultivating defensive alliances with surrounding Anatolian polities such as Phrygia.

The Urartian ideological system, insofar as it has been possible to reconstruct, strikingly resembles that of the Assyrians. In Urartian texts and art, it is clear that the kings conquered in the name of Haldi, the chief god of their pantheon. Haldi was a mighty war god who was depicted as a man, sometimes winged like Ashur, standing on a lion. The king served as Haldi's representative on earth and the patron of his cult; the king built and conquered directly in Haldi's name:

> *Through Haldi's might*
> *Menua, son of Ishpuini*
> *To Haldi, the lord*
> *A building, a shrine has set up*
> *A stronghold he has set up.*[2]

Haldi went forth, his weapon smote Hilaruada, son of Shahu, the king of the Meliteans' country [Malatya/Melid], subjected him before Sarduir, son of Argishti. Haldi is mighty, Haldi's weapon is mighty.[3]

Ishpuini, son of Sarduri, placed an inscription before the pedestal. He brought fine arms, fine goods, he brought standards of copper... he brought many goods. He established an *adani* at the Haldi gate. He gave them to Haldi the lord for his life ... through the favor of Haldi he made this citadel [*burganuni*]. ... Whoever removes this inscription from this place... may Haldi, Teisheba, Shiwini, the gods of the town of Ardini wipe out (his) seed on earth.[*]

Citadels and shrines were constructed, enemies defeated, offerings collected, and brutal death threats leveled – all in the name of Haldi. The parallels with the Neo-Assyrians and their god Ashur are obvious in these and other texts, for the Urartians were "massively indebted to Assyria from royal and religious iconography."[5] Although Haldi himself was only a minor god before the rise of the Urartians, the Urartian kings seem to have deliberately created a specific and new form of Haldi cult to empower themselves. M. Salvini argues that Haldi was intentionally adopted by King Ishpuini (r. 825–810 B.C.) as a deliberate and direct imitation of the Neo-Assyrian Ashur cult.[6]

Secondary states apparently were not afraid to fight ideology with an essentially derivative ideology – like fighting fire with fire, as it were. Here, a religious ideology evidently was crafted to fit specific political and military ends. The Haldi cult was most likely shaped and imposed from above, that is, from political leaders; it does not seem to have emerged from longer cultural traditions, as did the Ashur cult. In fact, Urartu provides a rare example in which we actually can trace the initial emergence of a powerful ideology and its usage. Usually, that story is completely lost in the mist of preliteracy.

Further Neo-Assyrian–Urartian parallels appear throughout the sources. The few surviving early Urartian texts were written in Assyrian cuneiform and composed in the manner of the Assyrian Royal Annals, arranged according to yearly campaigns. As the kingdom grew toward its height, its texts were

3.3. Bronze model of a city wall. From Turkey, Urartian. Line drawing by Andrew Welton.

written in Urartian, using a Hurrian script, perhaps an indication of growing Urartian assertiveness in the face of their rival and model. At the end of our study, we will see a similar process with an Islamic empire, which first used Greek as an administrative language but then switched to Arabic as assertiveness grew and identity hardened. The Urartian mode of conquest followed a familiar pattern: a powerful king who demanded unquestioned obedience led the conquest in Haldi's name, subordinated local rulers into his expanding state, demanded regular tribute, and later also began strategically deporting local populations. The Urartians learned well from their Assyrian teachers, and, it seems, even adapted some of the Assyrian innovations along the way, such as the policy of deportation.

The Urartian kingdom reached its height under its kings Menua (r. 810–785 B.C.) and Argishti I (r. 785–763 B.C.). During the reign of the Assyrian king Shalmaneser IV (r. 782–773 B.C.), Argishti I firmly held Syria and attacked the kingdom of Assyria from both east and west. The Assyrians were being attacked by many other local princes at this same time, as well as by rebelling governors, thanks in part to the new opportunities afforded by better harvests and growing populations throughout the Near East, as will be recalled from the previous chapter.

Urartian expansion continued westward until it was halted by the campaigns of Tiglath-pileser III. At the Battle of Kummuh in 742 B.C., Tiglath-pileser defeated Sarduri II (r. 763–734 B.C.), effectively ending the Urartian hold on northern Syria. At the same time, the Cimmerians, usually in the form of mounted nomadic raiders, attacked Urartu and several other Anatolian kingdoms, further hampering their ability to fend off the Assyrians. The Assyrian king Sargon II (r. 721–705 B.C.) bragged of plundering one of Haldi's cult sites and "godnapping" a Haldi statue in 714 B.C. Such "godnapping" was a typical feature of Assyrian ideological warfare.

Still, the Urartians survived into the seventh century, enjoying an impressive resurgence under Rusa II (r. 685–645 B.C.). One story that has been preserved for us hints at an event during the reign of Rusa II that shows another dimension of Urartu's relationship with Assyria. The story has come down to us in the Hebrew Bible, which says that Sennacherib was assassinated by his

"land of Ararat" (i.e., Urartu). We already know that the peripheral kingdom of Elam, before it was eliminated in 646 B.C., served as a refuge for Assyrian exiles and political dissidents; perhaps Urartu did as well. Mention of Urartu appears in later Neo-Babylonian texts, but specific details of its history after the fall of Assyria are difficult to confirm.

The survival and success of Urartu, even throughout the strongest period of the Neo-Assyrian Empire, demonstrates the effectiveness of resistance when it comes from a strongly united political and ideological system. Without this type of state consolidation, the chances of survival for a secondary state were rather slim within the Near East during this period.

COALITION AND COLLAPSE:
SYRIA AND ITS NEIGHBORS

We find a different situation when we move farther to the south, although still on the periphery of the Assyrian Empire. Ben-Hadad II of Damascus (r. 880–842 B.C.) was a bitter enemy of Ahab, king of Israel. After two years of fierce fighting, Ben-Hadad and a large coalition of "kings" (I Kings in the Hebrew Bible says that there were 32 kings) were defeated by Ahab and the Israelites. Ben-Hadad begged for peace, dressed in sackcloth. Ahab agreed to a truce, and an alliance was born, but it would last for only three years before Ben-Hadad and the Syrians began threatening Israel once again.

3.4. Pointed bronze helmet, Urartian. British Museum/Art Resource, NY.

However, there is much more to this short-lived alliance than just a cessation of hostilities among small kingdoms. During the three-year peace, Ahab fought alongside Ben-Hadad and many other petty kings for the survival of Damascus, Israel, and other small kingdoms in the area depended on such coalitions. At the Battle of Qarqar in 853 B.C., fighting against the Neo-Assyrians, their combined and cooperating armies checked the forces of Shalmaneser III.

Most smaller polities simply joined temporary coalitions, sometimes even aligning with their sworn enemies, to resist assimilation into the Neo-Assyrian Empire. In the short term, this method was fairly effective, prolonging the independence of some groups that otherwise would have immediately fallen to the Assyrians. However, the coalitions could not hold out, or hold together, indefinitely. Besides the fact that the coalition partners squabbled among themselves, the Assyrians also had the manpower and the will to come back again and again until the threatening coalition was eliminated. Although some coalitions could mount stiff military resistance, most lacked the unity of resistance that came from a unified political and ideological system. As a result, such coalitions almost always collapsed, and usually sooner rather than later.

Syria was a hotbed of anti-Assyrian coalitions. At the time of the Neo-Assyrian rise, the region consisted of many small kingdoms, which tended to unite in two coalition blocs – one in the north and one in the south. Most of these kingdoms had fairly short histories.

Although the coastal and inland regions of Syria had been united in several Bronze Age kingdoms such as Mitanni and Ugarit, the area was devastated during the turmoil at the end of the Bronze Age. Exactly what happened here during the ensuing Dark Age is, not surprisingly, a matter of much dispute, but it is clear that there was significant population growth during these centuries, as more and more pastoralists moved into the abandoned Bronze Age centers. One important group was the Aramaeans, who settled in Damascus as well as in other parts of the Near East. Here in Syria, these one-time "roving bands of marauders" were successful in setting up kingdoms in a way that they were not elsewhere, particularly in the region of Babylonia, as we see in the next chapter.[7]

A fairly clear picture of these small kingdoms in Syria emerges from the Assyrian Royal Annals dating to the ninth century B.C., for during the

the Phoenicians, were important suppliers of iron and timber to Assyrians and others. These annals are quite helpful, frequently in spite of themselves, especially if we are careful to read between the lines. If Shalmaneser III, for example, brags about his multiple campaigns against basically the same Syrian coalition – as he did in 853, 849, 848, 845, and 841 B.C. – we can be fairly certain that the coalition was strong enough to stand up to him for a time.

Shalmaneser III's reign witnessed both the zenith and the nadir of the Syrian anti-Assyrian coalitions. During his three-year campaign, which began in 858 B.C., he was halted by a northern Syrian coalition consisting of the kings and their armies from the small kingdoms of Sam'al, Patina, Carchemish, and Adini, among others. However, Shalmaneser was able to capture a palace at the site of Til Barsip from an Aramaean king, which he turned into an Assyrian provincial palace. A few years later, at the Battle of Qarqar in 853 B.C., Shalmaneser III was stopped again, this time by a southern Syrian confederation consisting of Syrians, Israelites, Cilicians, Arabs, Phoenicians, Egyptians, Aramaeans, and Ammonites, among others. This significant battle had more combatants than any previously recorded battle, according to the Kurkh Monolith, the Assyrian monument on which the text is recorded. It would take Shalmaneser four more campaigns before he actually captured the territory that he claimed in his Royal Annals.

Soon after the battle at Qarqar, Ben-Hadad II of Damascus betrayed the coalition and absorbed all of the southern Syrian states into his own

3.5. Orthostat showing an Aramaean horseman. BildarchivPreussischerKulturbesitz/Art Resource, NY.

kingdom. A secondary state was apparently in the making, but Shalmaneser III returned and defeated Ben-Hadad's forces. Ben-Hadad was followed on the throne of Damascus by a usurper named Hazael (r. 842–806/805 B.C., Fig. 3.6). He reignited the rebellion against the Assyrians and held out until after the death of Shalmaneser III, all while absorbing more neighboring kingdoms into his own. Shalmaneser's account of his eighteenth year mentions this rebellion, but the Assyrian text, as is frequently the case, only implicitly hints at the scale of the military resistance from the Syrian coalitions and glosses over the effective resistance that Hazael and his forces mounted:

> In the eighteenth year of my rule I crossed the Euphrates for the sixteenth time. Hazael of Damascus put his trust upon his numerous army and called up his troops in great number. . . . I fought with him and inflicted a defeat upon him, killing with the sword 16,000 of his experienced soldiers. I took away from him 1,121 chariots, 470 riding horses as well as his camp. He disappeared to save his life (but) I followed him and

besieged him in Damascus, his royal residence. . . . At that time I received
the tribute of the inhabitants of Tyre, Sidon, and of Jehu, son of Omri.[8]

Hazael, meanwhile, was also campaigning against Jehu of Israel, who had
refused to voluntarily join his coalition and had become a tribute-paying
Assyrian vassal instead. The coalition could not hold out with this type of
conflict among the kingdoms. Well before the close of the ninth century
B.C., the kingdoms of Syria had all collapsed into anarchy or been folded
into Assyrian provinces. The coalitions were not able to survive into the
subsequent period of Assyrian weakness; if they had, Near Eastern history
might have turned out rather differently. Subjugated Syrians did rise up in
rebellion later, forming some coalitions against Tiglath-pileser III and his
successors, but once again, they were eventually defeated, as we will see
shortly.

Overall, several influential groups were pulled together within the Syrian
coalitions. Although many would be folded into the Assyrian Empire and
completely disappear, the Aramaeans at least gave their language as a lingua

Empire were still speaking Aramaic as their first language centuries after the
Arameans had ceased to exist as a kingdom. Similarly, "Arab," a term that
literally means "nomad," first appears in Assyrian Royal Annals of the ninth
century. Dwelling in oases, some submitted to Assyrian rule, whereas others
remained independent, dominating the frankincense trade of northern Arabia,
just out of the Assyrian reach but still within its commercial networks. The
place of such peoples at the peripheries of many Ancient Empires, as soldiers
and traders, will be a significant one in centuries to come, as we shall see.

REVIVAL OF EAST–WEST TRADE:
THE PHOENICIANS/CANAANITES

The Phoenician city-states of the northern Levant eagerly joined the Syrian
coalitions, most notably at the Battle of Qarqar. However, the Phoenicians
ultimately would outlive the Assyrian Empire, and not just because of their
attachment to the short-lived coalitions. In many ways, the Phoenicians, the
most famous sailors and traders of the ancient world, profited greatly from
the Neo-Assyrian rise to dominance in the Near East. In direct response to
it, they intensified and expanded their older trade networks at the same time
they exploited new sources of raw materials. As they did so, they spread Near
Eastern culture westward as well as reconnected the Near East with the wider
Mediterranean world.

3.6. King Hazael of Damascus framed by a lotus flower. Erich Lessing/Art Resource, NY.

The Phoenician response to the Neo-Assyrian rise, unlike the Urartian, was built directly onto long-term traditions. It is important, then, to explore their response(s) in light of their *longue durée* history. The Phoenicians first appeared as Levantine traders and sailors in Bronze Age sources, where they were part of the larger group collectively known as Canaanites ("Phoenician" being a later Greco-Roman designation). Their major coastal centers, Tyre, Sidon, Byblos, and Arvad in particular, all enjoyed commercial contacts with Ugarit, the Hittites, the Egyptians, and the Babylonians. Most famously, the Phoenicians supplied lumber-poor Bronze Age kingdoms with beams of cypress and "cedars of Lebanon." They also provided luxury goods such as ivory, inlaid furniture, textiles, metals, and a purple dye extracted from the murex mollusk. During the Bronze Age, however, the East–West Mediterranean trade was dominated by the Minoans and then the Mycenaeans. The Phoenicians' seaborne trade was limited to the Eastern Mediterranean region. When extensive international trade died with the Bronze Age, an opportunity was created for these seaborne traders. When the demand for international trade emerged again with the Age of Ancient Empires, it was the Phoenicians who were the first to capitalize on it.

The Phoenician centers were able to maintain some elements of a Bronze Age Canaanite culture, even into the Dark Age and amid the widespread

destruction and contraction of culture. They continued to supply lumber
during the twelfth and early eleventh centuries B.C., as we know from the
Assyrian king Tiglath-pileser I (r. 1115–1076 B.C.), who received cedar and
tribute from Phoenician city-states:

> I marched to Mount Lebanon. I cut down (and) carried off cedar beams
> from the temple of the gods Anu and Adad, the great gods my lords. . . . I
> received tribute from the lands of Byblos, Sidon, and Arvad.[9]

A curiously detailed story from a few years after this shows Byblos in a
comparatively better position. A certain Wen-Amon, an Egyptian official
from the Temple of Amon at Karnak, went to Byblos to get lumber for an
Egyptian religious barge. The results were somewhat comical, as he faced a
series of setbacks while trying to get the lumber. After a humorous back-and-
forth argument with Zakar-Baal, the prince of Byblos, Wen-Amon described
his mission:

> I have come after the woodwork for the great and august barque of
> Amon-Re, King of the Gods. Your father did (it), your grandfather did
> (it), and you will do it too![10]

Zakar-Baal, not cowed by a declining Egypt, simply responded: "To be sure,
they did it! And if you give me (something) for doing it, I will do it!" Several
points are clear throughout this well-preserved story: Egyptian power was
certainly on the wane, and a Phoenician city-state was impressively assertive.
Compare the tone of the letters from the archive at Tell el-Amarna sent from
this area (see Chapter One) from just a few centuries earlier in which the
local princes simply described themselves as the dust beneath the feet of the
Pharaoh, and the like. Much had changed here since the Bronze Age.

The Phoenicians profited from some new trading opportunities during the
Dark Age as well. The United Monarchy of Israel emerged, for a time, as a
valuable trading partner when, under King David (r. c. 1000–960 B.C.) and his
son Solomon (r. c. 960–930 B.C.), Israel controlled the major trade routes from
the Red Sea to Syria. The Phoenicians supplied the timber, luxury goods, and
craftsmen for beautifying this new and relatively powerful kingdom, including
the cedar, carpenters, and masons for David's own house and for Solomon's
famed Temple at Jerusalem. Indeed, King Hiram of Tyre enjoyed friendships
or mutually beneficial trade partnerships with both David and Solomon at
a time when demand for his kingdom's goods might otherwise have been
minimal. Solomon, we are told, specifically looked for an "artisan skilled to
work in gold, silver, bronze, and iron, and in purple, crimson and blue fabrics,

trained also in engraving"; he found such a man in Huram-abi, a Phoenician from Tyre, who became the major artisan of the Temple.[11]

The Phoenicians were also a key link in the iron trade during this period. Iron was known much earlier, even in the Bronze Age, but it was not widely used. The Phoenicians played a key role in its diffusion during the Dark Age. Their first Mediterranean colonies, in Cyprus, Cilicia, and Crete, were founded for iron supply, beginning in the tenth century. As always, the real importance of a material or technology has less to do with its invention or discovery and much more to do with its actual and widespread use. The Phoenicians were vital in iron's diffusion and in the early ninth century were instrumental in meeting the growing demands of the Assyrian army for this metal.

It was the Neo-Assyrian rise to power that prompted the most influential of the Phoenician developments. The Phoenician response to the rise of the Neo-Assyrians was multifaceted. To begin with, a rising Near Eastern empire in the ninth century B.C. meant a drastic spike in the demand for raw materials, craftsmen, and luxury goods. The Phoenicians, in accord with their long-term traditions, were prepared to meet this demand. The Assyrian appetite, however, far exceeded anything seen before, and the Phoenicians had to adopt new measures to keep up with the demand. Founding far-flung western colonies was one of their most famous and innovative measures. From colonies on the north coast of Africa, in western Sicily, Sardinia, and southern Spain, the Phoenicians procured the raw materials and other commodities needed to meet the growing Assyrian demands. The Phoenicians must have anticipated a continuing demand, for nearly all their colonies "show signs of permanence from the outset, which reflects a firm determination to develop into populous colonies."[12] These colonies did much more than extract materials for the Near East; they spread Near Eastern culture with them. They also served as models for Greek colonies; Greek colonization would eventually surpass the Phoenician, as we will see in later chapters. Both changed the face of the Mediterranean. The Phoenicians also developed and spread the alphabet westward where it could be borrowed and adapted by Greeks, Libyans, Etruscans, Latins, and others.

There is much more to the story of these western colonies; they show us, again, the connection between the various levels of historical time, as explained in Chapter Two. With the population growing markedly over the late ninth and eighth centuries, colonization also served as a population outlet for so-called mother cities – that is, the cities that sent out the colonists. The later Greek colonization movement was also driven largely by such population pressures. The similar Phoenician and Greek actions were part of the larger human response to changes in climate, food supply, and population numbers.

3.7. Island of Arvad at the Lebanese coast. Erich Lessing/Art Resource, NY.

Phoenician colonizing in the western Mediterranean followed a basic pattern that reflected developments in the Near East. A primary phase, specifically in the ninth and early eighth centuries, saw the initial arrival of Phoenician traders and settlers. This was a direct response to the initial period of Assyrian expansion and trade demand. Carthage, the most famous of the western colonies, for example, was founded in 814/813 B.C. A second stage followed, during the eighth and seventh centuries, which in many cases saw notable growth of industrial and mercantile installations, leading toward a specifically urban culture. Right about the time that the Assyrian Empire was in its most expansive and decorative phase, the colonies were forming firm urban centers in the West that made supply more efficient. A final colonial stage followed, which saw the construction of great public works and urban centers, much of it in imitation of Near Eastern models. These urban centers, a direct reflection of the Near Eastern developments under way elsewhere, would serve as models for urbanization around the Mediterranean rim.

The colonies also provided a way for the Phoenicians to move beyond the reach of the Assyrian armies and tribute collectors. This was an option that other Near Eastern groups generally did not have. The timing provides a telling story. Their first western Mediterranean colonies were founded soon after they suffered both a defeat at the hands of Shalmaneser III in 842 B.C.

3.8. The wooden gates of Shalmaneser III with bands of relief decoration in bronze. Werner Forman/Art Resource, NY.

and then the additional ignominy of having to pay tribute from their wealthy commercial centers. Later, Tiglath-pileser III's expansion folded several Phoenician city-states into an Assyrian province. The Phoenicians would later enter a coalition with Egypt and Judah, but their unsuccessful rebellion was quashed by Sennacherib at the end of the eighth century B.C. Sidon was later completely destroyed by Esarhaddon, following yet another rebellion. The growth and sophistication of their western Mediterranean colonies corresponded in time to the grinding down of their cities back home. Although Tyre itself lived to see another empire, Phoenician culture survived most vibrantly in the colonies. Today, thanks to the work of archaeologists, we know far more about the Phoenicians from their colonies than from their central Canaanite cities.

The Phoenicians' response to empire, largely economic, had strong cultural ramifications. At the "big-picture" level, they reconnected the Near East with the Mediterranean, spreading the newly redeveloping culture of the Near

East to Greece, North Africa, and Italy. The Near Eastern and Mediterranean worlds would not be separated again. At the "micro-level," their importance can be seen in the use of an alphabet on this very page. What is clear to current historians, but was not to previous generations, is that the famous Phoenician expansion cannot be understood apart from the rise of the Neo-Assyrian Empire.

CONFLICT AND COVENANT: ISRAEL AND JUDAH

The history of the United Monarchy of Israel and the subsequent separate kingdoms of Israel and Judah during this period is best told with at least one eye on the *longue durée*. As with the Phoenicians, it is helpful to view their specific responses to Neo-Assyrian aggression in the light of deeper cultural patterns. Some of the most characteristic Jewish traditions and beliefs either emerged or were intensified and magnified with the rise of the Neo-Assyrians. The surviving accounts of Jewish interaction with the Assyrians, particularly as recounted in the books of Kings, Chronicles, and a few contemporary

Yahweh and his chosen people. Although the later histories put monotheism at Israel's ideological core from an early period, the fact is that polytheism dominated Israel's history, as the ancient writers themselves make quite clear. Exactly when the covenant with Yahweh became a central point of their story is a matter of much dispute among scholars, but all agree that there was a renewed and explicit emphasis on monotheism in response to the Neo-Assyrian threat. This primarily ideological response was critical to Jewish identity and may have been one reason the Jewish people survived as a people in the face of Assyrian hegemony and aggression.

Thanks to the lengthy accounts in the Hebrew Bible (or Old Testament), we know more about the history of Israel and the Israelites than about almost any other area or group from this time period. The amount of detail does not make the historian's task any easier, however, if that task involves not only determining how historically accurate the details are in the first place but also connecting Israel's stories to the larger picture of Near Eastern history. The history given in the Old Testament is an extremely focused one, narrowing in on the covenant with Yahweh. The Assyrians, Syrians, Phoenicians, and others do appear but essentially as props for telling the "real story." Conversely, Israel barely registers at all in the accounts written by its neighbors; it was hardly worthy of a mention except perhaps in a stray line declaring that some power had just handed it a devastating defeat. Not a single contemporary reference to kings David or Solomon, who took the United Monarchy to its height, appears in any surviving outside text. Outside of later Neo-Assyrian sources, there are only two or three brief references to Israel or Judah. Reading the text of the Old Testament in light of ongoing archaeological discoveries presents a whole series of thorny issues, many of them well beyond the scope of this study.

Israel's own accounts take them back deep into the Bronze Age. Abraham, their progenitor, was called by Yahweh out of Mesopotamian Ur to start a new people and was given an exclusive covenant and assurance of a Promised Land. After a period in Egypt when they had been enslaved, the "children of Israel" made their way to their Promised Land and began slowly wresting it away from its erstwhile inhabitants. The completely isolated and first definite reference to Israel outside of the Old Testament appears in a sentence in an Egyptian victory hymn dating to 1207 B.C., the fifth year of Pharaoh Merneptah. The line is hardly helpful: "Israel is laid waste, his seed is not."[13] It does, however, complement the picture given in the Hebrew Bible of a group of people – the Israelites – as inhabiting Canaan by this time.

Between 1200 and 1000 B.C., during the Dark Age, the Israelites won a series of military victories against various groups of Canaanites and took control of a fair portion of their Promised Land. Even by the mid-eleventh century, however, they still remained a set of villages with no single ruler over them; the most influential man among them at this time was the prophet Samuel. Eventually, in the face of expansionist pressure, as the Philistines moved up into the Shephelah and the Israelites expanded downward, conflict between the two groups became inevitable.

Faring poorly against the Philistines – they even lost their famed Ark of the Covenant – the Israelites decided that what they needed was a king and a real kingdom like their neighbors. Samuel reluctantly anointed Saul as the first king, setting up a dichotomy between the political and religious power bases that would characterize the subsequent history of the Israelite kingdom(s). Saul turned out to be a false start for the monarchy, and he ended up committing suicide as he was being routed by Philistines. The royal mantle then fell on King David sometime around 1000 B.C.

The real story of Israelite state formation began with David. David himself captured Jerusalem and made it his capital city. The reclaimed Ark of the Covenant was eventually brought to the city as well, and both Jerusalem and the Ark thereafter served as political and ideological indicators of state formation and Israelite identity. During this period, however, we begin to see the tensions between political and religious power, for it was a prophet, Nathan, who famously rebuked David for transgressions against Yahweh, foretelling divine wrath.

According to the ancient sources, David's son, Solomon, brought the United Monarchy to a comparatively formidable, if short-lived, height of power in this age of petty kingdoms. Solomon is described by a later Jewish chronicler, in exaggerated prose, as

> sovereign over all the kingdoms from the Euphrates to the land of the Philistines, even to the border of Egypt; they brought tribute and served Solomon all the days of his life.[14]

In addition to emphasizing his political power, the books of Kings and Chronicles in the Hebrew Bible lay out Solomon's economic and military power:

> Solomon gathered together chariots and horses; he had fourteen hundred chariots and twelve thousand horses. . . . The king made silver as common in Jerusalem as stones. . . . A chariot could be imported from Egypt for six hundred shekels of silver, and a horse for one hundred fifty; so through the king's traders they were exported to all the kings of the Hittites and the kings of Aram.[15]

Despite such accomplishments, Solomon encountered resistance from the defenders of the covenant with Yahweh. Earlier in his reign, Solomon himself had prayed to Yahweh for wisdom, we are told, so that he could "govern your people, able to discern between good and evil."[16] The standard of righteousness for Israel was one that hung over the heads of kings and commoners alike. During the later parts of his reign especially, "Solomon did what was evil in the sight of the LORD [Yahweh], and did not completely follow the LORD [Yahweh]."[17] A prophet, Ahijah, predicted disaster on the kingdom as judgment upon Solomon's wickedness. Both then and later, the fiercest defenders of Israel's religious identity were described more often than not as being strongly at odds with the political powers.

Solomon's vast expenditures ultimately resulted in large taxes being levied on his citizens, who grew increasingly disgruntled and eventually revolted, leading to the permanent division of his kingdom at the end of his reign. The northern kingdom became known as Israel, with its capital at Samaria, and the southern kingdom was called Judah, with its capital at Jerusalem. They are collectively referred to as the Divided Kingdoms, in contrast to the previous United Monarchy. The conflict between religious and political sources of power came to a head just as the Neo-Assyrians began their expansion, soon after this division of the United Monarchy into two separate kingdoms.

Nearly all of the kings of both kingdoms fell far short of the ideals of the covenant, "chasing after" the gods of their neighbors and "doing what was evil in the sight of Yahweh." The prophets continually called them back

3.9. Jehu, king of Israel, prostrating himself before King Shalmaneser III of Assyria. Line drawing by Andrew Welton.

to their religious ideology and identity. As the Neo-Assyrians rose and grew more powerful, the voices of the prophets became ever more strident in opposition to the kings of both kingdoms. Some of the most memorable stories from the reign of King Ahab (r. 869–850 B.C.), who ruled the northern kingdom of Israel during the expansions and encroachments of the Neo-Assyrian kings Ashurnasirpal II and Shalmaneser III, involve the Prophet Elijah directly rebuking the Israelite king for his sinful actions and challenging his false prophets and wrong gods. For Ahab had been seizing private property and generally acting as a typical Near Eastern monarch, but such actions were in direct opposition to Israel's religious ideals.

As the Neo-Assyrians put direct pressure on Israel and Judah, the kingdoms responded by sometimes rallying against and sometimes even allying with the Assyrians. Ahab, it will be recalled, was a senior partner in the anti-Assyrian coalition at the Battle of Qarqar. Jehu (r. 842–815 B.C.) of Israel, who may have come to the throne courtesy of Hazael of Damascus, later refused to join a Syrian-sponsored anti-Assyrian alliance and instead allied with Assyria's Shalmaneser III against his former ally. Jehu is a perfect example of an elite collaborator, who, like Udjahorresne, cooperated with the imperial aggressor. Jehu, however, ended up the double loser as he became a tribute-paying vassal to an otherwise-occupied Shalmaneser who probably did not lose much sleep when Hazael decided to exact his revenge by attacking Jehu and ravaging Assyria's vassal kingdom of Israel (Fig. 3.9). After Shalmaneser, the Assyrian threat declined for nearly a century, allowing the northern kingdom to recover, but the respite would be only temporary.

When Assyria reasserted itself in force under Tiglath-pileser III, new vari-
eties of prophets emerged within Israel and Judah in response. The prophets'
messages helped shape Jewish identity from that time forward and served as an
effective mode of ideological resistance to Assyrian might. The eighth-century
prophets were not just private counselors and critics of the king, as most earlier prophets had been, but opinionated leaders – public figures who delivered
their messages directly to the people as well. Some, such as Isaiah, remained as
valuable advisors to kings even while they addressed the people at large. They
lambasted the Jews as a whole for forgetting their covenant and for neglecting
social justice – not caring for, and even abusing, the downtrodden in their
own communities. Yahweh spoke through one prophet, Isaiah of Judah:

> When you stretch out your hands, I will hide my eyes from you; even
> though you make many prayers, I will not listen; your hands are full of
> blood. Wash yourselves; make yourselves clean; remove the evil of your
> doings from before my eyes; cease to do evil, learn to do good; seek
> justice, rescue the oppressed, defend the orphan, plead for the widow.[18]

> Thus says the LORD [Yahweh]: For three transgressions of Israel, and
> for four, I will not revoke the punishment; because they sell the righteous
> for silver, and the needy for a pair of sandals – they who trample the
> head of the poor into the dust of the earth, and push the afflicted out of
> the way.[19]

The prophets claimed that Israel's oppression by Assyria and others, past,
present, and future, was the will of Yahweh. Yahweh could and would bring
the Assyrians against the Jews as a purifying punishment. Yahweh, in fact,
was behind all historical events, Amos proclaimed:

> Is a trumpet blown in a city, and the people are not afraid? Does disaster
> befall a city, unless the LORD [Yahweh] had done it? Surely the Lord
> GOD does nothing, without revealing his secret to his servants the
> prophets.[20]

The campaigns of Tiglath-pileser III and his successors would push the religious ideology of the Divided Kingdoms to its limit. Both kingdoms went
back and forth between Syrian coalitions and Assyrian vassalage. One famous
example of both Jewish collaboration and internal Jewish division emerged
amid the international pressure of empire. Menahem (r. 745–738 B.C.) of Israel
submitted to Tiglath-pileser and then infuriated many in his kingdom while
trying to raise the expected tribute; consequently, he was assassinated. One

3.10. The Taylor-Prism, Neo-Assyrian, from Nineveh. Erich Lessing/Art Resource, NY.

of his successors, Pekah (r. 737–732), then threw in his lot with a brief-lived Syrian anti-Assyrian coalition. Angered that Jehoahaz I (r. 735–715 B.C.) of Judah refused to join the coalition, Pekah declared war on Jehoahaz to try to force him into the Syrian coalition. The prophet Isaiah clearly warned Jehoahaz not to do so, but he appealed to Tiglath-pileser III for help anyway. Tiglath-pileser responded by subordinating Israel; Jehoahaz then worshipped Ashur in the Temple at Jerusalem and took the oath of loyalty to him.

Responding to subsequent rebellion, the Assyrian kings Shalmaneser V and Sargon II invaded and utterly destroyed Samaria, the capital of the northern kingdom of Israel, deporting 27,290 people, who became known as the Ten Lost Tribes of Israel. The northern kingdom of Israel was finished – the Assyrians replaced the deportees with people from Babylonia as well as Arabs. Israel was now part of an Assyrian province.

The southern kingdom of Judah, meanwhile, voluntarily became a vassal state. Moments of resistance, though, were fanned by the voice of the prophets, reminding Jews of their covenant and calling for ideological resistance. One famous moment of Assyrian counterresponse was the siege of Jerusalem in 701 B.C. Accounts of this siege survive from both sides, oddly agreeing in most – but not all – particulars. The biblical book of Kings and the Prism of Sennacherib give alternate versions of why, exactly, Jerusalem was actually spared destruction (Fig. 3.10).

A culminating moment of Judah's ideological resistance against Assyria came in 621 B.C., just before the collapse of the Neo-Assyrian Empire (that event, incidentally, is not even recorded in the historical books of the Hebrew Bible). Josiah (r. 640–609 B.C.), a glaring exception to Judah's line of "wicked kings," carried out a radical religious reform and reaffirmation of the covenant, while simultaneously expanding against a weakened Assyria. A cleaning of the Temple, apparently, had uncovered a lost "Book of the Law" or "Book of the Covenant" (probably sections of the book of Deuteronomy). Josiah then destroyed the prevalent sites and symbols of other gods throughout Judah after a passionate and powerful call for covenant faithfulness:

> The king stood by the pillar and made a covenant before the LORD [Yahweh], to follow the LORD [Yahweh] keeping his commandments, his decrees, and his statutes, with all his heart and all his soul, to perform the words of this covenant that were written in this book. All the people joined in the covenant.[21]

it would long be remembered as such. Josiah extended his rule and reforms to all Israel, and his actions amounted to a bid for autonomy from the Assyrians, backed up by a strong religious ideology. The Jews would survive, thanks in part to their identity as People of the Covenant, that is, as People of the Book.

Israel's and Judah's enduring legacy – as well as a significant portion of the Hebrew Bible – emerged in response to the Age of Ancient Empires. The emphasis on the covenant with Yahweh from the time of the Neo-Assyrian revival forward, especially after the 722 B.C. destruction of the northern kingdom of Israel, is so strong that some scholars have argued that it was in fact the fall of the northern kingdom that prompted the first compilation of Israel's history and "the formulation of all historical experience as a direct reflection of the purity of its adherence to Yahweh's cult."[22] That is, all of their earlier history, parts of which were recorded in the Hebrew Bible, was at this point recast in the new mold of the ideologically potent covenant ideology; they then retrojected their covenant into their pre–eighth century past.

These are controversial conclusions that take us beyond the scope of this work. However, no scholar would deny that Jewish traditions were intensified and expanded in response to Neo-Assyrian imperialism. The Jews could and would remain a people and a faith even without a political unit. Their prophets would continue to call them to covenant faithfulness, and political and ideological forces would continue to clash. Nonetheless, a powerful ideology would help sustain, for a little longer, a people who had barely survived Assyrian assimilation and who would soon fall to the Babylonians, the next empire on the horizon.

CHAPTER FOUR

BEYOND THE NEAR EAST: THE NEO-BABYLONIAN AND EARLY ACHAEMENID PERSIAN EMPIRES

Says Darius the king: by the favor of Ahuramazda I am of such a kind that I am a friend to what is right, I am no friend to what is wrong. It is not my wish that to the weak is done wrong because of the mighty, that the mighty is hurt because of the weak. What is right, that is my wish. I am no friend of the man who is a follower of the Lie.

— Naqsh-I-Rustem Inscription of Darius I[1]

* How did the Neo-Babylonian Empire hold the former Assyrian territories?
* How does an "empire in denial" work?
* How did the past – or images of it – help shape the Neo-Babylonian Empire?
* How did the Persians build and hold together such a vast and diverse empire?

THE CHAOS AND FRAGMENTATION that had characterized the Near East before the Neo-Assyrians' rise did not return upon the empire's collapse. The fairly direct transition to the next empire (and the next . . .) reveals that the political organization of empire was impressed firmly on the Near Eastern landscape and beyond. Many familiar patterns persisted, even though subsequent empires would showcase the variety with which ancient empires consolidated their rule.

As one looks ahead from this point, two general trends appear. First, each succeeding empire would be larger than its predecessor and more diverse in its inhabitants, moving well beyond Mesopotamia. In fact, from the rise of the Achaemenid Persian Empire onward, there would be only one more ancient empire with its heartland in Mesopotamia. Second, there was a broad tendency for empires to expand westward: the Neo-Babylonian,

Achaemenid Persian, Alexandrian/Hellenistic, Roman, and Umayyad Islamic Empires would successively pull together regions of the eastern and western Mediterranean, even as some continued remarkable expansion to the east, even to India. Some of the peoples swept into the Age of Ancient Empires would resist this inclusion, and some empire resisters would, in turn, become empire builders themselves. The rise of the two great empires of this chapter, in fact, could be analyzed as additional case studies for significant response to the Neo-Assyrian Empire.

THE RISE (AND FALL) OF THE
NEO-BABYLONIAN EMPIRE

We have already seen that Babylon had a deep and rich culture of which its inhabitants were acutely aware. The Babylonian elite were self-confident in their sense of Babylonian identity, which did not tolerate outside rule well. Babylon was a definite prize to win but a difficult one to grasp. Assyrians' and others' efforts to take over and hold Babylon and surrounding areas present a saga going back to just after the collapse of the Bronze Age. A long and rather complicated story of Babylon from that point until the emergence of the Neo-Babylonian Empire can, for our purposes, be summarized briefly: 1) small, brief dynasties troubled frequently by Assyrians, Elamites, Aramaeans, and others (late twelfth–early ninth centuries B.C.); 2) recovery and cooperation/détente with the Neo-Assyrians (ninth century B.C.); 3) invasion and domination by Neo-Assyrians broken by periods of revolt and relative autonomy (late ninth–late seventh centuries B.C.); and 4) rise of Babylon's Nabopolassar and Assyrian collapse (626–612 B.C.).

Nabopolassar (r. 626–605) began the Neo-Babylonian rise by conquering several Assyrian provinces. He had started out as a local political functionary for the Assyrians and used his position as a springboard to betray and then expand against his weakened former masters. He allied with Cyaxares (r. 625–585), who was king of the Medes, a large tribal confederacy sharing linguistic and other cultural similarities with the Persians. The aid of the Medes, a growing strength, on the path toward emerging as a secondary state on the periphery of the Neo-Assyrian Empire was significant. Together the Neo-Babylonians and Medes took Nineveh, ending the Neo-Assyrian Empire in 612. One fragmentary inscription affords a glimpse of Nabopolassar's acceptance by the Babylonian elites after his victory over the Neo-Assyrians. The assembled body of elites publicly acclaimed him as ruler:

The princes of the land, being assembled, Nab[opolassar they bless?] . . .

> Bel (Marduk), in the assembly of the gods, [gave?] the ruling power to
> [Nabopolassar?] . . . With the standard I shall constantly conquer [your
> enemies], I shall place [your?] throne in Babylon. They kept placing the
> standard on his head. They had him sit on the royal throne. . . . O lord,
> O king, may you live forever! [May you conquer] the land of [your]
> enemies!
>
> May the king of the gods, Marduk, rejoice in you.[2]

As the Neo-Babylonians moved into the former Neo-Assyrian Empire and
set up their rule, they simply replaced the highest level of Assyrian political
and social elites, leaving the rest of the population to function pretty much
as before – a textbook case of elite replacement. There was, as might be
imagined, nothing along the lines of a grassroots Assyrian "nationalism" with
which to contend as they consolidated their own rule. As so often occurs,
life for the vast bulk of the population was essentially "business as usual,"
regardless of the actual empire in control. In their texts and imagery, the
Neo-Babylonians primarily stressed maintenance and continuity of structures

Nabopolassar was succeeded by his son, Nebuchadnezzar II (r. 604–562),
who brought the Neo-Babylonian Empire to its height of glory by beautifying
cities throughout the realm, ruling in the name of the Babylonian chief god
Marduk, and maintaining a sense of cosmos/order over the largest amount of
land and greatest population yet. The descriptions of his righteous reign call
to mind some Neo-Assyrian notions:

> In those days Nebuchadnezzar, king of Babylon, the judicious prince
> shepherd of the widespread people, who like the sun-god oversees the
> totality of the lands, who determines right and justice, who destroys
> evildoers and criminals.[3]

Neo-Babylonian history is essentially the story of Nebuchadnezzar's reign;
almost all else is curiosity. He is most remembered for his urban renaissance in
Babylon – the construction and repair of countless temples and the construction of the Ishtar Gate, one of Babylon's most beautiful and sacred treasures.
The later and universal attribution of the Hanging Gardens of Babylon to
him was possibly a mistake, but a thoroughly understandable one given his
legendary beautification of the city. Although his texts do not much emphasize this aspect, he was also a tireless warrior. For the first ten years of his
reign, he was constantly at war, especially with the Egyptians who, like the
Babylonians themselves, maintained a solid and self-assured identity in the
face of external interference.

During the course of his campaigns against Egypt, the troublesome polities of the Levant got in the way. Nebuchadnezzar removed Jehoiachin, the king of Judah (in 598/597), and put a puppet ruler in his place (Zedekiah), who later rebelled against him (587). This event signaled the end of Judah, which was then folded into a Babylonian province under a local elite collaborator. Many of its inhabitants were deported in the Assyrian style, the so-called Babylonian Captivity. Nebuchadnezzar also conquered Phoenician Tyre after a long siege. In the end, the drawn-out hostilities between Babylonia and Egypt gave way to a type of peaceful coexistence. Egypt would remain an independent kingdom until it fell later to the Achaemenid Persians.

Nebuchadnezzar, like all Neo-Babylonian rulers, personally emphasized his own peaceful achievements rather than his military exploits and conquests, showing a marked contrast with Neo-Assyrian precedents. Neo-Babylonian kings also avoided universalist titles, opting simply for the comparatively mundane "king of Babylon" over such Neo-Assyrian titles as "king of the world," "king of the universe," and the like. One historian suggests that these facts point to the "systematic denial of the fact of empire, contrasting with the very obvious exercise of it in practice."[4] Why would an ancient empire want to be an empire in denial? The same historian suggests a few possible reasons. The Neo-Babylonians' fairly short-lived empire did not actually exist long enough to work out a universal vocabulary of their own. Or perhaps they wanted to emphasize that their Babylonian "piety had triumphed over Assyrian hubris and savagery."[5] Such a stance obviously set them apart from their Neo-Assyrian predecessors and points to ways in which each successive empire brought in their own methods of empire formation and consolidation, even as all borrowed from their predecessors, as can be seen, for example, in the Neo-Babylonian deportation of inhabitants of Judah. There was much continuity from empire to empire, but there was no such thing as a static and standard Near Eastern Empire.

Nebuchadnezzar's spectacular forty-three-year reign was followed by a series of brief reigns (three kings in six years), which are more notable for petty palace intrigue than for some actual, although small, territorial gains. The next king worthy of note was the final one. Apparently seizing the throne by force, Nabonidus (r. 555–539) ushered in the last phase of the Neo-Babylonian Empire, aided by his adult son Bel-sharra-usur ("Belshazzar" in the Hebrew Bible book of Daniel). Nabonidus apparently had no relation to the royal family, and his hold on the throne was contested. His well-documented reign seems to have been challenged from inside and outside throughout. He campaigned for a long period of his reign against Arab tribes on his southern borders, leaving Bel-sharra-usur in charge of Babylon.

4.1. Stela of King Nabonidus, Neo-Babylonian dynasty. The Trustees of The British Museum/
Art Resource, NY.

His campaigns even pulled Yathrib (later known as Medina) into the Neo-
Babylonian Empire, incorporating an important trade depot directly into the
Near Eastern economic and political sphere.

LOOKING BACK AND LOOKING AHEAD:
NEO-BABYLONIAN RULERSHIP IN ACTION

In the latter parts of the nineteenth and in the early twentieth centuries (A.D.),
it was common for Near Eastern archaeology and European empires to move
along together somewhat symbiotically. Artifacts and even architecture from
ancient imperial sites built up many a museum back in imperial European
countries during Europe's so-called Age of High Empire. One of the more
famous and most grandiose "trophies" brought to Europe, in fact, was the
famous Ishtar Gate of Babylon. Brick by brick, the gate was taken to pre–World
War I Germany and reconstructed, where it still is today in the Pergamon
Museum in Berlin (Fig. 4.2). This imperial fascination with the distant tangible

4.2. The Ishtar Gate, built during the reign of Nebuchadnezzar II. BildarchivPreussischer-Kulturbesitz/Art Resource, NY.

past is nothing new. Empires, through symbols, imagery, and even material culture, have often aspired to re-create or renew moments of past glory. The past, tangible or not, is a dynamic tool that has the power to inspire, to encourage, and to legitimate current imperial rule.

Ancient empires have proven to be some of the most powerful models across time. The Roman Empire, for example, inspired, among others, Charlemagne's Frankish Empire, the Turkish Ottoman Empire, and the British Empire, which borrowed much of its imagery and artifacts. Alexander the Great's empire was a model for the Ottoman Empire as well as the Mongol Empire of Genghis Khan but in turn was itself modeled on the Achaemenid Persian Empire created by Cyrus the Great and his successors. The Achaemenid Persian Empire also served as an inspiration both for the Safavid Empire of early modern Iran and the modern nation of Iran. The Anatolian Hittite Empire was a model for the modern state of Turkey, which continues to employ its imagery freely. More recently, Saddam Hussein employed imagery from Nebuchadnezzar's Babylon in a bid to bolster his own national and international image.

The Babylonian Empire likewise looked back to the distant past for ideological legitimacy. Neo-Babylonian emperors even sponsored archaeological field excavations of sorts to back up their claims to rule. They searched out and unearthed old Bronze Age temple foundations to rebuild long-forgotten temples at their exact location as well as simply to find ancient remains and artifacts. Ancient inscriptions, broken statues, steles, architectural fragments, and other artifacts were all unearthed and placed in museums adjacent to the royal palaces. For the Babylonian kings, this restoration was a cornerstone of their imperial ideology. The corpus of Neo-Babylonian inscriptions is replete with examples of what they present as pious, antiquarian building work. This task, rather than offensive or defensive military exploits, was the real pride of the Neo-Babylonian kings.

> I, Nabopolassar, the obedient, the submissive, (the one) who reveres Nabu and Marduk, the shepherd who pleases Sarpanitum [Marduk's wife], who inspects the old foundations of Babylon, who discovers the original brickwork, who reveals the original eternal ground.... On that day I found a royal statue of (a king) who had gone before me, who had restored this wall, (so) I indeed placed it with my statue in a secure place

The Neo-Assyrians before them had rebuilt a few Bronze Age Babylonian temples as well, probably to encourage the support of the populace. But there was no precedent for the lengths to which the Neo-Babylonians pursued their distant past in their imperial project. As the kings discovered old dedicatory inscriptions at these excavation sites, they sometimes imitated their wording in their own inscriptions, using an archaizing script and language. They could also thereby bring back long-forgotten practices, as Nabonidus did:

> I discovered an old stele of Nebuchadnezzar [I, r. 1146–1123], son of Ninurta-nadin-shumi, a former king, which had an image of the entu-priestess fashioned on it. Moreover, her insignia, her clothing, and her jewelry were recorded (on it) and brought (these texts) into the Egipar. I brought out the ancient tablets and writing boards and restored the panels as they were (restored) in the past.[7]

Nabonidus is here placing his daughter in the position of entu-priestess, a long-defunct office. Such invocation of antiquity was central to legitimizing and reinstating the position. The inscription goes on to describe how Nabonidus discovered an ancient foundation for the temple and then restored it as it was in the past, bringing back, in effect, the "good old days."

This re-created or discovered past was to be an ideological model for the future, as suggested by a Nabopolassar inscription. The discovered inscription

is one of Naram-Sin, the grandson of Sargon I, from the late third millennium
B.C.:

> To the king of the land – be he a son or a grandson – who follows me and
> whom Marduk calls for rulership of the land: You should not concern
> yourself with might and power. (Instead) seek out the shrines of Nabu
> and Marduk in your heart that they may slay your enemies. . . . When this
> wall grows old and you remove its decay, just as I found an inscription of
> a king who preceded me and did not alter its location, (so should you)
> find the inscription (bearing) my name and set it in the (same) place as
> your inscription.[8]

The past provided stability, continuity, and legitimacy from the first Neo-
Babylonian king onward.

The key festival of the Neo-Babylonian year likewise emphasized the
crucial stabilizing role of the king by parading the distant past before the eyes
of the Babylonians while looking to a prosperous future. Like most ancient
emperors, the Neo-Babylonian ruler stood for and maintained a righteous
order. The New Year's festival, Akitu, was a vivid and visual illustration of his
roles as guarantor of order and righteousness. The festival itself, dedicated to
Marduk and his son Nabu, clearly reified the political, ideological, military,
and economic power of the king – a veritable festival of ideology, economics,
military, and politics (IEMP). At the festival, which could not be celebrated
without the presence of the king, the empire was symbolically placed on
strong footing for the year ahead. Some of its major rituals involved the re-
creation and actual performance of creation myths to connect Babylon with
deepest antiquity.

The first few days of the twelve-day festival were dedicated to the king's
ritual preparation, praying, and sacrificing at the temple of Marduk. Statues of
Marduk and Nabu were then paraded out of the city via the Ishtar Gate. The
procession went out to survey the fields, on which the agricultural and hence
economic life of the people depended. On the final days, the king returned
to the city accompanied by a great procession.

The ideology of the king as the rightfully chosen instrument of Marduk
was a central theme of the festival. One of the major rituals consisted of the
king being stripped of all his royal insignia, slapped in the face, and forced to
his knees before a statue of Marduk as a priest pulled on the king's ears until
tears formed. The king then delivered a solemn oath, swearing that he had
not affronted Marduk, humiliated the people of Marduk's city (Babylon), or
harmed the city in any way. The priest then would restore his insignia. The
blessing of Marduk would be evident for the new year in both crop production

and maintaining order throughout the land. A bountiful and blessed new year was the reward of Marduk on a king who pursued righteousness.

Politically, the whole ceremony impressed on the inhabitants of the city the legitimacy of the king, who defended right and justice. Mock battles were staged to demonstrate that order was based on military violence and suppression of enemies and evildoers. Some have interpreted these as a recognition by the Babylonians that violence was a necessary, if unfortunate, part of the building and maintaining of empire. Again, the theme of empire in denial seems to come forth. Scenes from the Akkadian creation epic *Enuma Elish* were dramatically performed during the festival to symbolize Marduk defeating primeval monsters of chaos and to connect the Neo-Babylonians with their earliest foundations and origins. Underscoring the political and military facets or imperial rule as well, the festival provided a setting for the king to display his troops and his recent trophies of war.

Outside of the highly symbolic and celebrated acts of pious restoration and directing of the new year's festival by the king, the actual day-to-day mechanics of Neo-Babylonian empire maintenance are difficult to recon-

point to much continuity with the Neo-Assyrian Empire. It is clear that the Neo-Babylonians continued elite replacement, giving the most important governmental and provincial positions to their own people, but relying on preexisting local elites to maintain order and continuity in their regions. One famous example is Adad-guppi, the mother of King Nabonidus. In a lengthy autobiographical inscription, Adad-guppi describes her fascinating and surprisingly long life, which stretched from the Neo-Assyrian Empire up to the final king of the Neo-Babylonian Empire. She lived to the age of 104, and, as she tells us, cared for a temple of the moon god Sin "for ninety-five years." Maintenance of a temple implied a fairly high social status, and the basic chronology of her life tells an interesting story, emphasizing some of the continuity from the Neo-Assyrians through the Neo-Babylonians.

Neo-Babylonian governors were probably much like Neo-Assyrian governors, and to them fell the duties of gathering the tribute and taxes necessary for maintaining the empire. With the Achaemenid Persian provinces following (although expanding and elaborating) Neo-Assyrian provincial patterns, it is safe to assume that the Neo-Babylonians also carried on much of the Neo-Assyrian structures in the intervening years. City dwellers had a comparatively impressive amount of clout within the Neo-Babylonian Empire, foreshadowing some important civic developments roughly akin to concepts of citizenship we will encounter in later empires.

Two non-Babylonian groups were prominent within the Neo-Babylonian provinces: the Chaldeans and the Aramaeans. Several leaders of both groups remained in power under the Neo-Babylonians, helping keep order at the local level. Chaldeans appear in cuneiform records in the ninth century B.C., but it is not known how long before that time they had arrived. They played a major role in Babylonian history as residents of its cities and even, at one point, contenders for the throne of Babylonia. Tending to be divided into three major tribes, they were governed at the local level by their own leaders. Their major importance was in trade, and they were vital to the caravan trade of the Arabian Peninsula and the Persian Gulf, through both of which the Babylonians themselves profited greatly.

For their part, groups of Aramaeans moved into the region of Babylon sometime in the eleventh century B.C. Here they did not develop into small kingdoms as Aramaean settlers did in Syria but rather remained as a settled agricultural people organized into villages, clans, or tribes, arranged under chiefs. As opposed to the Chaldeans, most of the Aramaeans remained outside the cities. Although some think they might have been related to the Chaldeans, others challenge this view. The Aramaeans at any rate did not possess the wealth or political clout of the more urban Chaldeans within the Neo-Babylonian Empire.

INTERLUDE: THE PEOPLE OF THE BOOK

Imperialism usually, if not always, contests the identity of subject peoples. The Jews again provide a good case study of response to empire. Spared, to a certain extent – apart from the incursion by Sennacherib in 701 B.C. – from the Neo-Assyrian campaigns and ultimate destruction in 720 B.C. of the northern Kingdom of Israel, the Jews of Judah rallied around the moral reforms proclaimed by their prophets and enforced by their King Josiah, as will be recalled (Chapter Three). However, with the Babylonian captivity, beginning in 587, their land lay in ruins: how were they to persist as a people lacking a land, a temple, or even a king? Their strong identity as a People of the Book, forged under the Neo-Assyrian and Neo-Babylonian onslaughts, was further strengthened even in the absence of traditional community markers. They now had to renegotiate an identity in exile, which they did as a People of the Book and a People of the Covenant. Much of the Hebrew Bible, in fact, reached its final form at this time during the sixth century. The voices and the writings of their prophets in particular were clear and full of promises to sustain them as a people. They could survive as a people and a faith even without a political unit and with only memories of classical identity markers of land, king, and temple. Theirs was a powerful ideology that persisted even lacking the economic, military, and political power to back it up. They were promised future blessings and prosperity as a people if they would repent, as their prophet Amos had assured at the close of his prophecy:

> I will restore the fortunes of my people Israel, and they shall rebuild the ruined cities and inhabit them; they shall plant vineyards and drink their wine, and they shall make gardens and eat their fruit. I will plant them upon their land, and they shall never again be plucked up out of the land that I have given them, says the LORD [Yahweh] your God.[9]

THE ENIGMATIC NABONIDUS AND THE PERSIAN TAKEOVER

The end of the Neo-Babylonian Empire came, as had the Neo-Assyrian demise previously, suddenly and fairly mysteriously. At center stage were the figures

the Neo-Babylonian throne was fairly violent, and he seems to have been challenged by the elites of Babylon for the whole of his reign. Not being a member of the royal family, he had to demonstrate his legitimacy in ways other than heredity. His own inscriptions have what one historian has termed an "apologetic" tone – that is, he is more effuse than any other Neo-Babylonian king in declaring that he has the blessing of the gods.[10] This was probably an attempt to ingratiate himself with the Babylonian populace – recall the crucial role the Babylonian elites played in acclaiming Nabopolassar at his ascension to the throne. Nabonidus likewise went to great lengths to find Bronze Age temple foundations so as to claim that a god had revealed their long-forgotten locations to him, demonstrating a legitimacy in line with the rich and powerful Babylonian past.

Significantly, however, the god he consistently chose to show his legitimacy was not Marduk but rather the moon god Sin, whose temple his mother, Adad-guppi, maintained. This specific loyalty seemed to have further alienated him from the Neo-Babylonian elite, many of whom were priests of the high god Marduk. His support of Sin, whom he called "lord of the gods" and "king of the gods," amounted to a type of henotheism, a firmly held belief in a single god that nearly eclipses other gods although not outright denying their existence. He dedicated numerous temples to Sin at Harran and Ur and thus was seen as betraying the chief god Marduk. He described his long absence from Babylon as a result of the impiety of the inhabitants of Babylon and other

4.3. Cylinder of Nabonidus. The Trustees of The British Museum/Art Resource, NY.

major cities, an enigmatic reference that probably refers to the widespread rejection of his high veneration of Sin.

His long campaign in Arabia, which made him even more unpopular back in Babylon, had several ramifications. It does seem to have been pressured, to an extent, by the priests of Marduk with whom he was particularly unpopular. Their anger, however, would have been more intensified because the Akitu festival could not be celebrated in his absence, risking serious calamity to Babylon and its empire. Nabonidus' campaigns, however, apparently had important strategic goals, which he was unable to communicate fully to the elites of Babylon. He likely saw the rising Persian aggression at his peripheries and found in Arabia an important zone of access to the Mediterranean, should northern Mesopotamia and Syria fall. His campaigns were potentially aimed at keeping the Mediterranean trade connection alive as well as designed to guarantee that the luxury trade that came through Arabia would continue to be dominated by Neo-Babylonians, especially the trade in frankincense.

Nabonidus returned to Babylon in 543 B.C. and desperately attempted to prepare against an attack by the expanding Persians. The Persians arrived in 539 B.C. Cyrus the Persian gives us his own account of what then happened:

He [Nabonidus] maliciously suspended the regular offerings and upset the rites. He plotted to end the worship of Marduk and continuously perpetuated evil against his city. Daily [he . . .] brought all his [people] to ruin by (imposing) toils without rest. . . . [Marduk] sought and looked through all the lands, searching for a righteous king whose hand he could grasp. He called to rule Cyrus, king of Anshan, and announced his name as the king of the universe.... And Marduk, the great lord, leader of his people, looked happily at the good deeds and steadfast mind of Cyrus and ordered him to march to his own city Babylon, set him on the road to Babylon, and went alongside him like a friend and companion. His teeming army, uncounted like water (flowing) in a river, marched with him fully armed. (Marduk) allowed him to enter Babylon without battle or fight, sparing his own city of Babylon from hardship, and delivered Nabonidus, who had not worshiped him, into his hands. All the people of Babylon, the entire land of Sumer and Akkad, rulers and princes, bowed down to him, kissed his feet, and rejoiced at his rule, filled with delight. They happily greeted him as the lord, by means of whose trust those who were as dead were revived and saved from all trial and hardship; they praised his name.[11]

The inscription continues, describing Cyrus' devotion to Marduk, honoring,

in agreement: the takeover was relatively peaceful, and the priests of Marduk cooperated with and even aided Cyrus, rejoicing that Marduk worship thus had been restored.

The problem with this straightforward version of events is simply that it comes completely from a propagandistic text of a Persian king. Cyrus' takeover of Babylon was presented as legitimate because he overthrew a "heretic" king and was even welcomed by the priests of Marduk; his account is even replete with the rhetoric of a Babylonian conqueror. Some recent historians are not so sure about this sequence of events, however. Cyrus had much to gain by presenting himself in this way – he did, after all, have to get the proud and self-assured Babylonians to submit to his authority, and this was something even the Neo-Assyrians had had serious trouble doing. Although the populace of Babylon did eventually submit to his rule and even acclaim him publicly, as was customary for new rulers, the on-the-ground details of Cyrus' takeover remain far from clear. This moment did, however, mark the real beginning of the Persian Empire.

THE RISE OF A MULTICULTURALIST EMPIRE: THE ACHAEMENID PERSIANS

The Persians are well attested as a unified and coherent polity beginning in the seventh century B.C. They had been one of many Indo-European language-speaking groups migrating in the eleventh and tenth centuries B.C., moving from central Asia into Elam and Iran, where they settled. After the Neo-Assyrian Ashurbanipal's sack of Susa ended the Elamite kingdom (646), the Persians seem to have moved toward a breakaway secondary state in response, uniting under a Persian family against the Assyrian threat. Their first real consolidator was Cyrus (r. 559–522), a local king of the small kingdom of Anshan, which was at that time subject to the king of the Medes. After he fended off an attack by and then defeated Astyages of the Medes in 550 B.C., Cyrus began consolidating a powerful kingdom with its heartland outside of Mesopotamia – the first such in the Age of Ancient Empires. He began to solidify rule with his capital at Pasargadae.

Cyrus' kingdom registered rather suddenly on the sixth-century political power scene. Croesus of Lydia (r. 560–546), an Anatolian kingdom and ally of the Babylonians, immediately moved to halt its rise. The Lydians had recently expanded, incorporating significant portions of western Anatolia. The Lydian territories in turn fell to Cyrus, including, importantly for later historical developments, the Greek city-states of western Anatolia, known by the Greeks as Ionia; these had just recently been subjugated by Croesus. Cyrus had, in fact, called on these Ionian Greek city-states to aid him by revolting against Croesus. Babylon itself came under Persian power soon thereafter, in 539. The story of Cyrus' rise, rule, and demise is replete with legends, mainly because of the interest shown in him by the Greek writer Herodotus, variously designated the "Father of History" and the "Father of Lies." We will meet Herodotus officially in the next chapter, but his famous *Histories* is one of our most important – and problematic – sources on the Persian Empire, particularly its western portions.

By all available indications, the Persian takeover of Babylon was a fairly bloodless affair, and it is widely believed that the priests of Marduk either welcomed Cyrus or at least did not encourage any significant resistance. In keeping with established imperial patterns of elite replacement, Cyrus removed the highest level of the Babylonian officials, keeping the local officials, essentially elite collaborators, in place to help him rule. Cyrus then turned eastward and conquered a significant portion of central Asia – Afghanistan, Turkmenistan, Tajikistan, pulling more people into the Age of Ancient Empires and taking his empire to limits never even dreamed of by the self-proclaimed "kings of the world" and "kings of the universe" before him. If we are to believe Herodotus, Cyrus himself met a macabre ending while fighting against Tomyris, Queen of the Massagetae/Scythians in central Asia.

Cyrus' son and successor, Cambyses (r. 530–522), is most noteworthy for conquering Egypt, bringing it firmly into the Age of Ancient Empires. He was able to conquer Egypt by building a powerful Persian navy for use against Egyptian naval power, the first to do so. In Herodotus' view, Cambyses was

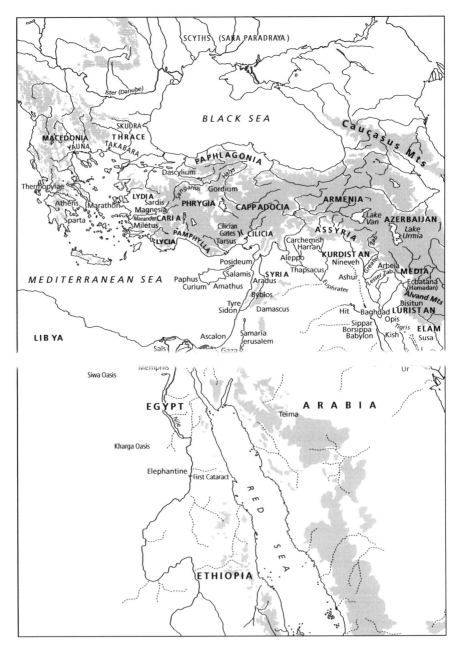

4.4. Map of the Achaemenid Persian Empire. In *Cambridge Ancient History*, Volume IV, Part I, pp. 2–3.

essentially insane, and consistently and senselessly provoked the Egyptians by his all-around insensitivity to their culture. According to Egyptian sources, however, Cambyses seems more in the mold of what would become a typical Persian ruler. The Persians became famous for fostering a rule that seemingly allowed for diversity, and the rulers often presented themselves in the fashion of local rulers, as Cyrus had done with Babylon. In Egyptian texts and inscriptions, Cambyses presents himself, in garb and rhetoric, as an Egyptian

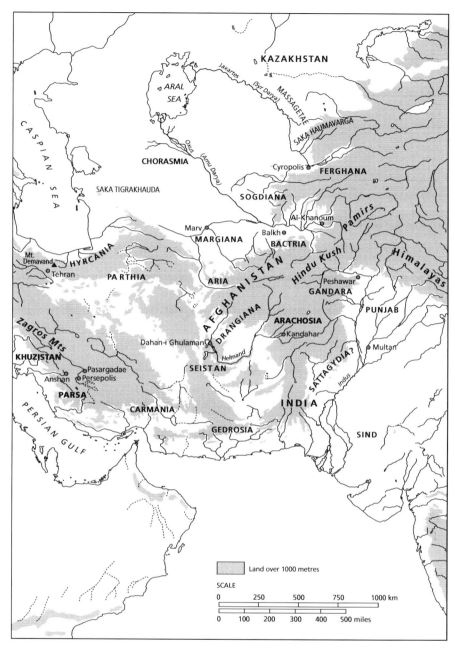

4.4 (continued)

pharaoh. It was he, it may be recalled, who gave the Egyptian elite collaborator Udjahorresne his honorific position, suggesting a ruler who was fairly
sensitive to local norms and mores and dedicated to a fairly smooth transition
to Persian rule.

The transition in rule after Cambyses, in Herodotus' telling, was bizarre.
To begin with, Cambyses met his end by falling off his horse in his eagerness
to stop a conspiracy. He was killed by his own weapon, reportedly fatally

wounded in the same spot where he had previously wounded an Egyptian sacred bull. The succession to the throne was surrounded by perennially engaging, if seriously questionable, stories – a disguised pretender to the throne recognized only by his ears (or rather lack thereof); a serious, if anachronistic, Persian debate over the best form of government – monarchy, aristocracy, or democracy; and, finally, a horse race to determine the winner of the throne in which the victorious stallion had been secretly primed by the smell of the genitals of his favorite mare. The ascension to the throne is shrouded in mystery still and probably involved serious intrigue and even assassination(s). What is certain is that after a year of fighting, Darius (r. 521–486) emerged as the winner and then proceeded to consolidate the Persian Empire with an effective mixture of almost Assyrian-style brutality and conciliation. His famous Behistun (or Bisitun) inscription, high up on a virtually inaccessible cliff, records his version of the events, a useful source to give at least some balance to Herodotus' lively story of his rise to the throne (Fig. 4.5).

Just as Cyrus was the major conqueror, so Darius was the real consolidator

continue, but he witnessed the last significant expansion of the realm. As the Behistun inscription reveals, he began his reign quelling revolts throughout the young far-flung empire. On his tomb at Naqsh-I-Rustem, Darius recorded that when he came to power, the earth was in "commotion" and that he had then "put it down in its place," clearly establishing order/cosmos in the place of chaos that had reigned at his ascension. Continuing the ruling strategy of his Persian predecessor in Egypt, he continued rule there by depicting himself as both an Egyptian pharaoh and warrior-monarch and a conqueror and foreigner.

Darius notably adopted and strongly promoted the new faith of Zoroastrianism, making it his central religious ideology. Zoroastrianism was founded in the sixth century by the Persian prophet Zoroaster (Zarathustra). It was Ahura-Mazda, the chief god of Zoroastrianism, Darius tells us in nearly all of his royal inscriptions, who had given him the throne; and it was in Ahura-Mazda's name and by whose favor that he ruled his massive Empire. By his own admission, he was the chosen consolidator but also a tool of expansion, advancing in the name of Ahura-Mazda.

> A great god is Ahura-Mazda, who created this earth, who created yonder sky, who created man, who created happiness for man, who made Darius king, one king over many, one lord of many.... Says Darius the king: By the favour of Ahura-Mazda these are the countries which I

4.5. Behistun inscription. Alinari/Art Resource, NY.

seized outside of Persia; I ruled over them; they bore me "tribute"; what
was said to them by me, that they did; my law – that held them firm;
Media, Elam, Parthia, Aria, Bactria, Sogdiana, Chorasmia, Drangiana,
Arachosia, Sattagydia, Gandara, India, Scythians . . . Babylonia, Assyria,
Arabia, Egypt, Armenia, Cappadocia, Sardis, Ionia . . . Thrace, *petasos*-
wearing Ionians, Libyans, Ethiopians, men of Maka, Carians.[12]

Zoroastrianism held at its core a concept of order, truth, and righteousness known as *Arta*. *Arta* descended from Ahura-Mazda, a powerful deity of
light and order. Ahura-Mazda had an evil counterpart in Ahriman, a god
of chaos, darkness, and the Lie, or *Drauga*. Denunciations of and warnings
against *Drauga* feature prominently in Persian texts from this period and after.
This dualistic religious system was central to Darius' own administration and
conquests:

> King Darius says: You who shall be king hereafter, protect yourself
> vigorously from lies; punish the liars well, if thus you shall think, "May
> my country be secure!"[13]

Darius and subsequent Persian leaders fostered a worldview in which the king
was head of the empire, chosen by Ahura-Mazda, with the voluntary support

4.6. Tomb of Darius II. Line drawing by Kathryn Brunk.

of the peoples under his rule. The followers of *Arta* were rewarded with the cosmic benefits of his empire (Fig. 4.6).

THE PRAGMATICS OF A MULTICULTURAL EMPIRE

The Persians recognized diversity in an unprecedented way throughout the Empire, but it also appears that many local native elites freely adopted Persian ways. On the whole, the iconography of kingship clearly shows a "Persian king supported by, and at the apex of, an Empire made up of many peoples whose individual character was emphasized, yet who were all drawn together in a harmonious union to serve their Persian ruler."[14] Yet were the actual pragmatics of empire so clear-cut as implied by the imperial line of Ahura-Mazda's *Arta* vs. *Drauga,* as laid out in the Behistun inscription?

One basic difficulty in assessing the Persian Empire as a whole is the disparity in source material from its various regions; the western sections, thanks to Herodotus and other Greek sources from around the time of the Greco-Persian War, tend to be far better documented. The eastern sections of the Persian Empire are hardly documented at all, in many instances, and hence it might well be misleading to generalize across the entire empire. Nonetheless, the general contours of Persian rulership may be sketched out, if cautiously. There are some generally recognized trends, however, that, although they were probably implemented variously according to local mores, nonetheless characterized the whole of the empire.

Darius put the Persian Empire on the firm administrative foundation it would need to survive for several centuries. He divided the empire into satrapies, ruled by elite Persians (satraps), who governed in the king's name. From various sources, it appears that the satraps shaped their rule according to preexisting local mores and were granted a certain measure of autonomy. The Persians continued the tradition of elite replacement, although we do know of one local collaborator who rose to the office of satrap for his aid during a struggle for the throne. The example of Udjahorresne also shows continuity with a fairly high-level official. Below the satraps were local governors who kept a close eye on local affairs; many of these were drawn from local populations. Partially to keep their eyes on such a vast empire, the Persian rulers constructed and maintained several capitals – Persepolis, Susa, Pasargadae, and Ecbatana; Babylon also served as a capital. They regularized taxation and communication by means of the Persian Royal Road, which, although based on some Neo-Assyrian precedents, was expanded by the Persians. Aiding communication throughout the empire, Aramaic continued as it had under the Neo-Assyrians as a lingua franca.

The artistic program of the Persian Empire reveals an unprecedented recognition of diversity. On royal panels, subject peoples appear in their local dress and *seem* to voluntarily support the righteous ruler: clothing styles, beard styles, hat types, and so forth show the remarkable degree to which the Persians understood the diversity of their empire. They presented each region as forming a vital part of the whole. Further, the Persians erected statues of Marduk in Babylon and statues of Persian officials dressed in Egyptian garb in Egypt.

The message being communicated, however, could be almost contradictory or at least paradoxical at times. On one stele in Egypt (Shaluf or Chalouf Stele), one side is written in Egyptian and in a mild tone of benevolent Persian rule. On the reverse side, the same inscription is translated into Persian, Median, and Assyrian, but the overall tone is more firmly one of master to subordinate. Resistance to the will of Ahura-Mazda, and thus the righteous order of the universe, at least as declared in some public inscriptions such as the famous Behistun inscription, tended to be met with an unmitigated harshness that would have made the Assyrians proud. A small group of scattered upstarts at and beyond their western fringe would soon find out that diversity did not necessarily mean tolerance, as we will see in the next chapter.

4.7. Procession of tribute bearers. Bridgeman-Giraudon/Art Resource, NY.

The kings did have close interaction with subject peoples and often appeared as supporters of local religions and customs. Jews in the Hebrew Bible books of Ezra and Nehemiah seemed to have had a remarkable degree of encouragement and support from the Persian king to practice their traditions and faiths locally. Although Aramaic, borrowed from the Aramaeans, was the most widely used administrative language of the realm, decrees appeared in multiple languages – Old Persian, Akkadian, Elamite. Inscriptions were translated into many other languages as well, so that the local elites could actually read the inscriptions – Egyptian hieroglyphics, for example, as seen earlier.

Taxation and communication were standardized throughout the empire at a level never seen before – and in a particularly impressive way given the empire's size and diversity. Taxation, also, was presented as a voluntary action (one necessary for the blessings of empire), and imperial reliefs show the tribute being brought from all corners of the empire via local sources of wealth (Fig. 4.7). Some peoples brought silver, some gold, some textiles, some incense, some animals (Fig. 4.8). The Persians themselves could be influenced by local styles and tastes, and they at times would actually borrow a local style for use more widely throughout the empire. In time, satraps of far western regions began copying Greek architectural styles even as they enlisted Greek mercenaries for their armies.

4.8. Reception Hall "Apadana," relief of tribute bearers. DeA Picture Library/Art Resource, NY.

RESPONDING TO EMPIRE

Following the reign of Darius, the empire essentially stopped expanding, although the challenges of internal administration persisted. Despite the tranquil and tolerant façade proclaimed in much of its artistic program, the Persian Empire was not immune from revolt and resistance throughout its existence. The famous revolts of the Greeks of western Anatolia are explored in detail in the next chapter. Elsewhere, during the reigns of Darius and Xerxes (r. 486–465), there were rebellions and revolts in the traditional hotbeds of Egypt and Babylon. As is often the case, it was areas with a strong sense of local identity and history that proved to be the most likely to revolt. It was revolts in these areas that delayed the famous Persian revenge on the mainland Greeks, as we will see, and distracted Xerxes during the second phase of the Greco-Persian Wars. Xerxes' successor Artaxerxes (r. 465–424/423) also crushed a revolt in Egypt. As we will see, the Persians were unsuccessful in getting all of the Greeks, to their west, to acknowledge their power; some Greeks, however, did readily submit to the Persian Empire and attach themselves to it. Others famously resisted.

The Jews seemed to have responded rather well to their rule by Persian Empire and were, as noted earlier, direct beneficiaries of its policies of tolerance and even support of subjugated peoples. A series of Jewish letters written in Aramaic by Jews living at a garrison in Elephantine Egypt give some indication of the length to which Persian leaders went to keep the Jews content: the Persian king Darius II (r. 424–404) even authorized a festival of unleavened bread for the Jewish garrison.[15] Further, as the biblical books of Ezra and Nehemiah record, the Persian king allowed the Jews to return to Israel, where they then rebuilt their temple. The Persian king then helped support their efforts against the resistance of surrounding peoples who were not eager to see the Jews reestablished in Jerusalem.

The Neo-Assyrians had indeed cast a long shadow across the Near East and even beyond. Their legacy continued as empire succeeded empire, each ruling and innovating in its own way(s) but all evidencing some familiar themes and dynamics. The dream of world conquest actually came closer and closer to reality, culminating in the spectacular display of power across space and time that was the Achaemenid Persian Empire. The legacy of resistance continued as well, both in the form of major and emerging empires and in the basic survival of groups like the Jews, whose ideology helped sustain and renegotiate an identity, even amid the subjugating and homogenizing forces of imperialism. A key development, to which we now turn, is the reaction of areas in the Mediterranean and the west to these new currents.

CHAPTER FIVE

THE CRUCIBLE OF HISTORY: EAST MEETS WEST

Although you know what it's like to be a slave, you've never experienced freedom and you have no idea whether or not it's a pleasant state. If you had experienced it, you'd be advising us to wield not spears, but even battleaxes in its defence.

— Herodotus, *Histories* 7.135[1]

* In what ways do philosophical ideas shape or influence historical action?
* How did external and internal factors, working together, shape Greek experience between the eighth and early fifth centuries B.C.?
* How did the Greeks' exercise of ideology, economics, military, and politics (IEMP) compare with Near Eastern patterns?
* How did Greeks manage to decisively defeat the Achaemenid Persian Empire and defend their homeland(s)?

O N 28 MAY 585 B.C. (or perhaps 21 September 582), Western philosophy and science were born, a little bit after 6:00 P.M. Thales of Miletus, one of the Seven Sages of Greece, had predicted a solar eclipse, and it had indeed occurred. He thus demonstrated that there was a rational order to the universe, thereby introducing science and philosophy to the world. From this crucial moment sprang mathematics, astronomy, geography, history, logic, political theory, and so much more.

This oft-told story is at once intriguing, instructive, and downright misleading. Like any catchy and tidy summary of pivotal historical moments, there is a kernel of truth here amid gross overstatement. The element of truth to the eclipse story is that small numbers of forward-thinking Greeks, living in cities such as Miletus, Samos, and Halicarnassus on the Ionian coast of

western Anatolia, did begin to think about the physical world in unprecedented ways during the sixth century B.C. They were attempting to discover
the natural and rational causes behind observable phenomena, whether the
cause of eclipses or the path of human evolution. Thales was a guiding light
in this broad movement, known by scholars as the Ionian Revolution. Within
these Ionian city-states, a constellation of factors came together in truly revolutionary intellectual and political movements. In addition to his astronomical
speculations, Thales also was an outspoken political thinker who argued for
the unification of the Greek colonies of Ionia against the expansion of Near
Eastern kingdoms and empires. In this latter effort, he failed, but understanding the intrinsic connection between his seemingly unrelated pursuits
in "science" and politics is central to grasping the place of the Greeks in the
story of the Age of Ancient Empires.

The Greeks, for a time, would break with a key Near Eastern pattern
central to our exploration. They came to downplay divine authority and
religious ideology (I) in favor of a much stronger emphasis on the political
(P). After a series of wars and then their eventual conquest from the peripheral

world, as we will see in the next few chapters.

Yet though the Thales story is often used to show that "Western thought"
was born in Greece, the Greek innovations in fact would not have been
possible without earlier Near Eastern precedents and influences. By the time
the Neo-Assyrians were at their height, the Near East and the Mediterranean
were, once again, linked together as they had been during the Bronze Age,
and much high culture flowed westward. Even before that, the Phoenicians
had carried much culture westward, both their own and some they borrowed
from elsewhere.

To the east of the Greeks, in western and central Anatolia, two smaller
kingdoms in succession helped mediate the connections between the Near
East and the Aegean. The western and central Anatolian kingdom of Phrygia,
famously ruled by a real King Midas (with a probably not-so-real Golden
Touch, as the famous legend goes) passed on to Greeks much cultural creativity originating in the Near East. The Phrygians had carved out an empire
in western and central Anatolia between the eighth and the sixth centuries
B.C., with the Assyrians initially to their south and east and the Greeks to
their west. This kingdom had significant interaction with both the Assyrians and the Greeks and, as a result, carried on a lively cross-cultural trade.
The Phrygians introduced Near Eastern artistic styles and technology such
as glasswork and metalwork to the Greeks (Fig. 5.2). The Lydian kingdom
that succeeded the Phrygians continued intense interaction with the Greeks

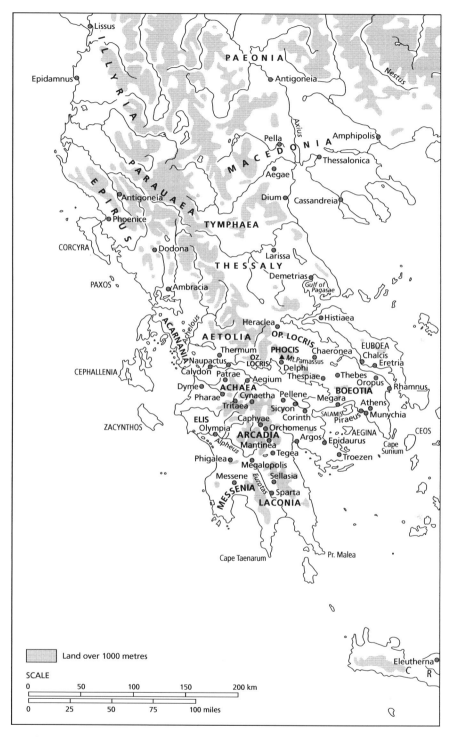

5.1. Greek mainland and Aegean map. In *Cambridge Ancient History*, Map 5. The Greek Mainland and the Aegean, Volume VIII, Part I, pp. 222–3.

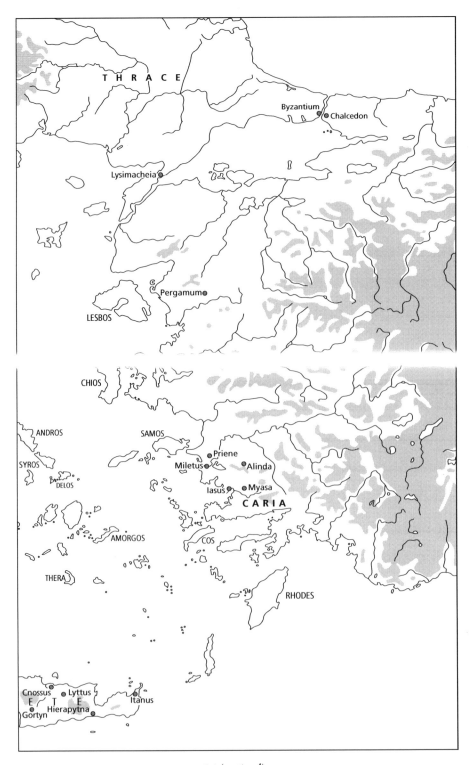

5.1 (*continued*)

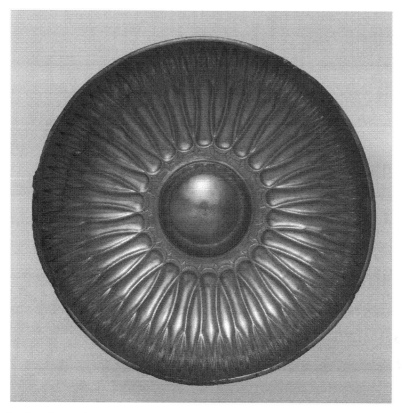

5.2. Bowl with a radiating petal design, Phrygian. The Metropolitan Museum of Art/Art Resource, NY. Gift of Mr. and Mrs. J. J. Klejman in Memory of Director James J. Rorimer, 1966.

to their west even as they resisted Assyrian expansion in the seventh century. Under their most famous king, Croesus (r. c. 560–546), they actually folded many Ionian Greek city-states into their growing, but soon-to-be-vanquished, empire. Their pressure on the Greeks in the early sixth century helped them raise revenue as Egypt, Babylon, and Media fought over the remains of the Assyrian Empire.

Beyond these smaller kingdoms and fledgling empires, but coming progressively closer over the course of the eighth to sixth centuries, the great empires of the Near East – Assyrians, Babylonians, Persians – cast looming shadows toward the Ionian city-states. In particular, some of the knowledge that sparked Ionian thought had been carried to the Aegean world by Near Eastern refugees and other travelers, particularly after the fall of Assyrian Nineveh in 612.

Yet there was, to be sure, something truly unprecedented and uniquely significant about what Thales and a few of his Ionian contemporaries were thinking and doing. As throughout history, diffusion of culture need not imply only mere imitation. Once in the Aegean, elements of Near Eastern culture could, and did, take on a life (or rather lives) of their own. The Ionians themselves were located at the peripheries of two rapidly changing worlds – Greece and the Near East. The blending could be formative, if at times a bit volatile. To understand the Ionian Revolution, therefore, we must first look westward from the Ionian coast, across the Aegean to some significant changes going on throughout the Greek mainland.

THE GREEK EXPANSION AND THE BIRTH OF THE POLIS

In Book Nine of Homer's *Odyssey*, the titular character, Odysseus, sails to the inhospitable land of the Cyclopes. Odysseus himself describes the brutal character of its one-eyed inhabitants: they do not plow, they have no institutions, no council meetings, each one is a "law for his own wives and children, and cares nothing about the others."[2] Furthermore, they live right near a wooded island, with a fine harbor and fertile soil and teeming with flocks of goats. Shockingly, to Odysseus, the Cyclopes have never attempted

could be exploiting its rich resources as well as sailing among "all the various cities of men."[3] In this telling encounter, Homer, as he often does, lays bare key assumptions of his own age – to be civilized implied sailing, colonizing, and exploiting resources available by sea voyages, near and far. Much had changed since we last encountered the Aegean world.

By the mid-eighth century, the so-called Age of Homer, inhabitants of the Greek mainland had already begun to emerge from the Dark Age. Following the collapse of the Mycenaeans in the twelfth century, as will be recalled from Chapter One, complex societies had vanished from the Aegean. The population of the Greek mainland had declined by up to 75 percent, institutional structures were drastically simplified, and literacy disappeared completely. Several outside wandering groups had moved into the Greek mainland, and a fairly diverse population was then settled throughout, with small-scale communities ruled over by a tribal chief or warlord (called a *wanax*) being the norm. However, by Homer's day, signs of rebirth were appearing everywhere, a fascinating mixture of Near Eastern and unique Hellenic elements.

New artistic expressions, in monumental architecture, on pottery, and in sculpture, heralded an emerging complex culture. Many of the initial artistic expressions closely followed the remarkable shifts that had begun in the Near East and Egypt during the previous century (Fig. 5.3). The use and imitation of Near Eastern styles, known as "Orientalizing," resulted in new types of

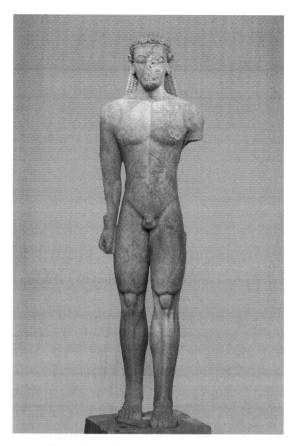

5.3. Kouros from Sounion. Vanni/Art Resource, NY.

pottery, sculpture, and glassware, vivid testimony to the revival of East–West contacts after several centuries of hiatus.

Writing and literacy suddenly returned, now with an alphabet the Greeks borrowed from the sea-faring Phoenicians and modified slightly. The most famous Greek writers launched enduring works and traditions in literature. Homer's epic poems, the *Iliad* and the *Odyssey*, give insight into his own age as well as into, but hopelessly jumbled together with, the previous Dark Age and Bronze Age, which had come to an end long before his time. A contemporary of Homer, Hesiod, wrote other famous surviving works of early Greek literature – *Works and Days*, which elucidates archaic Greek agricultural and social practices, and *Theogony*, stories about the origins of the gods and the cosmos.

Scale and patterns of settlement also changed drastically over the eighth and seventh centuries, as can be traced through archaeological analysis of burials. Population size throughout the western Aegean expanded markedly, no doubt partly because of the general climate change, the effects of which could be seen throughout the Near East and Mediterranean. Growing communities throughout the Greek mainland began to crystallize into the polis (plural poleis), the Greeks' most characteristic political institution. The rugged topography of Greece, mountainous with fertile valleys interspersed, helped shape the number, size and character of these growing communities, at least 750 of which are known. New communities were founded as well, and most preexisting communities grew with the general population expansion but could only do so up to a point.

The polis took a variety of forms throughout the Greek mainland and beyond. At times it functioned as a monarchy – as it did in the rare dual kingship in Sparta – but most of the time as an oligarchy. Only rarely did it take the shape of a democracy, as at Athens, and then usually only later in time. The form of the polis generally did not remain static; in many poleis, traditional oligarchies slowly gave way to assemblies of citizens. This process was well under way by the sixth century and furthered a growing sense that the inhabitants of a polis collectively owned the community. It also helped further the unprecedented rise of political power (P) at the expense of ideological (I)

The polis, like so much else in the Aegean world, also was shaped by outside models. Mesopotamians and Levantines had settled into city-states long before the Greeks, and it is likely that the Phoenicians provided the direct model for the Greek polis. There was something decidedly different about the Greek communities, however, something that has prompted many scholars to designate them "citizen-states" as opposed to more broadly defined "city-states." This translation of the term more accurately reflects that the polis was a people and not just a place. The ramifications of this important difference were huge.

Although only a minority of Greek poleis developed what we might call "democratic" institutions, many developed a concept of the free citizen as opposed to a subject of a divinely appointed (or divine) monarch. Ideological/religious power was thus relatively weak in these Aegean communities, compared with both their Bronze Age predecessors and contemporary polities to their east, be those Neo-Assyrian, Babylonian, Lydian, and so on. Political power and discourse came to the fore in a unique way among Greeks. Whatever the outright cause of this new development, it emboldened Greeks to action and defense against outside hegemony in a way that was pretty much unthinkable outside of this setting. Once again, an external model was appropriated uniquely in the peculiar political, geographic, and intellectual context of the Greek mainland of the eighth and seventh centuries.

So much about Greek culture reflects and is reflected in the political order of the Greek poleis. The ideals of political participation and visions of equality

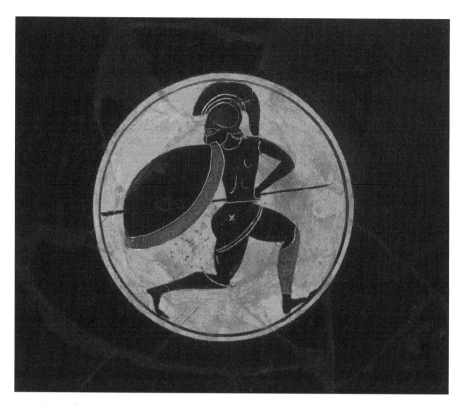

5.4. Oltos Painter (fl. c. 525–500 B.C.) Hoplite. Réunion des Musées Nationaux/Art Resource, NY.

registered rather obviously in their famous military organization as well. The characteristic Greek military formation, the hoplite phalanx, arose from a rich matrix of ideological and political forces (Fig. 5.4). The phalanx itself was a closely packed formation, consisting, at this early stage, of heavily armed infantryman (hoplites) lined up eight deep. The hoplites stood shoulder to shoulder in battle, each relying on the shield of the hoplite to their right for protection. The front line of hoplites would project long spears for the attack, and those in the rows behind would back them up, ready to take the place immediately of any who fell.

Building on ideals of wide political participation and visions of equality, the hoplite phalanx assumed a certain measure of trust and respect for one's equals, a morale built up in the relatively egalitarian setting community of the polis. The phalanx would not have been possible without all of these. The heavy and expensive armament was paid for by the hoplites themselves, a further factor in the diffuse political and economic system that made the phalanx possible. Drawn from a class of independent farmers who did not pay taxes to a monarch or rent to a local power figure, the hoplites controlled their economic surplus, which enabled them to buy armor and weapons in the first place. In most cases, there was little military training at all (Sparta might seem a famous exception, although in comparison to the modern soldier, the Spartan actually trained relatively little).

The success of the phalanx, then, lay in its basic organization, which directly reflected Greek political, social, and ideological norms. The stunning success of the Greeks against the Persians is a clear testimony to the effectiveness of this military formation. It might seem concise and attractive to simply explain how the Greek military organization led to their stunning defeat of the Achaemenid Persian Empire, but such an explanation would ignore the ideological, economic, and political forces that helped shape the peculiar military organization. The phalanx then is a microcosm of the IEMP model. Sources of social power, working together as we have seen throughout this text, did not simply build empires; they also helped resist and defeat them.

The expanding poleis, following the direct example set by the Phoenicians, began sending out overseas colonies, beginning in the early eighth century. Such colonization apparently was already common enough by Homer's day, hardly half a century later, that he could use it as a distinguishing point between savage and civilized. Some colonies provided surplus grain for the

and Levant, and all provided new homelands and opportunities for the growing number of inhabitants of the mother cities. In most cases, the connections to the sponsoring city dissolved fairly quickly, and colonies became independent poleis in their own right. Starting with a trading colony founded at Al Mina in Syria early in the eighth century, the Greeks then began to spread out in all directions. To the west, beginning in the second half of the eighth century, southern Italy and Sicily became prime targets for colonization. These areas absorbed so many Greek colonists over the next few centuries that southern Italy would later come to be known as Magna Graecia, or Greater Greece. Cities such as Naples (Italian Napoli, from the Greek neopolis, i.e., new polis) in southern Italy continue, both through name and surviving ruins, to attest to this early Greek phase. In time, Greeks would also colonize areas of France, Spain, North Africa, and along the shores of the Black Sea. However, the most important colonies, in terms of subsequent history, lay to the east on the Ionian coast of Anatolia and its adjacent islands.

THE IONIAN INTELLECTUAL REVOLUTION AND THE LIMITS OF PERSIAN TOLERANCE

Often, there seems to be a special place for peripheries in intellectual revolutions. Maybe this is because of the dynamic mixtures of cultures that tend to occur in frontier zones; maybe it is because revolutionary movements can thrive safely removed from power centers (which tend to prize order over innovation); maybe it is because of both of these and more. In the distant Greek colonies on the Ionian coast, a set of seemingly unrelated circumstances came together in the sixth century to allow the Ionian Revolution. In these Ionian centers, a "Greek" sense of political and intellectual independence perhaps had become more pronounced even than on the Greek mainland itself.

As with trade contacts and related influences, the intellectual movement spearheaded here by Thales of Miletus had deep connections with the Near East and Egypt. Scientific-type thought had a long history preceding his famous prediction of the eclipse and was both practical as well as theoretical. The identification of discrepancies between the solar and lunar calendar and the mathematical language used to describe the orbit of Venus were old news to Egyptian and Near Eastern thinkers by the eighth century. Fairly advanced geometry and surveying techniques had been put to practical use in the administration of the Neo-Assyrian Empire. This geometric knowledge was also applied to astronomy in making calculations for calendars. Refugees from Assyrian Nineveh also spread this knowledge westward, helping spark initial intellectual ferment in Ionia.

Although the Greeks traditionally have been given much, if not full, credit for the results, it is important to note how older ideas in a different cultural, political, and intellectual and institutional setting can help produce significantly new results. In Ionia, the institutional setting of the poleis encouraged relatively free discussion on a wide range of matters, allowing for openness and even audacity in their explanations of physical processes. The Greek political context encouraged rational debate and criticism of theory, well beyond what we might call politics, strictly speaking. The life of the polis was all-consuming. Some Ionians began to question, challenge, and debate traditional explanations of things, from the material origins of the universe to how political power works. Ideological explanations – and the power inherent in them – were far less pronounced than in the Near East.

A few key differences from their Near Eastern "scientific" counterparts thus came to characterize Ionian "scientific" pursuits. First, Ionians began to ask *why* things work the way they do in addition to the well-worn question of *how*. They were interested in questions of causation, not just description. Second, their explanations sought to leave the gods, strictly speaking, out of the explanations. Although no Ionian Greek thinker would qualify as an atheist and most were deeply religious, these thinkers sought explanations that did not simply invoke the gods when teasing out causation. Their explanations came to differ sharply from explanations of Homer, Hesiod, and other poets, for whom the gods simply caused everything. Third, they sought systematic theories to define the natural order. They looked for rational and consistent theories to explain the phenomena of the universe; their intellectual climate prized reason, logic, and relative intellectual freedom. Although surely the Ionians have, in some quarters, been overly praised retrospectively for their humanist, naturalist, and rationalist thought (we moderns like to praise past characters when they seem most like us – a process historians know as teleology), profound consequences did, in fact, flow from this new institutional setting for some old ideas. Additionally, with the power politics of the Age of Ancient Empires playing out before their eyes, traditional and conventional explanations were becoming inadequate for these profound, if a bit quirky, thinkers.

The real profundity of these thinkers, usually called "Pre-Socratics" (simply for coming before Socrates), is difficult to reconstruct from the fragmentary or cursory texts and traces they have left behind; taken together, however, they show early stages of rational thought and experimentation. A few foremost practitioners might serve as illustrations. Thales, for example, who dabbled in engineering and geometry in addition to his forays into

Egyptian and Babylonian thinkers as well as Hesiod had thought this before, but what Thales added was an explanation from natural causes. Previous thinkers simply saw water as an element of primeval watery chaos, as revealed in religious texts or mythologies.

Anaximander of Miletus (died c. 547), the most famous disciple of Thales, also speculated on the ultimate origin of things, but he instead traced the basic element to an infinite void around the world. He explored the origins of the material world through the separation of opposites, such as hot and cold, wet and dry. Notions of human origins that included a stage of fish have also been traced to him. Like most of the Ionian philosophers, he was a polymath, and he collected geographic information to form one of the earliest examples of a map.

Pythagoras of Samos did much work on fundamental laws of musical harmony, while discovering the famous theorem that still bears his name (Fig. 5.5). He also, incidentally, dabbled in mystery-type cults as well. There were others as well, such as Xenophanes of Colophon who mused on fossil remains as he traced the origin of the material world to earth and water. The key here is that each of these thinkers had the boldness to explore new ideas and propose new theories of origins or causation, not being strictly bound by traditional explanations or even traditional questions. They challenged old authorities while establishing new conventions in philosophy, science, and politics and also history. This is the point that the Thales eclipse tale actually gets right.

5.5. Bust of Pythagoras.
Scala/Art Resource, NY.

Some of these thinkers played active political roles as well. Thales, it will be recalled, argued for Ionian unification against outside aggression. Hecataeus of Miletus, a student of Pythagoras, played a public role in discussions about how to respond to the Achaemenid Persian expansion. The experiment in free thought played out in many different and seemingly unrelated directions. Crucially, while these revolutionary new thoughts were just beginning to move out of the very small intellectual circles, the "ivory towers" of Ionia as it were, the surrounding political landscape was drastically and rather suddenly revamped. Some key early thinkers, for instance, were at their intellectual peak just as Croesus of Lydia took over the Ionian poleis.

It wasn't just in Ionia at this time that such intellectual and philosophical leaps were being made. For difficult-to-pin-down reasons, there were a series of movements going on across the world in the sixth century B.C. – normally called by historians the Axial Age – among Greeks, Jews, Indians, and Chinese. Historians have long puzzled over the enduring intellectual ferment in the whole world during this particular century, for some of history's most significant and influential systems of thought emerged during this period, including the Pre-Socratic philosophers in the Greek world, the great exilic prophets of the Jews (including Jeremiah), perhaps Zoroaster in Persia, Siddhartha Gautama/Buddha and Jainism in India, and Laozi (Lao-Tzu) and Confucius in China. Many areas of the known world were shaped by the developments of this crucial century. All of these societies, incidentally, also were moving away from godlike kings and toward more centralized, bureaucratic states. Humans in various settings perhaps reacted to and against these developments by crafting enduring systems of thought that emphasized self-fashioning and personal transcendence. No one has ever put forth an air-tight case for interconnection among these global movements, however, and even though the interconnections between the Near East and the Aegean, at least, point to the importance of diffusion at least in two of the contexts, none of the others can be fit into a general pattern.[4]

In any event, by the middle of the sixth century, the Persians were expanding their hegemony. The Ionian Greeks, as well as the Lydians who briefly ruled them, were conquered by Cyrus. Most of the subjects of the Persian Empire, it will be recalled, apparently functioned reasonably well within and under the Persian system. Not all, of course, were as loyal (or as coddled) as that Egyptian sycophant Udjahorresne, but the revolts, as we have seen in places such as Egypt and Babylon, were surprisingly infrequent considering the size and diversity of the empire. The Ionian Greeks, however, presented some specific and unique ideological and political challenges. To begin with, their more "secular" political approach did not mesh well with the Persian ideological system in which the king/emperor represented a moral order ordained by Ahura-Mazda. The Behistun inscription lists Ionia among

> Within these countries, the man who was loyal, him I rewarded well; (him) who was evil, him I punished well; by the favor or Ahuramazda these countries showed respect toward my law; as was said to them by me, that was it done.[5]

The illustrations of the Behistun inscription vividly portray the punishment meted out to those who believed the Lie (*Drauga*) and went against the rule of Darius/Ahuramazda. The Ionians fell into this latter category when they revolted, placing themselves among those who called drastic divine vengeance down on themselves.

THE CRUCIBLE OF HISTORY

> Here are presented the results of the enquiry [from Greek *historia*] carried out by Herodotus of Halicarnassus. The purpose is to prevent the traces of human events from being erased by time and to preserve the fame of the important and remarkable achievements produced by both Greeks and non-Greeks; among the matters covered is, in particular, the cause of the hostilities between Greeks and non-Greeks.[6]

It is no coincidence that historical writing emerged at just this moment. Revolutionary Ionian thought might help provoke revolt, but at the same time, it would also help analyze the ensuing Greco-Persian War in critical, rational terms. Just as the philosophers of the Ionian Revolution represented an experiment in thought, so, too, did the birth of historical writing as we have come to understand it. Although we might see "science" and history as separate, the social, scientific, and political thought of the Ionians had a common foundation in rational thought aimed at exploring their world, its workings, and its sudden changes. It probably comes as no surprise that the earliest Greek historical writers, Hecataeus of Miletus and Herodotus of Halicarnassus, were both caught up in the Ionian Revolution.

Greek historical thought fit into basic patterns, just as we have seen in the Near East. Larger political and social changes of the eighth and seventh centuries B.C., it will be recalled, helped prompt a certain type of historical consciousness throughout the Near East. The Assyrian king Ashurbanipal constructed a famous library for preserving the past. The Babylonians were fascinated, indeed obsessed, with their own past and its reconstruction and preservation. The Hebrew historical writings appear at this same time as well, also in response to the early stages of the Age of Ancient Empires. Perhaps the historical distance between the height of the Bronze Age and the later emergence of empires inspired in people throughout the Near East, Aegean, and the eastern Mediterranean a sense of a history, a historical consciousness. They could see the remains of the distant past before them (no wonder they imagined their heroes as gods or demigods), and they could feel the distance between it and them; and this is a basic starting point for historical thinking. The Age of Ancient Empires inspired a desire to recover the past, and not to let it slip away again, as it had with the Dark Age.

In a similar way, the "Father of History," Herodotus of Halicarnassus, likewise was keen "to prevent the traces of human events from being erased by time."[7] The exact way in which he did that owed much to the Ionian Intellectual Revolution, however. In fact, a specifically Greek tradition in historical writing was just beginning as he wrote. One of the most famous pupils of Pythagoras of Samos, Hecataeus of Miletus, whom we have just mentioned, began to apply some of Pythagoras' theories to social questions. He was interested in questions of ethnography, geography, and politics, and, like many Ionians, he insisted on rational explanations of natural – in his case human, action.

> Hecataeus of Miletus speaks thus. I write what follows as it seems to me to be true; for the stories of the Greeks are varied, and, as is manifest to me, ludicrous.[8]

The myths of Greek origins and their past, such as those put forth by Homer and Hesiod in the eighth century, simply would not do for Hecataeus. He was fascinated with the Greek genealogies – stories of Greek families that could be traced back to divine descendants. His method was to discover historical facts of the family stories while peeling away some of the divine and mythic elements. In this way, he merely echoed the critical and rational approach of the Pre-Socratic philosophers. Herodotus later would lightheartedly criticize Hecataeus' approach, particularly his obsession with divine lineages, but this need not obscure the fact that he learned from Hecataeus the idea of presenting critical and rational inquiries in prose form (as opposed to poetry). In Herodotus, the gods still appear from time to time, but, as generally in Hecataeus, there is usually a clear distinction between divine forces and what can be explained in purely human and rational terms. This is precisely what distinguishes Herodotus' historical writing from accounts written before or elsewhere.

The major political events of his recent past provided him with the perfect opportunity to apply a new way of thinking about the human past. An intrepid

Persian, Egyptian, and others – in constructing his delightful narrative. In the *Histories*, he critically analyzes his sources and juxtaposes various positions, sometimes defending one over another and sometimes letting the reader decide among conflicting versions. Herodotus, as he states in the preface to his work, was loath to see the moment of the Greek clash with Achaemenid Persia become "erased by time" (as had so much of the Aegean Bronze Age) or mythologized beyond recognition (as in the tales of Homer, Hesiod, and other poets). His search for the distant cause of the war, owing something to both general Near Eastern historical consciousness and the Ionian intellectual revolution, produced the first great work of prose historical writing.

THE GRECO-PERSIAN WAR

Of all wars fought until this time, the Greco-Persian is the best documented, thanks to the creation and survival of Herodotus' *Histories*. This book is also the major source for the Achaemenid Persian Empire, especially its western portions. In and out of Herodotus' narrative appear the major causes of the war, some complementary, some not: unified Persian aggression against Ionian Greeks, senseless provocation of Ionian Greeks by "loose-cannon" Persian satraps and generals, provocation by brash Greeks, personal vendettas among rulers, and – his favorite – powerful Greek notions of freedom and liberty as articulated in resistance to an expanding, despotic empire. In the end, the disunified upstarts from the West, divided up into fiercely independent poleis, decidedly got the best of the superpower from the Near East. The Greek articulation of the ideology of freedom turned out to be another enduring means of empire resistance. Although Jews had fashioned a powerful identity as a people minus a polity, the Greeks' identity as peoples defending the liberty of their poleis proved equally effective and enduring.

Although Herodotus' narrative actually begins much earlier, the direct course of events leading to war picks up in the middle of the sixth century. In 546, Cyrus of Persia overran Lydia and the rest of western Anatolia. By 539, as will be recalled, Cyrus was given Babylon and then campaigned eastward during the 530s. What exactly he was doing in the eastern portion of his empire is difficult to determine because of the relative paucity of source material for these regions. He seems to have stopped the western expansion altogether at this point, probably seeing the Aegean as a natural frontier of the Achaemenid Persian Empire. Or perhaps this was due to a basic Persian tendency to campaign on only one front at a time, a characteristic that made expansion monodirectional as well as making reprisals slow in coming. Under Darius, however, the Persians would renew their expansion westward after 520. The question of why is a burning one for Herodotus.

Darius' expansion shows no conscious "Greek policy" before 500, however, although he was certainly interested in expanding Persian power westward into the Mediterranean. He already controlled Ionia and the large Greek islands near the Ionian coast and even enlisted some of their inhabitants to assist him for an invasion into Europe. His initial westward movements took him across the Danube and into what is now eastern Romania. As a universalist ruler, he was simply continuing to expand the realm. Yet was he independently planning an invasion of the Greek mainland itself? This question might be unanswerable, for the Greeks soon enough "invited" him directly into their world before, it seems, he even had a chance to look seriously in their direction.

The conflict began officially with the rebellion of his Greek subjects; Ionian boldness and audacity was, it seems, not limited to intellectual endeavors. The specific cause of revolt is difficult to pin down, however. As Herodotus relates, the revolt was partially in response to out-of-control and independently acting satraps and generals, as opposed to simply against a monolithic Persian hegemon. Samos, for example, actually was sacked against Darius' orders. Other Ionians revolted directly against local provocation by unreasonable Persian officials. Also, following a pattern we have seen with previous empire resisters such as the Jews, some squabbling Ionians invited some Persians in against their fellow Greek political foes. Although it took Darius five years to quell this rebellion completely, the outcome was really never seriously in question. Under Persian pressure, some Ionians had called on fellow "sons of Hellas" across the Aegean, on the mainland. Most of the mainland poleis more or less ignored Ionian calls for help, but the Athenians and the Eretrians did send aid for a highly visible and memorable symbolic action – the capture and burning of the Lydian capital turned Persian city of Sardis in 498. In Herodotus' vivid telling, when news of Sardis was brought to Darius, he first had to inquire, "Who are the Athenians?" before firing an arrow into the air and pledging vengeance against them.

It would be eight years before Darius sent a modest force of about twenty thousand directly across the Aegean. The army was intent on punishing Athens and Eretria but perhaps also on laying some groundwork for a later attempt to subjugate the Greek mainland. Vengeance struck Eretria first, and its population was promptly deported. The fleet then sailed to the Plain of Marathon, about 26 miles from Athens, where it was met

warriors. The militant Spartans to the south had promised aid but unfortunately were delayed while waiting out an auspicious moon phase (a memory the Athenians long harbored). What ensued was one of the most celebrated moments of military history as the outnumbered Athenian/Plataean force, heavily armed and held together by their tight hoplite phalanx formation, broke through the lightly armored, more mobile Persian ranks. The Greek forces then turned and enveloped the Persian center, and a veritable, highly lopsided, bloodbath ensued. Conservative estimates put the body count at somewhere between 6,000 and 7,000 Persian dead compared with only 192 on the Greek side. The famous story of the runner who rushed back to Athens after the Battle of Marathon, dying as he gasped, "Rejoice, we conquer!" is probably fictitious, even if the astounding scale of this victory is not.

This was the first major Persian setback in the West, and an angry Darius began planning a major invasion and campaign unambiguously aimed, this time, at outright conquest of the western Aegean and Greek mainland. On the Greek side, the memory of Marathon lived on as a significant boost to the Athenian spirit in particular, to continue to resist this outside invader now seemingly bent on subjugating the Greek mainland and adding it to his universal empire.

Meanwhile, an Egyptian revolt kept Darius occupied on another front, and he died in 486, with the Greeks still unpunished. His successor, Xerxes, clearly

5.6. Athenian mound (Soros), Marathon. Vanni/Art Resource, NY.

did not forget his father's wishes; in any event, he was bent on expansion himself. Herodotus records him as proclaiming:

> There has never been a time when we have not been at war . . . it is the god who steers us in the direction, and so we prosper as we follow his guidance time and again.[9]

The Persians expand, and Herodotus has Xerxes proclaim, "just because we wanted to increase our dominion." Such words might have been put into Xerxes' mouth by Herodotus who, influenced by Greek epic traditions, aimed to illustrate the hubris of Xerxes. Nonetheless, they do, in fact, fit the general Persian pattern, as revealed in inscriptions. After nearly a decade of campaigning elsewhere, Xerxes began raising, in 481, a massive army to invade and subjugate the Greek mainland. Herodotus also notes splits within the Persian elite that pushed their empire directly to attack. This time, the Persian invading force was somewhere around 100,000, according to the most convincing estimations (Herodotus' alternate figures of 1,700,000 and 5,283,200 Persian troops notwithstanding). Such a large force could not be supported by simply pillaging the meager Greek countryside, so it had to stick close to the coast to keep supplied from Persian bases.

The Greeks meanwhile had done surprisingly little to prepare for the ensuing invasion until Xerxes was actually raising his force. Some poleis, such as Thebes, and whole regions like Thessaly actually allied with the Persians. The Greek poleis were, after all, still the quarrelsome, scattered, and independent poleis they had always been, and besides, to the minds of some "sons of Hellas," this was primarily Athens' and Eretria's battle anyway. A leader of Athens, Themistocles, had encouraged the construction of a fleet, but not much else was done. As the Persian force advanced, however, the Spartans moved quickly, spearheading a Hellenic League against them. Given the topography of the Greek mainland and the supply needs of the huge invading force, the Greeks knew that the Persians would have to follow a fairly predictable path along the Aegean coast. The Spartans, under their leader Leonidas, opted not to await the army's impending arrival (or auspicious moon phases) and marched north to meet the Persians. Thermopylae (Hot Gates), a fairly narrow pass near the coast, became their site of choice, and six thousand to seven thousand Greeks from various poleis rushed there to help defend Hellas. Here, in narrow confines, only a fraction of the Persian

the Greek stand was impressive. In the end, three hundred Spartans and eight hundred other Greeks held the pass until a traitor revealed an alternate route to the Persians. All the defenders then famously fought to the death. Years later, Herodotus visited a memorial marker here, engraved with the names of the fallen. Like many Greeks, he committed at least the three hundred Spartan names to memory.

After Thermopylae, all of Greece north of the Isthmus of Corinth lay open to the Persians, who promptly burned Athens as revenge for the earlier burning of Sardis. The Spartans then argued for withdrawing the combined Hellenic forces south of the Isthmus, where they could be more easily defended beyond this narrow strip of land. Themistocles of Athens protested this abandonment of the north, however, and managed to trick the Spartans into joining the Athenians in a ruse at Salamis Bay. Luring the Persians into its narrow straits, the Greek navy was able to devastate the much larger, generally immobile fleet, using the same sort of tactics as they had on land at Thermopylae. With Xerxes himself watching from a nearby hillside, the Greeks won yet another unlikely victory.

Soon afterward, Xerxes fled back to Persia; in addition to this humiliating defeat, he had also received news of unrest in Babylon. He left one of his key leaders, Mardonius, in charge of about one hundred thousand men. The events at Marathon were partially repeated soon thereafter, this time mostly by the Spartans, and a force of about thirty-five thousand Greeks then handed the final stunning defeat to the Persians at Plataea in 479. This

5.7. Leonidas monument, Thermopylae. Vanni/Art Resource, NY.

would be the last large-scale attempt by the Persians to conquer Greece, although this was far from apparent to the Greeks at the moment. The Greeks collectively began preparing, in more earnest this time, for the next phase of the Persian onslaught. Although it never actually came, the threat of it and the preparations against it were some of the most formative factors shaping Greece for most of the fifth century, as will be seen in the next chapter.

To the Greeks, their victory struck a powerful blow for freedom against despotic rule and imperial expansion. At one point in the war, when a Persian military commander of Ionia asked some Spartans why they continued to resist the all-powerful Persian king who would probably give them high commands themselves if they would submit to him, the Spartans tellingly responded:

Although you know what it's like to be a slave, you've never experienced freedom and you have no idea whether or not it's a pleasant state. If you had experienced it, you'd be advising us to wield not spears, but even battleaxes in its defense.[10]

And Herodotus continued, commenting on this story

> once they [the Athenians] had decided that their preference was for
> Greece to remain free, it was they who aroused the whole of the rest of
> Greece . . . not even the fearsome and alarming oracles that came from
> Delphi persuaded them to abandon Greece; they held firm and found
> the courage to withstand the invader of their country.[11]

Further, the Greeks imagined that the hubris of Xerxes and the Persians had
violated physis, the fundamental natural law of the universe. Although in
the Persian worldview, the resistance of the Greeks constituted *Drauga*, in
opposition to the standard of righteousness, justice, and balance represented
by the rule of their Ahura-Mazda–appointed king, the Greeks imagined the
even higher law of *physis*. Their victory showed them that they and their ways
were in the right after all. A political notion of freedom (as opposed to a
strong religious ideology) worked together with military and political power
to make their resistance and ultimate victory possible.

course, acceptable. As we have seen throughout this text, such historical
events cannot simply be seen as the victory of one ideological/value system
over another or even, as is sometimes claimed, one form of military organization over another. The truth is far more intriguing. For, as we have seen, even
the hoplite phalanx, so effectively employed against the Persian force, had
the social and political makeup of the Greeks written into its very structure.
The Greek concepts of freedom, liberty, and equality, tried by fire under the
Persian invasion, would prove to be an incredibly resilient and effective means
of empire resistance, sustaining the Greeks in the face of imperial aggression.
However, the strong and unique military system was absolutely necessary to
back up these political notions. Without the phalanx, the Greeks would, no
doubt, have been completely defeated, perhaps even demoralized after the
first stage at Marathon. Without a solid group of hoplites wealthy enough
to purchase and maintain their own armaments, the phalanx and likewise the
resistance would have failed. The IEMP model helps explain effective resistance to as much as the formation of empires. It also helps show the peculiar
political emphasis prevalent among the Greeks.

POSTLUDE: EAST, WEST, AND ORIENTALISM

While East and West were being reintegrated, a parallel project was subtly
launched that continues to define East–West relations and representations.

To the Greeks, their victory came from their love of liberty and their self-professed superior and simpler mode of life. Whereas Herodotus portrayed the Greeks in terms of freedom, smallness, and practicality, he tended to color the Persians as tyrannical, excessively expansive, decadent, and opulent. This constellation of Western images of the East and contrasting images with the West – known collectively as Orientalism – would be revived and expanded in later centuries. This phenomenon has been explored by Edward Said in a famous book of this title. The West, he claims, has come to continuously represent the "East" as decadent, effeminate, corrupt, voluptuous, despotic, and culturally static and incapable of change. Although such stereotypes do no justice to the pictures of variety and dynamic changes we have observed throughout the Near Eastern scene, the representations Westerners continue to project of the "East" carry on in the tradition of Herodotus. One need look no further than the portrayals of Xerxes and the Persians in the A.D. 2007 film 300 to see such stereotypes portrayed in living color.

CHAPTER SIX

DEMOCRACY AND EMPIRE BETWEEN ATHENS AND ALEXANDER

And everywhere we have left behind us everlasting memorials of good done to our friends or suffering inflicted on our enemies.

— Pericles' Funeral Oration, from Thucydides' *Peloponnesian War* 2.41[1]

* Why and how did Athens become an empire?
* How did the Greeks' exercise of ideology, economics, military, and politics (IEMP) compare with Near Eastern patterns?
* Can a democracy run an empire?
* Why and how was Alexander successful? Why and how was he not?

FLUSHED WITH PRIDE FROM THEIR VICTORY over the Achaemenid Persian Empire, the Greeks confidently embarked on their most famous age. The cultural fluorescence of the half century following the Greco-Persian War stands as one of the most brilliantly creative moments in human history. In literature, history, sculpture, architecture, and more, Greeks – Athenians in particular – created monuments that continue to challenge, inspire, and awe. At the same time, the Athenians constructed a harsh empire; indeed, their beautification projects were indirectly funded by tribute they exacted from other Greek poleis. Their lead in resistance to the Persian Empire was a vital ingredient in their own short-lived bid at imperialism. Near Eastern imperial expansion once again drove empire formation on the margins. An empire resister became an empire itself.

Behind the gleaming white façade of fifth-century Athens, tension – creative and destructive – was the real theme of the age. The tension was political, cultural, and intellectual. Much of it followed from the Greco-Persian

War. In retrospect, the Greco-Persian War was over in 479. This, however, was far from clear to the Greeks at the time. The Persians could return at any time, and fears of an imminent invasion continued to fuel political turmoil and uncertainty for decades after the war. Significant skirmishes with the Persians actually continued in the years following the Battle of Plataea. The Ionians, still under Persian control, rebelled yet again, and other Greeks again came to their aid. Athens asserted herself as the real defender of Greek freedom, starting on the Ionian coast but then moving throughout the mainland as well. Their notion of freedom, ironically, became a major source of their imperialism. The Athenian imperial moment continues to beg the question of whether any strong ideology – even one ostensibly of freedom and liberty – joined with military, political, and economic power, can ultimately avoid the creation of empire.

Many Athenians, however, were not exactly comfortable with being – or being known as – an empire. From the rhetorically charged setting of fifth-century Athens, in fact, come history's first known debates over the morality of empire. Even as Athens gradually extended its economic, political, and military control over other poleis, it struggled to construct and maintain an ideological justification for empire. From where would the Athenians get an ideology of empire? The Ionian Intellectual Revolution had helped ensure that they would not conquer and rule other Greeks in the name of a god or gods. How long could Athens effectively maintain that its role as defender of Greek liberty entitled it to bald hegemony over other Greek poleis?

Such questions revealed a series of deep and enduring issues. Greeks, no less than Assyrians, Babylonians, and Persians, sought to maintain cosmos, and to defend it through justice and right. As throughout the Near East, the public works of sculptors and architects proclaimed assumptions about cosmos and justice. Now, however, we also have the insights of playwrights, philosophers, and historians; a rather different sort of picture emerges than we have seen before. Taken together, these works are at once a testimony to a glorious humane spirit and a relentless imperial drive. The famous tragedies of Aeschylus, Sophocles, and Euripides, spanning the better part of the fifth century, show an incessant search for cosmos and justice in a world of anxiety and tension. Their philosopher counterparts – Socrates, Plato, and Aristotle – slightly later pose their huge ethical questions, not surprisingly, amid immense political tensions and clashes. Timeless questions of justice enliven the deeply humane and analytical history of the Peloponnesian War, the great Greek war, written by Thucydides, an Athenian general and the greatest of the Greek historians. The enduring and variegated output of all of these minds in so many spheres reinforces the old adage that conflict is a veritable crucible of creativity.

About as quickly as it had begun, this brief and shining moment was over. The Greek world descended into nearly a century of chaos and bitter strife. Most notably, the Peloponnesian War saw the poleis engulfed in a nearly thirty-year bipolar struggle. The subsequent collapsing polis system provided a start for the world's most famous conqueror. Alexander of Macedon would oversee a final stage of the forced "unification" of the once-autonomous Greek poleis. He would then proceed to bring Greek culture far to the East, intensifying the ongoing integration of East and West. He would also, as we will see, bring ideological power (I in our IEMP model) back to the fore.

A GOLDEN AGE (AT ATHENS)

A set of common values lay behind the Greek literary and artistic achievement of this age. These were not exclusive to Athens, but this polis was indisputably the epitome, and it is impossible not to give it center stage. Core Greek val-

the artistic output of the age. At the heart of what has been called Greek "humanism" was a basic belief that the human is simple, yet ideal. In the relatively free air of the polis, citizens could strive to distinguish themselves artistically, athletically, rhetorically, or politically. The Greeks were extremely competitive, a trait that played out both on the "international" stage within the Aegean and beyond – in wars as well as the famous Olympic games – and in their interpersonal relationships (Fig. 6.1). Balancing this drive was the ideal of self-restraint; "nothing in excess," as tragedian and philosopher alike would maintain. One should strive to distinguish oneself, but to do so in such a way that showed self-restraint and that ultimately brought glory to the polis. There was always the danger of hubris lurking for those who simply aimed to outshine one's fellow citizens. Individual freedom and the restraint imposed by civic responsibility worked together, in the Greek mind, to produce the ordered, cosmic community of the polis.

These were murky waters, however, and defining and defending the limits of ambition and self-restraint produced lively and intense debates, particularly at Athens. Much of this debate focused on the public assemblies, where voting took place. Traveling teachers of rhetoric, known as Sophists, emerged at just this time to instruct in the art of how to convince. These rhetoricians established a strong reputation for their ability to teach how to sway voters and policy makers. With the heightened democratization of Athens, as we will see in this chapter, they became influential and controversial figures in public life.

6.1. Euphiletos painter. The Metropolitan Museum of Art/Art Resource, NY. Rogers Fund, 1914.

One of the central and pertinent debates at this time was over how to define justice and right. An ongoing struggle emerged over defining and distinguishing *nomos* (custom, convention, and law based on them) and *physis* (the natural order, and law based upon nature). The discussion was inspired in part by the Ionian Intellectual Revolution, which had done much to define and explore *physis* in rational terms. Critical, rational thought and discussion of it distinguished Greek from Near Eastern notions of cosmos and justice. The Sophists and philosophers such as Socrates and Plato often were at the center of these discussions, especially as they explored issues of justice, right, and morality. In the troubled political climate of the time, these were glaring issues for the citizens of the polis.

Vital political changes – particularly those at Athens – intensified and fueled discussion. By 462, the power of the traditional and aristocratic Council of Areopagus at Athens was severely limited, and more than ever before, citizens across the board had to accept the decisions of the majority. This was part of a larger movement of democratization, or the continued emergence of a more thoroughgoing democratic political culture. The ability to convince in public speech was at a higher premium than ever.

The physical appearance of Athens was also changing throughout this period. The beautification of Athens, through architecture and sculpture, is still the most visible sign of Athens' Golden Age. At one level, it was purely practical. Athens had been destroyed by the Persians during the Greco-Persian War. Much of what can still be seen today on the acropolis in Athens was the product of the fifth-century building program. Pericles, the greatest mid-fifth-century leader of Athens, was the major sponsor of the massive rebuilding and beautification efforts. The chief architects Ictinus and Callicrates and the head sculptor Phidias designed the Parthenon as a beautiful offering of thanks to the gods for the Greek victory in the Greco-Persian War; of course, to Athenians, it was only natural that such a monument should be at Athens, the real victor of the war (Fig. 6.2).

Athenian literature of the fifth century boldly set forth the tensions, balance, and splendors of the age, especially three key playwrights, Aeschylus, Sophocles, and Euripides, who produced memorable tragic plays. These

raising poignant questions of justice and cosmos. One can clearly trace a progressive secularization across the three playwrights in handling these issues. Their plays are especially important, because drama can both reveal and express the thoughts of the people at large and is an important lens into Greek minds during the vibrant and tumultuous fifth century.

Aeschylus, the first great Greek playwright, was himself a veteran of the Greco-Persian War. He fought at the Battle of Marathon and probably the Battle of Salamis Bay as well. Famously, his own tombstone records nothing of his work as a writer or his frequent victories at the Athenian play festival but only his prowess at Marathon, the proudest day of his life. Aeschylus wrote with, comparatively speaking, the most religious values of any of the playwrights. To him, the vicissitudes and tragedies of life can be ascribed to the justice of the gods. Throughout his works, he depicts the tense balance of "Nothing in Excess" so central to the Greek mind. His play *The Persians*, the only surviving Greek play with real historical subject matter, can serve as a case study particularly relevant to the subject and themes of our study. Although all other extant plays are set in the mythic or legendary past, Aeschylus sets *The Persians* in the Greco-Persian War. It was first performed a mere eight years after the Battle of Salamis Bay, which is a major piece of action in the play. In writing the play, Aeschylus presented himself with a perfect Greek challenge – to glorify Greece, Athens in particular, while maintaining emotional balance.

6.2. Parthenon. Slide by Celine Leon.

His praise of Athens in the play is strictly muted, and his techniques for maintaining balance are memorable. Obviously, the members of his Athenian audience did not need encouragement to praise their own glorious polis and its recent past. A play that merely elicited civic pride would have ended up encouraging hubris. Although he names multiple Persian warriors and members of the Persian royal family, he never records a single Athenian name. The great hero of Salamis Bay, Themistocles, is referred to simply as "a man." One can only imagine a live performance with the audience collectively mouthing the name of their great leader during the play. However, the balance appropriate to tragedy is maintained because the play does not merely become a paean of Athenian greatness.

Nor does Aeschylus exult over the fallen Persians. In fact, he aimed to move his Athenian audience to grieve the losses suffered by their enemies. This type of humane sympathy is directly in tune with Greek values. When word of the Persian defeat at Salamis Bay reaches Susa, a Chorus of Persian Elders exclaims:

> *Awful sovereign of the skies,*
> *When now o'er Persia's numerous host*
> *Thou badest the storm with ruin rise,*
> *All her proud vaunts of glory lost,*

> *Ecbatana's imperial head*
> *By thee was wrapp'd in sorrow's dark'ning shade;*
> *Through Susa's palaces with loud lament,*
> *By their soft hand their veils all rent,*
> *The copious tear the virgins pour,*
> *That trickles their bare bosoms o'er.*
> *From her sweet couch up starts the widow's bride,*
> *Her lord's loved image rushing on her soul,*
> *Throws the rich ornaments of youth aside,*
> *And gives her griefs to flow without control:*
> *Her griefs not causeless; for the mighty slain*
> *Our melting tears demand, and sorrow-soften'd strain.*[2]

The tone of the tragedy is fittingly somber. By moving his audience to grieve for the Persian dead even amid vivid memories of Greek victory, Aeschylus strikes a stunning balance. The moment that vessels clash at Salamis Bay is preceded by shouts of

> *Your country, save your wives, your children save,*
> *The temples of your gods, the sacred tomb*
> *Where rest your honour'd ancestors; this day*
> *The common cause of all demands your valor.*[3]

But then, immediately following a brief description of how the "beaks clash with beaks," the tone shifts to gloomy, and

> *. . . the sea no more*
> *Wears its accustomed aspect, with foul wrecks*
> *And blood disfigured; floating carcasses*
> *Roll on the rocky shores: the poor remains*
> *Of the barbaric armament to flight*
> *Ply every oar inglorious . . .*
> *Wailings are heard, and loud laments, till night*
> *With darkness on her brow brought grateful truce . . .*
> *Ah what a boundless sea of wo hath burst*
> *On Persia, and the whole barbaric race.*[4]

Throughout this and his other famous surviving plays such as *Agamemnon*, *Seven against Thebes*, *Prometheus Bound*, and *The Eumenides*, Aeschylus is exploring human action with universal implications. A deeply sensitive humanity comes across here as Greeks grieve for their fallen foes, rather than exulting over them as victims of divine wrath, vengeance, or chaos. He argues strongly, through his

6.3. Euripides bust. Wikimedia, public domain image.

work, that order and purpose in the universe do in fact transcend civic pride. Right is, for him, not a matter of might, nor is the polis and its traditions the basic reference. There are universal laws (*physis*) that transcend customs and civic laws (*nomos*). Like Herodotus, he accuses Xerxes of hubris. Like a Greek hero, Xerxes is punished in the end for his excessive pride and for going beyond the bounds set for him. Right has not come from simply carrying out the will of the god(s) who command conquest and the administration of justice in their name(s), as in the Near East, but from a broader sense of *physis*, religious, natural, and physical laws. The question is the same as we have seen throughout the Near East – how to define justice? – but the answer is starkly different.

Sophocles, the second great tragedian, experienced firsthand the triumphs and tragedies of the fifth century. Born during the Greco-Persian War, he was later chosen, at the age of sixteen, to lead a chorus that annually celebrated the Battle of Salamis Bay. A political advisor to Pericles, he also served as a Strategoi, one of ten generals, during the Peloponnesian War. His public career spanned almost the entirety of the fifth century. Not as tradition-bound as Aeschylus in his plays, Sophocles gives less room to the will of the gods in defining justice and right. In all of his plays, including *Oedipus the King*, *Antigone*, *Electra*, and *Oedipus at Colonus*, one can see intense passion under control. The plot of *Antigone* is timelessly poignant in its presentation of the conflict between *nomos* and *physis*. During the mythical Theban War, Oedipus' sons Eteocles and Polynices killed each other. Creon, their uncle and the new king of Thebes, forbade the body of Polynices to be buried, considering him a traitor. Antigone, the sister of Eteocles and Polynices, then proceeded to bury her brother Polynices, against the direct orders of Creon. *Nomos*, as represented by the decree of Creon, is pitted here against *physis*, the universal law that dead bodies should be kept from birds of carrion and that siblings have a duty toward one another. Only the temporal decree of the king has rendered Polynices the traitor, Antigone essentially contends; there is a higher law (*physis*), and the plot of the play unfolds as Antigone defies the king's temporal decree (*nomos*) and pays the price. Such scenes vividly mirror the ethical dilemmas of the age.

Factual details about the life of the final of our fifth-century playwrights, Euripides, are few (Fig. 6.3). According to one dubious but telling story, he was born in Salamis the very day of the famous naval battle. With a rationalism in line with the Ionians and ethics inspired by Sophists, he gives little room to gods, either avenging or aiding, in his plays, the most famous of which are *Medea, The Heracleida, The Suppliants, The Trojan Women, Hecuba*, and *The Bacchae*. His own cynicism probably comes through in lines such as one in *Hecuba*: "By *nomos* we believe in the gods and define justice and injustice by which we

midst of the Peloponnesian War. *Medea* was first performed in 431, the year of the outbreak of the war. Traditional standards of rightness and justice were being flaunted and transgressed almost daily. With characters like Medea, Euripides pushed traditional ethical standards to their limits; this sorceress kills her own children, but the audience could almost sympathize with her violent rage, a victim betrayed by her love.

CAN A DEMOCRACY RUN AN EMPIRE?
THE PELOPONNESIAN WAR

Even while Athenians were declaring their humane values to the universe through literature, architecture, and sculpture, they were busily constructing an empire. In fact, the funds for the beautification of Athens were indirectly procured as virtual tribute from Athens' subjects. The Athenian Empire continued a long-standing pattern in which beautiful building projects proclaimed the creation of an empire. Cruelty and cultural creativity went hand in hand, as among their Near Eastern counterparts. The task of working within a consistent ideological basis for empire was treacherous, and within Athenian discourse emerged the first known debates over the morality of empire. Was empire right? For Greeks? For anyone? Does might make right? Does *nomos* define justice? It is hardly surprising that the three famous Greek philosophers – Socrates, Plato, and Aristotle – thrived amid questions of justice, morality, and political power. The Age of Ancient Empires had, once again, opened up huge questions on justice and cosmos.

The Peloponnesian War might also be seen at this point as a peripheral offshoot of the expansion of the Persian Empire. As always happens on peripheries when cores expand, there was a struggle to see who would lead the resistance to or assimilation into the imperial power. As often happens too, that struggle soon became more important than resistance to or assimilation into the imperial power itself. The Peloponnesian War drew more and more people from the margins into the central struggle, including those from areas we will soon encounter, such as Macedon, Italy, and Carthage.

Athens' journey to empire actually began during the Greco-Persian War. As Xerxes prepared his invasion force, the Greeks, led by Sparta, established a defensive confederation known as the Hellenic League. All the members pledged, for an indefinite span of time, to fight the Persians "for the common freedom." Soon after the Battle of Plataea and the end of the Greco-Persian War, the Ionians revolted once more against their Persian overlords and called on help from the mainland. The Greek poleis significantly disagreed among themselves how they should respond this time. The Spartans cautiously argued against the outright defense of these hard-to-defend and far-flung city-states, pushing for a resettling of the Ionians on more defensible mainland Greek territories seized from a few poleis that had sided with the Persians. Athens protested the idea of moving the Ionians from what had been their ancestral homes for centuries by now. Several mainland poleis gave nominal aid, but it was Athens that again stepped forward as the defender of the Ionians, solidifying its own image as the real protector of Greece. Some poleis interpreted Athens' move cynically; they began to see the potential for Athens to abuse this position and violate the freedom and autonomy of other poleis in her self-proclaimed role as defender and protector of the freedoms of the "sons of Hellas," be they on the Ionian coast, the islands, or the mainland.

To help protect the Ionians and others from a Persian incursion, and citing Spartan reluctance to commit the Hellenic League to the defense of Greeks, Athens established a new league in 477. The Delian League was centered on the island of Delos, a cult site and strategic position in the Aegean, midway between the mainland and the Ionian coast. Members, who pledged membership indefinitely, sent funds or other material resources annually to the treasury at Delos to help in the collective defensive effort. Over the 470s and 460s, the Delian League sponsored significant action against the Persians — for example, in 469 at the Eurymedon River mouth in Pamphylia. The league also entangled Athenians farther afield. It became involved in the Levant, a move that, according to some, helped convince the Persian king

Artaxerxes I (r. 465–423) to lend full support to the Jewish efforts to rebuild their temple under the Jewish Achaemenid courtiers Ezra and Nehemiah. He needed strong support in this region. The Athenians continued to press the Achaemenids in Cyprus and even aided in an (unsuccessful) Egyptian revolt before a peace with Persia was finally agreed on, probably in 449. The evidence is inconclusive, but at this point, the Persians most likely gave up their claims on the Ionian city-states.

Athens, for her part, lost few opportunities to use its resistance and belligerence against the hated Persians to strengthen its relative position back home. All along, it continued to build up its powerful navy with Delian League funds, freeing other funds for construction and beautification. Once the actual Persian threat to Greece had essentially vanished, some poleis tried to withdraw from the league or resist its burdensome financial and political demands but were met with swift and decisive retribution. Athens made clear that withdrawal from the league was not an option. The league funds, handled by Athens, were becoming a not-so-subtle tribute system. Athenian epigraphy of this time, as well as historical accounts written later, refers to other Greek

treasury of the Delian League to Athens itself in 454, there was little room left for speculation; Athens was an empire in every sense of the term.

When resisted, the Athenians always were quick to point out that it was they who had defeated the Persians at Marathon, Salamis Bay, and elsewhere; they had saved "Hellas" even at the cost of their own city, and they continued to guard against Persian aggression; thus they were deserving of their prominent and important position over other Greek poleis. Sparta, slowly and reluctantly at first, became the champion of poleis resisting Athenian hegemony. They and others watched as Athens used Delian League funds to build the Long Walls, connecting Athens directly with her port, Piraeus. Athens continued to claim that this was necessary for defense against a Persian invasion. To many, however, the walls represented an aggressive defense against other poleis rather than against Persians; Athens was building a fortress. However, the response to Athenian measures was slow, and Athens for a time had a free hand. Thucydides is characteristically straightforward in describing the cause of the Peloponnesian War:

> The Athenians and Peloponnesians began it by breaking the Thirty-Year Peace that they made after the capture of Euboea. As to why they broke the peace, I have written an account of the complaints and disputes so that no one may ever search for the reasons that so great a war broke out among the Hellenes. For I consider the truest cause the one least

openly expressed, that increasing Athenian greatness and the resulting fear among the Lacedaemonians made going to war inevitable.[6]

War preparations proceeded along expected lines. Athens, as usual, dominated the sea, and Sparta the land. The so-called First Peloponnesian War already pitted the two powers against each other by 461. Athens, beginning in the same year, built the famous Long Walls to keep grain fleets coming steadily into Piraeus amid hostilities. The Spartans aimed to secure as many allies as possible to dominate the Athenian allies on land. Although there were many clear and hostile precedents, the major phase of the Peloponnesian War, known as the Archidamian War, began in 431.

Thucydides presents the story of the war powerfully, both through his own critical and masterful narrative and through the gripping speeches he records or puts in the mouths of speakers. The speeches are well worth quoting at some length. One of the most famous speeches from the ancient world (if not all of history – Abraham Lincoln, in fact, modeled his Gettysburg Address on it), was delivered by Pericles of Athens in 430, after the first year of open hostilities of the war. Pericles' speech is rife with the tension between *nomos* and *physis* as well as a Sophistic fascination with words (*logoi*) and deeds (*erga*). After a long and flourishing discourse which both explicitly and implicitly contrasts the free, ornate, and beautiful way of life of the Athenians with the, well, spartan life of the Spartans, Pericles gets to his surprisingly stark central point:

> Taking everything together then, I declare that our city is an education to Greece, and I declare that in my opinion each single one of our citizens, in all the manifold aspects of life, is able to show himself the rightful lord and owner of his own person, and do this, moreover, with exceptional grace and exceptional versatility. And to show that this is no empty boasting for the present occasion, but real tangible fact, you have only to consider the power which our city possesses and which has been won by those very qualities which I have mentioned. . . . Mighty indeed are the marks and monuments of our empire which we have left. . . . For our adventurous spirit has forced an entry into every sea and into every land; and everywhere we have left behind us everlasting memorials of good done to our friends or suffering inflicted on our enemies.[7]

The proof of the superiority of the Athenian way of life is simply her dominance over others, Pericles claims. The everlasting memorial erected in architecture, literature, and so forth made her a hegemonic "education to Greece." The ideology of freedom had become, ironically, a clear ideology of empire.

Throughout the war, the mantle of empire sat heavily on the Athenians. Thucydides records several flashpoints by way of debates. Early in the war, in 428, one of Athens' Delian League allies/subjects, Mytilene, a polis on the island of Lesbos, revolted. After quelling the revolt, the Athenians decided to kill the entire adult male population and sell the women and children into slavery. By the next day, however, some Athenian citizens had changed their minds and argued for a more moderate path. So, in Athenian fashion, two orators argued the dominant positions: a certain Cleon and Diodotus, a prominent Athenian political leader. After the speeches there would be a vote to decide the fate of the Mytilenians. These speeches present history's first extended debate over the morality of empire, and it is worth noting some rich and extended excerpts:

> **Cleon:** Personally I have had occasion often enough already to observe that a democracy is incapable of governing others, and I am all the more convinced of this when I see how you are now changing your minds about the Mytilenians. . . . What you do not realize is that your empire is a tyranny exercised over subjects who do not like it and who are always
>
> plotting against you; you will not make them obey you by injuring your own interests in order to do them a favour; your leadership depends on superior strength and not on any goodwill of theirs. . . . What we should have done long ago with the Mytilenians was to treat them in exactly the same way as all the rest . . . for it is a general rule of human nature that people despise those who treat them well and look up to those who make no concessions. . . . To feel pity, to be carried away by the pleasure of hearing a clever argument, to listen to the claims of decency are three things that are entirely against the interest of an imperial power. . . . For if they were justified in revolting, you must be wrong in holding power. If, however, whatever the rights or wrongs of it may be, you propose to hold power all the same, then your interest demands that these too, rightly or wrongly, must be punished. The only alternative is to surrender your empire, so that you can afford to go in for philanthropy.
>
> **Diodotus:** I have not come forward to speak about Mytilene in any spirit of contradiction or with any wish to accuse anyone. If we are sensible people, we shall see that the question is not so much whether they are guilty as whether we are making the right decision for ourselves. . . . Cities and individuals alike, all are by nature disposed to do wrong, and there is no law (*nomos*) that will prevent it. . . . In a word it is impossible (and only the most simple-minded will deny this) for human nature (*physis*), when once seriously set upon a certain course, to be

prevented from following that course by the force of law (*nomos*) or by any other means of intimidation whatever. . . . It is far more useful to us, I think, in preserving our empire, that we should voluntarily put up with injustice than that we should justly put to death the wrong people.[8]

Diodotus' measure passed, but just barely; and the majority of the Mytilenians were spared.

By 421, with each side having inflicted serious losses on the other, the short-lived Peace of Nicias was affirmed between the major belligerents and their respective allies. The first phase of the war, the Archidamian War, ended. A second phase of war broke out soon afterward. The Athenians had some initial success under a young, brilliant, if hot-headed and arrogant, leader named Alcibiades. Accused of religious sacrilege (probably deservedly), he fled to Sparta, however, where he aided them against his own polis. Defining and maintaining a just cause in a war like this was becoming more and more impossible.

In 416, a year before Alcibiades was exiled, one of the baldest statements of conflicted Athenian imperialism appeared in the Melian Dialogue, which would decide the fate of the inhabitants of Melos. As Thucydides relates, the Melians were originally a Spartan colony, and their crime was that they had "refused to join the Athenian Empire." They had in fact struggled to remain neutral for a time, but then, under strong Athenian pressure, they had reluctantly joined the Spartan cause. The dialogue begins with the Athenians demanding that the Melians submit themselves completely to their empire, whereas the Melians simply insist on neutrality. The Athenians tell the Melians early in the dialogue:

> You know as well as we do that, when these matters are discussed by practical people, the standard of justice depends on the equality of power to compel and that in fact the strong do what they have the power to do and the weak accept what they have to accept [or, "the strong do what they can, the weak do what they must"].[9]

A more bald statement of Athenian imperialism would be difficult to find. To the Melians' appeal to a higher standard of justice (*physis*, essentially) than "might makes right," the Athenian response is poignant:

> Our opinion of the gods and our knowledge of men lead us to conclude that it is a general and necessary law of nature (*physis*) to rule whatever one can. This is not a law (*nomos*) that we made ourselves, nor were we the first to act upon it when it was made. We found it already in existence, and we shall leave it to exist for ever among those who come after us.[10]

The Melians, in turn, refused to "give up in a short moment the liberty which our city has enjoyed from its foundation." The Athenians, unmoved by arguments about liberty other than their own, then successfully besieged Melos, killing all the men and selling the women and children into slavery. Athens had become an empire as brutal as any before it, only lacking a strong religious ideology to back up or drive its imperialism. The Athenians imperial ideology of freedom remained throughout paradoxical at best.

Athens, however, emerged as a very different kind of empire than the Near Eastern examples we have seen already in this study. Partly this is a matter of scale and homogeneity, which make Athens' activities less like other imperial conquests we have seen. It is, however, also partly a matter of ideologies, or rather scale of religious ideology. Pericles' funeral oration, the Mytilenian Debate, and the Melian Dialogue contrast obviously with the imperial ideologies of Assyria, Babylon, and Persia. Unlike the Near Eastern texts, Greek sources never say anything about seizing areas because the gods desire such (in fact, the Melian Dialogue in another section explicitly says that the gods do not care either way). Ashurbanipal would never have missed

would seem that the Greeks in fact did see state power differently from earlier Near Eastern Empires; or, to put it another way, for them, the P dominated over the I, E, and M. In this way, they anticipate what we will see in the rise of Rome, a story that Romans tended to tell in comparatively secular terms.

Not all Greeks made the transition to empire smoothly. Episodes like the Melian Dialogue, etched deeply into the Athenian collective memory through the vivid presentation of Thucydides, troubled many Athenians. In the midst of conflict, some searched for ultimate standards of right, particularly philosophers who were not content with justice and right as defined by public rhetoric. It was precisely at this time that Socrates began his famous quest for truth, having himself served as a hoplite in several battles of the Peloponnesian War. Both he and his famous student Plato would react strongly against both Sophistic rhetoric and the excesses committed and excused by Athens.

Plato, looking back at the Peloponnesian War, set out, in his famous *Republic* and in his many dialogues, to define the ideal society and its ethical and moral workings. His picture contrasted sharply with the Athens of his recent past. Both in his *Republic* and in his dialogue *Gorgias*, in fact, he presents central characters whose position is precisely that of the Athenians in their dialogue with the Melians; essentially "might makes right." Many have seen in one of these characters, Callicles in *Gorgias*, an uncanny resemblance to Alcibiades, the Athenian leader turned traitor. Plato, via his character Socrates, refutes both Callicles and several students of the Sophist Gorgias by defending an idea of absolute truth and goodness: "Then the belief that it is baser to do wrong than to suffer wrong and that equality is right appears to be founded in nature (*physis*) as well as in convention (*nomos*)."[11] Here and throughout this dialogue, Plato is defending a basic idea that it is better to suffer than to do wrong – a statement of an absolute ethical truth. The connections to Athens' immediate past were obvious. Plato ended up rejecting democracy altogether, advocating instead the rule of a philosopher-king who would reign with wisdom and reason. He remained to the end a defender of the polis but bitterly opposed to what he saw as the mob rule of democracy led by the demagoguery of rhetoricians and Sophists.

The latter years of the Peloponnesian War saw an Athens growing increasingly weaker than her confident and strident imperialist rhetoric. Sparta, however, was not able to cut off the Athenian grain supply defended by the Long Walls, and the war dragged on in Greece and in Sicily. In the end, it took Sparta actually pulling in the Achaemenid Persians under *shahinshah* ("King of Kings") Artaxerxes II (r. 405–359) to make Athens surrender in 404. The ironies here are many – an empire founded on an ideology of freedom was ultimately defeated by a Spartan coalition that had to depend on Greece's bitter enemy.

There was little to celebrate after the decades of devastating war. Sparta more or less dominated the whole of mainland Greece for almost half a century, although Athens made a few brief bids to renew her empire. Immediately after the surrender of Athens, Sparta imposed tribute on the subjects of the Athenian Empire. The Spartans provide yet another example of an empire resister becoming an empire in its own right, even if a short-lived one. To defend what was essentially their own empire, the Spartans continued to rely on Achaemenid Persian help. Persia, in fact, is the only candidate for a real winner of the Peloponnesian War in any meaningful sense, basically accomplishing what she had been unable to do over a century before during the Greco-Persian War. For her help in the Peloponnesian War, Persia was awarded outright control of the Ionian city-states. Like a puppet master, Persia almost playfully dominated the Greeks, even the apparently victorious Spartans. Athens, Corinth, Thebes, and Sparta continued to struggle among themselves for Greek dominance.

The Greek world never regained its former character; much had changed. The polis as a free, autonomous entity never really recovered, even if, as recent research shows, most Greeks individually were generally better off financially than before. The Greek population likewise expanded during this period. Greek border states, meanwhile, had learned much from their southern neighbors in terms of tactics, fiscal management, and political and military organization and were soon to outshine the poleis to their south. The pattern of peripheral states coming to center stage continued. Thessaly, for example, emerged as a powerful force on the fringe in the 370s. The most powerful polity to emerge was Macedon, whose "kind offer" to unify the poleis was met with some ideological resistance but not enough military. Someone, after all, had to take on the Persian puppet master.

THE EMPIRE STRIKES BACK:
ALEXANDER THE GREAT

One of the most famous stories about Alexander the Great is that he slept each night with two things under his pillow: a dagger and a copy of Homer's *Iliad*. To many Greeks, such stories would have affirmed images of Macedon and the Macedonians. In the eyes of Athenians and others, Macedonia was a backward, even rustic, region. Here, the Homeric notion of *arête* was alive and well – "excellence" in terms of manliness, prowess, dominance, and ability to get things done. To Alexander's own teacher, Aristotle, and his teacher,

manliness and the ability to get things done. Greeks saw Macedonia as living in a "semi-Homeric" world; that is, many of the changes in Greece since the Dark Age had not permeated the Macedonian polity. Perhaps worst of all to other Greeks, Macedonia did not have – and had never had – poleis. It was a kingdom. The philosopher Aristotle famously described the human as a "political animal," by which he meant a creature of the polis. Macedonians could not quite measure up fully. Then there were their all-night drinking parties (of which Greeks in principle approved, so long as you called it a symposium) flowing with unmixed wine (of which the Greeks definitely did not approve).

In the 350s, Philip II, king of Macedon, became embroiled in Greek affairs. He presented himself as a "unifier" of the Greeks, protecting Hellas from Persian abuses. The Athenian legacy lived on, as did a familiar pattern of empire formation through resistance. Philip borrowed Greek military organization but modified it in fundamental ways. He incorporated an effective cavalry, long part of Macedonian warfare, and lengthened the pikes wielded by the hoplites and increased the number of hoplites in each phalanx. When he moved against the Greeks, they, as always, disagreed on how to respond. Two major rhetoricians stepped in to present the terms of debate. Demosthenes, the greatest of all Athenian orators, in a series of brutal speeches known as the *Philippics*, castigated Philip as an illegitimate and bloodthirsty conqueror as well as an inept politician. He actually encouraged the Greeks to side with the Persians against the Macedonians. Isocrates, in his *Philippus*, called on Philip to relieve the misery of Greece by unifying it and taking on the Persians.

Whether conqueror or savior of Greece, in 338 at the Battle of Chaeronea, Philip defeated an alliance led by Athens and Thebes. At the head of the battle's key cavalry charge was his eighteen-year-old son, Alexander. Two years later, Philip lay dead at the hand of an assassin, and Alexander ascended the Macedonian throne, bent on continuing his father's "unification," but looking far beyond Greece. It is fairly clear that from his early life, Alexander dreamed of subduing the Achaemenid Persian Empire as well.

Alexander began his conquests immediately. He started with Thebes in 335, brutally crushing a revolt against him and sending a clear message to anyone considering asserting independence against this twenty-year-old. He then turned eastward on a series of famous campaigns from which he would never return home. Historians differ in their assessments of the Persian Empire at the time of his campaigns. To some, it was relatively weak, under a subpar Darius III; to others, the empire was not struggling at all, nor was its king. On balance, the evidence seems to favor a fairly thriving Persian Empire and a no-less-than amazing threat to it in Alexander.

Details from Alexander's campaigns reveal a fascinatingly complex and controversial story. They have to be pieced together from various biographical sources composed centuries after his death. Undoubtedly, he created a massive, if unwieldy, empire, stretching from Libya to the Hindu Kush and from the Balkans to the Sudan. But what was driving him and why was he so successful in his conquests? According to one older view, Alexander was a man of "Grand and Noble Vision," and his conquests were primarily a means to a noble end of spreading Greek culture eastward, and mixing it together with the best of Persian culture. As his biographer Plutarch, writing about four hundred years later, would claim:

> Believing that he had come as a god-sent governor and mediator of the whole world, he overcame by arms those he could not bring over by persuasion and brought men together from all over the world, mixing together, as it were, in a loving-cup their lives, customs, marriages and ways of living.[12]

Mixing the cultures of the Near East and Greece, then, was his way of realizing a sort of "Universal Brotherhood of Man."

Several vivid stories lend support to this view. After his decisive victory over the Achaemenid King Darius III at Gaugamela in 331, Alexander actually adopted Persian dress. His inner circle of leaders was not much impressed by this move, but it suggests that Alexander was experimenting with closing cultural gaps between the East and West. A few years later, after marrying a Bactrian princess named Roxanne, Alexander began to insist on *proskynesis*, the prostrating on the floor insisted on by Persian monarchs. Although this may well have been a perfectly practical move to garner the respect of the Persians, it suggested to his inner circle that Alexander was simply "going native," and they refused to bow before him. He granted Macedonians and Greeks exceptions, but continued to accept *proskynesis* from the inhabitants of the former Persian Empire. Whether it was his driving goal or not, Alexander did spread Greek culture far to the East, constructing Greek temples, gymnasia, and sculpture as far as present-day Afghanistan and beyond. It is widely believed, in fact, that Greek sculpture inspired the first sculptures of Buddha, which in subsequent centuries spread farther eastward to China and Japan (Fig. 6.4).

According to others, Alexander was not so much driven by a human

vine hero and thus invincible. His emphasis on ideology (I), then, presented both a challenge to the Greek emphasis on P and a reversion to much older norms. His fascination with Homeric tales was not just a leisure activity; he saw himself as a hero on par with Achilles. Early in his campaign, just after sending Darius III fleeing for the first time, Alexander made a mysterious trip to Egypt. While the Egyptians surrendered without a fight, Alexander continued westward, away from the Persians, toward an oasis and oracle at Siwa dedicated to the Egyptian deity Amon (Hammon). The passage there was a risky one and carried with it no outright military or political reward. However, the ideological payoff seems significant. Being greeted by the priests of Amon with "O *paidie*" (O, my son), which he heard as "O *pai dios*" (O, son of Zeus), Alexander took heart in identifying himself with the great divine heroes of old. The oracle supposedly also assured him that he would conquer the world. He now came to see himself as on par with, if not superior to, Near Eastern kings, through his connection to their gods. In doing this, he gave Greeks a strong organizing principle that they lacked – a centralized and motivating religious ideology to unite them. To the inhabitants of the Near East, he connected himself to deep-rooted ideologies. The successors to Alexander would continue to claim a semidivine status, connecting to age-old currents within the Near East and beyond. Religious ideology was a necessary ingredient of any empire that hoped to include parts of the Near East and Egypt.

6.4. Standing Bodhisattva Maitreya (Buddha of the Future). The Metropolitan Museum of Art/Art Resource, NY. Rogers Fund, 1913.

Alexander, according to this view, was shifting the foundations of social power back to I bases, where it had come, during the classical period of Greece, to focus on P. After a moment in which the P forms of power had flourished, the pendulum was swinging back to more traditional modes of power to rule and to reduce resistance. His biography is full of examples that defend this notion. In Egypt and Persia, he was accepted as a Pharaoh and an Achaemenid-style king. In 324, he even ordered the Greeks to worship him as a god. The Greeks would famously resist Alexander's insistence on being treated as a god at first. Within only a few decades of his death, however, divine and divine-right rulers would once again be the norm. This trend started in the Hellenistic period, as we will see, and then reached a zenith during the Roman Empire.

Other historians see him primarily as an incredibly charismatic leader, who inspired his troops by his fearless zeal and personal sacrifice on their behalf. Many stories support this view. He refused to drink water if his men were thirsty, to eat if they were hungry, and was loved by his men for his consistent personal sacrifice on their behalf. His indefatigable resolve is clear in his siege of Tyre in 333. This old Phoenician city-state, now a part of the Achaemenid Persian Empire, was particularly difficult to besiege because it was an island. Alexander simply turned the siege into a land battle, more to his liking, by building a half-mile land bridge connecting Tyre to the mainland. Tyre promptly surrendered and remains today a peninsula, as Alexander left it. In the same year, at the Battle of Issus, he sent Darius III fleeing eastward clear across the Persian Empire. A later mosaic from the Roman city of Pompeii captures, if nothing else, the reputation Alexander enjoyed as a charismatic leader. Note his position at the front of the charge against Darius, the wide-eyed steady gaze, his unprotected head, and the horror written all over the face of the Persian King of Kings, the *shahinshah* (Fig. 6.5).

The loyalty of his troops did run thin, however, after he defeated an Indian King, Porus, in 326, and showed signs of continuing to move eastward indefinitely. His troops threatened mutiny in 325, and Alexander had to relent, leading them back westward, across the Gedrosian desert (losing about three-

He possibly had plans, according to some ambiguous evidence, to move westward from Greece next, defeat the Empire of Carthage, and move to Italy where the city of Rome was on the rise.

A few historians claim that Alexander was simply a ruthless and bloody-minded conqueror, bent on subjugating others and maximizing his own power. These tend to minimize the foregoing perspectives. Such a view seems to ignore the rich complexity of power and rule, in general. The intricacy of power suggests that such views, although popular in some quarters, are just as wrong for Alexander the Great as they are for Charlemagne, Genghis Khan, Napoleon, or Adolf Hitler.

Alexander's success in creating an empire and ultimate failure in founding a lasting one show the workings of IEMP. The ideology of the divine or semidivine hero would inspire not only the immediate Hellenistic kingdoms and empires that emerged out of his own but most subsequent ancient conquerors, kings, and emperors as well. The ideology itself was a dynamic synthesis of archaic Greek and Near Eastern culture and epitomized the reintegration of East and West. With it, Alexander was able to inspire his own army and his conquered peoples. Without it, he could not have won the loyalty of his conquered subjects throughout the Near East.

As to economic power, Alexander more or less kept Near Eastern patterns in place. Tribute and booty enriched and heartened his soldiers for a time. His successors would continue to exact tribute in typical ways. They would

6.5. The Battle of Issus (Alexander Battle), mosaic. Scala/Ministero per i Beni e le Attivitàvulturali/Art Resource, NY.

erect with the tribute some of the most grandiose monuments of the ancient world. In fact, the Greco-Macedonian successors to Alexander's empire can claim more of the Seven Wonders of the Ancient World than any other group before or after, as we will see.

It would be difficult to overestimate the role of military power in his empire. Alexander continued, through subsequent centuries, as the very model of the charismatic military genius. Building on the military innovations introduced by his father, Alexander took the Greek phalanx even beyond the bounds of the Persian Empire to areas untouched by the great empires of the Near East. He has hardly been equaled on the battlefield, and he continued to inspire Roman generals and emperors, Muslim emperors, Byzantine emperors, Medieval English Kings, and Malaysian rulers centuries after his death.

His political power, however, is hardly worth mentioning, except to say that its very weakness was one of the most important reasons that his empire fragmented at his death. He provided for no strong political model other than the charismatic leader. No one could really fill his shoes. At his death, his successors were left to sort out how political power would work in this new world, this amalgamation of East and West.

The empires of Athens and Alexander were built at least partly on resistance to the Achaemenid Persian Empire, and thus the cycle of ancient empire continued. Internal and external factors came together to make both empires possible and, in their own ways, unique. They both reveal, thanks to new kinds of sources, a complex blend of intellectual and cultural forces behind the larger political picture. Alexander's Empire, though short-lived, was highly influential and represents a thorough combination of indigenous Greek and Near Eastern elements. To Greek culture, he gave a strong religious ideology that would have a long life in the Mediterranean and Near Eastern worlds. Under him, the Age of Ancient Empire had reached its farthest spread from West to East. Its continued progression westward would be a major theme in subsequent centuries as the Roman Empire arose in the West. First, however, we turn to the successor kingdoms and empires of those who followed Alexander.

CHAPTER SEVEN

"SPEAR-WON" EMPIRES:
THE HELLENISTIC SYNTHESIS

For now that there was no one to take over the empire, those who ruled peoples or cities could each entertain hopes of kingship and controlled hence-forward the territory under their power as if it were a spear-won kingdom.

— Diodorus of Sicily[1]

* How did the successors to Alexander consolidate power?
* In what ways did the Hellenistic world continue age-old patterns, and in what ways did it witness the start of new developments?
* In what sense(s) did empire shape the lives of individuals?
* How did sources of social power contribute to resistance to Hellenistic empires and kingdoms?

As ALEXANDER LAY DYING IN BABYLON, so one famous story goes, his generals asked him to name his successor; he replied, "the strongest." No doubt he suspected that there would be "'funeral games' in good earnest after he was dead" to determine whom that person would be.[2] A half century of violent struggles, however, was probably something neither he nor anyone else had anticipated. Every time one general would "hold his head above the others," a makeshift coalition would form against him. When the last of the Diadochoi, Alexander's officers who played key roles in these struggles, died in battle in 281, a single unified Alexandrine Empire was nowhere in sight. Instead, two estranged empires, the Seleucid and the Ptolemaic, and a varying number of smaller kingdoms would thereafter hold the fragments of the second largest and shortest-lived empire that the Near East and Mediterranean ever saw.

The Hellenistic era's importance to the Age of Ancient Empires lay not so much in producing renowned empires (the largest, the Seleucid, began its decline immediately after the death of its founder), but rather for the way it synthesized the worlds of Greece, Macedonia, the Near East, and northeast Africa. Its cultural, social, and economic reintegration of East and West would define the next half millennium of Near Eastern and Mediterranean history. The Hellenistic world laid foundations – often using very old materials – for all remaining ancient empires that followed it: the Roman, renewed Persian, the Byzantine, and, finally, the Islamic.

ALEXANDER'S "FUNERAL GAMES"

There was nothing foregone about the way the Hellenistic world took shape and under whom; contingencies abounded, with far-reaching implications. Frequent shifts at the top layer of historical time – the level of events – set the political scene in the topsy-turvy half century after Alexander's death. Wars, invasions, and assassinations often and suddenly upended most expectations

That Alexander's death launched a succession crisis would have surprised few who knew anything about Macedonian politics. Most Macedonian reigns were plagued by challenges at both beginning and end, if not frequently in between; how to establish and maintain legitimacy remained an overwhelming question. The initial battle lines among the Diadochoi were drawn between those who declared for unity at all costs and those who were content with, if not outright bent on, separatism and division.

The unity "camp" initially came together as collective regents for Alexander's son, Alexander IV, born just after his death, and Alexander's mentally impaired half-brother Arrhidaeus (declared Philip III). These two were proclaimed the joint rulers of the entire realm, a bizarre and unprecedented move designed to hold together opposing factions. The regency proved unstable from the beginning, and settlements at several "conferences" proved illusory as the Diadochoi turned on each other and new players joined the fray. The two most important "unifiers" to emerge over the first two decades were Antigonus "the One-Eyed," a satrap under Alexander, and Seleucus "the Conqueror," named satrap of Babylon just after Alexander's death. These two cooperated initially but soon fell out as wars broke out within the unity "camp."

The major initial "separatist" was Ptolemy, who initiated the most stable and long-lived of the successor kingdoms. One of Alexander's bodyguards, he immediately made for Egypt after Alexander's death and declared himself satrap and eventually Pharaoh. Two years later, he stole Alexander's embalmed body as it was being transported to Macedonia and brought it back to Egypt. Alexander had once expressed a desire to be buried at the Siwah Oasis, lending some legitimacy to the body-napping. The body never actually made it to Siwah, however, but was put on display in a mausoleum in Alexandria. In Macedonian tradition, burying a leader was a symbol of legitimate succession. Alexander had done so after both Philip II's assassination and the death of Darius III, in effect declaring himself the true Macedonian and Achaemenid heir. Ptolemy thus proclaimed his own separate kingdom, the Ptolemaic, as the legitimate successor state.

As the other Diadochoi were jockeying for position, an old conundrum returned: how to reconcile the perennial Greek desire for autonomy with rule by distant leaders. Freedom once again returned as a major slogan and, ultimately, a tool of empire. Diadochoi who desired Greek support or wished to incite rebellion against their rivals proclaimed "freedom of the Greeks," a refrain that would resonate for centuries among would-be hegemons in this region. Hardly coincidentally, the two first Diadochoi emperors, Antigonus and Ptolemy, were also the first to declare freedom for the Greeks. In 314, Antigonus "the One-Eyed" publicly proclaimed a resolution that:

> All the Greeks should be free, exempt from garrisons, and autonomous. The soldiers carried the motion and Antigonus [the One-Eyed] despatched messengers in every direction to announce the resolution. He calculated as follows: the Greeks' hopes for freedom would make them willing allies in the war, while the generals and satraps in the upper satrapies, who suspected Antigonus of seeking to overthrow the kings who had succeeded Alexander, would change their minds and willingly submit to his orders when they saw him clearly taking up the war on their behalf. . . . Ptolemy heard of the resolution concerning the freedom of the Greeks which the Macedonians with Antigonus had passed, and drafted a proclamation in much the same words to convey to the Greeks that he cared no less for their autonomy than did Antigonus. Each side saw that to gain the goodwill of the Greeks would carry no little weight, and so they vied with each other in conferring favours on them.[3]

Although not all scholars necessarily share Diodorus' cynicism, most contend that Greek autonomy under these terms presented at best a thorny dilemma: for a leader or leaders to be able to confer or proclaim freedom assumed that he or they also had the ability to take it away. Was this really freedom, or was it thinly veiled hegemony? One scholar simply calls it a tautology.[4] Some Greeks would respond to a similar affirmation of Greek freedom a few years later by erecting an altar to Antigonus and his son Demetrius "the Besieger," who they presented as their godlike saviors and sacral mediators. This is probably best explained, as mentioned in the previous chapter, as a reversion to the ideological (I) forms of power. Seen in this light, the claiming of divine status, as we will see, is part of a general shift back to religious ideology to the fore after the Greeks had tended to emphasize the political (P).

With solid Greek support, Antigonus consolidated a unified kingdom that stretched from the Aegean to the Hindu Kush. He seemed set to make a bid to restore Alexander's empire, but his move signaled to others that he was "lifting his head" a bit too high, and so other Diadochoi collectively declared war on him. In 311, the major players came to terms (creatively known as the "Peace of 311"). The peace was tense, short-lived, and suggested that multiple kingdoms would be the only feasible outcome of Alexander's "funeral games." Separate leaders were declared for Europe (that is, Greece and Macedonia), Asia, and Egypt. All the signees mutually pledged the obligatory "freedom of the Greeks."

Up until this point, most of the Diadochoi continued to maintain that assassinated in 317), waiting for him to come of age and receive his father's realm. None of them had yet taken on the official title of king (*basileus*), even if some were acting like kings. When the young teenage Alexander IV and his mother Roxanne were murdered in 310, the fiction was called off: "for now that there was no one to take over the empire, those who ruled peoples or cities could each entertain hopes of kingship and controlled henceforward the territory under their power like kingdoms that had been conquered in war (won by the spear)."[5] Not long afterward, in 306, Antigonus "the One-Eyed" and his son Demetrius "the Besieger" each claimed the official title *basileus*, the first of the Diadochoi to do so; their fortunes were riding high. All the other major players assumed the title over the next few years, however, and the battles continued. Five years later (301) at the Battle of Ipsus, one of the largest land battles in ancient history (as many as 150,000 took to the field), the apparent "frontrunner," Antigonus "the One-Eyed," and his dream of a single unified empire were trampled by Indian elephants, and Seleucus "the Conqueror" took control of Asia.

In 281, the last of Alexander's surviving generals faced off at the Battle of Corupedion, even though both were around eighty years old at this time. Seleucus won and was well positioned to reunite all of Alexander's empire minus Egypt, even calling Macedonia "his land," according to a recently discovered Babylonian chronicle. However, he was assassinated by a renegade and outcast son of Ptolemy (Ptolemy "the Thunderbolt"), who was also vying for the Macedonian throne, laying to rest any lingering dreams of unity under one of the Diadochoi. Thus, once again, a fairly random event changed the course of the age.

The following year, another contingency helped put the final pieces into the Hellenistic political puzzle. Wandering Celts/Gauls suddenly appeared from the north and began to devastate Macedonia and Greece. The Celts struck down Ptolemy "the Thunderbolt" (including sticking his head on a pike) and then proceeded to overrun the Balkans, one of the few times in the ancient world that Macedonia did not hold up as a buffer for Greece.

Subsequently, in a single vital move, the Aitolians, leaders of a federal league in central Greece, defeated roving bands of Celts, and saved the nearby shrine of Delphi. The league then proclaimed itself the "savior of Greece" and emerged as the preeminent power in central Greece. Meanwhile, Antigonus Gonatus "the Knock-Knees," the son of Demetrius "the Besieger" and grandson of Antigonus "the One-Eyed," who had been remarkably ineffective on the political scene up to this time, scored a major victory over the Celts, and thus secured the coveted Macedonian throne and began the long-lived Antigonid dynasty.

The political shape of the Hellenistic world came together in a way no one could have foreseen even two years earlier. The Seleucid Empire dominated Asia, the Ptolemaic Empire continued on in Egypt, and the Antigonids ruled in Macedonia. Central Greece was dominated by the Aitolian League, which, along with another old Greek League, the Achaean League, revived at around the same time, would govern all of Greece proper. The funeral games were over, but the clashes of empires had only just begun.

THE HELLENISTIC IEMP SYNTHESIS

The Hellenistic king, the *basileus*, ruled over a kingdom, a *basileia*. The *basileia* was a collection of subjects rather than a distinct territory or place, per se; it was enlarged by conquering new peoples, hence a "spear-won" kingdom. The Hellenistic empires and kingdoms were thus almost constantly at war with one another. Their political and economic systems depended on new conquests, which in turn affirmed the sacral and even divine status of the heroic conquering military leader – a dynamic IEMP synthesis, with the I component more central. Greek, Macedonian, and Near Eastern social patterns – at the middle layer of historical time – converged with the top-level political events to fashion the Hellenistic world. While there were, of course, peculiarities to each of the Hellenistic empires and kingdoms, there were some remarkable consistencies across the board.

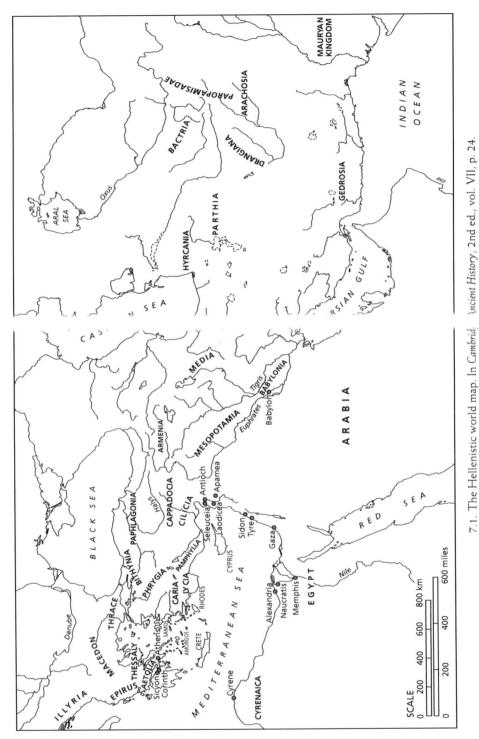

7.1. The Hellenistic world map. In *Cambridge Ancient History*, 2nd ed., vol. VII, p. 24.

7.2. Tetradrachm of Seleucus I. The Metropolitan Museum of Art/Art Resource, NY. Purchase,
H. Dunscombe Colt Gift, 1974.

Following traditional Near Eastern patterns of elite replacement, Hellenistic conquests put Macedonians or Greco-Macedonians on all the thrones
of these kingdoms and empires and in most top administrative, bureaucratic,
and social positions. Like many modern Western expatriates living in less
industrialized countries, Macedonians and Greeks were attracted to far-flung
regions by the new opportunities and potential for higher relative political
and social status.

Previous generations of scholars claimed that there was a radical separation between the Macedonian/Greek rulers and the diverse native populations,
with the native peoples consistently being exploited and excluded. Recent
views suggest a more symbiotic relationship between rulers and ruled, varying, of course, across time and space. In Ptolemaic Egypt, for example, a
native priesthood ran a local bureaucracy, which was arranged on patterns
close to traditional Egyptian administrative frameworks. The Seleucid army
gainfully employed many Persians, even putting some in fairly high positions. Macedonians and Greeks generally made out quite well in these new
settings, however, and their regular emigrations from the Aegean prompted
demographic and social shifts in all areas touched by Alexander's conquests.

The Hellenistic political systems depended on the powerful resurgence
of divine rulership ideology. Sacral monarchy, as we have seen, had deep
and strong roots in ancient mentalities, a central part of the ideological and
social structures. Even among the Greeks who had prized P component of

IEMP, there was a sense, perhaps subconscious, that their civic life had been missing something in the centuries since they had disposed of their kings, their sacral mediators. The Macedonians, who maintained their kings, had probably never completely lost this dimension of monarchy.

Philip II was probably tapping into such a *mentalité* when he paraded himself along with images of the Olympian gods just before his assassination. Alexander encouraged – or at least did not actively discourage – reverence of himself as a god. Ptolemy I, "the Savior," first proclaimed a ruler cult to Alexander; Ptolemy II then proclaimed his father, Ptolemy I, a god after his death, and a long tradition began. A ruler cult emerged among the Ptolemies that owed much to both divine pharaonic imagery and Macedonian hero worship (Fig. 7.3).

Although a bit slower to institute overt ruler cult, the Seleucids would also do so in time, based in part on older Achaemenid principles. Antiochus III, "the Great" (r. 223–187), was the first known Seleucid to institute a state cult to himself and his ancestors. Soon, a high priestess to the divine ruler was functioning in every Seleucid satrapy. Later, the Romans would learn much

ideological patterns returned.

At times, ruler cult was imposed from the top down, but it could spontaneously arise from below as well. Demetrius "the Besieger" was greeted by the citizens of Athens when he arrived there (in 291):

> How the greatest and dearest of the gods have come to the city! . . . His appearance is majestic, his friends all around him and he in their midst, as though they were the stars and he the sun. Hail son of the most powerful god Poseidon and Aphrodite! For the other gods are either far away, or they do not have ears, or they do not exist, or do not take any notice of us, but you we can see present here; you are not made of wood or stone, you are real. And so we pray to you.[6]

This hymn was sung not only in public but also in private homes, Athenaeus relates. Embracing Hellenistic rulers as divine was not simply a matter of bald imperial hegemony, even among the freedom-loving Athenians. The cynical approach to this moment is poignantly summarized by the famous twentieth-century historian E. R. Dodds, "When the old gods withdraw, the empty thrones cry out for a successor, and with good management, or even without management, almost any perishable bag of bones may be hoisted into the vacant seat."[7]

Hellenistic economic patterns echoed both Macedonian and Near Eastern practices. For the Macedonian part, the economy followed trends that

7.3. Detail of Ptolemy III Euergetes I and goddess. DeA Picture Library, Art Resource, NY.

have been termed "Heroic" or "Status-Distributive." All the land ultimately belonged to the king who conquered or inherited it; the king, or rather his favorites to whom he parceled land grants out as gifts, then exacted tribute from all agricultural proceeds from the land. Tax farmers bid on the right to collect the tribute/taxes, most of which made their way back to the imperial treasury in the form of precious metals. Following traditional Near Eastern imperial economic arrangements, the ultimate goal was simply to expand the royal treasury. This was why Alexander consistently found immense hoards of gold and silver in each Achaemenid royal city. The Hellenistic emperor or king, like his Achaemenid counterpart, generally expended but a small portion of the treasury hoard on public monuments to bolster his image and on defense to keep his *basileia* intact.

Tariffs and custom dues further expanded the royal treasury. The Hellenistic monarchs followed older Near Eastern patterns here more so than anything from classical Greece. In classical Greece, tariffs were low and fairly limited – no more than 5 percent: Greek citizens were never favorable to them. In contrast, the Ptolemies were particularly famous for their high rates and complex tariff and custom structure – tariffs on imported olive oil or wine were known to reach as high as 50 percent. Nonetheless, a vibrant international trade continued apace, and some private citizens amassed unprecedented amounts of personal wealth through it. More capital was available and more broadly than ever before; in the end, a select few were able to take advantage of it, and, even amid abundant wealth, the gap between the very wealthy and the poor widened, and general standards of living probably declined for the masses during this period.

The area of monetary policy had no long-term traditions behind it. Alexander and his successors literally monetized the economy of the Near East, especially within the cities. Coinage itself was invented around 600 B.C., just before the rise of the Achaemenids, who minted coins, but on a limited basis, generally only enough to pay mercenaries or bribe Greek politicians. Alexander coined massive amounts of money, releasing more than $300 billion worth of gold and silver from Achaemenid imperial treasures onto the Mediterranean and Near Eastern markets. His successors continued the patterns, and in many areas, the economy was monetized for the first time ever, as the use of currency now went far beyond just troop payment to daily business interaction. Most of the Hellenistic kingdoms and leagues adopted a single

and streamlined trade interactions among them. Always the separatists, the Ptolemies adopted a different measure for the tetradrachm (13–15 g).

Plunder and warfare were considered morally superior to any other mode of economic expansion, such as streamlining production or market ventures. Warfare thus remained a normal way of life in the Hellenistic world. There were, in fact, only four short periods of peace between 323 and 150 B.C. – 299–297, 249–248, 205–204, and 159–149.[8] Conquest also ensured a steady flow of slaves – Aristotle called them "animated tools" – into Hellenistic kingdoms and empires. Such would set a pattern and a precedent for the Roman Empire, as we will see, which captured staggering numbers of slaves in its earliest years.

The Hellenistic militaries continued some classical Greek and Near Eastern patterns, while innovating in some basic areas. Following Near Eastern examples, Hellenistic armies had much more diversity and relied even more on mercenaries than did classical Greek or Macedonian armies. No longer were citizen-soldiers the core of the fighting force, even though the Greek hoplite phalanx (with Macedonian modifications) remained standard. Although Alexander had made good use of cavalry, his successors generally did not. The numbers in Hellenistic armies dwarfed those of the classical Greek world, and the period saw some of the largest land battles in antiquity.

War was for the *basileus* the foundation of his royal power as well as divine authority. His was the law of the sword and of the spear, and his victories on the battlefield solidified his political legitimacy as well as his position in the royal cult: conquests contributed to a "royal mystique, coupled with a theology of victory."[9] As with the Assyrians, warfare was part of Hellenistic religious faith. Military victories boosted political and ideological prestige, filled the royal treasury, and added to the tax roll; this IEMP synthesis ran through all the Hellenistic empires and kingdoms.

EMPIRE AND THE CITY

After his first military victory, at age sixteen, Alexander founded and named a city after himself; Alexandropolis would be the first of many cities to bear his name. His father, however, did not approve – not because he objected to such apparent egotism (if not hubris) – Philippi and Philippopolis eloquently attest to that, but because it was the Macedonian monarch's distinct prerogative to found cities and thus immortalize his own name. In the end, Philip let the city – and its name – stand. It became a mixed city, settled by both Macedonians and Illyrian locals, presaging the characteristic Hellenistic city to come, which looked both forward and backward. Its specific type of synthesis and cultural mixing came to characterize all cities thereafter in the Age of Ancient Empires; yet the founding of cities followed centuries-old Greek and Near Eastern patterns, such as colonization and the specific use of monumental architecture.

Several hundred cities were founded during the period, bringing Greek culture to the farthest corners of the Hellenistic world in a dynamic process known as "Hellenization." Hellenization could be seen in the civic layout and architecture of these new foundations as well as heard in the koiné dialect of Greek being spoken on the streets and in the marketplaces. Cities such as Alexandria, Antioch, and Pergamon, the capitals, respectively, of the Ptolemaic Empire, the Seleucid Empire, and the Attalid Kingdom (later carved out of the western Seleucid realm), were many times larger in population than the largest of their classical Greek counterparts. Several major cities boasted several hundred thousand inhabitants. Most of the cities arose in the Seleucid realm; the Ptolemaic Empire had comparatively far fewer, although the few were important vehicles of Hellenization.

These cities were not, however, simply carbon copies of classical Greek originals; like so much else in the Hellenistic world, they were a palpable synthesis of Greek and Near Eastern culture. In the eastern part of Bactria (in modern Afghanistan), excavations of the ruins of a city have told a multi-faceted tale of synthesis. Ai Khanoum, as the site is now called, was a Seleucid fortified town constructed over a previous Achaemenid site. At the eastern extremity of the realm, it had all the major accoutrements of a Greek city –

7.4. Bactrian coin. Line drawing by Andrew Welton.

Greek-style temples, gymnasium, theater, and so on – but it also had a Persian-style palace and Mesopotamian-style temples, signs of the acculturation that ran parallel to Hellenization (Fig. 7.4).

In some ways, Hellenistic cities were, in fact, a reversion to something and their actual form was well known to the Age of Ancient Empires. Extravagantly adorned cities had long symbolized and proclaimed the creation of major empires and kingdoms. Indeed, to compete in this world as well as to be taken seriously by its inhabitants assumed the construction of impressive monumental architecture. The speed with which the Hellenistic monarchs turned to the task of building large monuments shows that they grasped its vital importance. During the comparatively peaceful decade following the Battle of Ipsus, all the Hellenistic kings feverishly worked on major monuments, the size and scale of which represented a throwback to an earlier era in the Near East.

The theme of recovery of a lost world was, in fact, a major one of the age. Hellenistic monarchs constructed great libraries and museums, repositories of texts and objects for preserving – or restoring – a previous era. The largest and most famous library was at Alexandria, but Pergamon had a fabulous one as well, and there were others at Pella and Antioch. Earlier ancient empires likewise longed for bygone eras and strove to recover them – recall the Neo-Assyrian library of Ashurbanipal and the museums of the Neo-Babylonians (Chapters Two and Four). Recovering the relics of a previous great empire could help buttress the grand claims of one's own. As we have seen before, the past thus legitimates imperial claims. The Hellenistic libraries presented new opportunities as well to assert Greek culture as superior to indigenous cultures, as at Alexandria. Much later, when nineteenth-century empires such

7.5. Pharos of Alexandria (reconstruction after Adler). Foto Marburg/Art Resource, NY.

as the Napoleonic and, especially, the British deliberately employed ancient Roman imperial imagery, they were carrying on ancient techniques.

Such nostalgia, coupled with a desire to distinguish themselves (they were heirs of Alexander, after all) against a fabulous imperial past in the Near Eastern and Egyptian areas they now ruled, fueled the Hellenistic world's famous fascination with gigantism. Theaters and temples, for example, were built much larger than their classical counterparts. Part of this was practical – cities now had to accommodate much larger populations – but many monuments simply point to a central Hellenistic tendency toward hugeness. Alexander himself supposedly had plans to build a tomb for his father on a scale with the largest of the Great Pyramids of Egypt. The first list of "Seven Wonders" – all notable for grand scale – was composed in this period as a gazetteer of "sites that must be seen," clearly demonstrating a Hellenistic fascination. The list varied slightly over time, but three on the list date to this period.

These three monuments display a consistent theme across several Hellenistic Empires and kingdoms. The Colossus of Rhodes was built to celebrate a moment when Ptolemy I ended a siege of the island by none other than Demetrius "the Besieger," one of many such conflicts in the first few decades after Alexander's death. The 107-foot-high statue, the tallest of the ancient world, later inspired the design of the American Statue of Liberty. The Temple of Artemis at Ephesus was built on an older temple base but was now much larger and much higher than ever before, earning it a place on the list. Pharos Lighthouse at Alexandria was somewhere around 400 feet tall; in its day, there were only two structures slightly taller than it was – two of the Great Pyramids of Egypt (Fig. 7.5). For a period of such lackluster empires – by the standards of the entire Age of Ancient Empires – such gigantism is in part a testimony to the great wealth of the period, but that in itself is hardly enough to explain the unusual size of these monuments. The weight of imperial history was heavy on the shoulders of the Hellenistic rulers; such monumental architecture was a clear way to establish their place within the Age.

How did all of these changes affect the actual workings of a Greek city? One of the richest – and most heated – debates among Hellenistic historians concerns the fate of the polis, the citizen state. Was it working in Greece? Was it replicated in any of the new city foundations? The traditional view is that the polis was defunct under Hellenistic emperors, kings, and leagues and

views have contended that the polis system was actually working in this period as well as it ever had.[10] Leading scholars continue to line up on both sides, with some scholars arguing strongly that whatever else may still have been working, the "polis mentality" itself was clearly defunct.[11] Whichever view is correct, none deny that the vast majority of the inhabitants of the Hellenistic world were simply subjects rather than citizens. Or, to put it another way, Greek architecture at Ai Khanoum did not a polis make.

THE INDIVIDUAL IN THE HELLENISTIC WORLD

The Hellenistic world affords some of history's earliest glimpses of the impact of empire on individuals. Much evidence survives for some, but not all, areas of the Hellenistic world. For Greeks, empire often meant a relative lack of personal external political involvement; they were now subjects rather than citizens. Or, as some would have it, the inhabitant of this world was now a *cosmopolites*, "a citizen of the cosmos." The upshot, often, was radical individualism, expressed in ways ranging from extravagant ostentation to an introspective inwardness, supported by philosophical speculation and/or religious fervor. The imperial system, be it the Ptolemaic or Seleucid, was hardly up for political discussion and discourse, and so the usual response was simply to find one's own place under the circumstances and in the cosmos ("it's all about you").

The literature of the period presents several aspects of these changes. In fifth-century Athens, as will be recalled from Chapter Six, the tensions between distinguishing oneself and the lurking danger of hubris, between emphasizing one's individuality and representing the collective good of the polis community, fueled the famed tragedians' fire. Now, with empires, large kingdoms, and panhellenic leagues as the dominant political units, the social and religious tensions that had electrified the atmosphere of the polis were essentially dead. Cultural patronage now focused heavily – if not exclusively – on the monarch's court. Almost all Hellenistic tragedians, for example, were panegyrists – set praise speechwriters – for Hellenistic sacral monarchs.

On the other hand, New Comedy, a distinctive Hellenistic genre best represented by the plays of Menander (rediscovered in the twentieth century, partially in a mummy case), explores stock characters consumed with everyday problems. The genre is dominated by characters preoccupied and obsessed with their own affairs – money, sex, marriage – and rarely if ever worried about the larger political world around them, the very touchstone of classical Athenian comedy. By fifth-century Athenian standards, such characters would have been dismissed with the term *idiotes*, that is, a private, self-absorbed, and often reclusive human, as opposed to an engaged citizen. Literature was thus either consumed with glorifying distant divine monarchs or exploring the mundane lives of individuals.

New philosophical schools arose to help the individual find his or her place in a broad and often confusing imperial world. Epicureanism and Stoicism taught adherents to deal with a world in which political and social control were beyond their grasp. Epicureanism, called with some justification "the only missionary philosophy produced by the Greeks," was launched in Athens by Epicurus of Samos (341–270). In his view, pleasure (*ataraxia*) or imperturbability was the highest good. Contrary to common assumptions, this did not in principle lead to hedonism ("eat, drink, and be merry, for tomorrow we die"); the best life, in fact, was one of withdrawal from the fortuitous world and one that avoided anything arousing strong emotions. True pleasure was to be found in the intellectual pursuit of wisdom, either in isolation or in a community of low-intensity friendships.

The real numbers (comparatively, of course – when have philosophies ever gripped the masses?) were with Stoicism, considered one of the most "popular philosophies" of all time. Founded by Zeno of Citium (335–263), it got its name from its original meeting place, the *Stoa Poecile* (Painted Porch) in the Agora of Athens. Its major goal was *apatheia*, indifference to the vicissitudes of life; true virtue was living in accordance with the will of divine Nature expressed as *Logos*, the rational order of the Universe. One Stoic teacher, Chrysippus, used an example of a dog tied to a cart behind a horse to illustrate the Stoic life. The dog could choose to resist the inevitable movement of the horse, or it could save itself much anxiety and trouble by resigning itself to trotting along wherever the cart went. Thus, the *Logos* guides humans, and they should simply find and submit to the divine will to avoid a life of pain and stress. The Stoic teacher Cleanthes clearly summarized Stoic philosophy in his "Hymn to Zeus":

> *Nothing occurs on the earth apart from you, O God,*
> *Nor in the heavenly regions nor on the sea,*
> *Except what bad men do in their folly;*
> *But you know how to make the odd even,*
> *And you have wrought together into one all things that are good and bad,*
> *So that there arises one eternal Logos of all things,*
> *Which all bad mortals shun and ignore,*
> *Unhappy wretches, ever seeking the possession of good things*
>
> *By obeying which they might enjoy a happy life.*[12]

Popular religions, often known as Mystery Cults, also began to spread broadly in the Hellenistic world and would later have a definite showing in the Roman Republic and Empire. Although there was much variety among them, some common elements included an emphasis on individual emotional involvement and beliefs about immortality, personal salvation, and a blessed afterlife. Most had personal initiation rites as well as detailed cosmologies that helped people understand their place, as individuals, in the cosmos. Although Hellenistic philosophies emerged almost exclusively in Greece, popular religions sprung up throughout the Near East and Mediterranean. A cult of Cybele or the Great Mother, which emphasized death and resurrection, came from Phrygia. Isis worship, focusing on the Egyptian goddess as a loving mother and personal savior, enjoyed great popularity in Greece and elsewhere. Mithraism, a military cult whose adherents included King Antiochus I of Commagene, a small Hellenistic kingdom in what is now modern Turkey, developed in the late Hellenistic period from a form of Persian Zoroastrianism. The Dionysiac cult, dedicated to the god of wine, was built on old Greek practices but added personal initiation rites during the third century as it spread throughout the Hellenistic world. These all bear witness to the cultural synthesis and absorption that were hallmarks of the Hellenistic age.

7.6. Bust of philosopher Zeno of Citium. Réunion des Musées Nationaux/Art Resource, NY.

To many inhabitants of the Hellenistic world, however, life's true meaning was probably pursued in the enjoyment of the simple pleasures of life, as one touching tomb inscription declares:

> *Traveler, feel no regrets as you pass by my monument:*
> *I've no cause for lamentation, even in death.*
> *I left children and grandchildren, grew old enjoyably*
> *With the same dear wife; married off three sons,*
> *Rocked their babies asleep on my lap, so often,*
> *And none of them got sick, none died: no grief.*
> *So now they in their turn have poured wine for my painless journey*
> *Sent me off to that sweet sleep among the holy dead.*[13]

Not that much really distinguished the *cosmopolites* from the *idiotes* (the self-absorbed private person). Both were in basic ways a far cry from the *politikes*, the ideal politically engaged citizen of an earlier Greek era.

RESISTANCE AND REVOLT: MAURYANS
AND MACCABEES

Resistance to the Hellenistic Empires followed some familiar patterns – the presence of empire sharpened some strong identities in response even as it also tended to homogenize others. As always, within and beyond the far-flung borders of empire were peoples with histories, traditions, and identities that did not mesh well with the demands of the empire and who were not willing to submit to its all-encompassing rule and demands – or who could be provoked, after long periods of peaceful coexistence, by shifting expectations and demands.

Like the Achaemenids before them, both the Seleucid and Ptolemaic Empires faced resistance and breakaway movements. Regions fairly regularly calved off the Seleucid Empire, especially along its eastern flank, starting soon after the inception of that empire. In Parthia and Bactria, breakaway king-doms seized significant portions of the empire beginning just after 250; parts of these regions were recovered only temporarily, and with great difficulty.

kingdom centered in Ctesiphon that would last for the next 450 years, long outliving the Seleucid Empire. For several centuries, Greeks ruled eastern breakaway kingdoms known as Indo-Greek and Graeco-Bactrian kingdoms. The Attalids of Pergamon, who ruled one of the most important Hellenis-tic dynasties, began their rule by breaking away from the western Seleucid empire. The Ptolemies always found it challenging (and expensive) to con-vince the native Egyptian priesthood to submit consistently to their rule; priests, as local administrators, played a leading part in any native revolt. For just about two decades at the end of the third and the early second centuries, upper Egypt even managed to break away under Nubian pharaohs, supported by native priests.

Two specific case studies of resistance exemplify central themes of this study. Beyond the eastern Seleucid frontier, the Mauryan Empire emerged at almost exactly the same time as the Seleucid, and partially in resistance to Seleucid imperial formation, becoming the first polity to rule virtually all of the Indian subcontinent. On the western side of the Seleucid Empire, the famous Maccabean Jewish Revolt produced an independent Jewish kingdom, showing, once again, the vitality and viability of Jewish identity and ideology in the Age of Ancient Empires.

Parts of northwestern India (modern-day Pakistan) had been part of the Achaemenid Empire for several centuries when Alexander arrived there in 327. Before that, regional states had emerged there by around 600. Alexander's two years of campaigning in this region, moving within and beyond what had been the Achaemenid satrapy of Gandhara, were the most difficult of his career. He conquered several of what the Greeks called "autonomous cities," independent polities ruled by neither the Achaemenids nor any of a number of small kingdoms of northern India. When Alexander departed India, under threat of mutiny by his men, he left governors to rule the area. Immediately after his death, these governors abandoned their posts, leaving behind an ambiguous and somewhat confused political situation in the northwest of the subcontinent.

Just a few years later, in 321, Chandragupta, a young member of the Maurya family of central northern India, usurped the throne of the Nanda (centered in the modern Bihar state), a small but growing kingdom well beyond the farthest reach of Alexander's campaigns. Some maintain, in fact, that rumors of Nanda's growing strength were a real factor in Alexander's refusal to advance farther. After securing his base in the Nanda heartland and the Ganges Plain, Chandragupta began a campaign of expansion to his northwest, taking advantage of the power vacuum created by Alexander's conquests and the subsequent departure of his governors. Seleucus "the Conqueror" meanwhile solidified his hold on the region, and Chandragupta had to retreat but returned in strength in 305.

The outcome of the subsequent battle between Chandragupta and Seleucus remains unclear, but it is likely that Chandragupta won. Seleucus ceded significant portions of what are today eastern Afghanistan, Baluchistan, and Makran to Chandragupta, who in turn gave Seleucus five hundred elephants (one of which trampled Antigonus "the One Eyed" to death at the Battle of Ipsus in 301). The foundations of India's first empire were now laid across the entire northern part of the subcontinent. Chandragupta's grandson, Ashoka, brought most of the Indian subcontinent into the Mauryan Empire, which at its height was substantially larger than the Seleucid Empire (Fig. 7.7). Diplomatic relations, trade, and correspondence with the Seleucid and other Hellenistic kingdoms continued thereafter until the breakup of the Mauryans in 185 B.C.; it would then be about a half millennium before the subcontinent would see another empire.

Although some of Chandragupta's imperial project can be traced to expansive trends within the Nanda kingdom he conquered, many scholars believe that resistance to Alexander's incursion and then the Seleucid Empire were necessary catalysts for India's first large-scale empire. The autonomous cities and smaller kingdoms of northern India did not necessarily resist Chandragupta's move to fold them into his empire, preferring his rule to that of Macedonians from far to the west. As one historian of India put it, the people of northwest India, perhaps, realized that "emotional love of independence was no match to the disciplined strength of a determined conqueror"[14] such as a Greek or Macedonian, and thus they readily gave their aid and loyalty to Chandragupta, becoming part of the Mauryan Empire. As a Hellenistic historian put it, Chandragupta proceeded to organize a "disciplined army" of the "freedom-loving people of the Punjab," effectively unifying them as empire resisters.[15] Although many other factors contributed, resistance to one empire had, once again, helped create another empire; this one ranked among the largest of the premodern world.

On the opposite side of the Seleucid Empire, another influential response played out a little over a century later. The Jews, one of the most consistent threads of resistance running through the Age of Ancient Empires, were caught up, like many other subgroups within the Seleucid and Ptolemaic Empires, in the currents of Hellenization. Merely eight years after Alexander's death, the Jews first appeared in Greek literature in a reference that tellingly relates Jewish identity and empires:

> But when later they [the Jews] fell under foreign domination as a result
> of mixing with outsiders, under the rule of the Persians and of the
> Macedonians who overthrew them, many of the ancestral customs of
> the Jews were disturbed.[16]

Whether they acknowledged it or not, most Jews accommodated to the Hellenistic world quite early.

The basic political narrative of Jews under Hellenistic rulers is fairly straightforward. In 332, Alexander seized the region – where the kingdoms of Israel and Judah had once flourished – from the Achaemenid Persians. From 320 to 312, the Jews were under the Ptolemies; from 312 to 301, they were under the Seleucids; from 301 to 200, under the Ptolemies once again; and from 200 to 167, under the Seleucids once again. The simple facts speak clearly of the area's status as a contested arena between the two empires. Among the Jews, pro-Seleucid and pro-Ptolemaic factions strove for political advantages from the empires as these battled back and forth across the Levant. By and large, both the Ptolemies and the Seleucids allowed the Jews some level of political autonomy with local political representation through their high priest, a hereditary office held for life and an important political link between the distant Hellenistic monarchs and the rank-and-file Jews.

Meanwhile, the Jews in diaspora carved out a niche as one of many thriving subcultures. Babylon, Alexandria, Cyrene, Antioch, and Ephesus all had sizable Jewish communities; Alexandria, in fact, was the largest center of Judaism in the ancient world from this time on into the late Roman

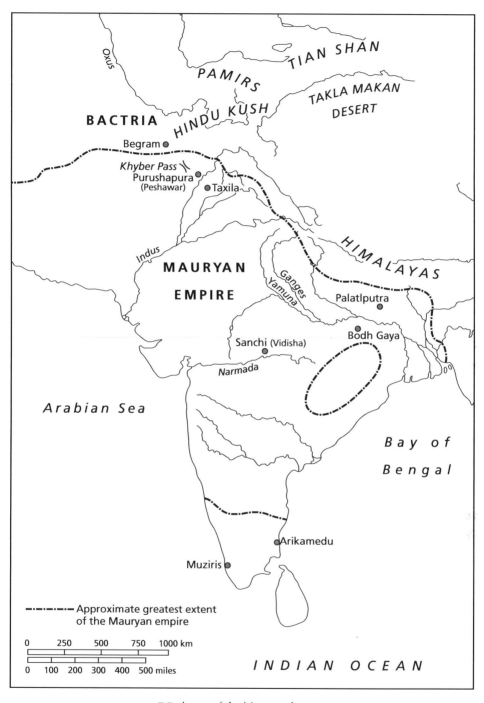

7.7. A map of the Mauryan dynasty.

Empire. Diaspora Jewish life was less politicized and tended to be more closely associated with synagogue worship and Torah reading. Surrounded by Greek institutions, language, and culture, the Jews consciously and even unconsciously adapted their traditional ways to the prevailing culture. Most obviously, they lost their native language of Hebrew. One source claims that Ptolemy II had their Scriptures translated into Greek for them, but it is more likely that the *Septuagint*, as this translation is called, was done at local Jewish initiative.

During the reign of Antiochus IV "Epiphanes" ("God Manifest") (r. 175–164), the Jews launched a powerful revolt that led to their independence as a kingdom officially outside of Seleucid rule (Fig. 7.8). This was one of the most significant and successful revolts in the Hellenistic period. For several decades after they became Seleucid charges in 200, the high priest dynasty enjoyed solid and mutually beneficial relations with the Seleucids. A series of quarrels broke out, though, among rival claimants to the office of high priest. Unable to solve their disagreements, the respective squabbling sides appealed to the Seleucid ruler for support. Antiochus' brutal response shocked the Jews

was in no mood for Jewish squabbles, and so he suddenly attacked the Jews harshly, massacring and enslaving them after they staged a civil disturbance. Explanations for his harsh reprisals range widely. Some have ascribed to him an almost missionary zeal to Hellenize Judaea by bringing it out of perceived cultural isolation and backwardness. Others claim he was simply hard pressed for money and coveted the Jewish temple treasures; others maintain he was punishing the Jews for not keeping up on their tribute/tax payments. By some estimations, he was simply a madman, and no further explanation need be sought.

At all events, his measures were unprecedented in the ancient world up to his time – it appears that he was trying to wipe out a religion and perhaps an *ethnos*. He prohibited central Jewish religious institutions: circumcision, Sabbath observance, and temple sacrifice. He reportedly instituted a "Cult of Olympian Zeus" in the Jewish Holy of Holies, commanded Jews to eat pork, and even reportedly sacrificed a pig on the temple altar in Jerusalem.

Jewish reaction was swift and violent; a guerilla movement sprang up to resist Antiochus Epiphanes, based in the rural Judean hinterlands. A certain Mattathias from the Hasmonean priestly family and his five sons, the most famous of whom was Judas ("the Hammer") Maccabeus, organized the movement and carried out a decisive revolt against Antiochus and the Seleucids – the Maccabean Revolt. Mattathias' rallying cry of resistance will sound familiar, coming from antiquity's original "People of the Book": "Let everyone who

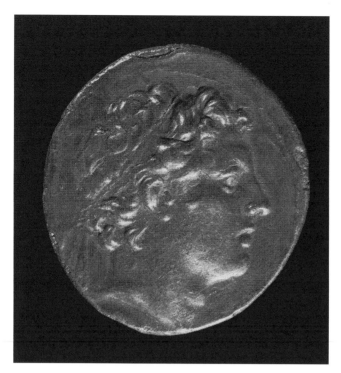

7.8. Antiochus IV Epiphanes. Erich Lessing/Art Resource, NY.

is zealous for the Law, and supports the covenant, come out with me"; "Now, my children, show zeal for the law, and give your lives for the covenant of our ancestors."[17]

Jewish ideology was central in the resistance, and the military might shown by the Jewish resistance was impressive. Antiochus' response to the revolt was brutal but ultimately unable to quell it. Grotesque martyr stories still proliferated centuries later, producing our own word "macabre" from Maccabee. In the end, Antiochus Epiphanes retreated and relented in 167, and the Hasmonean dynasty in Mattathias' line took over the high priesthood and ruled the semiautonomous Hasmonean kingdom for more than a century, until the arrival of the Romans.

The Jewish resistance accomplished an ambiguous independence for the Jewish *ethnos* from a vast empire. The Maccabean Revolt helped define Jewish identity and character for ages to come. The celebration of Hanukkah continues to commemorate the rededication of the Jewish Temple during the revolt. Yet the Jews would continue to Hellenize throughout the whole period – they continued to use Greek names for their children, to exercise and to read at Greek gymnasia, and so on. In general, the diplomatic relations between the Hasmoneans and the Seleucids were smooth throughout this period, and both sides profited from it.[18]

Various sects of Judaism sprung up at this time – Pharisees, Saducees, Essenes, Therapeutae – some explicitly accommodating to Hellenization and some solidly anti-Hellenistic. What is known of each of these groups shows the influence of Greek philosophical ideas on even the most ardent anti-Hellenistic of the groups, however. Jewish identity was in flux and was far from monochrome, but Jewish ideology, once again, proved to be a powerful force of resistance to empire.

The later history of the Hellenistic empires and kingdoms is a central part of the story of the rise of the Roman Empire, to which we now turn. Hellenistic squabbles would prove to be the ultimate undoing of this world. The rising empire in the West was only too eager to interfere in Hellenistic affairs. The Seleucids, a mere shadow of their earlier self, lasted until 63 and the Ptolemies until 31 B.C. But the Hellenistic world, a synthesis of Greece, Macedonia, the Near East, and Egypt, would leave a very deep mark on Rome and all other ancient empires yet to come.

CHAPTER EIGHT

THE WESTERN MEDITERRANEAN
AND THE RISE OF ROME

Lucius Cornelius Scipio Barbatus, Gnaeus' begotten son, a valiant gentleman and wise, whose fine form matched his bravery surpassing well, was aedile, consul, and censor among you; he took Taurasia and Cisauna from Samnium; he overcame all the Lucanian land and brought hostages therefrom.

— Tomb from Rome, early third century B.C.[1]

* How and why did Rome go from a small village in central Italy to master of the entire peninsula?
* How did Roman imperialism compare with previous examples?
* How did Roman thinking on cosmos/order and justice compare with previous examples?

THUS FAR IN OUR STUDY of the "irreversible fact" of empire, we have traced a chain of causation in the Near Eastern and eastern Mediterranean worlds. The basic story has gone something like this.

As the Dark Age ended, due in part to a general climate change in the ninth century, the Neo-Assyrian Empire forcibly united the Near East, prompting a range of ideological, economic, military, and political responses from surrounding peoples. The Babylonian and then Achaemenid Persian Empires followed the Neo-Assyrian, expanding the arena of the Age of Ancient Empires well beyond its Mesopotamia heartland. The Mediterranean was pulled in early on, as the Phoenicians responded to the Neo-Assyrian rise by taking to the sea. Greeks soon followed the Phoenician example, and the Aegean, southern Italy, and the Ionian coast of Anatolia were all joined together. The Greco-Persian War pulled Greeks directly into the power politics of the Near East; Greek resistance to the Achaemenid Persian Empire in turn led

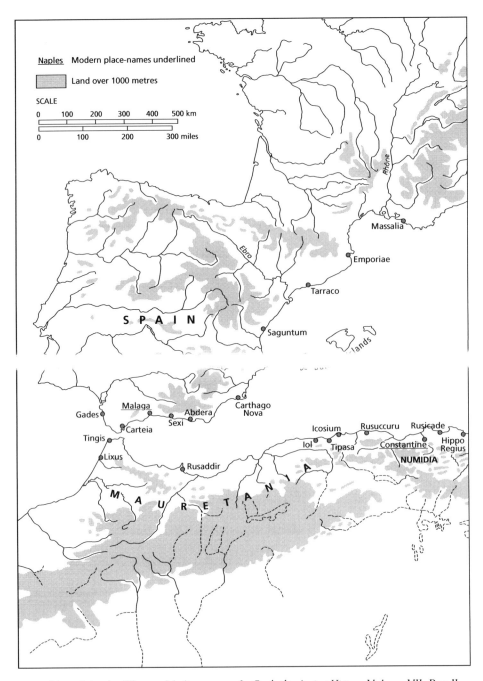

8.1. Map of the the Western Mediterranean. In *Cambridge Ancient History*, Volume VII, Part II, pp. 488–9.

to one of history's most famous cultural Golden Ages as well as the creation of the Athenian Empire. Alexander the Great staged his own resistance to the Achaemenids and, in turn, further integrated East and West. The ensuing Hellenistic empires and kingdoms then continued the legacy of empire, resistance, and integration.

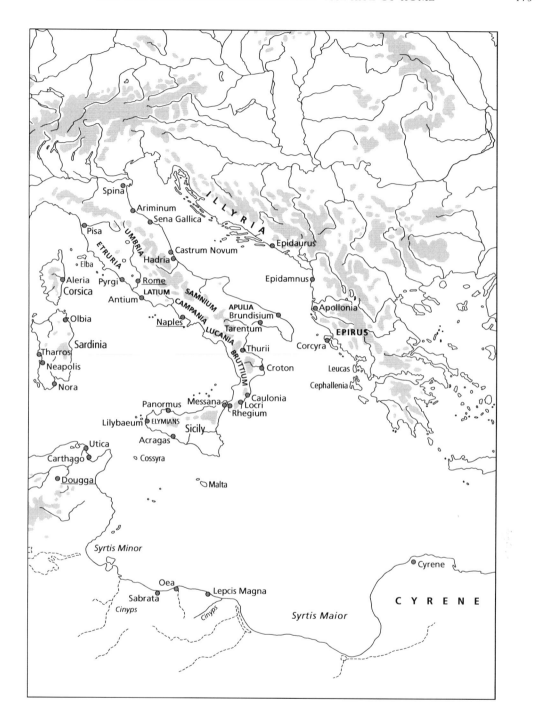

The culmination of the Age of Ancient Empires, though, was yet to come. An empire larger than Alexander's and longer lasting than all prior ancient empires combined was coming together in the West, specifically in Italy. Although it is possible that Alexander had plans for the Western Mediterranean, no Near Eastern empire had yet managed to incorporate any part of it. For a time, Rome would have as a western rival the old Phoenician colony of Carthage, which was expanding across and beyond North Africa. It was the Romans, however, who ultimately united the Eastern and Western Mediterranean, building an empire stretching from Britain to the Tigris and from the Sahara to the Danube. This would be the first – and last – time in history that the Mediterranean was ever politically unified.

Rome emerged from humble and shadowy beginnings. As far as anyone can tell, it began as a small village on the Tiber, founded around the same time that the Neo-Assyrians were hitting their imperial stride far to the east, although neither knew anything about the other. As Darius was crushing "the Lie" throughout his immense realm, the Romans were enjoying an urban revolution, details of which are still being pieced together by archaeologists. As the Athenians were reaching the apex of their Golden Age, the Romans were erecting their first written law code, the Twelve Tables. The Achaean League was formed at the moment the Romans became the masters of the entire Italian Peninsula and embarked on the first of a series of successful wars against Carthage. Many familiar patterns appear in this story, whether

or simply because some dynamics of empire are uniform across time and space. Rome's rise to empire also showcases how differences and variety enliven not only the study of various empires but of history in general.

THE WESTERN MEDITERRANEAN SETTING

As was the case throughout the eastern Mediterranean and the Near East, the eighth to sixth centuries were a time of major adjustment in the western Mediterranean. The general climate shifts that preceded the Neo-Assyrian rise prompted changes in the West too, but not of exactly the same sort. To put it another way, changes at the deepest level of historical time (ecological) were fairly consistent across the board, but those at the next two levels (social structures and events) were rather different. As in the Near East, there were notable population expansions and demographic shifts. Here in the West, however, there emerged at this time no major urban centers comparable to those of Assyria, Babylon, or Persia.

Instead, smaller, politically autonomous societies, largely agricultural, and a variety of languages, political organizations, and ways of life proliferated. These societies were not cut off completely from the recent changes in the wider world around them; some had themselves migrated in the not-too-distant past, and most interacted at various levels with some well-established groups entering their world from the East. Thus, although there was no direct contact between the Assyrians and, say, small communities throughout northern and central Italy, there were certainly many indirect connections. Interactions with and among three groups in particular set the western Mediterranean stage: the Phoenicians, the Greeks, and the Etruscans.

As we saw in Chapter Three, the Phoenicians, our first group, reestablished East–West trade after it had folded along with the Bronze Age. By the eighth century, they dominated the Mediterranean long-distance metal trade, part of their response to the rise of the Neo-Assyrian Empire. The Phoenician city-state of Tyre was the major colonizing power and came to have either a port or a colony at one-day sailing intervals all the way across North Africa as well as some in Spain, southern France, and on various Mediterranean islands. One of its colonies, Carthage, probably founded in the last years of the ninth century, has left archaeological remains beginning from the later eighth century.

As one sits on the high coastal promontory of what is now Sidi Bou Saïd, Tunisia, looking southward along the shore of the Gulf of Tunis where the settlements of Punic Carthage once stretched out, it is easy to appreciate the Phoenicians' choice of this site (Fig. 8.2). Sheltered from the open sea and with a nearby promontory for lookout, it was a natural place to build a city. It became a profitable trading center and a city-state in its own right, absorbing portions of the local population. The influence of the Near East was, naturally, direct here for a time, and Carthaginian culture continued to be Orientalizing even after direct contact with Tyre died out (Fig. 8.3). By the sixth century, Carthage had colonies of its own. By the fifth century, it was a major Mediterranean power; soon thereafter, it began its rivalry with the growing city-state of Rome.

The second group, the Greeks, under population pressures and desiring a piece of the long-distance metal trade, began their first wave of western colonization in the eighth century. Like the Phoenicians (imitating them, in fact), they founded colonies on promontories and along coastlines; again like the Phoenicians, they spread Orientalizing culture from Near Eastern sources to the West. Euboean Greeks established the first Greek colony in the West, Pithekoussai, on the largest island in the Bay of Naples around 760 B.C. The wealthiest of the Greek colonies, Syracuse, was founded soon thereafter on Sicily by Corinthians in 734 B.C. Like their Phoenician counterparts, Greek colonies usually became autonomous. By the seventh century, colonies were sending out colonies of their own. In the sixth century, Greeks launched their last great wave of colonization, founding colonies in southern France, Corsica, and Spain. The colonies variously interacted with local inhabitants, sometimes remaining strictly separate, sometimes intermingling.

8.2. Looking southward to Carthage from Sidi Bou Saïd. Andrew Welton.

Although we know from exactly where (and often precisely when) the Phoenicians and the Greeks entered the western Mediterranean, the origin of the third major group, the Etruscans, is a bit less certain. Their language, non-Indo-European and unrelated to the Italic languages around them, does not provide much clue for their ultimate origin.

It is possible that they simply emerged as a group within Italy, inspired by sophisticated Orientalizing culture encountered by way of Greek traders, themselves strongly influenced by the Near East. Along with material culture and decorative styles, they also borrowed the idea of the alphabet from western Greeks. Ancient sources, as well as recent DNA studies, however, point to an origin in Asia Minor or the Aegean, and the issue is by no means resolved. In any event, the Etruscans emerged by the eighth century as the most powerful group in north and central Italy. Their central region, Etruria, is rich in copper and tin and gave the Etruscans trade and political clout. Never a unified state and thus not a true empire, the Etruscans were essentially a loose group of city-states that shared a common language and culture. In each of their city-states, the local aristocracy remained powerful and controlled

8.3. Dougga monument with Near Eastern decoration. Slide by Mark W. Graham.

their trade with the western Greeks. Trading with settlements in southern France by the middle of the seventh century, the Etruscans introduced wine and olive cultivation into the western Mediterranean, forever revamping the landscape and patterns of life there. Their influence on small villages, such as

Rome, throughout northern and central Italy was profound. Elements of town planning, temple architecture, religious and divination practices, political offices, and much more were borrowed from the Etruscans or modeled on them. Centuries after the Etruscans faded from the scene, the Romans would continue to ascribe to them any part of their own culture of whose ultimate origins they were uncertain.

The interactions among these three groups, and with the indigenous inhabitants of the western Mediterranean, evolved over time. Early on, in the eighth and seventh century, there was relative harmony as trade relations expanded. By the sixth century, however, tensions arose as competition over resources intensified. The Aegean Greeks continued to send out colonies, and their colonies continued to send out colonies. Meanwhile, Carthage was expanding in several directions, and conflict became inevitable. When Greeks founded colonies at Massilia (modern Marseille, France) and on Corsica near the beginning of the sixth century, the western Mediterranean got a bit crowded for some. The Carthaginians and the Etruscans allied together against the expanding Greeks and fought a naval battle against them near the Greek colony of Alalia, on Corsica, in 535 B.C. The Greeks actually won the battle but lost so many ships that they had to give up their colony (a "Pyrrhic victory"). The Etruscans then took over Alalia, and hostilities continued. Greek colonies also fought among themselves and sometimes even pulled the Aegean poleis into their squabbles.

A couple of inscriptions dating to the late sixth century give rare but significant insight into the treaties and alignments at this time. The first is a treaty between Rome and Carthage reportedly inscribed on bronze tablets and recorded by the Greek historian Polybius. The inscription dates to the first few years of the Roman Republic and records the Romans' and Carthaginians' declarations of mutual friendship and disavowing of actions that would interfere with one another's interest.

This Romano-Carthaginian treaty clearly shows the recognized importance of Rome in the eyes of one of the three major players soon after its declaration of the Republic, as we will trace later. Trade interests were primarily at stake, with the Carthaginians preserving their trade with the power that was now coming to dominate central western Italy.

A second treaty, recently unearthed, is a set of bilingual inscriptions from Pyrgi, an important Etruscan commercial port and religious cult center. The dual inscriptions in Etruscan and Punic script are on gold leaf and record dedications to the Phoenician goddess Astarte and the Etruscan goddess Uni as an assurance of a treaty between the Etruscans and Phoenicians.

Together these bring to light the mixture of regional alliances, political tensions, and economic competition that shaped the world within which Rome arose.

ROMAN BEGINNINGS: INSIDE AND OUTSIDE

Beginning probably sometime in the eighth century B.C., Rome began expanding from a small village near the mouth of the Tiber River in central Italy into a fairly respectably sized city, eventually incorporating several surrounding settlements. It was founded on the Palatine, one of seven hills among which lay a swampy valley primarily used as a burial ground. The position of the village of Rome was strategic – at the lowest fordable point on the Tiber and near a juncture of trade and communication between Etruscan-dominated northern Italy and the Greek-influenced south (*Magna Graecia*). Because it was located near the coast, the Romans came into contact with Phoenician and Carthaginian traders as well.

The inhabitants of the small village of Rome were initially poor and thatched huts. Several huge changes over this period, however, uncovered by the archaeologist's patient spade, demonstrate that some pivotal shifts were already under way in this settlement. All of these reflect changes at the middle level of historical time – the level of social structures. First, the landscape was massively altered in response to key political and ideological developments. For instance, the nearby swampy valley was drained and land-filled for public use by the seventh century. This civil engineering project required strong political leaders to mobilize; it has been estimated that the landfill project required 10,000 cubit meters of earth. The Cloaca Maxima, the great sewer of Rome, was built in the valley, where it remains to this day (Fig. 8.4). The foundation for the Forum, which would serve as the nexus of social, economic, and political exchange throughout Roman history, was also created as part of this project.

Second, new types of domestic architecture began to appear. Corresponding to the growing complexity of political hierarchy, some large stone houses with baked tile roofs were built. These houses represent both a jump in structural complexity and vocational specialization. Building them required specialists, and their presence suggests a growing and very visible hierarchy in Roman society. Most of the Romans continued to live in mud huts with thatched roofs, but a clear demarcation can now be seen with the building of these wealthier homes.

8.4. Tiber River outlet, water conduit from Roman Forum; Cloaca Maxima. SEF/Art Resource, NY.

Third, a clear and centralized state religion emerged. Although the earliest Romans would have had a long-standing religious system, evidence for it is scanty and details are highly controversial. Clear evidence of a state religion appears by the sixth century – the massive Temple or Capitol of Jupiter Optimus Maximus (Jupiter the Best and Greatest), built on the Capitoline Hill, was the focus of both political and religious life. This capitol/temple, following the Etruscan model, was the most impressive of its type in the extended region and declared strong ideological and political messages (Fig. 8.5). Just as in the Near East, religion and politics were inextricably interwoven in this new show of strength. Rome, of all the small indigenous villages of central and northern Italy, was demonstrating strong signs of change and complexity, hinting perhaps at even larger things to come.

Lastly, Rome's boundaries expanded to include a large area dominated by the new capitol/temple. The city grew to include settlements on several hills, with the filled valley in between. A ring of walls demarcating and protecting the growing settlement was also built and has been discovered by archaeologists. A single and respectable city-state had emerged from several villages with a focal point in the Forum and in the Temple of Jupiter Optimus

8.5. Etruscan temple. In *Cambridge Ancient History*, Volume VIII, Part II, 2nd ed., 1989, p. 79, Figure 27b.

Maximus. By this time, Rome had elaborate trade contacts with surrounding communities, throughout the Etruscan world, and with Carthage and the Greeks.

These four changes reveal action at the middle level of historical time, that is, social structures. The results, as usual, were just as dramatic at the top level, that of events.

Reconstructing the earliest events of Roman history is notoriously difficult, and much of it lies outside of the focus of this book; but there are tantalizing clues that suggest why Rome would later develop as an empire. At a time when Assyrian kings were proclaiming their deeds and motives to the universe in long royal inscriptions, the Romans were writing almost nothing.

Few – and only very fragmentary – inscriptions survive from the first several centuries of Rome's existence. Many famous legends of early Rome are readily available, but thorny source problems abound. To begin with, these legends were not written down until several centuries after the events supposedly occurred. The earlier ones in particular often say much more about the much later political context within which they were written down than about the famous events they supposedly record. There is still clear value in these tales, recorded by Livy in his *ab Urbe Condita* (*From the Founding of the City*), when taken together with the archaeological material mentioned earlier. Treated with proper caution, they can reveal age-old Roman mind-sets, mentalities, and worldviews, some of which lay behind Roman imperialism. Indeed, it would be impossible to understand Rome's rise without them.

Whereas archaeology can help uncover early ideological and structural changes, Livy's tales give the names and dates. Rome was supposedly founded in 753 B.C., year 1 of the Roman calendar, by its namesake, Romulus. He and his twin brother Remus, born to Mars and a Vestal Virgin, were discovered in a floating basket and suckled together by a she-wolf (just like the foundation legend of Sargon of Akkad from centuries earlier), before being raised by a herdsman and his wife. During a jealous quarrel, Romulus killed his brother and then established the city. According to legend, although not according to recent scholarly investigation, the early city of Rome was permeated by Etruscan cultural and political influence.

The early Romans moved from battle to battle, defending and extending their fledgling city. Livy's year-by-year (almost blow-by-blow) description of these battles would grow tediously monotonous if he did not intersperse his history with memorable tales of the early city's pivotal events. A few of these stories are worth considering a bit, leaving aside questions of their authenticity for the moment.

One famous story reveals, perhaps, a reason Rome was able to move beyond its original Palatine setting to subsume other surrounding communities. In the same year that their "city" was established, the Romans, Livy relates, found that "there were not enough women, and that, added to the fact that there was no intermarriage with neighboring communities, ruled out any hope of maintaining the level of population."[2] After trying various means to solve this problem, the Romans hosted a feast to the god Neptune and invited all the surrounding communities. At a signal, the Romans seized women from among their neighbors, the Sabines, and forcibly made them their wives. Not long afterward, the Sabine army descended on Rome seeking revenge. As the two armies come together, the Sabine women, "with loosened hair and rent garments," then

> braved the flying spears and thrust their way in a body between the embattled armies. They parted the angry combatants; they besought their fathers on the one side, their husbands on the other, to spare themselves the curse of shedding kindred blood. "We are mothers

8.6. Bronze statue known as "Lupa Capitolina" representing a she-wolf nursing the Roman twins Romulus and Remus. Vanni/Art Resource, NY.

now," they cried; "our children are your sons – your grandsons: do not put on them the stain of parricide."[3]

The daring move worked, and both sides immediately concluded a peace. "Indeed, they went further: the two states were united under a single government, with Rome as the seat of power. Thus the population of Rome was doubled," says Livy.[4]

Who knows if anything remotely close to this episode ever actually occurred. What it faithfully records, however, is a deep-seated Roman tendency to incorporate outsiders, thereby expanding. This, in fact, would be the story of Rome over and over again in subsequent centuries, as it expanded toward empire. The Romans would usually also find a way to gain the upper hand; others joined Rome rather than vice versa. Even when Rome defeated another city, they would often extend a similar offer: if you can't beat us, join us. "A result of the fall of Alba was an increase in the size of Rome. The population was doubled," writes Livy, in a typical description.[5] Rome's power and size thus expanded throughout central Italy and then beyond.

Another famous story explains the establishment of the Roman Republic, in 509 B.C. According to Livy, a group of Roman and Etruscan aristocrats and princes, together besieging the nearby city of Ardea, were given some leave time; several of them decided to throw a party. Drunk, they soon took to arguing heatedly over who had the best wife. At the suggestion of one Collatinus, they decided on a way to actually solve the argument: sneak back to Rome after dark and spy on all of their wives. One after another, they discovered the wives partying on into the night themselves, flaunting stereotypical Roman social norms. Finally, Lucretia, the wife of Collatinus, was discovered spinning wool by candlelight – an excellent Roman matron indeed. Collatinus, of course, won the contest hands down, but the sight of his comely and excellent Roman wife incited lustful desire in Sextus Tarquinius, a prince and son of Tarquinius Superbus, a foreign-born king (*rex*). A few nights later, Sextus managed to slip into Lucretia's private quarters. He then threatened to kill her if she did not yield to his sexual advances; all in vain, for the excellent Lucretia stood firm. Finally, after he threatened to kill her and place a dead naked male slave by her side thus destroying her honor publicly, Lucretia finally yielded. The next day she sent for both her father and her husband and told them of Sextus Tarquinius' vile deed. Plunging a knife into her heart, she then fell down dead. Collatinus immediately began rallying the Romans together, pledging to rid Rome of the Etruscan tyrant Tarquinius Superbus and thus remove the rule of kings over Romans forever. With a certain Lucius Junius Brutus leading the rebellion, Tarquinius Superbus and his sons were expelled from Rome, and the republic was established with Collatinus and Brutus as the first two consuls. If nothing else, this story shows the importance that Romans placed on the defense of public honor and pursuit of duty, traits that again probably lay behind Rome's expansion. Like British imperialists, several millennia later, Romans liked to invoke their devotion to honor and duty in establishing a just – but no less imperial – rule.

Gripping, and rather dubious, stories aside, the late sixth century probably did see the formation of the Roman Republic, even if the exact details are probably unrecoverable. The characteristic social and political arrangements of the Roman Republic seem to have emerged fairly early on, by most estimations. Rome's social relations intersected with her foreign affairs; often, external and internal affairs shaped each other, a crucial connection throughout Roman history. One famous aspect of political power and social prestige in Rome was the patron–client relationship that connected many of Rome's free inhabitants to one another in an informal trust based on reciprocal obligations, favors, and services. The patrons provided protection, and the clients gave their loyalty and support. The patron would display his status in the number of his clients, who were required at times to gather around him in public and even go to his house to greet him each morning.

This basic social relationship generally informed Rome's dealings with other communities. When asked for aid, especially from the Greeks, the Romans always felt that their honor was at stake; it was their duty to come to the aid of anyone who needed it, and the Greeks skillfully manipulated Roman policies and tendencies. Again, the parallels with the British Empire, several millennia later, are many. Although there were probably earlier examples, the first documented case is from 390 B.C., when Rome established a friendship (*amicitia*) with Caere, a neighbor to the northwest of Rome. Many others, including Greek communities, would follow soon thereafter. Less conciliatory in form was the Roman ritual of *deditio in fidem*, which was often forced after a decisive victory by the Romans. Through the ceremony, the leaders would hand over its people, possessions, lands, buildings, and so forth to the Roman people.

Roman society generally was divided formally between patricians and plebeians, often the patrons and clients, respectively. At least as early as the foundation of the republic (and probably before), there emerged a clear distinction between those of a certain wealth, property, and political status (patricians)

the Palatine might be one visible indicator of this social demarcation. Over time, the fortunes of some patricians fell and those of some plebeians rose, so these labels did not remain clear wealth designations. Nonetheless, social status was written into one's paternal lineage, and this could not be changed. Once a patrician, always a patrician; once a plebeian, always a plebeian.

The patricians held most of the Republican political magistracies at first; in fact, their name comes from the Latin *patres*, "Fathers," the holders of senatorial offices. The customs, traditions, and institutions strongly favored the patricians, but the plebeians were able to gain more representation over time. In Livy's telling, the plebeians used a clever strategy to wrest power from the hands of the "Fathers." The patricians relied heavily on the plebeians in their constant military campaigning, so the plebeians used their leverage in several "strikes," refusing to fight in ongoing campaigns until they received better political and legal representation. The plan worked, and over the first half of the fifth century, the plebeians were able to negotiate a pair of major concessions that probably saved the republic. The first was the creation of the office of "Tribune of the Plebs," an important representative who initially could protect individual plebs from abuse by magistrates by literally interposing his sacrosanct person, meaning that he could not be physically harmed without terrible cosmic repercussions. In time, and through a natural extension, the Tribunes were given the right to veto any decision in the Senate, a potent position from which they could both temper the power of senators or patricians in general and defend the interests of the plebeians at the same time.

Other political compromises and concessions continued to shape Rome over the course of the fifth and fourth centuries B.C., arising out of what is collectively known as the Conflict of the Orders. Gradually, high political and religious office came to the plebs as Rome came under intense military pressure. The Twelve Tables, a heavily debated yet major source for social and economic conditions of the fifth century B.C. and the most important piece of writing from the early republic, were carved around 450 B.C. Throughout, internal and external affairs were linked – for campaigns to continue, the plebeians had to be satisfied; for them to be satisfied, concessions had to be made by the aristocracy. This give-and-take was the social glue that bound Roman society together. The need for cohesion among the groups spurred the development of crucial civic institutions; with this cohesion, Rome was a formidable force.

The political offices, although now more responsive to the bulk of the citizens, remained largely in the hands of the patricians. Once elected to an office (or magistracy), one became eligible for the Senate; once appointed to the Senate, one served for life unless removed for improprieties. The Senate was Rome's chief governing body, controlling public finances, foreign affairs, and ratifying legal decrees. Voting for the various magistracies took place in two assemblies, composed of all citizens, the *Comitia Centuriata* and the *Comitia Tributa*. In time, the various offices came to be ranked in what would be called by the late third century the *cursus honorum*, the course of honors. In practice, it was never a rigid system, but the relative importance of each office was fairly consistent. The competition for office was fierce and public, and rising through the ranks of the *cursus honorum* was a primary means of attaining coveted glory. The various offices appeared during the sixth through the fourth centuries and were generally held for one year.

The office of quaestor, probably Rome's oldest, administered the finances of the state treasury. The aedile supervised public works, public games, and the grain supply. The praetor served as judges in the law courts and could convene the Senate. When no consul was present in the city, the praetors would assume his administrative duties. The most important officials were the consuls; two were elected annually. These were the chief magistrates who presided over the Senate, initiated legislation, and served as generals in the frequent military campaigns. They, along with praetors, held the *imperium*, the supreme state command (and the origin of our word "imperialism").

There were two additional offices, which were different from the others in that they were not annual appointments. Two censors were elected every five years to revise lists of senators, fill vacancies in the Senate, conduct the census of citizens for tax purposes, and perform ritual purifications. The office of dictator, founded soon after the establishment of the republic, was given absolute control of the state in times of intense crisis. The office, expectedly rare, could be held until the end of the crisis or up to six months.

The competition over the magistracies, as we will see, was also both cause and effect of Roman expansion. To gain honor, one had to climb the ranks. Distinction on the battlefield could help one rise up the ladder. Internal and external affairs again joined together.

THE ROOTS OF ROMAN IMPERIALISM

In Book VI of his history of the rise of Rome, the Greek writer Polybius reveals what he saw as the secret of Rome's success in expanding so far beyond its city limits – its very constitution. By this, he meant not a document or charter but rather the way in which Roman society was constituted, how it was put together. He saw three elements as working together to make Rome

led the legions with absolute power on the battlefield; only the Senate could advise and fund war. The people declared war and ratified peace treaties; the people also elected all the officials and thus could bestow either honor and punishment on them. These three elements, he claims, presented a most compelling balance of power:

> These, then, are the powers which each of the three elements in the system possesses to help or harm the others; the result is a union which is strong enough to withstand all emergencies, so that it is impossible to find a better form of constitution than this. For whenever some common external threat compels the three to unite and work together, the strength which the state then develops becomes quite extraordinary. No requirement is neglected, because all parties vie with one another to find ways of meeting the needs of the hour, and every decision taken is certain to be executed promptly, since all are cooperating in public and private alike to carry through the business in hand.

> The consequence is that this peculiar form of constitution possesses an irresistible power to achieve any goal it has set itself.[6]

Polybius, viewing Rome as a successful second-century B.C. Mediterranean empire, no doubt idealized and oversimplified a rather complex and often messy political system. Nonetheless, what many historians think he got right is both that successful expansion was built directly into the Roman system and that a good defense ended up being a great offense, so to speak. Romans had the power to accomplish any goal they set; their expansion was thus the result of a goal to unite the world, in Polybius' telling. Rome was, in effect, a competitive oligarchy in which a person could rise through the ranks and distinguish oneself through conquest of neighbors. And there was almost always a war going on.

Was this frequent warfare a cause of Roman expansion or simply an effect of Roman expansionism? Historians have long debated this and related questions. The crux of their debates is the cause of Rome's initial expansion; was it hardwired into the Roman social structure and ethos and thus in one sense inevitable, or was it ad hoc, simply happening as decisions were made on the field and in the Senate and as events unfolded over time?

In the view of some historians, Rome was actually fearful, hesitant, and reactive, rather than active, in expanding throughout the Italian Peninsula. These scholars, claiming that there is little proof for a Roman plan for or drive to conquest, point instead to historical contingencies on the spot that tended to push, pull, or coax the reluctant Roman state into conflicts. Most of these historians point to the sack of Rome by the Gauls, a barbarian group, in 390 B.C. as a significant turning point in the Roman psychology of conquest. The Romans at that moment developed a dreadful fear of powerful neighbors and thereafter sought to keep any threat neutralized – a defensive imperialism of sorts. Uncannily victorious in such defensive conflicts (and here Polybius' argument from Roman constitution fits nicely), the Roman state effectively expanded, but not necessarily by Roman choice or plan, and eventually ended up with an empire, quite by accident (but here Polybius' arguments do not fit so well).

Other historians claim that war, conquest, and aggression were actually deeply ingrained in Roman social fabric, and thus expansion and a "will to power" were always vital parts of who the Romans were. Imperialism was thus part of their "national habit" from their beginning or at least from a very early point; their empire, acquired over centuries, was, in effect, simply waiting to happen. According to Polybius, his study "should leave my readers in no doubt that the Romans had from the outset sufficient reason to entertain the design of creating a world empire and sufficient resources to accomplish this purpose."[7]

Still other historians have proposed various combinations of these two options, such as the view that individual decisions over time shaped evolving social structures and foreign policy. Any consensus among scholars is hard to come by, but it is difficult to deny that Roman social structures played some part in their remarkable expansion, whether conscious or not.

8.7. Lucius Cornelius Scipio tomb. Scala/Art Resource, NY.

In the next chapter, we consider more specific examples of Roman imperialism, for as the Romans encountered the Hellenistic world, a whole new
set of factors come into play. However, for the period up to their acquisition
of the entire Italian Peninsula, we can begin to see some roots and trace some
patterns. It would be difficult to find more concrete illustrations of Roman
imperial roots than a set of inscriptions from the tomb of the Scipios, a patrician family with a deep, long, and illustrious history. The inscriptions begin
in the early third century (Fig. 8.7).

Lucius Cornelius Scipio son of Gnaeus
Lucius Cornelius Scipio Barbatus, Gnaeus' begotten son, a valiant gentleman and wise, whose fine form matched his bravery surpassing well,
was aedile, consul, and censor among you; he took Taurasia and Cisauna
from Samnium; he overcame all the Lucanian land and brought hostages
therefrom.

Lucius Cornelius Scipio son of Lucius, aedile, consul, censor

This man Lucius Scipio, as most agree, was the very best of all good men
at Rome. A son of Barbatus, he was aedile, consul, and censor among
you; he it was who captured Corsica, Aleria too, a city. To the goddess
of Weather he gave deservedly a temple.

Lucius Cornelius Scipio, son of Lucius, grandson of Publius, quaestor,
tribune of the soldiers. Died at thirty-three years. His father vanquished
King Antiochus.[8]

Note that, in all of these inscriptions, there is an emphasis on taking land,
capturing cities, dedicating temples, vanquishing kings, desiring honors and
office. The connection between holding office and carrying out conquest is
particularly striking. Even the final Lucius Cornelius Scipio, who apparently
did not accomplish much himself, is remembered simply via the offices and
conquests of his father and grandfather. To gain glory, one had both to
conquer enemies and to surpass countrymen in political office. The potential
ramifications for Roman expansion are fairly obvious.

This need not imply that Roman warfare was random and that conquests
were up for grabs for anyone who wanted to raise an army and enhance his
own prestige, at least not at this stage of Roman history. As was true in the
Near East, there was a foundational logic and cosmic order to Roman warfare
and expansion. Like the Assyrians or the Persians, for example, the Romans
were also deeply concerned with notions of justice and righteousness, in both
peace and war, but they defined them rather differently. Livy traces such
traditions of justice back to an early point in Roman history, claiming them
as the basis for later thought and action:

It was not enough, he [Ancus Marcius, an early Roman king associated
with restoration of Rome's religious traditions and observances] thought,
that wars should be fought; he believed that they should also be formally
declared. . . . The procedure was as follows: when the envoy arrives at
the frontier of the state from which satisfaction is sought, he covers his
head with a woolen cap and says: "Hear me, Jupiter! Hear me, land of
So-and-so! Hear me, O righteousness! I am the accredited spokesman
of the Roman people. I come as their envoy in the name of justice and
religion, and ask credence for my words." The particular demand follows
and the envoy, calling Jupiter to witness, proceeds: "If my demand for
the restitution of those men, or those goods, be contrary to religion
and justice, then never let me be a citizen of my own country." . . . If
his demand is refused, after thirty-three days (the statutory number) war

is declared in the following form: "Hear, Jupiter; hear Janus Quirinus; hear all ye gods in heaven, on earth, and under the earth: I call you to witness that the people of So-and-so are unjust and refuse reparation. But concerning these things we will consult the elders of our country, how we may obtain our due."[9]

If a majority of the elders then decided and voted that the Roman cause was just and righteous, war was declared. Livy explains further how a college of fetial priests were responsible for handling the laws of declaring wars and making treaties, and ensures his readers that "the same formal procedure was adopted by subsequent generations."[10] The simple fact, though, that he had to describe the ceremony in such detail implies that it was long forgotten by his own day. But such passages might well reveal an earlier situation; they did, no doubt, resonate with the justice-conscious Romans even of Livy's own day. Fetial priests were for centuries a key to Roman relations with foreign states, even into the empire. We will explore in the next chapter the extent to which debates over justice informed the early Roman Empire, once it is

Roman imperialism resembled Near Eastern in many ways, but several basic differences stand out. First, religious ideology does not seem to have played as prominent a role in Roman expansion. Note that, even in the declaration of war passage quoted earlier, the conquest is not being commanded or mandated by Jupiter. The gods are actually invoked by the messenger as witnesses to a wrong; the ultimate decision to go to war rests with a council of elders. Romans hardly, if ever, mention conquering in the name of Mars, Jupiter, or any other god. Whereas one has to work hard to ignore or downplay the frequent references to conquests in the name of Ashur, Marduk, or Ahura-Mazda in Near Eastern sources, one looks in vain for Romans presenting their gods' commands as reasons for expansion. The Romans did not abandon religious ideology, of course; in fact, they could celebrate major conquests with the construction of a temple, an act of fulfilling vows made to gods. They fought with the gods' assistance because they thought that they only fought just wars and fulfilled their end of the *pax deorum*, the peace with the gods.

A second major difference is that rather than elite replacement, the Romans worked out a system that could be called elite co-option. Conquered or subordinated elites usually were granted real political power (as opposed to, at best, honorary positions, as with Udjahorresne). In fact, the Roman imperialist system came to depend on foreign elites left in place or given key political offices after inclusion in the Roman sphere. Many of these elites

seemed gladly to join Rome and share its interest. Conquered elites and their
subjects often received either Roman citizenship or, from the fourth century
onward, the semicitizenship status of *sine suffragio* – that is, citizenship minus
the right to vote. On the pragmatic side, these foreign elites helped Romans
control their local populations, known as *amici* (friends) or *socii* (allies). Rome
always seemed able to draw on a supply of allies and would eventually out-
last its foes by sheer replenishable manpower. The allies were able to enjoy
the spoils of war as well, and it could be a mutually beneficial system. The
bond was firm, and it was notably rare for any of the allies to rebel or try
to break away from the Roman alliance, although renewals for *deditio in fidem*
rituals were not unknown. The Romans combined a policy of noninterfer-
ence in local affairs with the ability to bring overwhelming force to bear on
defectors.

When provoked, and especially when defending her friends, the Romans
could be as brutal in conquest as any; they were not necessarily a kinder,
gentler empire-in-the-making. In the early third century, for example, they
enslaved more than sixty thousand people during the course of a single war
(the Third Samnite War). Outright and even unprovoked brutality appeared
from time to time, increasing dramatically in the third and especially the
second century. Questions of whether that change was merely due to new
opportunities, deeper structural changes, or basic instincts to conquest simply
bring us back to the basic debates over imperialism in the first place.

In large part through their alliance system and the conquests flowing
from it, Rome found itself in control of all of Italy by 264 (Fig. 8.8). The
acquisition came in parts, but the bulk came in the seventy years before
264 B.C., by way of responding to calls for aid: for instance, the Capuans
called in Rome against the Samnites c. 343; the Thuriians called in Rome
against the Lucanians and Tarentum in c. 282. In both of these examples, the
threatened communities initiated a friendship with Rome, and thus became
her client, while the Romans, collectively, were loath to miss a chance to
defend Roman honor, and, individually, to miss a chance for martial glory.

With each new conquest and acquisition, the Romans left their characteristic marks – highly visible symbols of their power over the landscape. Signs of
their land division, road building, and city foundation are still evident today,
even after nearly two and half millennia. In all instances, they proposed what
they saw as a rational and logical system for ruling effectively. As they came
to control new land and then establish colonies, the Romans would divide
up the colonized land, marking it out as squares and rectangles through
a process known as centuriation. Aerial photographs can still pick up the
marks of Roman centuriation, or at least continuations of long-term patterns

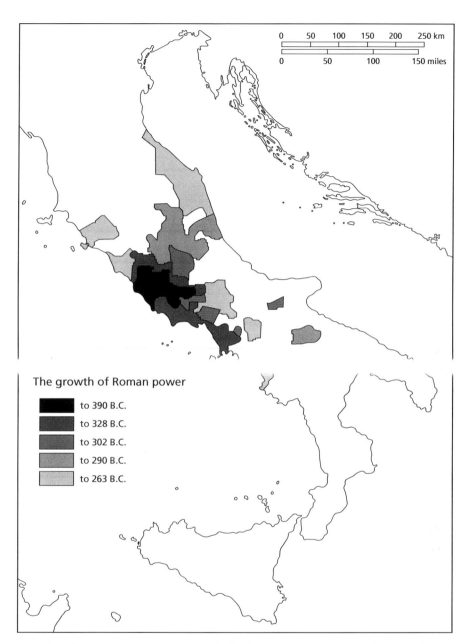

8.8. Map of growing Roman power in Italy. In *Cambridge Ancient History*, Volume VII, Part 2, 2nd ed., 1989, pp. 588–89.

(Fig. 8.9). The practice began in the fourth century B.C. and continued on, with each new land acquisition, into the official empire, giving far-flung regions as much of a Roman look as possible.

Rome's road building, the most famous of its engineering projects, began in earnest in the fourth century B.C. and came to connect all of her distant holdings, communities, and allies. The most famous early Roman road, the

8.9. Centuriation. Photo by Francesca Radcliffe © 2003.

Via Appia (Appian Way), was begun in 312 and connected Rome to Capua; stretches of it are still in active use today. Their road-building techniques were borrowed originally from the Etruscans, but the Romans brought the practice to unprecedented heights of sophistication and scale. Roman road building made a strong statement about the layout of the cosmos and Rome's central place within it. All roads did, in fact, lead to Rome, at least those in the Italian Peninsula. Practically speaking, the roads were also a necessary result of, and means for, Roman expansion; they were constructed, like America's Interstate Highway system, for military transport. Roads brought together military power with economic and political, as they also functioned for trade and for communication (Fig. 8.10).

City planning also began at a fairly early stage and, in time, would become one of the most characteristic expressions of Roman expansion (Fig. 8.11). As Rome came to control external communities, a veritable architectural repertoire emerged, consisting of a forum, a capitol, and assorted temples, along with civic streets, sewers, and various other monuments. For preexisting communities, this repertoire often was added onto existing structures. The canon of monuments for a Roman city became more elaborate over time as the Romans themselves borrowed much from the Greek communities that they incorporated. During the period of the official empire, the repertoire came to

8.10. Roman road in Ostia. Slide by Mark W. Graham.

8.11. Roman civic plan. Barbara McManus Picture, the VRoma Project.

include luxury buildings such as bathhouses, theaters, and amphitheaters as well, as we shall see.

Desire for personal military glory and political honor, readiness to incorporate and draw on outsiders, a tendency to view aid as patronage, dread of powerful neighbors, eagerness to defend public honor and perform duty – these are some of the many factors through which Romans initially came to play a central role in the Age of Ancient Empires. If our working definition of empire holds, Rome was well on its way there, through its "system of interactions" that exerted "political control over the internal and external policy – the effective sovereignty" of many non-Roman communities.

Of the multiple small indigenous settlements in central and northern Italy, it was Rome that rose progressively to subsume all the others. Notably, it held them all, as we will soon see, through some ups and many bitter downs. These peoples usually seemed willing to belong to the growing Roman polity and even eager to help it attain its goals. Although it will be recalled that the Achaemenid Persian leaders were keen to proclaim that they held an empire of willing subjects, it seems that the Romans were the first actually to come close to attaining that goal. By all appearances, these communities and peoples generally were not constrained by obvious and, by now, stereotypical shows of authoritarian force. Yet the imperialism that developed was as real as any we have seen, even if it does not furnish quite as many images of naked bodies hanging on spikes, skin being ripped off and used as building decoration, heels crushing the skulls of "evildoers," and brutal massacring of neutral and unthreatening communities. Our very words "empire" and "imperialism" are, for good reason, rooted in Roman culture and the language from which they ultimately derive. A new type of empire – but no less an empire – was on the rise and soon would be making its way eastward, toward empire's original home.

CHAPTER NINE

IMPERIUM SINE FINE: ROMAN IMPERIALISM AND THE END OF THE OLD ORDER

This will be your genius — to impose the way of peace, to spare the conquered, and to crush the proud.

— Vergil, *The Aeneid* 6.853

* How did the expansion affect or reflect basic social arrangements at the center?
* What might all this mean for the exercise of social power in the growing empire?
* To what extent could contemporaries grasp the implications of a shift in the deeper two levels of historical time?

PERIODIZATION AND TERMINOLOGY can seem arbitrary. Take, for example, the possible answers to the question "When did the Roman Empire begin?" One perfectly acceptable answer would be that it began in the third and second centuries B.C., as Rome expanded beyond the Italian Peninsula to Spain in the West and into the Hellenistic East. Yet it also would be correct to say that the empire began precisely in 27 B.C. when Octavian reached a critical agreement with the Senate known as the Constitutional Settlement of 27 B.C. and received the title of Augustus. The former answer is describing an empire in action, the latter the Roman Empire as a distinct historical period following the end of the republic. These two answers are, in one sense, closely interrelated; in complex ways, Rome's expansion throughout the entire Mediterranean precipitated the collapse of the republic. Rome was, in fact, remarkably expansive during the republic even if not particularly expansive at all during the period of the Roman Empire.

Thus, we have an expansionist empire without an emperor during the republic, a period followed by a hardly expansionist Roman Empire. To keep things straight, it is helpful to think of "empire" simply in terms of our working definition throughout this text and "Roman Empire" as a distinct historical period to which we turn in Chapter Ten.

Whatever the terms we use, Rome entered a new phase following its acquisition of the Italian Peninsula. By the middle of the second century B.C., she was engaged in near-constant warfare throughout the Mediterranean. An ideology of *imperium sine fine*, imperial power without limit, without bound, can be traced to at least the second century B.C., and would continue to dominate Roman thought for centuries. According to this ideology, Rome was an organic entity that never had to define frontiers as it fulfilled its destiny to expand throughout the whole world, the *orbis terrarum*. It was not limited by time or space. As Jupiter promised the Romans in Vergil's *Aeneid*: "I set no limits to their fortunes and no time; I give them *imperium sine fine*."[1]

This era raises again the question of whether new opportunities for conquest merely made a deeply embedded Roman "will to power" more apparent or whether there was a fundamental shift in Roman expansion as a true imperialism emerged. In this chapter, we explore two major signposts of Roman imperialism: Rome's conflicts with Carthage and her acquisition of much of the Hellenistic East. We then analyze how Roman dealings abroad indelibly shaped the exercise of social power at Rome itself; the republic was transformed from the inside out as much as from the outside in.

ROME VERSUS CARTHAGE

In 264 B.C., with Rome's ascendency in Italy undeniable, she began a series of conflicts with Carthage. The parallels between these two cities that would become such bitter foes are striking. They were both founded within a half century of each other, one late in the ninth century, the other around the middle of the eighth century. Their interior social arrangements were fairly similar: both city-state institutions dominated by landed aristocracies. By the end of the sixth century, both were also independent, Rome having broken free from a king (*rex*) and Carthage gaining independence from its mother city of Tyre. We have already seen in the previous chapter how the two cities entered into a treaty of friendship at that time, right at the dawn of the Roman Republic. By the third century, both were notably powerful and expansionist as well. Although they were bound together by various treaties and alliances stretching almost right up to the outbreak of war, conflict was soon to break out.

9.1. Rome's first silver coin. Drawing by Andrew Welton.

century. It is difficult to trace the internal history of Carthage because of a lack of written source material, but there are hints. Contemporary evidence from the Roman side is hard to come by as well. Later Greek and Roman authors wrote much, but often unconsciously retrojected their own immediate context centuries back into the Roman past, making it difficult still to sort their own pressing and immediate issues from the real concerns of those on the spot. However, one bit of evidence speaks volumes about Rome's growing self-confidence at this moment. In 269 B.C., Rome issued her first silver coins (Fig. 9.1). Unlike the bronze pieces they first issued several decades earlier, silver could circulate broadly throughout the Mediterranean. These coins featured Hercules, the Wolf and the Twins, Mars, and Winged Victory goddesses, images that "serve to remind us that coined money was a medium through which a state could advertise itself to the world at large."[2] Rome was increasing in boldness and in awareness of her significant power; it was now proclaiming these broadly and Carthage was reading the message directly on the coins it acquired through its extensive trade.

It is not clear, though, that either side was intent on war with the other. The fact that they were bound together by treaties until virtually the outbreak of the conflict makes premeditation seem unlikely. A by-now familiar set of circumstances, however, pulled Rome into conflict or gave it an excuse to flex its muscles abroad, depending on one's viewpoint. Trouble began in Sicily, right between the two growing powers. Syracuse, a Greek colony turned polis, attacked Messana, another Greek colony immediately across from the toe of Italy. Messana had a checkered history: it was destroyed by Carthage in the early fourth century, rebuilt, and then ruled by Syracuse, only to then be seized by some Campanian Italian mercenaries known as Mammertines. In 264, Syracuse attempted to retake Messana from the Mammertines, who in turn called on Rome, their powerful neighbor, for help. Duty- and honor-bound to defend anyone who called on them for aid, of course, the Romans immediately came to the defense of the city.

Carthage, fearing Roman meddling within her own sphere of influence, sought to keep Rome out of Sicily. The First Punic War (264–241 B.C.) then erupted between Rome and Carthage. The war spread well beyond the Sicilian front and into the western Mediterranean. Rome, by building a navy very quickly, was eventually able to pull out a naval victory against Carthage, the dominant naval power of the day. Through her victory, Rome acquired Sicily, Sardinia, and Corsica, in addition to indemnities paid by Carthage. Rome was solidly on the world stage now and had begun acquiring an overseas empire (whether she wanted to or not and whether she called herself an empire or not).

Rome's status as a rising power thereafter involved her more and more beyond Italy and the surrounding islands. Carthaginian bitterness over the terms of the treaty ending the First Punic War continued to grow apace. Desiring a power base against Rome, Hamilcar Barca, a major Carthaginian commander of the First Punic War, began concerted expansion in Spain. His son, Hannibal, would continue Carthaginian expansion in and consolidation of territory and peoples within Spain. Growing nervous of Carthaginian success in Spain, and claiming violation of a treaty fixing the Ebro River as a boundary between the Roman and Carthaginian interests, Rome declared war on Carthage in 218, expecting an easy victory. The Second Punic War (218–201 B.C.) had begun.

An easy victory it certainly was not to be, however. Led by Hannibal, one of history's most able and famous generals, the Carthaginians made a surprise offensive against Rome from the north, crossing the Alps into Italy with elephants (probably only two survived the crossing), and proceeded to devastate the countryside. For about a decade and a half, Hannibal campaigned throughout Italy, north to south, never losing a battle and handing the Romans some stunning losses. One of these, Cannae (216 B.C.), might still hold history's record for the most casualties in a single day of battle, by far the majority of them Romans (as many as eighty thousand total). Hannibal, however, never managed to take the city of Rome.

Despite the many setbacks, the Romans were able to hang on, largely because almost all of their "friends and allies" (i.e., clients) throughout the peninsula remained loyal and kept sending auxiliary troops. Hannibal's strategy depended on these groups bolting from Rome at his first victory, but he completely underestimated the strength of the alliance system, and the Romans kept coming back from defeat with their seemingly endless manpower supply. In all, Rome fielded at least 10 percent of the Italian population. Hannibal could hardly have anticipated this; never before had conquered peoples fought so tenaciously for their conqueror even as that conqueror clearly was beaten time and time again. We have seen, by contrast, how quickly the Neo-Assyrian Empire vanished as soon as it was put to the test; its subjects gladly helped dismantle it as soon as the empire hit a serious outside challenge.

Winning battle after battle but not ending the war, Hannibal was recalled to Africa to help save Carthage after the Romans decided to invade rather than keep trying to defeat Hannibal in Italy. Publius Cornelius Scipio "Africanus" took the war to North Africa, and he then decisively defeated Hannibal at the Battle of Zama in modern-day Tunisia in 202 B.C. As a result of their victory, Rome acquired Spain, gained some toeholds in North Africa, and received more cash payments from Carthage. Defeated again, Carthage was left weak but still intact and independent. Meanwhile, Hannibal ran into strong opposition in Carthage and slipped off to the Hellenistic East where he spent several decades fighting Roman interests until his end, which came at his own hands as Romans were about to capture him. The specter of Hannibal long hung over the Romans; centuries later, Roman parents put their children to bed at night, warning them that Hannibal – like our boogeyman – would "get them" if they did not go right to sleep.

SYMPLOKÉ: ROME AND THE HELLENISTIC EAST

> There can surely be nobody so petty or so apathetic in his outlook that he has no desire to discover by what means and under what system of government the Romans succeeded in less than fifty-three years in bringing under their rule almost the whole of the inhabited world, an achievement which is without parallel in human history.[3]

Born just after the Second Punic War (the exact year is uncertain), Polybius was in a perfect position to directly view Rome's rise to ruler of the Mediterranean world. He was actually an important figure in this story. He participated in the Achaean League's resistance to Roman involvement before he was deported to Italy as a hostage. Befriended by Scipio Aemilianus (adopted grandson of Scipio Africanus), he became completely enamored of the Roman system, as we saw in the previous chapter. When he described Rome's swift takeover of the Mediterranean world, he used a beautifully evocative Greek metaphor – *symploké*. A weaving term, it describes the way in which individual threads come together to form a whole piece of cloth or fabric. As he saw it, the rise of the empire had woven local, previously unconnected histories and events together into a single universal history. The fifty-three years he refers to above is roughly the period between the start of the Second Punic War and the Battle of Pydna in 168 B.C., a decisive moment in Rome's acquisition of significant parts of the Hellenistic East.

Direct Roman political engagement with the Hellenistic world began just before the First Punic War. Pyrrhus, an Alexander imitator and king of Epirus, invaded Italy from just across the Adriatic Sea. Called in by the inhabitants of Tarentum in southern Italy, he briefly got the support of some Italic and Greek groups there. In a series of battles, in 280 and 279, he defeated the Romans, but with such a great loss of his own men that his name still lives on in our term "Pyrrhic victory," that is, a battle that is technically won but at such tremendous and devastating cost it is hardly worthwhile.

Rome and Carthage both became involved in alliances with the Hellenistic East later in the century. During the Second Punic War, for example,

9.3. Baal-Tanit, the major Carthaginian goddess at the time of the Punic Wars. Slide by Mark W. Graham.

Philip V of Macedon was allied with Carthage, and Rome was allied with the Aitolian League. Immediately following the Roman victory in that war, Hellenistic cities and kingdoms, eager to get one up on their own Hellenistic neighbors, began to call on Rome for aid. Rhodes, for example, did so in 201 B.C., just several months after the Battle of Zama.

It took Rome only thirty-five years after the end of the Second Punic War to become master of the Eastern Mediterranean as well, largely in response to these calls. As seen in the previous chapter, there is wide disagreement over when and how Rome became imperialistic or an empire. A further, nuanced dimension of this debate highlights Roman involvement in the Hellenistic world. Some, as will be recalled, simply maintain that Rome had a deeply engrained "national habit" of conquest to begin with and thus her involvement in the East merely continued a long story.

To another group of historians, however, its interaction with the Hellenistic East was actually the beginning of Roman imperialism. These historians differ on the specifics of the process, even if they generally agree on the time frame and context. One view holds that Rome's involvement in the Hellenistic East was not premeditated at all and certainly was not part of any Roman plan to take over the world, retrospective ideologies of *imperium sine fine* notwithstanding. The Greeks coaxed the Romans into their world and then took full advantage of their aid and protection for their own purposes.

The Romans, for their part, feared for their reputation if they did not respond, and then did so in the Roman way, which involved patronage. Roman hegemony, however reluctant, followed in the wake of this aid.[4] Another view holds that the Romans were deeply enamored of Greek culture, and that imperialism thus followed distantly on philhellenism, the love of things Greek. The Romans actually were anti-imperialist and emerged on the Hellenistic Greek scene as starstruck champions of Greek culture, its freedom and liberty in particular. Again, however, their involvement in the East led to acquisitions and patronage, and they were stuck ruling over the Greeks. A third view contends that Rome's initial and passive involvement in the East created in her an "unsatiable passion" for conquest; she acquired a new militarism and imperialism on her involvement there. Imperialism thus followed from her engagements in the East and need not be read into the Roman past. Support for all three of these positions (and others) can be read at various levels in available sources.

The story of Roman entanglement in Greek affairs is both fascinatingly complex and frustratingly confusing. Touching on only a few highlights, although necessary here, runs the risk of making a labyrinthine set of circumstances and actions appear artificially straightforward. Several milestones and banner moments can help illustrate the major themes and how this empire connects to our overall story of ancient empires. We begin in 197/196, just a few years after the Second Punic War. Titus Quinctius Flamininus fought the Battle of Cynoscephalae against Philip V of Macedon. A significant number of Greeks were allied with Rome against Philip. Just after the Roman victory, thousands of Greeks gathered into a stadium to hear from a Roman herald what would happen next. The proclamation was read:

> The Senate of Rome and Titus Quinctius Flamininus the proconsul, having defeated King Philip and the Macedonians in battle, leave the following states and cities free, without garrisons, subject to no tribute and in full enjoyment of their ancestral laws: the peoples of Corinth, Phocis, Locri, Eubeoea, Phthiotic Achaea, Magnesia, Thessaly and Perrhaebia.

Following the announcement, there was shock and exhilaration:

> The greater part of the crowd could not believe their ears, for what had happened was so unexpected that it was as if they were listening to the words in a kind of dream.

But what Romans meant by freedom and what Greeks understood by the term could be significantly different. Roman patronage always came with strings attached and with long-term reciprocal obligations not yet apparent to the euphoric masses. Even Polybius was probably constrained by his own love for the Roman system, as he wrote:

> For it was a wholly admirable action in the first place that the Roman people and their general should have made the choice to incur unlimited danger and expense to ensure the freedom of the Greeks, more remarkable still that they devoted to this ideal the force sufficient to bring it about, and most remarkable of all that no mischance intervened to frustrate their intention. Instead, every factor combined to produce this crowning moment, when by a single proclamation all the Greeks inhabiting both Asia and Europe became free, with neither garrison nor tribute to burden them, but enjoying their own laws.[5]

It would be a while before many Greeks began to realize that there were other ways to build an empire than through garrisons, tribute, and imposition of a uniform law code. In the meantime, however, under the banner of the "liberation of the Greeks," the Romans continued to expand, responding to

By the time of the decisive Battle of Pydna (168 B.C.), the other side of the Roman coin was clearly showing. Perhaps the Romans were not just into philanthropy after all. The Roman conqueror at Pydna, Aemilius Paullus, defeated King Perseus and the Macedonians, and Romans revealed a side of outright expansion and unprecedented brutality. On his way back from Pydna, Aemilius Paullus enslaved one hundred fifty thousand, sacked seventy Greek cities in retaliation for their support of Perseus, and celebrated a three-day triumph, an official victory procession, in Rome. It took three full days to display publicly all the booty from the campaign, much of it going to Paullus himself.

An episode just after Pydna demonstrates clearly the new Roman outlook and attitude. Antiochus IV "Epiphanes" of Syria was about to attack Ptolemy VI of Egypt, and the Roman Senate did not approve. Under command of the Senate, an ambassador named Gaius Popillius Laenas was sent to order King Antiochus to leave Egypt immediately. When Popillius delivered the Senate's demand to Antiochus, the latter declared that he needed some time to consult on the matter. Then Popillius stepped forward:

> Happening to have a vine stick in his hand, he drew a circle around Antiochus with it, and ordered him to give his answer to the letter before he stepped out of that ring. The king was taken aback by this haughty proceeding, but after a few moments' hesitation he replied that

he would do whatever the Romans demanded. Then Popillius and his
aides shook him by the hand, and one and all greeted him warmly.[6]

Many were fairly shocked at the arrogance of a Roman ambassador in the
face of a Hellenistic king, and equally so that such a king would acquiesce
so swiftly to such a demand. The strength of Rome was clearly becoming
recognized throughout the Mediterranean world. Also telling is the warm
and friendly response by Romans once Antiochus assented to their ultimatum.
The Roman way of dealing seems to have changed in fundamental ways by
this point. Yet at the same time, the tendency of Romans to receive warmly
those who recognized themselves as Rome's subordinates is as old as Rome's
patron–client system itself.

The decades following Pydna saw continued devastation and brutal
assault. Carthage, which Rome had left a weak but still a sovereign state,
was attacked again by Rome in 146 B.C., in an unprovoked and completely
lopsided rout usually elevated to the title of the Third Punic War.

> The whole city was therefore utterly blotted out of existence, and it was
> decreed that for any person to settle on its site should be an accursed
> act.[7]

The Romans devastated Carthage such that few traces of Punic Carthage
remain (although the oft-told story that the Romans then sowed its fields
with salt is simply a modern myth that will probably never die). In the same
year, Romans sacked Corinth for its support of a revolt of the Achaean
League, putting the majority of its male inhabitants to the sword and selling
the women and children into slavery. Previous distinctions between the
imperialism of second century Rome and that of fifth century B.C. Athens
were becoming negligible by this point.

The responses to Roman actions varied widely. Some Greeks actually
embraced their new masters, just as some had embraced Philip II of Macedon
about a century earlier. Most had, after all, been under outside masters since
then, and so the difference probably did not seem all that significant. When
fully appeased, in fact, the Romans could be surprisingly warm and kindly
masters. In many cases, elite co-option won over the local elites, who stood
to gain much by their support of Roman rule. Many, like Polybius himself for
example, seemed sincerely to fall in love with the Roman system. He became
a collaborator in imposing Roman rule on Achaea and enjoyed friendship
with the highest levels of Roman elites. In other cases, the local elites might
not have embraced Rome per se but ceased resisting the inevitable. Attalus
of Pergamum, for example, simply bequeathed his whole kingdom to Rome
upon his death in 133 B.C.

In other cases, Hellenistic Greeks bitterly opposed the Romans. The most famous example was in 88 B.C., when Mithridates of Pontus, a small Hellenistic kingdom, ordered the Greeks of Asia Minor to kill Romans and Italians living among them. Long victimized by Roman tax collectors (*publicani*), they responded enthusiastically with a massacre that left eighty-eight thousand dead. The shocked Roman response here is rather telling:

> We did not retain possession of you when you became our subjects . . .
> but made you free and autonomous . . . not as tributaries, but as clients.[8]

Even at this point, the Romans saw their rule as innocuous, a favor to clients, who were subjects nonetheless. In this way, the parallels with previous empires come out clearly. Assyrians, Persians, and Athenians, for examples, certainly thought that they were doing their subjects a favor. Did a Roman client actually have freedom and autonomy? By whose definition? Again, Roman self-perception could clash markedly with Hellenistic understanding of what the Romans were about. Whereas Romans noted their acts of patronage, many inhabitants of the East saw patronizing acts.

many and varied. Some of the kingdoms were incredibly wealthy, and there was much material attraction. Generals competed tooth and nail for commands in this area, knowing full well the glory and wealth to be gained for themselves and/or their soldiers. Italian traders began pouring eastward as well. Because traditional Roman mores strongly forbade patricians and senators from gaining profit in speculative trade, an entire social class, the equestrians, emerged to take advantage of the lucrative markets. Qualifications for entering this class at this point was the ownership of a minimum of four hundred thousand sesterces, and more were clearing the bar all the time with expanded markets and opportunities. The equestrian ranks also swelled with the profits and the proceeds from tax farming; they would bid on contracts for extracting taxes from the unallied conquered. Some historians of an older generation even claim that it was these commercial interests that actually caused Roman imperialism in the first place. According to this view, espoused by some Marxist scholars, Rome was actually pressured abroad by Roman merchants and the rise of the Roman commercial class. Rome's political and military presence was initially intended merely to protect Roman trade interests, but then ending up sticking around. "The flag followed trade," as some theorists of empire like to describe this dynamic in more modern contexts.

A whole new phase of Greek cultural influence also flowed from Rome's involvement in the Greek East. Although Rome had been influenced by Greek culture since its early days, this era saw unprecedented intensity and diversity. Greek temples, political practices, religious expressions, and literature had a

9.4. Maison Carrée, Roman temple in Greek style. Slide by Céline Léon.

tremendous influence on Romans (Fig. 9.4). Philhellenism hit a new high,
aspects of which we will explore in later chapters. With it also came a new
emphasis on the charismatic general in the stamp of Alexander the Great
and the downplaying of traditional Roman mores of leadership. Note the
two statues in Figures 9.5 and 9.6. The Barberini Togatus clearly shows a
traditional Roman, ancestor busts in hand and fully clad in a toga. The Tivoli
general, by contrast, is barely and provocatively covered by a disheveled toga;
signs of his ancestors are nowhere in sight. He is the conquering, charismatic
individual, sporting, teasingly, the heroic nudity of Alexander. Conservatives
protested Greek influence loudly, but Greek styles came to permeate Roman
society. The stodgy Senator Cato the Elder would pronounce in the early
second century B.C. that "if ever Romans became infected with the literature
of Greece, they would lose their Empire."[9] Maybe they did gain the whole
world by losing their own Roman soul, but they certainly did not lose an
empire in the process.

THE LATE REPUBLIC AND THE END
OF THE OLD ORDER

Whatever the cause of the expansion, it was now rapid and continuous, and
there was no official plan in sight for dealing with the changing circumstances.
Two Punic Wars had nearly doubled Roman territory; the eastern expansion

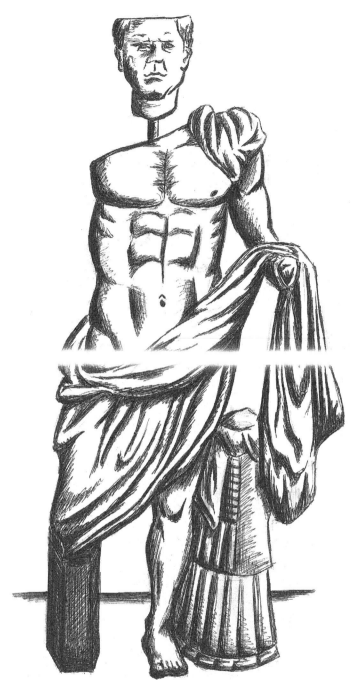

9.5. Tivoli general. Line drawing by Stephanie Espeland.

went far beyond that. Roman centuriation, road building, and city building would soon be stamping the Roman (or now Greco-Roman) look around the Mediterranean. Distant areas were transformed by all of this, but at the same time, so was Rome. Rome's involvement abroad transformed her internally in ways far beyond the ken of contemporary observers.

Ancient and modern assessments of the late republic have dwelt much on its powerful demagogues and warlords/generals – far too much, in fact, in light of other significant dimensions of this rich period. Much has been written about the "Great Men" of this famous age, but, until fairly recently, far less has been published on the larger ideological, economic, military, and political forces surrounding them. Most historians at the time could only make sense of ongoing changes in moral terms. To them, greedy individuals simply were ruining the republic. One should always be cautious of ancient writers (or modern commentators for that matter) who make sense of social and cultural changes purely in moral terms. The accounts of the historians Sallust, Livy, and others rarely, if ever, go beyond moralizing in their analyses of the late republic. The historian Plutarch, looking back on the second century B.C. from the perspective of the late first and early second century A.D., is typical of this type of view:

> The Roman Republic had grown too large to preserve its original purity
> of spirit, and the very authority which it exercised over so many realms
> and peoples constantly brought it into contact with, and obliged it to
> adapt itself to an extraordinary diversity of habits and modes of living.[10]

Historians continue to debate this famous age: was it an era of selfish individualists, would-be saviors of the empire, pragmatic realists, or something else? Looking at the intricate connections among the various levels of historical time is helpful in answering such questions.

Underlying changes were going on beneath the surface, both as cause and effect of the famous historical events. Changes in agriculture and farming registered somewhere between the ecological and social structure levels of historical time, and were triggered in part by the events. Transformations at the different levels of historical time are multidirectional. At a basic level, the influx of war booty set up a cycle that revamped Roman demographic and economic structures. As more slaves and goods poured in, more Roman soldiers, settlers, and traders tended to move out. The wars continued to provide the means to acquire slaves but demanded more and more commitment from Rome's small farmers, the backbone of the Roman economy and the mainstay of the Roman army. By custom, to serve in the Roman legions, one had to own land, even if a small plot. Farmers made the best soldiers, in the minds of conservative Romans. The traditional image of the free farmer going off to war and then returning to his small plot (like Cincinnatus) was deeply embedded in the Roman mind. Such small farm plots originally dominated the Italian countryside, producing the cereal crops that were the Roman staple. Between

9.6. Roman man holding busts of his ancestors. Scala/Art Resource, NY.

the third and first centuries, some changes, although uneven in impact, were altering Roman demographics.

The extent is debated, but slave labor for agriculture began to rise. Slaves had been used on a modest scale in Roman agriculture before. The best slave productivity, it was found, could be had on large farms overseen by hired foremen. As a result, farm sizes began to increase dramatically as small farm plots were bought up and folded into larger and larger farms. "Get big or get out," as Earl Butz, U.S. secretary of agriculture under Richard Nixon and Gerald Ford, used to say.

A large number of slaves worked on these plantations – *latifundia* as they were called – of 300-plus acres. By some modern estimations (probably too high, according to very recent research), slaves came to make up as much as one-third of the Italian population eventually. The slaves and farms were owned by patricians or wealthy plebeians such as the equestrians. Landowner-ship was always *the* premodern basis of wealth, and it was also a useful avenue to social respectability for the equestrians, who well knew how the established aristocracy looked down on the entrepreneurial basis of their wealth. Feeling compelled to sell their small plots, some free peasants and small farmers took to the growing cities to find work, where they were known as *proletarii* (Karl Marx would base his proletariat on them); others moved out to new overseas holdings.

Roman slavery did not emerge at this moment. Rome was already a slave society by the fourth century, but the second century saw a general shift in scale in response to conquest. The extent of this shift is hotly contested among recent scholars, although none doubt that changes were occurring. Never based on race or ethnicity, Roman slaving was through war and trade. The treatment of slaves varied considerably: they could be practicing doctors and teachers living comfortably as part of an aristocratic *familia*, but most often they were employed in agriculture or, worse, mining. The latter was brutal work, characterized by severe exploitation and short life expectancy. Slaves could be freed, however, through a process known as manumission, and their descendants could become part of Roman society as freedmen.

The agricultural activity on the *latifundia* differed notably from earlier periods as well. The real money was now in olives, wine, and, most of all, ranching (especially sheep and horses). These were luxury goods that were consumed by the small number of Italian elites. The small-plot free farmers primarily had grown their own cereal crops, staples for these inhabitants of the Italian Peninsula, but increasingly grain came from outside the peninsula. Areas such as Sicily, North Africa, and western Anatolia would become the key grain producers for Italy.

The senatorial aristocracy and equestrians made out well in this broad transformation of agriculture. In addition to their expanding personal land-holdings, many had also long been farming the *ager publicus*, the public land owned, in theory, by the people of Rome. The wealthy often treated the agricultural proceeds from this land entirely and illegally as their own private property, and the Senate, for fairly obvious reasons, turned a blind eye toward this misuse of public land. At the same time, the free urban and rural poor often found their situation worsening, even as Roman conquests produced a seemingly endless inflow of wealth, which was distributed unequally in Italy. Some free poor, in fact, found their own plight so desperate that they actually joined slave revolts, such as the famous one under Spartacus in 74–71 B.C.

Romans at all levels began to respond to these broad changes without grasping their full implications. Their responses proposed from every conceivable angle to restore the republic but often exacerbated existing problems. This was the events level of historical time. The most famous early political response was that of the brothers Tiberius and Gaius Gracchus. Ancient sources as well as modern accounts differ widely in assessing them – were they altruistic social reformers or would-be tyrants?

The brothers had an interesting pedigree that they used to full advantage. Their father was a famous censor and twice consul – particularly noteworthy for a plebeian – and their mother was a daughter of Scipio "Africanus." The brothers distinguished themselves as well – Tiberius, for example, was the "first over the wall" at Carthage in 146. Both married women of the highest nobility, Gaius into the family of the wealthiest Roman of his time. Thoroughly connected to the senatorial aristocracy, but still plebeian, they had the best of both worlds in that they could hold the highly influential office of Tribune of the Plebs. It was from this platform that both proposed their respective reforms.

Commission to redistribute the *ager publicus*. This meant seizing it from the nobility, whose exclusive and illegal use of the land had become traditional. Tiberius had seen firsthand the impoverishment of Rome's common citizens and the parallel growth of slave labor while traveling in northern Italy. By putting the *ager publicus* into the hands of landless Romans, the plan could accomplish several things at once: put more small farmers back on the land, thereby increasing the military draft pool and decreasing dependence of Italy on outside grain.

Technically, a reformer aims to re-create a previous situation, and Tiberius no doubt thought that this was what he was doing. In his mind was probably a very traditionalist and conservative plan to revive Rome's "hardy peasantry" and thus solve many social and agrarian problems. He wanted to turn back the clock to a time when he imagined Rome working well. Such attempts, however, have always evidenced one or both of the following: either the "Golden Age" to which reformers want to return is heavily idealized or dreamed up altogether or the attempts to "restore the past" simply end up creating something new. Tiberius' proposals evidenced a good bit of both.

The Land Commission did manage to attract the support of a handful of powerful and reform-minded senators. Emboldened, Tiberius then took his reform program directly to the popular voting assemblies. In doing this, however, he bypassed the Senate, and many senators felt slighted, to put it lightly. Further, as a tribune in 133, Tiberius illegally removed a colleague tribune who opposed him. He was ready to push his traditionalist agenda across via nontraditional measures: innovate to restore. Most senators did not share either his method or his dreams. Then several historical contingencies suddenly converged and emboldened him further. News arrived in 133 B.C. that king Attalus of the Hellenistic kingdom of Pergamum had bequeathed his kingdom to Rome. Tiberius jumped on the opportunity and proposed that money from Attalus' bequest be used to fund his commission and provide start-up grants to landless Romans, particularly veterans. Also, between 135 and 132 B.C., a slave revolt in Sicily disrupted the grain supply and demonstrated how susceptible Italy was by relying so heavily on grain from outside the peninsula. The restoration of the small-time farmer would help guard against such emergencies in the future.

Tiberius' supporters were mainly drawn from the rural poor who would often flock into the city when key measures were at stake in the voting assemblies. When one crucial election was held at harvest time – and thus with little hope of Tiberius' power base being present – he turned, in desperation, to the urban poor to help push his measures through. In the end, Tiberius was killed – clubbed down by senators with help from some equestrians as well. His assassination was a deeply serious one: the sacrosanctity of the Tribune of the Plebs had been violated.

His younger brother, Gaius, Tribune of the Plebs a few years later, set out to complete Tiberius' reforms. He proved to be even more bold and radical in challenging the power of the senators. He fought to remove them from courts that tried senators' abuses in provinces – too much solidarity, he suspected. Realizing even more than had his older brother the importance of the equestrians, he courted them by formally recognizing them as a political entity with status and by proposing that they get extended tax-collecting rights abroad. To attract more commoners to his cause, some of whom would have been clients of his senatorial foes, he attempted (unsuccessfully) to extend citizenship rights and subsidized the price of grain, which eliminated the fluctuations in price that could at times put the cost of food beyond the reach of the poor. He also founded an overseas colony at the site of Carthage in 122, obviously ignoring the curse leveled against anyone who would dare resettle it. Carthage became Rome's first overseas colony; many would later follow. With all of these measures, Gaius was building a bloc against the senators who opposed his plans. The Senate responded by putting forth their own partisan tribune, and the back-and-forth spiraled. Gaius had proposed one overseas colony; the senator-backed tribune then proposed twelve domestic colonies, and so on. In the end, Gaius was assassinated, just as his brother had been, a second blow to the sacrosanctity of the tribune. Some of the Gracchan reforms, however, such as the Land Commission, lived on.

Both reformers were, it seems, attempting to preserve the Roman constitution by forcibly adapting it to new circumstances that no one at the time
fully understood. The Gracchi exposed many deep fissures in Roman society.
Among them was a divide in Roman society between *populares*, aristocrats who
solidified power by working directly through and catering to the people, and
optimates who dominated the Senate and stood for the status quo. Although the
terms were not immediately used this way, they generally came to designate
distinct factions in an ensuing age of strife and civil war.

Resulting shifts in the exercise of social power register clearly in a succession of powerful generals who, like the Gracchi, were responding to the
deeper structural changes. The first in a succession of Great Men/rogues was
Gaius Marius, an equestrian as well as a *novus homo*, the first man in his family to
reach the Senate. Marius rose to the top through his military prowess, holding
the office of consul seven times between 107 and 86 B.C. He attempted to
resolve some of the same problems that had troubled the Gracchi. One plan,
with significant consequences for the republic, was simply to recruit landless
men (*proletarii*) to serve in his army and to pay for soldiers' equipment. The

before, but Marius, in effect, created an early professional army and set up a
situation in which much loyalty was given directly to the general who could
reward his soldiers through conquests rather than to Rome, per se. Rome, or
at least Marius, now had a standing army that needed to be kept busy through
war to be paid. The soldiers also served as an engineering force, constructing
roads, bridges, and so on. However, there was still the big question of what
to do with soldiers once they returned home from campaigns. Not all of them
received land handouts for their conquests, and the real problems continued.

Marius' sympathies lay with the *populares*, but an *optimate* rival arose in
Lucius Cornelius Sulla. Sulla won prestige during the Social War (91–89), a
rare revolt by Roman allies who then were granted full citizenship. The year
that war ended was the year Mithridates massacred the 88,000 Romans in
Asia Minor. Sulla immediately proposed to lead a campaign of conquest and
revenge against him. He got the charge from the Senate, but a tribune then
transferred the prestigious command to the aging Marius instead, amid riots
in the assembly. In response, Sulla marched on Rome (the first Roman to do
so), took control of the city, and compelled the Senate to pass his reform
package as he murdered those of his enemies that he could catch. An army
forcing the Senate's hand was a far cry from Polybius' idealized balance of
powers in the Roman constitution.

Sulla then left on the campaign himself, and in his absence Marius seized
Rome in 87, killing some of his own opponents and declaring Sulla an outlaw.
When Sulla successfully completed his campaign in the East, he returned

to fight the "Marians," partisans of Marius (who himself had died in the meantime). He set a dangerous precedent by publishing a proscription list, a list of citizens who were declared outlaws and who could thus be killed or have their property seized with impunity; all his Marian political foes appeared on it. Declaring himself dictator, he established a harsh and bloody order that he saw as a necessary means of restoring the republic; he then retired from public life.

One young Marian, Julius Caesar, barely survived the proscriptions: at one point, so the story goes, he eluded Sullan strongmen by hiding in water and breathing through a reed. From an elite and well-connected family, he rose through the *cursus honorum* a little more than a decade after Sulla's dictatorship. He was accused of taking part in the famous Catiline Conspiracy, a violent *popularis* attempt to redistribute land and cancel debts. He was never brought to trial, but Cicero, the leading orator statesman of the late republic who got his real start condemning the conspirators, remained always convinced that Caesar was actually guilty.

In 60 B.C., as an ambitious and talented young politician, Caesar teamed up with the two leading men of the age, Gnaeus Pompey and Licinius Crassus, to form a powerful republican coalition (sometimes anachronistically called the "First Triumvirate"). Pompey was Rome's most able general at the time, famous for defeating Mithridates of Pontus and adding enormous amounts of territory to Rome's *imperium* as well as subduing Mediterranean pirates. Crassus was among the most wealthy men in Rome and a moderately able military leader. These two together had crushed the famous Spartacus slave revolt (74–71 B.C.), which left six thousand slaves and the freemen who fought beside them crucified along the Appian Way.

The threesome of Caesar, Pompey, and Crassus pulled together obvious elements of ideology, economics, military, and politics (IEMP). All of them had a great deal of economic and political clout. Pompey had the military acumen in spades, and Caesar the political. None of them had it all. The ideological base, such as it was, should probably best be understood as an almost Alexandrine drive for conquest and glory. Honoring one's ancestors and gaining offices honorably were hardly to the fore at this point.

After serving a year as consul in 59 B.C., Caesar was given a multi-year command in Gaul with four legions under him (about five thousand men per legion) and two more raised in 58. Statistics from his campaign loudly proclaim the immense shift in scale of Roman imperialism: one million "barbarians" killed and around one million enslaved. He later wrote *Gallic Wars*, which tells in straightforward language the details of his campaign, which brought significant western territorial gain to the empire. He by no

9.7. Julius Caesar, marble head. Vanni/Art
Resource, NY.

means hides the fact that he was bent on Roman expansion and personal glory.
Meanwhile, Crassus was off on the eastern frontier fighting the Parthians, who
had reestablished a Persian empire to replace the Hellenistic Seleucid Empire;
we will hear more about the Parthians in the next chapter. Crassus' force was
routed at the Battle of Carrhae in 53 B.C.; he was killed in its aftermath, the
standards of his legions were captured, and his severed head ended up as a
prop in a performance of Euripedes' *Bacchae*. The Parthian Empire might resist
Roman hegemony, but it held tenaciously onto its Greek culture.

After Crassus' death, civil war broke out between the two remaining
triumvirs. In 49 B.C., Caesar was declared an outlaw by the Senate. Crossing
the Rubicon, the river that marked the boundary between Italy and Gaul,
he essentially declared war on Pompey and the Senate. In the end, Pompey
ended up fleeing to Egypt, where he was killed by the Ptolemies. Caesar was
now alone at the top.

Caesar's run as sole ruler of Rome was decisive but brief. In 46 B.C., he
declared himself dictator for ten years; and in 44, he declared himself dictator
for life. To protect himself, he assumed the inviolability and sacrosanctity of
the tribune. An Alexandrine ideology of charismatic leadership is obvious in
his reign. For example, he was the first Roman to have images of himself put
on coins, by decree of the Senate; coins were supposed to be decorated with
the heads of gods. It is probably not surprising that the historian Plutarch

paired Julius Caesar and Alexander the Great together in his famous *Parallel Lives of Greek and Roman Citizens*.

On the Ides of March, 44 B.C., Caesar lay dead, assassinated by a group of senators led by Gaius Cassius Longinus and Marcus Junius Brutus, the latter supposedly descended from the Brutus who had helped rid Rome of its king (*rex*) to set up the republic. In their minds, Brutus and Cassius were saving the republic by getting rid of yet another tyrant.

Bring back the republic they did not, however. A century of attempts to "save the republic" consistently ended in bloodletting, and no scheme really stood a chance of turning back the clock. Long before Julius Caesar, Sulla, or Marius, traditional republican institutions were stretched well beyond recognition. Memories of them, real and imagined, would continue to inspire and rebuke Romans in the decades and even centuries ahead. Rome was now a Mediterranean-wide empire, not just an Italy-based republic; it would shortly have an emperor and would be proclaiming itself more and more the *imperium sine fine*. The expansion of its empire was intrinsically connected to the collapse of the republic. A reconfiguring of Roman IEMP was well under way, details of which will become clear at the beginning of the period to follow, the Roman Empire. Assigning responsibility or blame to a few individuals misses significant parts of the historical picture, as does restricting the story to Great Men. Rome was undergoing huge social transformations, the types of which can only be appreciated at all three levels of historical time. Moralists might continue to hold forth about the "good old days," but by most sober historical measures, Rome's best days actually were just about to begin.

CHAPTER TEN

THE NEW POLITICAL ORDER:
THE FOUNDATIONS OF THE PRINCIPATE

In my sixth and seventh consulships, after I had extinguished civil wars, and at a time when with universal consent I was in complete control of affairs, I transferred the republic from my power to the dominion of the senate and people of Rome.

— Augustus, *Res Gestae*[1]

* How and why did Octavian/Augustus succeed where Julius Caesar had failed?
* To what extent did the rise of a Roman emperor signal a shift in the exercise of social power in the Roman world?
* What held an empire of 50 to 70 million people together?
* To what extent was this empire like or unlike the Near Eastern and Hellenistic empires that came before it?

IN THE EARLY SECOND CENTURY, the brilliant, if cynical, historian Tacitus summed up the reign of Rome's first emperor in his typically poignant and laconic fashion:

Augustus enticed the soldiers with gifts, the people with grain, and all men with the allurement of peace, and gradually grew in power, concentrating in his own hands the functions of the senate, the magistrates, and the laws. . . . At home all was peaceful, the officials bore the same titles as before. The younger generation was born after the victory of Actium, and even many of the older generation had been born during the civil wars. How few were left who had seen the Republic![2]

Like other Roman moralists, Tacitus focused exclusively on Great Men and their actions that drove the nails in the republic's coffin. Although his terse summation here might lack balance, it would be difficult to fault Tacitus too much for putting Augustus front and center. Augustus was one of the most brilliant and skillful leaders the ancient world ever saw, from almost any perspective. Wherever one chooses to begin the Roman Empire, with the rise of Augustus/Octavian, Rome finally came to have a true emperor.

It is not possible to properly understand even such a noteworthy figure as Augustus without considering the larger social forces that came together before, during, and after his long and fruitful reign. This is not to take anything away from his personal administrative genius – in fact, it is fairly certain that without Augustus, the Roman Empire would never have come together as it did, and today, needless to say, we would be living in a rather different world. Without a dynamic fusion of power sources, however, Augustus could not have succeeded in putting the Roman Empire on a solid footing that would hold directly for well over two centuries and even much longer in a modified form. His empire was different in some basic respects from all other empires we have studied, even as it continued some familiar, age-old patterns.

The Principate, as historians term the two-and-a-half-century-long age that Augustus initiated, witnessed the transformation of the Mediterranean world. Never before had this world been united under a single government, and it never would be again after the Roman political system came apart. Somewhere between 50 and 70 million people would find themselves bound together under an emperor whose realm stretched from Morocco to Mesopotamia and from the Sahara to Scotland. The conquests dropped off precipitously during the Principate, and Rome was left to define itself while defending far-flung frontiers, beyond which lived the "barbarian." Age-old patterns of life shifted in both obvious and subtle ways – forms of entertainment, patterns of settlement, means of food production, engagement in local politics. The next two chapters, in different ways, trace these changes concomitant with empire.

MR. IEMP: OCTAVIAN/AUGUSTUS

Just before his death in A.D. 14, Augustus looked back on his long reign (31 B.C.–A.D. 14) and composed a record of the highlights; it is the most famous inscription of the ancient world. His account, published throughout the empire just after his death, is a remarkable document. The wording of it echoed traditional Roman self-congratulation as well as, in a certain sense, the imperial pronouncements of earlier Near Eastern emperors. Although the title is usually shortened to *Res Gestae* (literally, *Deeds* or *Achievements*), the full title is worth recording here: "The Achievements of the Divine Augustus, by which he Brought the World under the Empire of the Roman People, and of

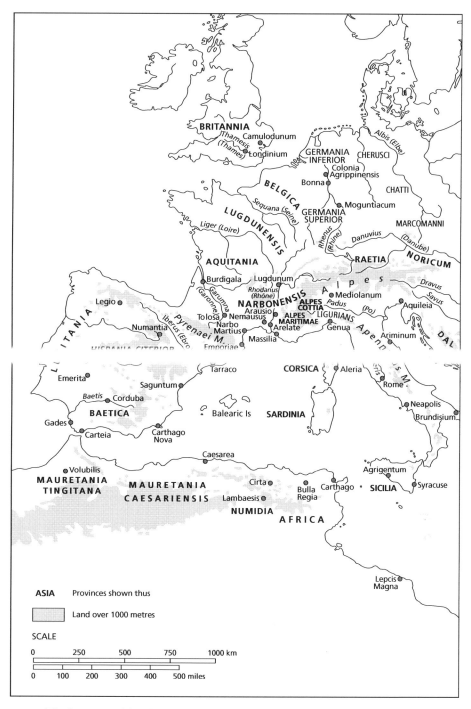

10.1. The Roman world at the time of Augustus. *Cambridge Ancient History*, vol. 10, pp. xvi–xvii.

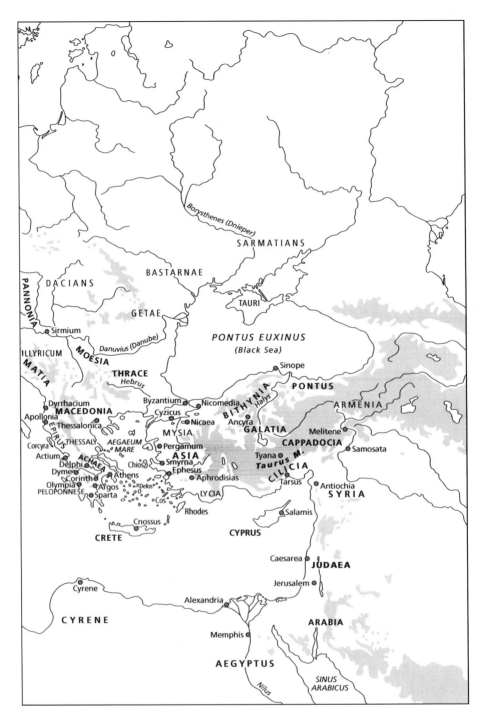

10.1 (*continued*)

the Expenses which he Bore for the State of Rome." One could hardly ask for a more succinct statement of ideology, economics, military, and politics (IEMP).

Octavius, as was Augustus' given name, was the grandnephew and adopted son of Julius Caesar. Upon his adoption by Caesar in 44 B.C., he became

Octavian(us). The heir to Caesar's wealth and the potential heir to his warlord status, Octavian did not long delay after the assassination of his adopted father to claim both. Within a year of Caesar's assassination, the ambitious young Octavian marched on Rome and was declared consul. He was just nineteen years old. Almost immediately, in 43 B.C., he, along with Mark Antony and Marcus Lepidus, formed a triumvirate to confront the forces of Brutus and Cassius, the assassins of Caesar who claimed to be restoring the republic. The net result was another bloody round of civil wars. One of their first tasks was the punishment of Caesar's assassins. The triumvirs then divided the Roman provinces among themselves to administer. After some initial shifts and wranglings, Antony received the eastern provinces, Octavian ended up with most of the west (Italy, Gaul, and Spain), and Lepidus was given North Africa.

As with the First Triumvirate, the power-sharing agreement was not to last for too long. Another bloody round of proscriptions and warfare erupted within a decade, pitting the forces of Octavian and Antony against each other. Lepidus was deprived of power by Octavian in 36 B.C. and watched round of late republican civil wars. Antony, meanwhile, allied with Cleopatra VII, the final and most famous ruler of Ptolemaic Egypt. Capitalizing on Antony's apparent Orientalizing in Egypt, offensive to conservative Romans, Octavian declared himself the real champion of their traditional values. The opposing forces met at the pivotal Battle of Actium in 31 B.C., off the western coast of Greece. Octavian's forces, led by his general, Marcus Agrippa, were victorious. As had Caesar, Octavian found himself alone at the top. Cleopatra's and Antony's suicides soon thereafter put the final Hellenistic kingdom into Rome's hands — the circle of lands (*orbis terrarum*) around the Mediterranean was now complete. The Mediterranean was now truly *mare nostrum*, "our sea," as the Romans affectionately called it.

The basic facts of Octavian's storied rise to the top of an empire are easy enough to relate. What demands more explanation is his curiously long tenure in power. Doing so takes us directly to the core themes of this study. A dynamic combination of IEMP, unusually well documented, not only kept him alive but also ushered in what was arguably the most glorious age of Rome.

Octavian's political program hinged on radical innovations presented as republican renovations. His political power, in form and effect, flowed directly from the republic. He was following in the tradition of the Gracchi brothers — radical reform that, while claiming to restore or re-create a previous situation, actually ended up creating something new. This need not imply that Augustus, any more than the Gracchi, was pulling the wool over his countrymen's eyes. His attempts to restore were arguably sincere. On coins and monuments, Romans would continue to describe their polity as the *Res Publica*, the republic, for centuries to come. Modern historians, benefiting from the perspective that only comes from temporal distance and needing clear chronologically demarcated periods, do not.

Just a few years after Actium, in 27 B.C., Octavian appeared before the Senate and proposed to lay down all of the titles and powers he had accumulated since he first marched on Rome and attained the consulship. Declaring the republic officially restored after more than a century of civil strife and chaos, he then offered to retire from public life. One might think that the Senate would have jumped at this chance. Had not many of its members bristled when Caesar snatched too much power from this illustrious body?

In fact, the opposite occurred. The Senate refused his offer to retire, begged him to stay in office, extended his consulship, and voted him even more honors and powers. This crucial moment, known as the Constitutional Settlement of 27 B.C., solidified the rule of the empire under an emperor. The Senate had meanwhile been packed with supporters of Octavian, and thus it is no surprise that they moved toward consolidation of his power. The challenges to traditional exercise of social power in Rome had proven too much and new configurations were emerging. Again, the political basis of his power cannot be understood simply in terms of the actions of a single Great Man. The Senate promoted the Constitutional Settlement, recognizing, albeit implicitly, the role of social power.

The Senate then conferred on Octavian the title Augustus, a Latin term rich with both ideological and political connotations. The title communicated a sense of dignity, reverence, and admiration (as its English cognate "august"); but its ultimate root *augos* spoke directly of divine power (as in the word *augury*) and growth and expansion (as in *augment*). He now ruled by divine-bestowed power as "one who awakens life and dispenses blessings"; his new title was "synonymous with being god present."[3] Near Eastern and Hellenistic traditions of divine authority and divine appointment were now alive and well in the Roman world; the age-old association of ideological and political power would now bear much fruit in the Roman West. Always eager to maintain republican forms, Octavian himself preferred the title *princeps*, literally "first-citizen" or "leading statesman," an appellation with solid and long-term resonances in the Roman Republic.

The *Res Gestae* emphasized Augustus' salvation of the Roman community through his achievements, the services he bestowed on the republic and the enormous influence with which he had been entrusted to guide Rome. He was careful to explain and justify his overwhelming power in deeply republican terms. The *Res Gestae*, in effect, proclaims the ideological basis of his rule. The document presents a fundamental contrast with Tacitus' cynical view from a century later: "concentrating in his owns hands the functions of the senate, the magistrates, and the laws. . . . How few were left who had seen the Republic!" In Augustus' own telling, he had actually "brought back into use many exemplary practices of our ancestors which were disappearing in our time."[4] He was restoring the republic, he claimed, not hoodwinking the Roman populace. "After I had extinguished civil wars, and at a time when with universal consent I was in complete control of affairs, I transferred the republic from my power to the dominion of the senate and people of Rome."[5]

There was hardly a better way to emphasize his restoration of the republic than to declare the favors he had bestowed upon the Senate and explain how he cooperated with the senators to restore Rome to its "former glory." Because, in the Constitutional Settlement, he had attempted to give all his own titles and power back to the Senate, he could now claim that he held his position "by the will of the Senate," and he was thus a constitutionally legitimate ruler.

political power from his reign onward; it would remain a prestigious body, however, that would handle a considerable amount of routine business under the empire.

One of the most important powers the Senate conferred on Augustus, and one he used to great effect, was the power of a tribune. This power was vital, because it theoretically allowed him to veto any measure proposed by the Senate. He actually did not spend much time at all wrangling with the Senate, because senatorial proposals were usually in keeping with his general program. Tacitus would read this as Augustus himself actually coming to take on the functions of the Senate. In Augustus' own telling, he could wield tribunician power while keeping to Republican traditions. It was in reference to this and other powers that he claimed: "I would not accept any office inconsistent with the custom of our ancestors."[6] Yet having a single ruler with this type of power was unprecedented; renovation had become innovation once again.

Members of the Senate, in turn, became his personal administrators, many of them receiving bureaucratic positions in Rome and throughout the provinces. The provinces themselves were divided into two types. The more peaceful were placed under control of the Senate, and the more volatile (as well as extraordinarily wealthy) provinces remained in the control of the emperor himself as imperial provinces. In Chapter Eleven, we consider provincial administration in more detail.

Most obviously, in terms of political power, Augustus solidified the position of emperor, which would be consolidated as a regular office under his successor, Tiberius. The period from the Constitutional Settlement until well into the third century A.D., saw a variety of emperors, ranging from so-called Good Emperors (i.e., Augustus, Vespasian, Nerva, Trajan, Hadrian, Antoninus Pius, Marcus Aurelius) to those who continue to live in infamy (i.e., Caligula, Nero, Domitian, and Commodus). Several dynasties came and went in these early centuries, the most important of which were the Julio-Claudian, in Augustus' line, and the Flavian, in Vespasian's, and the Antonines, in Nerva's. The succession was not always smooth – in fact, the year A.D. 69 is infamously known as the "Year of the Four Emperors" because of the violent civil wars surrounding the ascension to the office – but the Principate remained largely intact until the third century, an era that would shake the empire at its very foundations.

Augustus' military reforms likewise stabilized and solidified an empire. By 30 B.C., just after Actium, all the competing armies of the late republic had been demobilized. A big question remained, however. With several competing army options, which ones were the soldiers who stood for Rome, the real veterans among the competing mercenaries? Augustus skillfully solved this quandary by recognizing all discharged veterans as legitimate Roman soldiers. If a soldier had fought on the side of Antony, he was still considered a legitimate veteran upon retirement. This meant land and cash for all, regardless of prior loyalties. It was a decisive move, which strongly solidified his support among the soldiers: all had fought for Rome, the move implied, and all deserved the fruits of their labors upon decommissioning. He thereby averted dangerous bitterness among military men, whose general disfavor he could not afford. In the short run, the long-standing land problem, exacerbated rather than solved by the warlords of the late republic, was effectively addressed, for a time. As throughout Roman history, military reforms were often directly tied to land issues.

Up to this point in its history, Rome did not have a truly professional standing army. Late republican warlords starting with Marius challenged Roman mores by recruiting their own soldiers from among the populace to meet immediate needs, and there were many problems flowing from this, as will be recalled. Throughout republican history before this, the Roman fighting force was essentially a citizen militia that came together to face a threat and then disband and return to small farms. Augustus set up Rome's first official standing army, three hundred thousand strong, which was tasked with maintaining and defending Rome's far-flung frontiers. All members of this force swore a personal oath of loyalty to the emperor himself, as had always been done to republican generals; the army was Rome's, but it was, in basic fact, the emperor's own personal force. The army had long been the most expensive item in the imperial budget. Imperial Rome's political and economic character would shape and be shaped by this new army.

The imperial army served a different purpose than its republican counterparts. It was now generally not a fighting force of ambitious generals conquering new lands, eager for glory, power, and wealth. It was not even a tool of expansion, although the Roman ideology of *imperium sine fine*, imperial power without limit, remained intact (at least for a century or two). It was now primarily a defense force. Augustus emphasized in his *Res Gestae* that he had expanded the frontiers of the empire as far as they should go. His successors generally followed him, and the Principate saw only a few noteworthy conquests – in Britain, Dacia, southwest Germany, and Mesopotamia. The drive for valor was not altogether dead among the emperors, as these conquests attest, but no longer were warlords competing for conquests. The frontiers of the empire would remain generally stable for a time, and the army was there to ensure that.

much prosperity and standardization to the empire. The abuse of provincials in the late republic was notorious, and Augustus regularized the tax structure of the empire, decreasing opportunities for extortion by tax collectors (*publicani*). Regularizing the tax structure was essential for two basic reasons: it discouraged revolt, and it helped replenish the imperial coffers, which could now no longer depend on the loot and booty that came from conquest and expansion. With the political peace came more vigorous trade throughout the Mediterranean and environs. The famous Roman road network was expanded and maintained, bringing prosperity and distant goods to an unprecedented number, especially the equestrians, many of whom continued to enjoy lucrative trade opportunities. Local elites (decurions) were increasingly co-opted into the Roman system in part by such new opportunities. We explore this elite co-option, an obvious divergence from the Near Eastern elite replacement, in the next chapter. Many inhabitants of the empire, but surely not all, benefited from this new system.

In his *Res Gestae* as well as other inscriptions, statues, and sculptures, Augustus presented a staunchly pious image – the centerpiece of his ideological program. The peace of the empire depended on *pax deorum*, the peace of the gods, or with the gods. In 12 B.C., with the death of Lepidus who had held the position up to that time, Augustus took on the office of *pontifex maximus*, chief priest, or, literally, the chief bridge builder between the gods and man. Rome would prosper in peace only so long as the gods were at

10.2. Ara Pacis of Emperor Augustus. Scala/Art Resource, NY.

peace with Rome. One of his most famous monuments, the Ara Pacis, the Altar of (Augustan) Peace, visually proclaimed to the people of Rome that Augustus had preserved their ancestral religion and ushered in a new era of safety and prosperity (Fig. 10.2). The traditional symbol of peace throughout the Roman world was the shutting of the doors of the Temple of Janus in Rome. Although these had been shut only twice in Roman history, Augustus records, they were closed three times during his reign. A plethora of new temples appeared and old ones were repaired – a new day was dawning, with the blessing of the gods on Augustus and Rome.

Augustus was not just a representative of the gods. His very title, as noted earlier, bespoke divine authority, if not the very presence of a god. The Romans had never deified a living person before. Julius Caesar was deified just after his assassination. Octavian, then, began his campaign as *divi filius*, the son of a god. He himself made much of this connection. Many peoples of the empire recognized him as a god, although it is doubtful that he absolutely insisted on it. In the Hellenistic East, he was hailed as a savior, with full divine connotations. His deification in the Hellenistic world followed long-established patterns of ruler worship, and a cult sprang up to him. In the West, the cult of the *genius*, or guardian spirit, of Augustus emerged as well,

10.3. Ara Pacis – detail of procession of Augustus' family. Alinari/Art Resource, NY.

in Gaul and elsewhere. Augustus did not suppress this honor and worship; his program, in fact, built on this ideological power. The military accorded him such intense loyalty that it was a fine line, if one at all, that separated military allegiance from cult to the emperor. In the next chapter, we explore the Imperial Cult, or the cult of *Roma et Augustus*, in the more characteristic form it took after Augustus' death.

Like some modern Western politicians, Augustus styled himself a "family values candidate." He was the ultimate defender of *mos maiorum*, the mores or ways of (our) ancestors. This rich concept motivated and inspired traditional Romans with its emphasis on preserving the religious values of their past. He put forth legislation punishing adultery as well as extended special privileges to freeborn women who bore three or more children. The piety and values of his own family are a central theme on the panels of the Ara Pacis (Fig. 10.3).

Historians have long debated how to assess all of Augustus' measures and programs. One can read his measures in a variety of ways. Most would agree that a late Republican warlord had stabilized the Mediterranean world by becoming Rome's first emperor, putting it on a course that would bring peace and prosperity to the empire for centuries to come. But it is far from unanimous why Augustus pulled this off and how he was able to do so. Was he a selfish megalomaniac, the savior of an Empire, a pragmatic realist, a complex combination of these, or maybe something else altogether? The answers to these questions will continue to fuel debate and discussion of one of the greatest and best-documented figures from the ancient world. Yet as much as he seems to loom large as a solitary mover of history, IEMP analysis shows that there were, as always, larger forces shaping the history. His success can clearly be measured and expressed in terms of these.

PAX ROMANA

The famous eighteenth-century English historian Edward Gibbon, the man who actually coined the term *Pax Romana*, opened his famous historical work on the Roman Empire with fulsome praise for the system Augustus had put together.

> In the second century, the Empire of Rome comprehended the fairest part of the earth, and the most civilised portion of mankind. The frontiers of that extensive monarchy were guarded by ancient renown and disciplined valour. The gentle but powerful influence of laws and manners had gradually cemented the union of the provinces. Their peaceful inhabitants enjoyed and abused the advantages of wealth and luxury. The image of a free constitution was preserved with decent reverence: the Roman senate appeared to possess the sovereign authority, and devolved on the emperors all the executive powers of government.[7]

Such peace and prosperity, Gibbon claims, flowed from the genius of Augustus: "Happily for the repose of mankind, the moderate system recommended by the wisdom of Augustus was adopted by the fears and vices of his immediate successors." Even bad successors could not unravel Augustus' remarkable system, at least for a few centuries.

The Roman peace brought a remarkable level of communication, trade, and cultural unity to the Mediterranean world. The Romans pulled together under a central government an astounding diversity of topographies, religions, languages, and histories. The extent to which the empire actually created social, cultural, and economic unity in this diverse world – a process historians refer to as "Romanization" – is a matter of much fruitful debate. Although the Roman Empire was fairly nonexpansionist relative to the late republic, it had acquired much territory and peoples that now had to be integrated into the empire. Dynamic and creative tensions between local mores and unifying Roman culture expressed themselves in myriad ways.

Observers like Gibbon were (and are) unable to appreciate the marked changes at the structural level of historical time, which were both cause and effect of the notable political developments and events. Political and economic changes registered in drastic demographic shifts. For example, the population of the empire under the Principate was somewhere between 50 and 70 million, with most inhabitants (at least 80 percent) living in rural areas. The populations of these rural areas expanded rapidly because of more extensive food production and various opportunities that came with it.

Recent archaeological work has shed much light on the changes at the structural level. Such information simply cannot be found in the ancient texts that Gibbon knew so well. To take but one instance, a series of North African surveys in the late twentieth century, the UNESCO Libyan Valley Archaeological Surveys, revealed how one semidesert region was able to produce remarkably during the Principate.[8] Roman engineers designed apparatuses to capture and store flash-flood water for later use, which allowed the semidesert to bloom in a way it has not since, even with much effort. Such amazing engineering feats shaped the demographics throughout the empire. Significant populations arose within what were once extremely sparsely populated regions (and that returned to such after the retreat of the Roman system in

leader Muammar al-Gaddafi, who wished to know how Romans had lived so successfully in the pre-desert. Even with modern technology, the Roman achievement in this area has not been replicated.

The integration of varied regions allowed the Romans to pull together both rare and staple resources into a standardized and stable economic system during the Principate. The results were felt for centuries. For example, Egypt and North Africa produced much grain and olive oil for the empire; Spain produced olive oil, minerals, and silver. Many regions produced distinctive marble types to beautify public and domestic buildings in the city of Rome itself and throughout the empire. The Romans were, in fact, the first people in history to specialize in polychromatic marble decoration. Colorful marble from all over the Roman Empire still adorns such memorable monuments as the Pantheon in Rome, the House of Love and Psyche in Ostia, and the Library at Ephesus. Roman marble decoration remains a vivid and tangible testimony to what was a vast and integrated empire (Fig. 10.4).

The city of Rome continued to attract people from all the empire's regions. It became history's first megalopolis, with a population reaching about 1 million in the early Principate, with much dependence on goods produced throughout the empire. A significant portion of the city's population was on the grain dole, relying for survival on the grain fleets from North Africa. Acting as a Hellenistic-style benefactor, the emperor became the personal patron of the urban poor throughout the empire, but especially in Rome. Not all Romans

10.4. House of Cupid and Psyche. Slide by Mark W. Graham.

approved of this type of welfare system (Tacitus, predictably, dissented), but for a time it alleviated many problems inherited from the Republic.

Rome remained a city of avid consumers of the goods produced throughout the empire. One striking testimony to this is Monte Testaccio, a 100-foot-high mound outside of Rome that served as a dump for broken amphorae, the large vessels used to transport wine and olive oil into Rome during the empire. One recent estimate is that 25 million amphorae make up the mound, visible still to this day.

The cities that sprang up throughout the empire bear eloquent testimony both to the unity of the empire and the shifts it was witnessing at the structural level. Many Roman cities appeared where no cities had been before, especially in the west. Older cities were revamped to make them look more like standard Roman cities. Most Roman cities had small populations by modern standards (ten thousand to twenty thousand inhabitants or even fewer on average), but they were the major expression of Romanization on the landscape of the Mediterranean world. One can still observe these symbols of Roman power today throughout Europe, North Africa, and parts of the Middle East. Most cities became, in effect, "little Romes," boasting a canon of architectural and engineering accoutrements. Temples, baths, latrines, triumphal arches,

10.5. Tricapitol of Sbeitla; an example of syncretism of Roman and local cultures. Slide by Mark W. Graham.

theaters, amphitheaters, houses, aqueducts, and more were remarkably uniform and similar in construction from England to Syria. Bath, England, gets its name, in fact, from one important building here. Even allowing for some very real regional variation, Rome was stamped, seemingly indelibly, on a broad landscape.

Much of the construction was done at local initiative, with guidance and occasional support from the central government. Provincial elites, as we will see in Chapter Eleven, largely ran the empire at the local level for Rome. They funded the bathhouses and theaters, and employed architects from far beyond their own regions. These co-opted elites were vital to imperial governance and were the means through which a shockingly small administration was able to administer such a diverse and far-flung empire. In this sense, as in others, Rome was a different kind of empire in the ongoing Age of Ancient Empires.

INTO THE ARENA: A MICROCOSM OF IMPERIAL SOCIETY IN THE PRINCIPATE

The late first/early second–century (A.D.) Roman satirist Juvenal no doubt exaggerated in his most famous line: "The people that once bestowed

10.6. El Djem amphitheater. Slide by Mark W. Graham.

commands, consulships, legions, and all else, now meddles no more and longs
eagerly for just two things – bread and circuses!"[9] His line does, however,
communicate, amid talk of imperialism and conquest, the very real importance of the grain dole and entertainment to the imperial Roman public. A
characteristic form of entertainment by his day took place in the amphitheater, famous as the site of the gladiatorial games and public sport executions.
The largest of these was in Rome (the Flavian amphitheater, or Colosseum),
built in the later first century. Major cities throughout the empire, particularly
its western sections, followed suit, constructing amphitheaters that were not
much smaller. A closer look at the amphitheater can elucidate Roman imperial
society, for it was a microcosm of empire.

The games boldly proclaimed empire, Romanization, clear Roman social
hierarchies, and Roman visions of history. It would be difficult, in fact, to find
a single other phenomenon that reveals so much about Roman imperial life.
The very tensions introduced by Romanization, between Roman diversity and
unity, were often powerfully displayed in the arena itself. Individual gladiators
often used the specific weapons and armor of peoples conquered by Rome,
sometimes deep in Roman history. Gladiators could dress anachronistically
as long-subdued peoples, such as Thracians, Samnites, Germans, or native

10.7. Gladiator from Ephesus. Slide by Mark W. Graham.

Spaniards, and carry weapons specific to each of these peoples. The games themselves, then, potentially declared an empire made up of a variety of conquered peoples. In addition, one type of show, the *venationes*, or hunts, proclaimed Rome's conquest of nature. The *venationes* involved the slaughter of exotic animals that proclaimed both Rome's imperial reach to exotic climes and its subduing of the natural world itself.

Along with this diversity and conquest, the games proclaimed a unified Roman sense of consolidation and order. There were strict codes of conduct and honor by which gladiators fought and died. The codes, which determined even the kneeling stance of a gladiator about to be killed as well as the means by which the sword would be plunged into him, were Roman in essence. Thus, the message was clear: the conquered lived, fought, and died by the codes through which the Romans themselves had civilized the world. For it was now the Roman way that dominated the once-independent peoples portrayed in the arena. Decurions were the major funders and supporters of these shows, likewise demonstrating Roman power in their regions, and even their own

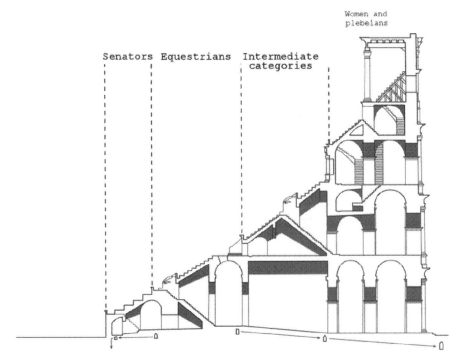

10.8. Amphitheater seating chart.

personal role in maintaining it. The Romans might not be expanding much anymore, but they could continue to proclaim their dominance over others, even if it took going into the distant past to find peoples so as not to be offensive to groups now fully integrated into the Roman system.

The shows also strongly reified Roman social hierarchies. The very spatial arrangements in the amphitheaters displayed the major Roman social divisions (Fig. 10.8). All present were arranged according to their standing in the Roman social order. Those in the arena, be they criminals (who were supposed to die) or gladiators (who were not), were distinct from Roman society as neatly arranged in the seats above. Those in the seats were arranged strictly according to their status. Closest to the arena were the senators, and behind them were the equestrians, then the plebs, and finally, in the farthest seats, the general poor, the women, and the slaves. The message was crystal clear, and internalized by the people of all social classes present.

When he was present, the emperor himself presided at the games, seated at the most prestigious place in the amphitheater and surrounded by the imperial family. His famous power over life and death, given by hand signals to contestants, demonstrated vividly his power over his subjects. Such power was, as always, hard to pin down concretely. Bad emperors generally got assassinated, and Roman emperors did not really have a free hand to do

10.9. Gold Stater of "barbarian" leader Vercingetorix (obverse). Réunion des Musées Nationaux/Art Resource, NY.

whatever they wished at any time. Faulty popular conceptions of notorious twentieth-century autocrats have sometimes left moderns with the impression that such leaders simply do whatever they want when they want to do it. Such is a rather simplistic view of imperial power that lacks critical nuance, as misleading for the modern as for the ancient world. During the Principate, at least, emperors followed Augustus in emphasizing that their power came "from the people." Here in the amphitheater, the dynamic relationship between *princeps* and people played itself out visibly. The approval or disapproval of the crowd at the amphitheater did, in fact, sway the decisions of emperors. The amphitheater thus gives insight into the complex dynamics of social power as few written sources could.

"BARBARIANS" THROUGH ROMAN EYES: THE ROMANS ENCOUNTER "THE OTHER"

Beyond the frontiers of the empire lay Barbaricum, the abode of the "barbarians." These peoples would test the inclusiveness of the Roman system. The Romans might have been more inclusive than any empire before its time, but there were limits, despite continued and strident Roman claims to universality. Roman relations with barbarians before and during the Principate helped define imperial Roman identity as much as it helped shape barbarian identity.

The concept of the barbarian is an invention of the Greco-Roman world. The word is Greek and based on a repeated nonsense syllable ("bar-bar") mirroring the supposed meaningless speech of non-Greek speakers. The Romans inherited many such Greek stereotypes and projected them onto people at and beyond their frontiers. To the Roman mind, the barbarians were the ulti-mate "Other," the people against whom the Romans could measure, and thus define, themselves. Moderns struggle to make sense of barbarians because images of them range in our minds from bloodthirsty, hairy, stinky brutes to Romantic noble savages, and from the rapists and pillagers of classical civilization to the inspiration for nineteenth- and twentieth-century German nationalism.

Romans classified such peoples in an eternal present. Whereas Romans had a history and were therefore historical peoples, they saw the barbarians as timeless and therefore without history or development. To writers like Pliny the Elder, a first-century naturalist, barbarians as groups neither disappeared nor changed. Pliny presumed to rely, ultimately, on references in Herodotus, written more than five centuries earlier, to make sense of peoples at Rome's frontiers in his own day. A few centuries after Pliny, when barbarians them-selves began to compose their own histories, they did so essentially in Roman terms, and thus passed on Roman (and Greek) stereotypes. Efforts to get at barbarian identity, in any meaningful sense, are frustrated at every level.

The barbarians exposed a critical tension in Roman imperialism. The Romans, from earliest times, seemed eager to incorporate outsiders. The his-torian Livy records many early Roman stories that showed Rome's willingness, if not eagerness, to incorporate outsiders. In fact, it was a very strength of the Roman system, Livy implies, that the Romans were not ethnocentric but rather allowed foreigners to become Romans. The story of the Sabine women is perhaps the most famous of Livy's stories that make this point.

Roman incorporation of outsiders continued at all social levels into the later republic and early years of the empire. This is well illustrated in a famous speech the emperor Claudius (r. A.D. 41–54) delivered in the Senate in 48. Trying to convince skeptical senators to allow inhabitants of a distant Gallic province into the ranks of the Roman Senate, Claudius argued:

> For surely we have no regrets in going clear up to Lugdunum [modern Lyon] for members of our order. Assuredly, Conscript Fathers, it is not without some hesitation that I cross the limits of the provinces which are well known and familiar to you, but the moment is come when I must plead openly the cause of Further Gaul. It will be objected that Gaul sustained a war against the divine Julius for ten years. But let there be opposed to this the memory of a hundred years of steadfast fidelity, and a loyalty put to the proof in many trying circumstances. My father, Drusus, was able to force Germany to submit, because behind him reigned a profound peace assured by the tranquility of the Gauls.[10]

Claudius himself recognized a long history of Romans incorporating outsiders, even those once considered barbarians.

Yet the Romans also came to imagine that certain peoples were simply incapable of appreciating the privileges of the Roman system and were thus best left outside of the frontiers of the empire and/or strenuously resisted if they should encroach on them. Romanization was not for everyone, despite traditional Roman claims to the contrary.

The Romans had no clear idea where the barbarians had actually come from when they settled along their frontiers (or, rather, Roman frontiers settled among them). Jordanes, a later Roman writer and himself a Goth by ethnicity, colorfully described the origins of his people:

> Now from this island of Scandza, as from a hive of races or a womb of nations, the Goths are said to have come forth long ago under their king, Berig by name. As soon as they disembarked from their ships and set foot on the land, they straightway gave their name to the place.[11]

Modern historians are not so likely to imagine such fanciful beginnings for any barbarian group. Three general models now explain how different groups of barbarians came to be – a process known as ethnogenesis. Some groups simply claimed descent from a legendary family. At some point in their history, these groups claimed to have descended ultimately from a famous family or legendary ancestor. Such claims are hard to substantiate historically, but they were believed and served to unite people groups into coalitions such as Goths, Lombards, and Franks. Other groups came into being more or less spontaneously with the emergence of a particularly charismatic figure who united various peoples together into a single moving or fighting force such as the Huns. A final model of ethnogenesis points simply to decentralized peoples who united politically, disbanded, and then united at other times as need or emergency arose. Groups such as the Slavs and Alamanni probably entered into history this way.

Most if not all of the barbarian groups emerged as mixed groups of people, coming together for purposes of warfare or to meet some basic needs. Romans, however, generally viewed barbarians as pure and unmixed. As Tacitus relates in his *Germania*:

> For myself, I accept the view that the peoples of Germany have never contaminated themselves by intermarriage with foreigners but remain of pure blood, distinct and unlike any other nation. One result of this is that their physical characteristics, in so far as one can generalize about such a large population, are always the same: fierce-looking blue eyes,

reddish hair, and big frames – which, however, can exert their strength
only by means of violent effort.[12]

Most modern archaeological study, on the other hand, points invariably to
mixed groups of people with rather flexible identities.

Difficult questions of actual origins of groups aside, most of the barbarian
groups on Rome's frontiers shared similar social patterns, as demonstrated
by archaeological evidence. Barbarians generally lived in small communities
of farmers or herders (or both). They dwelt in small huts, with families
organized as free women and men arranged in nuclear households. The status
in the communities was usually based on wealth (measured in terms of cattle)
and military prowess in maintaining and increasing that wealth. Warfare was
central to their way of life, but most barbarian groups had long histories
of peaceful trade interaction with Romans. The trade interactions shaped
the barbarians as well, pulling them into Roman networks of exchange and
shaping their demographics and settlement patterns. Thus, even as Romans
came into contact with such groups, they were inadvertently involved in their
transformations, making Roman observations of the "timeless barbarians" that
much more suspect.

Hostile encounters with barbarians helped define Roman identity as well.
One of the most poignant and long-term Roman historical memories was
the sack of Rome by Gauls (Celts) in 390 B.C. Some historians have even
traced Roman defensive imperialism directly to this moment. The best way to
keep from being threatened by any powerful invader was to neutralize the
threat. The Gallic sack of Rome was remembered centuries later during the
Principate as a defining point in Roman history. A second disaster, during
the reign of Augustus, would also linger long in the Roman collective memory. In A.D. 9, a German named Arminius, himself a Roman equestrian who
commanded troops in the Roman army as a tribal leader, defeated the forces
of Varus, Augustus' general, and annihilated three legions in the Teutoburgian
Forest.

A new type of empire had joined the Age of Ancient Empires, in name and
deed. Although there were many differences between this empire and those
that came before, basic similarities and continuities appear when analyzed
through the lens of IEMP. Augustus' success, as much as that of Ashurbanipal
of Assyria, is at bottom a testimony to his skillful employment of the four basic
power sources, although his knowledge of them no doubt remained tacit. Tacit
knowledge, when acted on by someone with Augustus' influence and power,
produced results felt by millions upon millions both inside and outside the
frontiers of the empire. This power came along with being a Roman emperor,

but an emperor who owed much to republican, Near Eastern, and Hellenistic precedents.

The emergence of a true empire was connected to deeper changes in the Roman world as well as the ancient world in general. The reconfiguring of IEMP had begun in the republic, but the results were felt acutely with the birth of the Principate. Augustus' responses and those of his successors were themselves part of long-term transformations, a fact that neither he nor his contemporaries could ever grasp on the spot. One need not share the total cynicism of Tacitus to recognize that a new Rome had emerged. How would the far-flung inhabitants of the Mediterranean world respond to this new face of Roman rule?

CHAPTER ELEVEN

RULING AND RESISTING
THE ROMAN EMPIRE

*But now a clear and universal freedom from all fear has been granted both to the world
and to those who live in it.*

— Publius Aelius Aristides[1]

*Neither East nor West can sate their appetite. They are the only people on earth to covet
wealth and poverty with equal craving. They plunder, they butcher, they ravish, and
call it by the lying name of "empire" [imperium]. They make a desert and call it "peace."*

— Briton Chieftain Calgacus[2]

* To what extent did the 50 to 70 million inhabitants of the Roman Empire
  accommodate themselves to Roman rule?
* Was cosmos/order worth the cost of "liberty"? To whom? To whom not?
  Why?
* How did the Imperial Cult connect with the imperial political program?

IT WOULD BE DIFFICULT TO PORTRAY the themes of this chapter more
succinctly than do the two speech excerpts that open this chapter.
Publius Aelius Aristides, a provincial Greek and a leading literary figure
of his day, addressed Rome itself during the reign of the "Good Emperor"
Antoninus Pius (r. 138–61). His panegyric, a speech of elaborate praise,
gushes with appreciation for the empire:

> All localities are full of gymnasia, fountains, monumental approaches,
> temples, workshops, schools, and one can say that the civilized world,
> which had been sick from the beginning, as it were, has been brought by
> the right knowledge to a state of health. . . . Thus it is right to pity only

those outside your hegemony, if indeed there are any, because they lose such blessings.[3]

The empire, Aristides exults, had brought cosmos through a civic culture that blossomed with vivid symbols of Romanization. *To Rome* presents a perfect example of elite co-option, in direct contrast to the long tradition of elite replacement in the Age of Ancient Empires. Rome preferred to win over, rely on, and reward the urban provincial elite throughout its realm rather than simply replace them with ethnic Romans or Italians. Many provincials, in turn, seemed to identify readily and gladly with the Roman Empire, as had a few generations of Aristides' family by this point. By all appearances, they embraced the empire and made it their own. Rome had earned their love and sincere praise.

Calgacus, a Briton leader, is known only from this single speech in Tacitus' first historical work, *Agricola*. The oration calls his fellow Britons to fight fiercely to remain "the most distant dwellers upon earth, the last of the free" from Roman domination.[4] It rousingly contrasts traditional Briton freedoms

if any – of this speech Calgacus actually gave is wide open to question; Tacitus was certainly not there, and its rhetoric smacks of the historian throughout in its denunciation of the Principate. Yet somewhere between Tacitus' starting claim that "this is the substance of what he is reported to have said" and Calgacus' spirited "On then into action; and as you go think of those that went before you and of those that shall come after,"[5] it is certain that Tacitus has picked up on some very real reactions to Roman rule.

Just a few pages prior, Tacitus described what imperialism looked like among a nearby group of Britons. Tacitus, once again, reveals the dark side of the *Pax Romana*, and in unforgettably poignant terms. Amid the "temples, market-places, and town houses" the Romans provided them, the Britons "went astray into the allurements of evil ways, colonnades and warm baths and elegant banquets. The Britons, who had no experience of this, called it 'civilization,' although it was a part of their enslavement."[6] The famous architectural and cultural amenities of empire, unprecedented blessings to the whole world in Aristides' view, are bald tools of hegemony in the view of others.

In Chapter Ten, we looked at the political and structural changes that came with the Principate and the *Pax Romana*. In this chapter, we take a closer look at the actual mechanisms of local control, political and religious/ideological, as well as the varied responses by peoples who found themselves, wittingly or unwittingly, under Roman rule. To what extent did the 50

to 70 million inhabitants of the Roman Empire accommodate themselves
to Roman rule and expectations? Not everyone, of course, felt the same way
about inclusion into empire. Outright revolt and explicit resistance was rather
rare, however. The few examples stand out in telling and bold relief against
the backdrop of *Pax Romana*. As throughout this study, resistance reveals
almost as much about empire and about the integration of sources of social
power as do the actual dynamics of empire at the center.

POWER AND THE PROVINCES

Compared with other ancient empires we have studied, as well as by any
modern standard, the official apparatus of Roman imperial control was notably
minimal and unimposing – a bare-bones provincial administration with a
fairly simply tax collection and census structure run largely by local elites. A
nuanced blend of formal and informal mechanisms and widely diffused power
channels helped hold the vast empire together with a tiny bureaucracy. Roman
legionnaires generally remained on the frontiers and in a few particularly
problematic areas, so most inhabitants of the empire rarely saw military figures
unless they happened to live near a major highway. Simply put, the Principate
was not held together by a menacing military presence or even the imminent
threat of spectacular and brutal force. Compared with prior empires such as
Babylon and Achaemenid Persia, both of which were constantly putting down
revolts and insurrections in some region of their empire at any given time,
Romans rarely resorted to shows of force within their empire. What, then,
besides a *princeps* and unprecedented peace, held it all together?

The basic building block of Roman imperial administration was the
province, through which the emperor controlled the cities. As Rome began
acquiring overseas territories during the republic, a unique provincial system emerged, apparently without any premeditation or plan. The provincial
system developed naturally, following typical transitions of Roman conceptions of space and power. *Provincia* once simply denoted a general sphere of
action and duty, as a secondary definition of province still does in English.
Gradually, it primarily came to define a specific geographic area as a unit of
imperial control. By the second century B.C., Rome had clearly designated
and demarcated provinces. With the rise of Augustus, there were thirteen and
at his death twenty-eight. By the time of Hadrian (r. 117–138), there were
forty-five.

The natural transfer in concept from the general sphere of one's influence
to the actual space over which that power was exerted had important parallels.
It might be recalled from the introduction that a similar transition shaped the

meaning of the word "empire" itself. *Imperium* once denoted for Romans of the republic not a territory or a polity but rather the sphere or realm of authority given to a magistrate, particularly a consul. A Roman republican leader, then, had both *imperium* and *provincia* long before an empire actually existed. Over time, *imperium* came to refer to imperial rule over a (however ambiguously) bounded territory, and thus an empire as we now understand it. A similar transition occurred with the *conventus*, a conceptual sphere of legal jurisdiction that evolved into a clearly bounded administrative subdivision within some provinces.

As soon as *provinciae* became provinces, so to speak, the Senate appointed officials to staff them. During the republic, a praetor ruled each province, and all the provinces were under direct senatorial control. Emperors governed imperial provinces through procurators. The provinces, as we saw in Chapter Ten, were also divided into senatorial and imperial provinces, depending on the wealth and risk potential of that particular province. Egypt, for example, remained an imperial province because of both its lucrative resources and its long tradition of stubborn cultural and political independence and revolt.

for the success of the Principate cannot simply be sought in the formal and direct mechanisms of empire. The real key was elite co-option, as seen with Aristides. Without the explicit and dedicated support of the provincials, the empire would not have lasted as long as it did. Recall how quickly subversion arose within the Assyrian and Achaemenid Persian Empires at the first sign of challenge and stress. The Assyrian Empire more or less disappeared immediately with a serious revolt, and the Persian essentially collapsed after only two major battles. Their inhabitants were simply subjects, unlike Rome's inhabitants, and did not actually internalize the ideologies of their rulers and realms.

The Roman Empire, then, was not held together like a modern police state by a sea of bureaucrats and local spies, although a small number of bureaucrats and internal spies (known as *frumentarii*) certainly existed. A few statistics highlight Rome's extremely rare accomplishment. Recent estimates hold that there was only one Roman official for every four hundred thousand subjects. One historian puts it in poignant, almost tangible terms: the Romans held together an empire of at least 50 million, stretching from England to Mesopotamia, with an administration smaller than that of a modern American research university.[7] No other empire in history, before or after, has done so much (for better or for worse) with so little. The inhabitants of the empire were not overwhelmed by the number of officials or the constant threat of coercive violence.

The most important of the co-opted local elites were the decurions (*decuriones*), or city councilors, who ran local government throughout the empire. Such openness to provincials within the system enabled the Roman state to create locally competent administrators who were responsible to imperial authorities. They met together in a *concilium*, a council that represented local interests to the imperial center at Rome. They collected imperial taxes, erected the still-ubiquitous honorific inscriptions and statues, organized the Imperial Cult, as we will see subsequently, and put on gladiatorial games throughout the empire. Such provincial elites also began making a mark in the Senate almost from the dawn of the Principate, and, by the middle of the second century, almost half of the senators were from outside of Italy. Several provincials, such as Hadrian and Trajan from Spain and Septimius Severus from North Africa, became emperors in the first and second centuries. By the third century, it was hardly even noteworthy for a provincial to hold the office of emperor.

The decurions and other local elites were granted full Roman citizenship. This was a further critical distinction from all previous empires and a highly effective means of creating a sense of belonging and identity among such far-flung and incredibly diverse peoples. Up until the early third century A.D., as we will see in Chapter Twelve, Roman citizenship maintained its privileged character. It was highly sought after and considered a great prize to those who attained it. Aristides saw this unprecedented phenomenon as critical to the Roman order:

> But there is that which very decidedly deserves as much attention and admiration now as all the rest together. I mean your magnificent citizenship with its grand conception, because there is nothing like it in the records of all mankind. Dividing into two groups all those in your empire – and with this word I have indicated the entire civilized world – you have everywhere appointed to your citizenship, or even to kinship with you, the better part of the world's talent, courage, and leadership, while the rest you recognized as a league under your hegemony. . . . No one worthy of rule or trust remains an alien, but a civil community of the World has been established as a Free Republic under one, the best, ruler and teacher of order; and all come together as into a common civic center, in order to receive each man his due.[8]

Those considered the best were recruited into informal, but essential, service. They could be given citizenship individually or collectively. Whole communities could be recognized formally with privileged status and their magistrates given automatic citizenship. Individuals who performed some noteworthy act for the empire could be granted citizenship. Their identification as Roman citizens assumed some level of internalization of the empire's vision to preserve and better the cosmos. Without such confidence in it, Rome could not have built and maintained the ancient world's largest and longest-lasting empire.

Citizenship and elite co-option also played key roles in Rome's reach outside of its provincial network. Client kings, allied rulers beyond Rome's frontiers, entered Roman politics in similar ways to other elites. The "King, Ally, and Friend" (*Rex sociusque amicus*), as the Romans termed the client king, did not pay taxes but helped protect Rome's frontiers, supplied auxiliary troops, and supplied specialist local knowledge, when needed. The relationship that Romans had with the client kings was generally a harmonious and mutually advantageous one, but it was invariably unequal. As we have seen before (Chapter Eight), the Romans naturally perceived foreign relations in terms of patronage and clientage. Roman relations with foreign peoples, no less than between elite and common within her empire, continued age-old Roman social patterns. By the Principate, most client kings had been granted full Roman citizenship. By the end of the first century A.D., many had even

The Romans often engaged client kings in areas that they initially deemed too expensive or too risky to conquer or control directly. At times of stress or transition within a client kingdom, however, the Romans would often attempt to annex it formally as a province. Ambiguities in dynastic succession, revolts against leaders, and unrest that could potentially disrupt adjoining provinces all served as causes or pretexts for annexing a client kingdom as a province. Annexation worked best, obviously, after time as a client kingdom had partially Romanized or pacified its kingdoms and peoples. The transition was generally peaceful, but not always, as we see later in this chapter.

With the formal and informal mechanisms in place, what role, then, did the *princeps*, the centerpiece of the Principate, assume in provincial administration? Generally, he worked in an advisory capacity and kept information flowing to local and provincial administrations. Communication from the central government, which helped build consensus with provincials, elite or not, flowed through a variety of media: letters of advice, general edicts, statues, and coins picturing victories and proclaiming honorific titles and honors (Fig. 11.1). It would be difficult to overestimate the important role such communication had in shaping the empire and solidifying in the minds of the inhabitants that the emperor was maintaining order and cosmos. The message was clear and widely diffused, touching each inhabitant of the empire.

11.1. Bronze coin of the city of Alexandria, reign of Emperor Hadrian, A.D. 134/135. British Museum/Art Resource, NY.

Aristides summarized imperial letter writing well during the Principate by claiming that the emperor

> Has no need to wear himself out traveling around the whole empire. . . . It
> is very easy for him to stay where he is and manage the entire civilized
> world by letters, which arrive almost as soon as they are written, as if
> they were carried by winged messengers.[9]

Yet the emperors generally were not micromanagers. They were usually keen to advise on local affairs when called on and to stay abreast of potential problems, but they usually let local elites handle the bulk of the empire's administration. If it wasn't broken, as the old saying goes, it did not need fixing.

One famous and detailed set of letters, exchanged in the early second century A.D. between Emperor Trajan and Pliny the Younger, the governor of the province of Bithynia on the Black Sea, gives rare insight into the level of the emperor's engagement at the local level. The letters assume, unsurprisingly, the importance of maintaining the civic amenities of the empire, the well-known external symbols of Romanization. To illustrate with several random but typical examples from the letters: the governor Pliny queried Trajan on reconstructing a run-down public bath, instituting a firefighting force, maintaining an aqueduct, and repairing structural damage in a theater. Trajan's responses to Pliny's questions are terse, but telling:

> If the construction of a new bath will not overtax the resources of Prusa,
> then we can acquiesce in their aim – provided that no assessment is

11.2. Roman bath, Bath, England. Slide by Mark W. Graham.

levied for it, and that it does not force them to curtail basic operations later on.

Your idea that a corps of firemen could be formed at Nicomedia has many precedents in its favor. But we need to keep in mind that your province and particularly the cities in that area have had trouble with just such outfits. Whatever name, for whatever purpose, we give to people who band together, they will turn into political groups in no time at all.

Arrangements should be made to supply water to the town of Nicomedia. I have every confidence that you will set to work with the diligence that is called for. But, good lord, part of that diligence should be to find out whose fault it was that the Nicomedians wasted so much money up till now.

Since you are on the spot, you are in the best position to resolve what should be done about the theater under construction at Nicaea. . . . It is not possible that you have no architects; there are men with experience

11.3. Antonine baths, Carthage. Slide by Mark W. Graham.

and talent in every province. At least you shouldn't imagine that it saves
time to have them sent from Rome, as we usually get them from Greece
ourselves.[10]

Trajan is clearly interested in the affairs of local provincial life (and he may
well have been exceptionally so), but he prefers to let this local governor take
care of his own problems whenever possible. Over the course of the second
century, there was a growing tendency for provincials to lean more and more
on the authority and charity of central imperial power.[11] In the next chapter
we explore some of the ramifications of this in its third-century context. By
any modern standard, central government remained minimalist.

   It is tempting to ask to what extent the inhabitants of the empire outside
of the elite circles embraced this system and internalized it. Being excluded
from official mechanisms of power and usually from citizenship, unfortunately,
also excluded one from historical sources, making such questions difficult to
answer. Local elites probably shared more in common, generally speaking,
with distant elites than with the local masses who shared their language and
other aspects of local culture. Yet the very amenities of empire praised by
Aristides and castigated by Tacitus touched many outside of strictly elite
circles. The poor, at least the urban poor, attended gladiatorial games, went

11.4. Zaghouan aquaduct, Tunisia. Slide by Mark W. Graham.

to the baths, and so on. The values of Roman imperial society were proclaimed to them through edicts, coins, and statues. We will never know exactly how they interpreted and appropriated these images, but most indications show that the poor also internalized Roman ideology and acted on behalf of the empire, if not identifying strongly with it.

As we will see in the next chapter, however, it is certain that people throughout the empire did not forget their local identities, language, burial practices, dress, and other characteristics while under Roman rule (Fig. 11.5). Take, for example, Egyptian mummies from the Principate that show obvious continuity of local mores. There was always tension and mixing, more apparent at certain times and places than others, between local cultures and the homogenizing forces of Romanization. Note the Roman-style paintings on the faces of the same mummies. Tacitus might tell us of average Britons adopting Roman language, education, and dress, so that "those who just lately had been rejecting the Roman tongue now conceived a desire for eloquence. Thus even our style of dress came into favour and the toga was everywhere to be seen."[12] Plenty of other peoples, however, from commoners to elites, clung to their traditional ways, or joined them together with prevalent Roman culture and did not simply jettison their local manners and mores altogether.

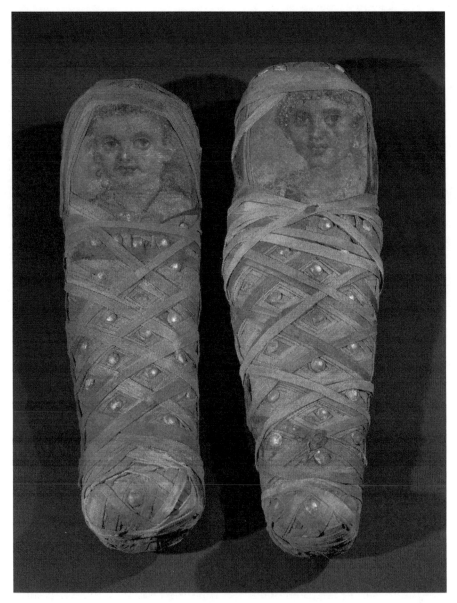

11.5. Funeral portraits of the children of Aline from Hawara, Fayum Oasis, Egypt. Erich Lessing/Art Resource, NY.

THE IMPERIAL CULT AND ROMAN RULE

All inhabitants of the Roman Empire, no matter how diverse they might have been, shared two basic assumptions. First, their safety and prosperity depended ultimately on the favor of the gods. Second, as attested by the fact that their political magistrates were one and the same as their priests, politics and religion were inextricably linked. Although these assumptions were, of course, far older than the Roman Empire, both informed the specific

11.6. Horse with twins mosaic, Carthage. Slide by Mark W. Graham.

and official religious form of the Principate, the Imperial Cult. Starting with
Augustus, the emperor himself was responsible for guaranteeing the safety and
prosperity of the empire as well as serving as its chief religious functionary, if
not a god himself. Augustus officially recognized the Imperial Cult in honor
of Julius Caesar (*Divus Iulius*), deified after his assassination, but it reached
its most characteristic expression in the Cult of *Roma et Augustus* soon after
Augustus' death.

The Imperial Cult rightly has been called "Rome's main export to the
empire,"[13] and it was a major means of both Romanization and imperial
control. It was a perfect complement to mechanisms of provincial control
and elite co-option. The same local elites discussed earlier were its main
functionaries, and the *concilium*, the provincial council, administered it along
with its other functions such as tax collection and census taking. Local elites
readily associated themselves with Roman power by identifying with it. It
was, therefore, a major element of ideological unity throughout the empire.

Its spread and expression throughout the empire, however, were far from
consistent, mirroring the complex central to local (and vice versa) power
relationships in the imperial system itself. In the Hellenistic East, for example,
where ruler cult had a venerable history, provincials seemed to have acted
on their own initiative, even spontaneously, in celebrating the cult of the

emperors, often in terms with which they were long familiar. Local initiative also helped solidify the Imperial Cult and imperial rule in areas of Gaul and Spain. In regions perceived as backward or non-Romanized, however, the cult could be encouraged or even forced to further Romanization, much as the London Missionary Society once explicitly pushed Christianization for the sake of encouraging "civilization" in a certain empire almost two millennia later. Archaeologists have long noted that the earliest inscriptions of the Imperial Cult often appear in "wild and wooly" regions of the Roman Empire.

The Imperial Cult blended Near Eastern, Hellenistic, and Roman traditions. Working within long-standing religious and political patterns of the Age of Ancient Empires, the emperor personally brought cosmos and abundance to the empire:

> What prayers ought cities to make to the power above, save always for the emperor? What greater blessing must one ask from the gods than the emperor's safety? Rains in season, abundance from the sea, unstinting harvests come happily to us because of the emperor's justice. In return, cities, nations, races, and tribes, all of us, garland him, sing of him, write of him."[14]

As with Egyptian *ma'at* and Persian *Arta*, for example, natural abundance flowed from the emperor's justice. The empire he established brought cosmos and order to the very universe itself:

> Before the rule of Zeus, as the poets say, the universe was full of strife, confusion, and disorder . . . but when you assumed the presidency, confusion and strife ceased, and universal order entered as a brilliant light over the private and public affairs of man, laws appeared and altars of gods received man's confidence.[15]

Even taking account of rhetorical flourish, the cosmological continuity with earlier epochs is clear – the preservation of cosmos brought both political power and natural abundance. The gods had brought laws and altars, clearly picturing assumptions about the union of religion and politics throughout this realm.

The people expressed their loyalty to the empire and emperor through elaborate rituals and sacrifices with roots deep in traditional Roman state cult. The proper performance of particular acts guaranteed the safety of the state and the vital *pax deorum*, the peace of the gods, or with the gods. Ritual rather than belief, per se, were at the cult's center – the correct sacrifice or libation at the right time and place, the specific and set formula for the correct holiday or festival, the celebration of the emperor's birthday. The sacrifices were carried out by the priests/magistrates on behalf of the whole community.

Although belief is familiar as a religious category in the modern West, the Romans were less concerned about an individual's personal beliefs and far more interested in getting the ritual and the formula correct. Pliny the Elder (the uncle of Pliny the Younger), a first century Roman writer, describes the importance of ritual to religious expression:

> It is a general belief that without a certain form of prayer it would be useless to immolate a victim, and that, with such an informality, the gods would be consulted to little purpose. And then besides, there are different forms of address to the deities, one form for entreating, another form for averting their ire, and another for commendation. We see too, how that our supreme magistrates use certain formulæ for their prayers: that not a single word may be omitted or pronounced out of its place, it is the duty of one person to precede the dignitary by reading the formula before him from a written ritual, of another, to keep watch upon every word, and of a third to see that silence is not ominously broken, while a musician, in the meantime, is performing on the flute to prevent any other words being heard. Indeed, there are memorable instances recorded in our Annals, of cases where either the sacrifice has been interrupted, and so blemished, by imprecations, or a mistake has been made in the utterance of the prayer.[16]

The acts, not the state of mind, were the key issue. Many, no doubt, did believe that the whole system worked, but the gods were not primarily looking for assent or sincerity.

For living emperors, sacrifices were devoted to his *genius* or guardian spirit; most emperors were officially deified after death. The line between worshiping the *genius* of the living emperor and the living emperor himself was a gray one, however, and we already saw in the previous chapter how Augustus began a tradition of taking on the language and imagery of divinity. His followers in office generally did the same, as will be seen later when the emperor Caligula commanded statues of himself as Zeus be placed in the Temple at Jerusalem. Prayer even directly to the emperor himself was common and perfectly natural, then. Witness, once more, Aristides:

> No one is so proud that he can fail to be moved upon hearing even the mere mention of the Ruler's name, but, rising, he praises and worships him and breathes two prayers in a single breath, one to the gods on the Ruler's behalf, one for his own affairs to the Ruler himself.[17]

RESISTING ROMAN RULE

Challenges to Roman rule during the Principate stand out for two basic reasons. First, they are the proverbial exception that proves the rule, and therefore invite analysis and discussion of the norm. Second, given the nature of literary historical sources from any period, war, revolt, and subversion tend to dominate, for obvious reasons, in a way that peace, tranquillity, and quietude generally do not. However, disruptions of the *Pax Romana* helpfully reveal the limits of Rome's power mechanisms as well as illustrate recalcitrant pockets of localism within and around the empire. Two famous armed revolts broke out in the A.D. 60s that can serve as case studies: revolt in Britain demonstrates that not everyone was eager to be a part of the empire, on Roman terms; the Jewish revolt can show, among other things, how seriously Romans could underestimate or misunderstand the potential of local ideology for resistance. Ideological resistance took more subtle forms than outright revolt as well, as we will see in a famous piece of anti-imperial resistance literature.

In A.D. 43, the emperor Claudius invaded Britain, conquering peoples and territory as well as establishing client kingships in a rare show of expansion under the Principate. One group from southeast Britain, the Iceni, voluntarily allied with Claudius but then broke off the alliance four years later. After their ensuing defeat by the Romans, their leader, Prasutagus, was declared a client king, probably reflecting Roman preference to make client kingdoms out of potentially difficult areas as opposed to immediately annexing them as provinces. Apparently, Prasutagus performed well his task of pacifying his region; when he died in 60, leaving his daughters as coheirs of his kingdom along with the emperor (Nero), Roman officials immediately tried to annex the whole kingdom as a province. The death of a client king was just the type of opportunity that the Romans would seize in attempting to annex a region as a province. The absence of a male heir – and thus the prospect of a client queen – probably did not sit well with the Romans either.

The Iceni resisted annexation, and Roman officials on the spot responded harshly. Prasutagus' widow, Boudicca, was subsequently scourged and the daughters were raped, to name a few of the outrages recorded in Tacitus' *Annals.* Led by Boudicca, the Iceni then revolted and inspired nearby groups and kingships to join them in a bid to "reclaim their freedom" (Fig. 11.7).[18] At first enjoying some success in sacking Roman settlements in Colchester and London, the Iceni killed as many as eighty thousand Romans. With a ready supply of legions to bring in, however, the Romans soon put down the resistance, and Boudicca poisoned herself. Tacitus' own father-in-law,

11.7. Boudicca statue, London. Slide by Mark W. Graham.

Agricola, was sent as governor to subdue the whole province (hence the title of Tacitus' first historical work).

The resistance – if not the famous speech – of Calgacus followed soon afterward. His Caledonian Confederation frustrated Agricola's efforts in the north but was quickly put down as the resisting peoples of Britain were conquered, pacified, and brought – whether they liked it or not – into, or back into, the Roman Empire. Tacitus, ironically, praises his beloved father-in-law's measures even as he continues to denounce the results.

On the other side of the empire, in Judaea, a rather different revolt broke out six years later. A little bit of context will help set the stage for this revolt in light of this chapter's themes. For a little over a century following the Maccabean revolt of 168/67 B.C., the Jews maintained an independent kingdom among the Hellenistic polities and monarchies. In 63 B.C., the Romans, led by Pompey, intervened in a Jewish dispute. As usual, Roman aid meant Roman patronage, and Judaea was declared a client kingdom. From 37 B.C. until 4 B.C., the Jews were ruled by Herod the Great, who had attained his position as client king with the help of Mark Antony. He later solidified his rule by supporting Octavian's winning side at Actium. Herod became a valuable partner with Augustus and Rome in ruling this potentially volatile region. A decade after Herod's death, however, Judaea and several adjoining regions were formally annexed as a Roman province, in A.D. 6.

In A.D. 41, the "Bad Emperor" Caligula ordered statues of himself portrayed as Zeus put in the Jewish Temple, for reasons which still are not entirely clear. A widespread revolt immediately erupted among the Jews; Judaea was then pacified and returned to client-kingdom status. But just three years later, in 44, it was annexed once again as a province by the emperor Claudius. The back and forth highlighted ambiguities in Roman power here. By 66, Jews were in open rebellion against the Romans.

There never really was a unified resistance here, because the Jews were divided strongly along several lines. Various sects and factions – Sadducees, Pharisees, Zealots, Essenes (but, note well, no "Judean People's Front" or "People's Front of Judaea") claimed competing loyalties. There was a marked divide between the Jewish elite and the common people as well, perhaps more so than elsewhere. Generally, the Jewish elite cooperated with the Romans at trying moments. The "people," at large, however, often did not. The Jewish masses were the driving force of revolt against the Romans, and they refused to be persuaded even by their own local leaders. A strong religious ideology nurtured a robust sense of political and cultural independence.

One of the elite Jewish leaders and himself a noteworthy historian, Josephus, initially led the resistance against Rome. After a defeat at Gamla, however, he defected to Roman rule and then set out to persuade the rest of the Jews to break off their revolt. As priest and a Pharisee, and thus himself a serious supporter of Jewish laws and traditions, Josephus passionately pleaded with the Jews to submit to the Romans, using a curious blend of arguments: Yahweh was now on Rome's side and, in fact, dwelling in Rome; the Jews should follow their own ancestors, and thus their own tradition, and submit to Rome; and natural law (*physis*) itself demands that the weaker submit to the stronger, a "might makes right" argument that probably owes something to the Greek historian Thucydides:

> From every side fortune had passed to them, and God, who had handed
> dominion over from nation to nation, round the world, abode in Italy.
> It was an immutable and unchallenged law among beasts and men alike,
> that all must submit to the stronger, and that power belonged to those
> supreme in arms. That was why their ancestors, in soul and body and
> in resources far superior to themselves, had submitted to Rome – which

11.8. Titus coin with Jewish captive. Line Drawing by Andrew Welton.

they could not have borne to do if they had not known that God was on the Romans' side.

His pleas fell on the deaf ears of many of his countrymen, and they continued in open resistance to the Romans. In 70, Titus, the son of the emperor Vespasian, besieged Jerusalem; the city was destroyed, and the temple was burned down, never to be rebuilt.

Josephus quotes one Roman procurator to the effect that "there would be continual revolts while the Sanctuary remained as a rallying-point for Jews all over the world."[20] The Romans seem to have seriously underestimated the power and nature of Jewish ideological resistance, for the destruction of the temple did not end Jewish resistance. A few years later, a group of Jews held out famously at Masada (A.D. 74). Their leader, a certain Eleazar, sounded a note not much different from Calgacus' speech (and perhaps just as crafted by the recorder) – "hitherto we have never submitted to slavery, even when it brought no danger with it: we must not choose slavery now, and with it penalties that will mean the end of everything if we fall alive into the hands of the Romans."[21] He urged his fellow resisters to serve only God and His Law, reflecting the heart of Jewish resistance. The legendary resolve of the 960 Jews at Masada, who committed mass suicide rather than submit to the Romans, amazed and impressed the Romans. Once again, the Romans had clearly underestimated the potential of ideological resistance. More than a half century later, in 132/135, Bar Kokhba, "son of a star," claimed to fulfill an ancient Jewish prophecy and led another major revolt.

The Romans suppressed it with some difficulty. As before in Jewish history, however, lacking a polity, Jewish identity as the "People of the Book" lived on. In fact, once again absent the physical temple as a focus of identity, it might well have become even stronger.

There are many ways of analyzing these revolts – far too many, in fact, to do them justice in this brief survey. Even at a glance, however, the similarities and differences elucidate patterns of resistance. Each of these revolts were provoked by offensive actions by individual Romans and not necessarily by general imperial policy – in Britain, the brutal responses of local Roman officials; in Judaea, the harsh measures of a temperamental emperor and then local Roman officials. Each can also be viewed as revolts in regions on the ambiguous fringes of Roman territory and control. For each, their official status between province and client-kingship had recently been in flux. Traditional freedoms were lost, regained, and lost again, provoking much resentment. It was unusual for a people to go back and forth between provincial and client-kingdom status like this. There were critical differences as well, however. The Jewish resistance had strong religious/ideological basis, whereas the revolt of the Iceni showed little indication of deep-seated ideological resentment against imperial rule per se, as much as understandable response to an inconsistent and harsh local administration.

Resistance to the empire could take on more subtle forms. The biblical book of Revelation (The Apocalypse) contains a coded denunciation of the empire written during the reign of the "Bad Emperor" Domitian (r. 81–96). The entire book, the most famous piece of apocalyptic literature from the ancient world, is, at one level, probably a veiled anti-imperial polemic and an attack on the Imperial Cult. Many Hellenistic Jewish and early Christian writings were apocalyptic – that is, they looked toward the suspension or end of the present cosmos and the establishment of an eternal kingdom. Needless to say, that eternal kingdom was not Rome but another that would overthrow it or replace it. In a general sense, then, Jewish and Christian apocalypse was almost invariably literature of resistance. Although it had an older history going back into the Hellenistic world, the apocalyptic genre flourished anew in both Jewish and Christian circles just after the destruction of the temple.

With such a potentially volatile and dangerous message, apocalyptic literature usually employed esoteric and indirect reference. Toward the end of Revelation, for example, the writer powerfully predicts the destruction of Babylon the Great, "dwelling place of demons, a haunt of every foul bird, a haunt of every foul and hateful beast" from whose power "the merchants of the earth have grown rich." A closer look at the passage reveals that "Babylon"

11.9. Masada. Picture by George Klaeren.

is a coded reference to something else beside the famous Mesopotamian city. The kingdom is doomed, and soon no more will these merchants buy the

> cargo of gold, silver, jewels and pearls, fine linen, purple, silk and scarlet, all kinds of scented wood, all articles of ivory, all articles of costly wood, bronze, iron, and marble, cinnamon, spice, incense, myrrh, frankincense, wine, olive oil, choice flour and wheat, cattle and sheep, horses and chariots, slaves – and human lives.[22]

Marble, wine, olive oil, grain, slaves, and more? – only one polity on earth had ever commanded this basic list of goods, and it was not Babylon. The message was thus a veiled attack on Rome itself. In the next chapter, we explore in more detail the place of Christianity in the empire.

Such passages and others we have seen throughout this chapter raise a basic but critical question: should they be read as references to empire in general, to the Roman Empire itself, or a given emperor in particular? It is worth noting, for example, that Aristides was writing under the "Good Emperor" Antoninus Pius. Some of his panegyric, although certainly not all, can be read as optimism about the reign of that particular emperor, one of the real highlights of an otherwise brilliant second century.

Tacitus' *Agricola* explicitly and often denounces the "Bad Emperor" Domitian. Tacitus opens the work ostensibly praising his immediate age as the dawning of a "most fortunate age" of the emperor Nerva (r. 96–98), which supplanted the previous era when "the voice of the Roman people, the liberty of the senate, and the conscience of mankind" were eradicated by the cruel tyrant, Domitian. His criticism, then, is aimed specifically at that emperor. Other passages of the work show a keen ability to critique the whole Roman imperial system from the perspective of those being subjugated. Recall his harsh invective against Romanization ("the Britons . . . called it 'civilization,' although it was part of their enslavement"). His take on client kingship hits the same note: "It is an ancient and now long-established practice of the Roman People to use even kings as instruments of enslavement."[23] Such passages clearly denounce the empire itself, much as Tacitus does in the *Annals* when he blasts the Principate, starting with one of the best of the "Good Emperors," Augustus himself.

This chapter challenges two major modern assumptions. The first is that politics and religion are distinct spheres of activity. Although the modern Western world arguably functions this way, the ancient world certainly did not, as this study maintains throughout. Imperial control was both political and ideological/religious, down to the very same people who carried out political and religious functions. The imperial project and the Imperial Cult were bound together inseparably. We do not do the ancients justice nor can we ever expect to understand them if we impose our own notions of separation of politics and religion onto them.

The second is that people invariably chafe under empire. The nineteenth and twentieth centuries, perhaps justifiably, have given empire a bad name in our world. No modern polity would own the title. Rome did, however, and did so proudly. It is hard for us to imagine people living happily under an empire. If we (just briefly) leave our modern distaste for empire aside and study the ancients in context, it is clear that many, and probably most, embraced the empire and what it stood for, at least during the Principate. Why and how this happened is one of the longest-running, most heated, and most meaningful debates among historians of the Roman Empire. As this study suggests throughout, there is much at stake in this debate. By its very nature, this text can only introduce the basic terms of a rich discussion.

It might be objected that this explanation takes ideology too seriously while ignoring the very real economic benefits that held the provincials close to Rome. Local elites did, in fact, gain much from their co-option by and identification with Rome. Josephus, the Jewish historian and Roman collaborator, for example, was given an imperial house in Rome, a tract of land in Judaea, and a lifelong pension for his efforts. Like Polybius, the Hellenistic historian of Rome, he became entranced with the Roman system, and enjoyed friendship with some of Rome's best and brightest, including Titus, the son of the emperor Vespasian and then emperor himself. Some historians rightly make much more of the material connection than does this particular chapter. It would be simplistic to begin and end, however, with the claim that Rome basically wooed the elites with material resources while duping them and others with ideology, or the smokescreen of ideology.

One brilliant recent study explores in much detail how Rome at its center built a powerful consensus with its far-flung inhabitants.[24] Many inhabitants of the empire, at all social levels, came to see that Roman rule was natural and justified, and worthy of great praise. These peoples internalized Roman imperial ideology – they came to believe that the empire was the best of all possible worlds, or, as Aristides contends, the best the world had ever seen, and they vigorously defended it. Recall that a media innovation of the Persian

peoples under its suzerainty. The Roman Empire actually accomplished what the Persian claimed through their inscriptions and reliefs – Rome was building on such older precedents, but it is certain that it inspired more confidence than any empire before it.

None of this, again, need imply that Romanization and Roman rule eradicated local cultures through all-encompassing hegemony. Peoples throughout the empire, at all social levels, could make sense of the symbols of imperial control in a variety of ways. They could, and surely did, make imperial control work to their own advantage. To say that they embraced the empire does not imply that they were passive, duped, and ignorant. Exploring this particular dynamic, however, is easier for the third century, as we will see in the next chapter, when the benefits of the empire – ideological, economic, military, and political – were harder to come by than in the heyday of the *Pax Romana*.

Contrary to a popular notion, sources never speak for themselves. Nonetheless, sometimes it is best, even if just for the sake of furthering discussion, to let the ancients have the last word. Petilius Cerialis, a Roman general, had just suppressed a brief revolt in Gaul in A.D. 70. He then turned and addressed the subdued locals, at least according to Tacitus:

> Tyranny and war always existed in Gaul until you yielded to our author-
> ity. And we, although we have been provoked many times, have imposed
> upon you by right of conquest only this one demand: that you pay the

costs of keeping peace here. For peace among different peoples cannot be maintained without troops, and troops cannot be maintained without pay, and pay cannot be found without taxation. In other respects we are equals. You yourselves often command our legions and govern this and other provinces. You are in no respect excluded or shut out. Although you live far from Rome, you enjoy as much as we do the benefits of praise-worthy emperors; on the other hand, the cruel emperors threaten most those closest to them. You must resign yourselves to the extravagance and greed of your masters just as you resign yourselves to barren years or excessive rains or any other natural disaster. As long as there are men, there will be vices. But they are not everlasting, and they are balanced by intervals of better government. . . . But if the Romans are driven out – may the gods forbid! – what situation could exist except wars among all these races? The structure of our Empire has been consolidated by 800 years of good fortune and strict organization, and it cannot be torn apart without destroying those who tear it apart. And you especially will run the greatest risk, for you have gold and natural resources, which are the chief causes of war. Therefore love and cherish peace and the city of Rome which you and I, conquered and conqueror, hold with equal rights. Let these examples of good fortune and bad fortune warn you not to prefer rebellion and ruin to submission and safety.[25]

CHAPTER TWELVE

IMPERIAL CRISIS AND RECOVERY

When another king of Rome will rule, then ruinous Ares with his bastard son will bring the disorderly races against the Romans, against the walls of Rome. And then suddenly there will be famine, plagues, dreadful lightning bolts, horrible wars, and destruction of cities.

— 13th Sibylline Oracle[1]

* Why did the *Pax Romana* come to an end?
* How and why did Christianity become a powerful force within the empire?
* How and why did Romans respond to it?
* How did the Roman Empire recover from crisis and with what results?

IT IS THE NATURE OF A HISTORICAL ERA or epoch that it can be seen only with distance and hindsight. Romans of the first few centuries of the empire never saw themselves as living in a specific era as such. Yet humans like – and need – clearly defined periods to make sense of the past. Often when people look back on an era, whether historians or not, they tend to idealize it. Thus emerge, but only in retrospect, "Good Old Days," "classical periods," and "Golden Ages." Recall, for example, how Hellenistic scholars invented the Classical Age of Athens or how Tacitus (and any number of late republican and early imperial writers) idealized the republic. They waxed nostalgic about its virtues and freedoms, wielded it as a bludgeon against their contemporaries, saw it as the height from which their culture only continued to plummet. Their language comes fraught with value judgments, as talk of rise, decline, and fall always does.

In the same way, many third-century Roman writers looked back wistfully at the first and second centuries and painted their own day in grim and gloomy shades, as does the anonymous author of the 13th Sibylline Oracle that opens this chapter. The Augustan period so despised by historians like Tacitus became, to early-third-century historians like Cassius Dio, a period to admire and to strive to emulate for the order and stability it brought. The first and second centuries, with some exceptions, became a veritable classical age, in retrospect.

Even nostalgic writers, however, sometimes get it right. The Roman Empire faced such serious and unprecedented problems and disasters in the third century that modern historians simply encapsulate the century with unambiguous terms such as "chaos," "anarchy," "crisis," and "disaster." By the end of the third century and the beginning of the fourth, however, two nostalgic emperors managed to restore cosmos and the empire. They did not, despite their efforts and intentions, bring back the *Pax Romana* any more than Augustus restored the republic. They effectively replaced the Principate with a new form of empire and thus a new imperial era, which historians today call the Dominate. This crisis and recovery make up the main story line of this chapter.

Another story line begins entirely separately from this central narrative but slowly intertwines itself around it, eventually becoming inextricable. This story, the rise of Christianity, adds multiple dimensions to this new form of empire that, in the long run, was more influential and arguably more significant than the Principate itself.

THE "THIRD-CENTURY CRISIS"

During the reign of Marcus Aurelius (r. 161–180), the last of the "Five Good Emperors" whose reigns spanned the second century, problems were already emerging. Military threats were commanding more attention and resources than they had since the late republic. Germanic peoples threatened provinces along the Danube, keeping the emperor personally occupied there for a significant part of his reign. Two groups, the Marcomanni and Quadi, even besieged Aquileia, one of the empire's larger cities, which was affectionately known as *Roma Secunda* ("Second Rome").

On the eastern frontier, Rome faced renewed threats from Persia, still ruled by the long-lived Parthian Arsacid dynasty. In quick succession in the 160s, the Parthians seized the Roman client kingdom of Armenia, defeated the Roman governor of Cappadocia and invaded the province of Syria.

In addition, plague ravaged the empire during most of the years of Marcus Aurelius' reign, killing as much as one-third of the empire's population, and eventually perhaps even the emperor himself. Signs of inflation and debasement of currency presaged cataclysmic economic problems that would hit in force in just a few decades.

The immediate aftermath of his reign saw more problems. Marcus Aurelius' successor and son, Commodus (r. 180–192), was the worst emperor in over a century. Civil wars broke out right after Commodus' assassination. The following year, a provincial governor actually purchased the office with a highest bid and held it for a few months before he also was assassinated. The *Pax Romana* was over.

The Principate did not die yet, however. An able emperor, Septimius Severus (r. 193–211), began the brief Severan dynasty and addressed the political and military problems. Of North African (Punic) descent, Severus was a highly regarded military leader and governor of the province of Pannonia Superior on the Danube when he was proclaimed emperor.

A few of his military reforms as emperor particularly stand out: he created several new legions along the Danube for defense against invasion, raised the pay of the army (for the first time in more than one hundred years), and

being shaped more and more by the army by this time, so the changes were mutually beneficial to him. His reputed final words to his sons speak volumes: "do not disagree, enrich the soldiers, ignore everyone else."[2]

Severus' son and successor, Caracalla, promulgated an edict that signaled several important turning points for the empire. Issued in 212, it extended citizenship to virtually all free inhabitants of the empire:

> I give thanks to the immortal gods, because [when that conspiracy occurred] they preserved me, thus I think that I should be able [magnificently and piously] to make a suitable response to their majesty, [if] I were able to lead [all who are presently my people] and others who should join my people [to the sanctuaries] of the gods. I give to all of those [who are under my rule throughout] the whole world, Roman citizenship. . . . The [whole population] ought [. . .] already to have been included in the victory. [. . .] My edict will expand the majesty of the Roman [people].[3]

There was much more to this edict than goodwill – it was, in fact, a clear IEMP (ideology, economics, military, and politics) gesture. Note that he starts with ideology; pleasing the gods, by expanding the citizen base of the Imperial Cult, would help maintain *pax deorum*, the peace with the gods. The move was economic as well – only citizens had to pay a special inheritance tax, and thus the edict immediately increased imperial revenue, desperately needed to pay the military.

Several important political changes flowed from granting citizenship en masse. All new citizens literally added the emperor's name to their own, as was traditional for a grantor of Roman citizenship. Caracalla's move, then, linked all free persons of the empire more directly to himself, binding together more closely than ever before the fate of the empire and the emperor himself, for better or for worse. For most of the third-century successors of Caracalla, it would be for the worse.

The move had several other important social ramifications. Obviously, it devalued citizenship, an element of elite loyalty. However, Romans, always status conscious, simply reconfigured social status, and the traditional divisions of *honestiores* (upper class) and *humiliores* (lower class) simply became the new primary distinction. The edict also recognized and formalized Italy's relative decline in status within the empire. Of all regions of the empire, Italy had always had the highest concentration of citizens, because of special mass citizenship grants during the republic. Now, provincials were necessarily on par with Italians. The center was not holding.

The Severan dynasty ended with an assassination in 235, and the most tumultuous period began. Here IEMP analysis can be of great use, for it can reveal imperial weakness as well as strength. This period of crisis vividly demonstrates how interrelated and integrated the sources of social power actually were, or at least needed to be, to maintain strong imperial power. They can be distinguished for the sake of illustration but never truly separated.

Modern historians revealingly call the third-century emperors the "soldier emperors" or the "barracks emperors." Most rose and fell as military strongmen or as their armies overthrew one another. It would be difficult to illustrate the political problems at the center more clearly than with a chart of their reigns, dates, and causes of death (Fig. 12.1). Military power was now paramount in politics, and the delicate IEMP balance of the Principate was ending. Between 235 and 284, there were twenty officially recognized emperors – an average reign of about two and a half years per emperor.

Meanwhile, trends toward localism challenged the political unity of empire, largely in response to the political problems at the center. In two noteworthy cases, local empires were carved out of Roman territory, one in the West and the other in the East. Both raise serious questions about the actual depth of Romanization throughout the empire. In the West, during the 260s, Postumus, a military commander under the emperor Gallienus (r. 253–268), established himself as emperor over a breakaway empire in Gaul, Britain, and Spain. Postumus ruled over an *imperium Galliarum*, a Gallic empire,

Roman Emperors from 180-284 A.D.

Reign	Emperor	Reason for Death
180-192	Commodus	Strangled by Courtiers
193	Pertinax	Murdered by Guards
193	Didius Julianus	Murdered by Soldiers
193-194	Pescennius Niger	Killed in Battle
193-197	Clodius Albinus	Killed in Battle
193-211	Septimius Severus	Died Naturally
211-217	Caracalla	Murdered by Soldier
211	Geta	Murdered by Caracalla
217-218	Macrinus	Murdered by Army
218	Diadumenianus	Murdered by Army
218-222	Elagabalus	Murdered by Guards
222-235	Severus Alexander	Murdered by Army
235-238	Maximinus Thrax	Murdered by Army
238	Gordian I	Committed Suicide
238	Gordian II	Killed in Battle
238	Pupienus	Murdered by Guards
238	Balbinus	Murdered by Guards
238-244	Gordian III	Killed in Battle
244-249	Philip Arabus	Killed in Battle
249-251	Decius	Killed in Battle
251-253	Trebonianus Gallus	Murdered by Army
253	Aemilianus	Murdered by Army
253-260	Valerian	Died in Persian Captivity
253-268	Gallienus	Murdered by Army
268-270	Claudius II	Died of Plague
275-276	Tacitus	Murdered by Army
276	Florianus	Murdered by Army
276-282	Probus	Murdered by Army
282-283	Carus	Struck by Lightning (or arson?)
283-284	Numerian	Murdered by Prefect (?)
283-285	Carinus	Murdered During Civil War

12.1. Roman emperors from A.D. 180 to 284. Compiled by Elizabeth Mubarek.

which lasted for about a decade and a half before the Romans ended it. Constantly at war with the Roman Empire, he was supported by the local elites. He set up a local Gallic Senate, and claimed all the major imperial titles and offices: tribune, consul, *pontifex maximus*, as did his successor emperors in his breakaway empire. His power base remained in Gaul, and neither he nor his few successors tried to move into Italy. His administration and army were made up almost entirely of peoples of Gallic descent, and he even recruited Gallic legions from beyond the northern frontier.

Just a few years later, another short-lived empire began expanding within Rome's eastern periphery. Palmyra, Syria, held a special status as one of a group of free cities (*civitates liberae*) — cities within Roman frontiers that had local autonomy and were not subject to the provincial governor and taxes. Material culture suggests that Palmyra's elites identified closely with Rome during the first two centuries of the empire; they built Roman buildings, dressed, and were buried as traditional Romans. Third-century local elites, however, began sporting decidedly non-Roman dress, as seen on some sarcophagi, suggesting

12.2. Gravestone with funerary banquet, Palmyra, second or third century A.D. The Metropolitan Museum of Art/Art Resource, NY; Purchase, 1902.

a growing sense of cultural independence from Roman cultural influence (Fig. 12.2).

As an established trade and communication center near the frontier, Palmyra played a critical defensive role. Its importance grew after 226, when the Parthian Arsacids were overthrown by a new and vibrantly expansive Persian dynasty, the Sasanids, which we explore in more detail in the next two chapters. The Romans bestowed several honorific titles on one of Palmyra's leaders, Septimius Odaenathus, the most important of which was *corrector totius orientis* (free leader of all the East). The title recognized him as the key defender of the entire eastern frontier, yet still independent as the leader of a free city.

After his death, his wife, Zenobia, ruled with Roman favor as a defender against Sasanid expansion (Fig. 12.3). She raised some initial suspicion, however, when she passed her husband's title on to her son. The Romans conferred such titles on individuals, and they were not hereditary. Some have inferred that she was simply carrying on local Palmyrene traditions, which kept such titles in the royal family. The Romans tolerated Palmyrene expressions of independence, however, as long as they did not thwart Roman agendas. Unlike with the Gallic Empire, which was viewed as an enemy power from

12.3. Queen Zenobia with an attendant. Relief from Palmyra, third century A.D. Bridgeman-Giraudon/Art Resource, NY.

the start, the Romans were more likely to negotiate and compromise with Palmyra.

Compromise proved impossible, however, when Zenobia, self-proclaimed "Queen of the East," began expanding her Palmyrene realm into Egypt and Asia Minor. Palmyrene elites threw in their support, again raising the question of how deep Romanization actually was. Zenobia marshaled an interesting blend of Roman and non-Roman titles and imagery in her bid at empire. She assumed the title "Augusta" and gave her son the title "Augustus," suggesting real imperial aspirations in Roman terms. Connecting herself directly to the pre-Roman imperial past, she stylized herself as Cleopatra and used Ptolemaic imagery to inspire specifically local loyalty as she claimed areas once part of the Ptolemaic kingdom. After resisting the Palmyrene Empire for five years (267–272), Roman armies ended it. Zenobia's life was spared, however, probably because Romans were keen to appease local elites who had sided with her.

Military threats plagued the frontiers throughout the third century. In one of the most ignominious moments, the Roman emperor Valerian (r. 253–260) was captured by the Sasanids, and, quite literally, became the Sasanid emperor Sapor's footstool until he died in captivity (Fig. 12.4). His flayed skin was then dyed red and hung in a temple. The Gallic and Palmyrene empires were, in fact, both responses to this political disaster at the top. Germanic peoples attacked Gaul and northern Italy as well, moving toward the city of Rome. In the next chapter, we trace the long-term effects of these movements.

Of all the challenges facing the empire, the economic problems probably had the deepest roots. Because military expansion had slowed down with the Principate, the stream of war booty into Rome's coffers had stopped rather suddenly. The occasional Principate-era conquest such as Britain yielded little in comparison to the earlier conquests of the Hellenistic kingdoms. The standing army, always Rome's largest expense, continually ate away at the imperial treasury. If this were true in peacetime, how much more now in times of instability and war?

In a vicious cycle, debasement of currency and rampant inflation flowed from, as well as exacerbated, these and other problems. The silver coinage, the primary means through which the central government met its expenses and paid the army, was the hardest hit. Most inconveniently, the silver mines of Spain, under imperial control, were being exhausted right about this time. Debasement of the silver coinage began as early as the reign of Marcus Aurelius, when the silver content of the *denarius*, the standard silver piece, dropped to around 75 percent, down from 90 percent in the emperor Trajan's day. By the end of Septimius Severus' reign, it was at only 58 percent, and with Caracalla it went down to 50 percent.[4] Eventually, the *denarius* became a bronze coin merely washed in silver. Caracalla attempted to solve the financial problems by introducing a new coin denomination, the *antoninianus*, which was declared double the value of the *denarius*, but only 1.5 times the weight. Its silver content simply decreased proportionately to that of the *denarius*. The results are easy enough to imagine.

Rampant inflation was plaguing the economy at the same time. The purchasing power of 400 *denarii* in the second century was equivalent to that of 75,000 *denarii* by the late third century.[5] Scholars debate to what extent the currency debasement and the inflation were directly related, but it is certain that they were both ongoing and intimately connected to the web of problems in the empire.

Financial problems at the top predictably played out at the local level as well. Maintaining the bath buildings, theaters, amphitheaters, aqueducts, the grain supply, and other accoutrements of the empire was expensive. In

12.4. Shapur receiving the surrender of Valerian at Naqsh-I-Rustem. Line drawing by Andrew Welton.

the previous centuries, local elites often footed part of the bill as a form of euergetism or benefaction, but there was always the expectation that the central administration would provide funds and support in time of need. Over the course of the second century, as seen in Chapter Eleven, the reliance on the central government gradually increased. Two trends converged in the third century – central resources were drying up, and the local administrations were expecting and demanding more from the central government. With more military action, there was also more movement of troops. Local cities had to pay the cost of armies moving through them, which tended to devastate local economies as well.

The local councilors, as will be recalled from Chapter Eleven, collected taxes for the empire. They also were personally responsible for making up any deficits. With the financial problems often making it difficult or impossible to raise taxes, many councilors and decurions simply abandoned their largely volunteer posts and moved to rural villas in the countryside. The shift to the countryside marked a structural and demographic trend that continued into subsequent centuries. The reign of the city as the exclusive repository of elite culture was thus on the wane in many (but not all) regions.

It is hardly surprising that these political, military, and economic challenges seriously strained imperial ideology. Although the changes here are difficult to trace closely because of a general decline in the number of inscriptions in general, the Imperial Cult lost momentum as a unifying element in the empire. With the quick turnover rate of emperors, it grew increasingly difficult to inspire and maintain worship of the emperor at either local initiative or central suggestion. Rampant civil war and frequent invasions clearly showed that the *pax deorum* was insecure, if not lost altogether.

Emperors sought to regain divine favor in a variety of ways. Some attempted to experiment with the imperial religion. The emperor Marcus Aurelius Antoninus, a.k.a. Elagabalus (r. 218–222), a priest of the sun god also named Elagabalus, declared his deity the supreme god of the empire, even above Jupiter. Although Elagabalus was an extremely unpopular emperor, his move reveals a structural shift in ideology or *mentalité* under way within the Roman world at this time. More leaders were exalting one high god over all others, a stance technically known as henotheism. A "One God, One Emperor" model was gradually arising. The emperor Aurelian presented the god Elagabalus as Sol Invictus, the Unconquered Sun, and adorned his temple with his images.

The emperor Decius (r. 249–251) attempted to buttress the imperial cult in a more traditionalist way. As we have seen before, however, staunch traditionalists often end up proposing radical and unprecedented measures to forcibly restore a real or imagined past. Decius began his reign just a year after Rome officially celebrated its first millennium (753 B.C.–A.D. 247). Such anniversary celebrations often encourage nostalgia for the past or loathing of the current moment. The millennial celebrations coincided precisely with a series of military setbacks that further suggested that the gods were upset with Rome. Decius attempted to stabilize the empire by demanding that everyone sacrifice to the gods through the Imperial Cult. In 249, he issued an edict declaring that everyone must obtain a *libellus*, a certificate proving that he or she had sacrificed to the gods on behalf of the empire and emperor. One example from Egypt survives on papyrus:

> *First band*: To the commission chosen to superintend the sacrifices at the village of Alexander's Isle. From Aurelius Diogenes, son of Satabous, of the village of Alexander's Isle, aged 72 years, with a scar on the right eyebrow. I have always sacrificed to the gods, and now in your presence in accordance with the edict I have made sacrifice and poured a libation and partaken of the sacred victims. I request you to certify this below. Farewell. I, Aurelius Diogenes, have presented this petition
>
> *Second band*: I, Aurelius Syrus, saw you and your son sacrificing.[6]

For most of the inhabitants of the empire, this was probably a source of some comfort, and at worst a minor inconvenience, but it was undoubtedly another innovation carried out in the name of tradition. Although sacrifice was standard for priests of the Imperial Cult (indeed, the *pax deorum* depended on it), never before had the people at large been required to sacrifice and prove it. There was one growing and increasingly influential group, however, that had a serious problem obeying this edict. To their story we now turn.

THE RISE OF CHRISTIANITY

Jesus of Nazareth was born in the client kingdom of Judaea, on the eastern edge of the empire sometime during the final three years of the reign of Client King Herod the Great (37–4 B.C.). He was about ten years old when Judaea was formally annexed as a province. At around the age of thirty, he emerged as a preacher and miracle worker, wandering primarily throughout rural regions of Judaea and Galilee, making the astounding claim that the long-awaited Kingdom of God had been inaugurated by his coming. His apocalyptic preaching, which did not look kindly on the current order and did not treat favorably some provincial Jewish elites, was a potential risk to these people who gener-

status quo, coupled with Jesus' remarkable claims to have a special relationship with God, eventually got him denounced to the Roman authorities by the Jewish provincial elites. The governor, Pontius Pilate, ordered his crucifixion during the reign of the emperor Tiberius (A.D. 14–37).

After his death, a small but passionate group of his followers, believing he had risen from the dead, continued his ministry far beyond Jesus' earlier rural Galilean ministry. After spending several years in Jerusalem, the followers of Jesus expanded the movement into towns throughout Asia Minor and Macedonia. Initially, a version of Judaism (among many), the movement expanded theologically as well, because it welcomed gentiles without forcing them to adhere to the Law of Moses and the rite of circumcision. In Antioch, Syria, around A.D. 45, outsiders called the group "Christians,"[7] and the moniker stuck. A member of the Jewish elite, Paul, converted to Christianity and became its leading missionary, traveling to cities in Asia Minor, Greece, and eventually to Rome itself. Paul helped expand the movement by dispensing with the requirement to follow Jewish law, enabling the movement to expand dramatically its appeal among non-Jews. By the reign of the emperor Nero (r. 54–68), the movement was visible enough in the city of Rome itself to attract the emperor's attention.

Christianity emerged similarly to what historians call "popular religions," religious groups with broad and wide appeal. The Imperial Cult, of course, did not dismantle or even discourage other religions, and these were left to flourish throughout the empire. In fact, the empire gave them a significantly broader and more diverse audience. Popular religions, unlike the state religion, focused on deities and heroes who were not part of the official Roman pantheon. They emphasized the individual more so than the preservation of the state and the *pax deorum* per se. In a way that was irrelevant to the state cult, they often spoke in terms of individual and personal salvation and a blessed life after death. A famous description of the cult of Isis, one major popular religion, presents a Roman about to be initiated. Note the clear emphasis on the individual himself:

> And now the promised beneficence of the ever-present goddess [Isis] drew near, and there appeared the priest who held in his hands *my fate and my salvation* [emphasis ours]. Equipped exactly as she had ordained and promised, he carried in his right hand a sistrum [silver rattle] for the goddess and for me a garland – rather a crown, as befitted the victory vouchsafed me by the great goddess's Providence.[8]

The popular religions reflected the political and cultural milieu both of the Hellenistic world and the Roman Empire. Isis worshipers, for example, devoted themselves to native Egyptian deities Isis and Osiris; Mithras worshipers to a Phrygian (western Anatolian) god associated with sun worship; Cybele devotees to another Anatolian set of deities, Bacchic cult to the Greek god of wine, and so forth (Fig. 12.5). All of these had devotees and cult sites throughout the empire, far from their original homes. Cult sites to Mithras, for example, may be found from London to Rome to the eastern frontier.

The Romans responded to Christianity in basically the same way they responded to any religious cult. As long as the group did not upset the civic order, it was more or less ignored. The Romans, as will be recalled from Chapter Eleven, were not that interested in what people believed, and so it was actions that caught the attention of authorities, and only when they seemed to threaten order. Local provincial leaders generally handled any problems on an ad hoc basis. Suppression of religious groups was rather rare and tended to be fairly local and short-lived when it happened at all.

Contrary to some common notions, there was no general, empire-wide persecution of Christians before the middle of the third century. Ancient sources allow a few glimpses of early local persecutions. Tacitus records the first imperial persecution, in the city of Rome, in 64. He puts most of the blame for it on the emperor Nero, who probably used the Christians as a scapegoat to deflect charges that he had started a destructive fire in Rome. This persecution did not reflect general policy and is best seen as idiosyncratic to Nero. Almost a half century later, in his famous interchange with the emperor Trajan (r.

12.5. Reclining Attis from Campus Magna Mater, Ostia; Popular Religion deity. Slide by Mark W. Graham.

98–117), the governor Pliny asked the emperor for a policy to deal with Christianity, which was "spreading not only to the cities, but also to the villages and even to the farms" of his province. Trajan replied:

> It is not possible to establish a general law which will provide a fixed standard. However, these people are not to be searched out. If they should be brought before you and proved guilty, they must be punished, with this proviso, however, that anyone who denies that he is a Christian and proves this by his action, that is, by worshipping our gods, even if he has been suspected in the past, should obtain pardon because of his repentance. But pamphlets published anonymously should have no place in a criminal proceeding, for this is a very bad precedent and not in keeping with the spirit of our age.[9]

This passage has been and will continue to be much interpreted and debated in its particulars. The absence of a general Roman policy is, however, clear enough.

Christianity did, though, pose some fundamental challenges to Roman social order, which can help explain the persecutions when they did come. In its earlier years, Christianity stood opposed to the Roman social hierarchies and values with such self-abasing teachings as "let the greatest among you be as your servant." The Roman Empire exalted elite values, which were honored and shared throughout the empire, both by the elites who espoused them and the commoners who took them for granted. Christianity was at odds with these values and also in giving uncharacteristic privileged status to women, as church functionaries and martyrs.

The story of Perpetua, a famous North African martyr of the early third century, illustrates how Christianity could threaten the Roman social fabric (Fig. 12.6). Arrested and imprisoned, she refused to renounce her faith. In her remarkable prison diary, she describes an interchange with her father who had come to visit her:

> While we were still under arrest my father out of love for me was trying to persuade me and shake my resolution. "Father," I said, "do you see this vase here, for example, or waterpot or whatever?"
>
> "Yes, I do," said he.
>
> And I told him: "Could it be called by any other name than what it is?"
>
> And he said: "No."
>
> "Well, so too I cannot be called anything other than what I am, a Christian."
>
> At this my father was so angered by the word "Christian" that he moved towards me as though he would pluck my eyes out.[10]

Perpetua was defying her father, a direct challenge to the Roman value of *patria potestas*, the power the Roman father had over his children, even married ones like Perpetua. Christianity thus challenged Roman social order. In the end, Perpetua gladly embraced martyrdom. Such Christian exaltation of martyrdom likewise upended the Roman system of glory and shame. Christians found glory and honor in the arena of amphitheaters where traditional Romans could see only shame and dishonor. Christians could seem inherently antisocial.

Christian self-identification vis-à-vis the empire varied widely. We have already considered Christian apocalyptic writing, such as the book of Revelation, which anticipated the overthrow of the empire and establishment of a better world. Some Christian writers continued to emphasize the distinction between Christians and the Roman Empire. Tertullian, a late-second- and early-third-century church writer from North Africa, summarized succinctly his attitude toward the Roman state:

> As those in whom all ardor in the pursuit of honor and glory is dead, we have no pressing inducement to take part in your public meetings; nor

12.6. Saint Perpetua and Saint Felicitas. Alinari/Art Resource, NY.

is there aught more entirely foreign to us than affairs of the state. We acknowledge one all-embracing commonwealth – the world.[11]

Elsewhere he prodded his fellow Christians in a similar vein:

From so much as a dwelling in that Babylon of John's revelation we are called away. . . . You are a foreigner in this world, a citizen of Jerusalem, the city above. Our citizenship, the apostle says, is in heaven.[12]

Such sentiments were necessarily offensive to the Romans who had sacrificed much to bring and maintain cosmos and stability.

Others Christian voices sounded a rather different note. A bishop of Sardis named Melito argued in a letter addressed to Marcus Aurelius that Christianity was not exclusive of empire but had long been a great benefit to it:

Our philosophy first grew up among the barbarians, but its full flower came among your nation in the great reign of your ancestor Augustus, and became an omen of good to your empire, for from that time the power of the Romans became great and splendid. You are now his happy successor, and shall be so along with your son, if you protect the philosophy which grew up with the empire and began with Augustus. Your ancestors nourished it together with other cults, and the greatest proof that our doctrine flourished for good along with the empire in its noble beginning, is the fact that it met no evil in the reign of Augustus, but on the contrary everything splendid and glorious according to the wishes of all men.[13]

The empire would actually continue to prosper if it supported Christianity – a far cry from the empire as Whore of Babylon.

The Christian stance toward the Imperial Cult necessarily was more unanimous. Whereas an adherent of Isis or Mithras could freely give worship in the Imperial Cult, a Christian could not. There was potential, especially at times of stress, for Christians to be singled out from among other popular religions as dishonoring to the Cult of *Roma et Augustus* and thus disruptors of *pax deorum*. Christians were accused of atheism, an odd-sounding charge to modern ears, but perfectly understandable in its context. They denied not only the power but also the existence of all known Roman deities. No other popular religion did this.

When Decius demanded that all inhabitants of the empire sacrifice in the Imperial Cult and prove it, Christians stood out, everywhere. At the same time, the third century was one of the greatest growth periods in Christian history, and Christianity was now a visible and rapidly growing movement. Estimates vary widely and evidence is difficult to come by, but over the course of the third century, the Christian population likely went from under 1 percent of the population to perhaps as high as 10 percent. The coincidence of a problematic century and a religion that denied gods that seemed to rise almost out of nowhere resulted in the first empire-wide persecution of Christians. Surely the Christians had disrupted the *pax deorum*.

The Decian persecution was harsh, but actually short-lived, and within a few years of its outbreak, a subsequent emperor, Gallienus (r. 260–268), issued an edict of toleration. Christians could worship publicly again. Incidentally, the oldest church building known was built just before the Decian persecution and apparently was active up until the reign of Gallienus, when it was buried during a Sasanid siege of Dura Europos, Syria, in 256/257, a fortunate preservation for twentieth-century archaeologists.

Christian church construction expanded rapidly after the Decian persecution, and sources speak of other impressive church buildings from the latter half of the third century, showing a religion with significant social and economic power; this was far from a hidden movement. Christianity was growing in numbers, organization, and confidence at the same time that the Roman Empire was struggling.

Church hierarchy and organization were in a continuous process of development, but by the third century, the churches had a firm and integrated structure throughout the empire. They also boasted an impressive communication network; many of the leaders' letters still survive. One bishop, Cyprian, later executed in the persecution initiated by Decius, claimed to get news from Rome's northern frontier via church channels even before his provincial governor.[14] This was a testimony both to the coherence of the church and the general breakdown of imperial networks. The church was enviably organized, coherent, and unified; it could not possibly avoid the gaze of attentive emperors.

THE DOMINATE: COSMOS RESTORED

In 284, a soldier from the Balkans rose to the emperorship in what promised

survived, however, and helped put the empire on the track it would take for the next several centuries in the West as well as the next millennium in the East.

Diocletian joins a list of radical Roman revolutionaries who were, to their own minds, staunchly conservative traditionalists – Tiberius and Gaius Gracchus, Julius Caesar, Augustus, and others. With all his measures, he was aiming to restore the Roman Empire to its former glory. Yet drastic times called for drastic – and unprecedented – measures to bring back the elusive Good Old Days. Diocletian, like Augustus, utilized the sources of social power to save the Roman Empire by transforming it (or should that be – to transform the Roman Empire by saving it?).

In the political ideology of the Principate, the emperor, as *princeps*, was the first among equals, one of the people. Augustus had walked the streets of Rome freely and mingled among the people. The third century had demonstrated consistently, however, that being visible and accessible also meant being within easy reach of the assassin's blade. In an attempt to restore the safety and dignity to his office, Diocletian assumed a new aura and with it a new title: *Dominus Noster*, Our Master. This title bespoke a fundamental distance between himself and the people. He was not, then, a first citizen, but a lord who dominated the people from a (safe) distance. One approached the *Dominus* through several layers of bureaucrats and bodyguards and, once in his presence, with *proskynesis*, prostrating oneself before him. As *princeps* was

12.7. The Tetrarchs. Alinari/Art Resource, NY.

to Principate, so *dominus* was to Dominate, the name historians give this new era of the Roman Empire.

To solve the problems of a fragmenting empire, Diocletian instituted the Tetrarchy, a short-lived but very significant political configuration that helped stabilize the empire politically (Fig. 12.7). There would be two emperors, one in the West and one in the East. Each emperor had the title Augustus, and under each Augustus was a junior colleague know as a Caesar. These four figures together would rule the empire, hence Tetrarchy, "rule of four." If an Augustus died or was assassinated, the transition to a Caesar as the next Augustus would be smooth. The Tetrarchy responded directly to the political problems at the top. Diocletian also recognized additional new capitals for the empire, one at Nicomedia in the East and one at Trier in the West, conveniently located near problematic regions needing oversight and surveillance.

The net effect of Diocletian's political reforms was firm centralization and stabilization. The picture of the empire was now less about far-flung loyal elites voluntarily keeping their empire running and more about heavy-handed rulers and compliant subjects. To keep an eye on local affairs, Diocletian increased

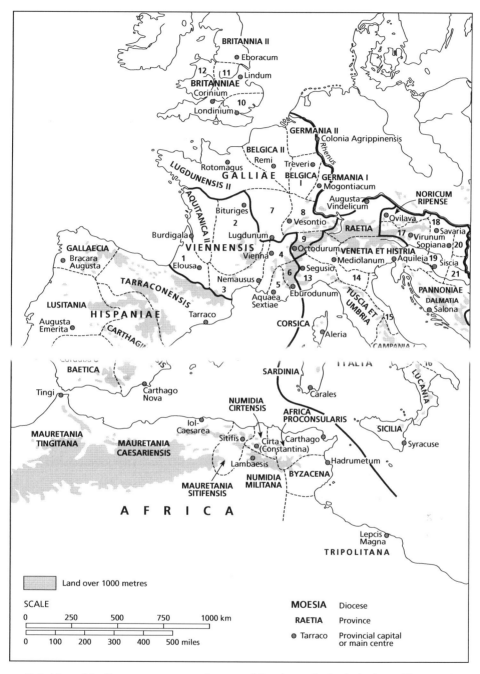

12.8. Map of the Roman provinces at the time of Diocletian. In *Cambridge Ancient History*, vol. 12, 2nd ed., pp. 210–11.

the number of provinces by dividing the existing 48 into 104; each governor now had a smaller area to maintain. He then grouped the provinces together into 12 supraprovincial units known as dioceses (Fig. 12.8). Each diocese was ruled by a vicar who looked over the governors within his diocese, reporting directly to the emperor. Political and provincial organization and bureaucracy

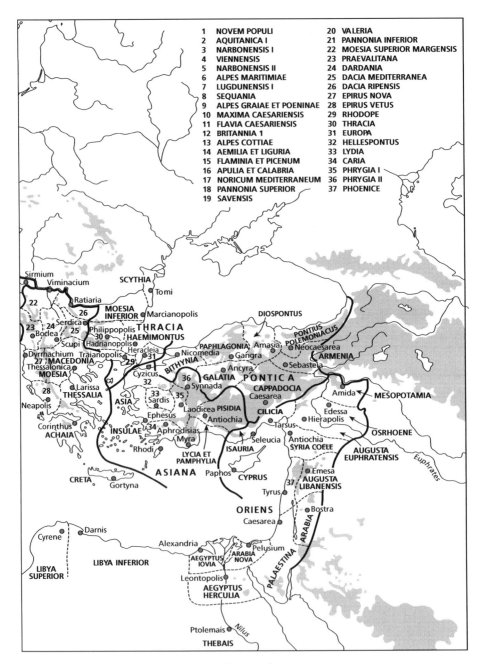

1	NOVEM POPULI	20	VALERIA
2	AQUITANICA I	21	PANNONIA INFERIOR
3	NARBONENSIS I	22	MOESIA SUPERIOR MARGENSIS
4	VIENNENSIS	23	PRAEVALITANA
5	NARBONENSIS II	24	DARDANIA
6	ALPES MARITIMIAE	25	DACIA MEDITERRANEA
7	LUGDUNENSIS I	26	DACIA RIPENSIS
8	SEQUANIA	27	EPIRUS NOVA
9	ALPES GRAIAE ET POENINAE	28	EPIRUS VETUS
10	MAXIMA CAESARIENSIS	29	RHODOPE
11	FLAVIA CAESARIENSIS	30	THRACIA
12	BRITANNIA 1	31	EUROPA
13	ALPES COTTIAE	32	HELLESPONTUS
14	AEMILIA ET LIGURIA	33	LYDIA
15	FLAMINIA ET PICENUM	34	CARIA
16	APULIA ET CALABRIA	35	PHRYGIA I
17	NORICUM MEDITERRANEUM	36	PHRYGIA II
18	PANNONIA SUPERIOR	37	PHOENICE
19	SAVENSIS		

12.8 (*continued*)

were now more complex and elaborate than ever before. The emperor was at once more distant and more involved.

A military strongman, Diocletian recognized as much as anyone some growing problems with the traditional military organization. Threats on the frontiers had proved too much for the stationary frontier army. His greatest military innovation was to recognize a twofold division of the army: a traditional frontier force (*limitanei*) and a new mobile force (*comitatenses*) that could

12.9. Diocletian's Triumphal Arch at Sbeitla, Tunisia. Slide by Mark W. Graham.

move quickly to meet interior threats or to supplement the *limitanei* at points of invasion. His successors would formalize the system further, but his reforms served as the basis for the late Roman army.

Diocletian was somewhat less adept at solving economic problems. Simply pinning rising prices on "persons of unlimited and frenzied avarice," he passed one of the most famous – and least effectual – economic decrees of the ancient world. The Maximum Price Edict of 301 put a price cap for the whole empire on approximately a thousand items, services, and wages. Although it proposed memorably harsh penalties (i.e., capital punishment for charging above the maximum price for grain), the edict was forgotten within a few years. Diocletian also experimented with currency reform to solve the debasement problems. Efforts to stabilize the silver currency did not register, in part because a stable ratio of the "silver" coins to the *aureus*, a gold coin, was not worked out.

In an attempt to bolster the ideological base of the empire, Diocletian championed the Imperial Cult with a vengeance. Once more, his stilted conservatism shows through:

> The immortal Gods in their Providence have so designed things that
> good and true principles have been established by the wisdom and

deliberations of eminent, wise, and upright men. It is wrong to oppose
these principles, or desert the ancient religion for some new one, for
it is the height of criminality to try and revise doctrines that were
settled once and for all by the ancients, and whose position is fixed and
acknowledged.[15]

Rome had experienced much religious change and transition in its long history, but Diocletian the traditionalist imagined only a single standard, and he
was attempting to set it firmly in stone. Although the above edict, from 301,
is directly addressing the Manichees, a cult from Persia, it reveals Diocletian's
general approach to which he would remain consistent. He was also certain
that Rome's problems showed a clear breach of *pax deorum*; there was only one
solution.

There is no doubt that the immortal gods, as always friendly towards
Rome, will be reconciled to us only if we have ensured that everyone
within our empire pursues a pious, religious, peaceful life, and one thoroughly pure in all regards. . . . For our laws safeguard only what is holy
and venerable; and it is in this way that the majesty of Rome, by the
favor of all the divine powers, has attained its greatness.[16]

Christian notions of pious, religious, and purity obviously did not square with
Diocletian's, but he did not go after the Christians immediately upon assuming
the purple. One church writer claims that a glimpse of a Christian church
towering higher than his imperial palace at Nicomedia prompted him to
persecute Christians. In 303, he and his colleagues launched what is known as
the Great Persecution, the first Christian persecution in about half a century.
It proceeded over several years to confiscate copies of Christian Scripture,
dismantle church buildings, and arrest and punish local church leaders and
then laypersons who would not honor the Imperial Cult publicly. His attempt
to eradicate Christianity ultimately failed, however; the Christian church was
simply too large and too well organized by the early fourth century.

Diocletian retired in 305, confident that he had restored both cosmos and
empire. He had reigned for more than twenty years, the first emperor since
Antoninus Pius (r. 138–161) to do so. He had not, in fact, brought back any
semblance of *Pax Romana*; civil war broke out once again after his retirement.

In this next round of civil war, Constantine, the son of a Tetrarch, emerged
as a frontrunner. Constantine had a history of visions connected with a
protective deity, initially Apollo, who guided him into battles. At the Milvian
Bridge (312), a crucial battle to determine who would be the Augustus in the

12.10. Christ monogram (Chi-Rho) in a wreath. Vanni/Art Resource, NY.

West, as contemporary biographers relate, he was inspired by a vision from Christ.

The sources differ on the details, but all feature a sign of a cross and a Chi-Rho sign, or Christogram, made up of the first two letters of Christ's name in Greek (Fig. 12.10). Neither of these had been common Christian symbols before this, but both quickly became at once Christian and imperial symbols. In one report of the vision, Constantine and his whole army saw the sign of the cross in the sky with the message, "In this sign conquer." He did indeed conquer, technically becoming the first crusader, literally one who conquers under the sign of the cross. The year after this battle, he issued an Edict of Toleration, which extended toleration to all religions and restored Christian church property lost during the Great Persecution.

Monotheism at the top, as we will see in the next two chapters, added a dynamic political and ideological dimension to empire. Christianity also was one faith that transcended local loyalties and guaranteed some support from all regions and social levels of the empire. Its exclusive nature focused religious energy as did no other religion at this time. Debate has long raged

12.11. Medallion with the sun god on his chariot, east front of the Arch of Constantine. Vanni/Art Resource, NY.

as to what extent these might have been inducements to Constantine's own conversion.

Some historians see his conversion as a continuation of the trend toward and beyond henotheism visible already in the third century, and thus not as radical as it might first appear. It was not much of a stretch for the idea of one high god above all others (henotheism) to give way to belief in only one god, period (monotheism). Constantine's father was a devout worshipper of the sun god, Sol Invictus, and manifestations of a sun god continue to appear within Constantine's visual program long after his conversion to Christianity (Fig. 12.11).

In the tradition of Augustus, Constantine also proposed a series of moral and social reforms. Some he aimed at families, such as a series of laws against adultery and the exposure of infants, that is, leaving unwanted children out to die. Others were aimed at public institutions and outlawing crucifixion. With the latter, the cross could more easily become a broad Christian symbol, which it was not until Constantine supposedly saw its image in the sky.

Like Augustus, he also had to present bold new imperial features cautiously, without offending other traditionalists. Constantine avoided revolt

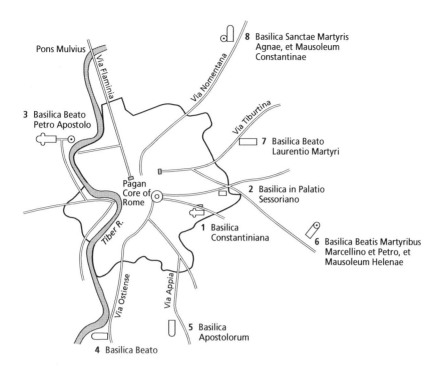

12.12. The Christian basilicas of Constantinian Rome. Their locations and ancient Latin names are shown on the map, and their modern Italian names given below the map. Map courtesy of Charles Matson Odahl, *Constantine and the Christian Empire*, Second Edition (London & New York: Routledge, 2010), p. 147.

by the aristocracy of Rome through skillful and cautious measures. For example, he kept the title of *pontifex maximus*, because he probably suspected that abandoning it outright would have signaled to many in the empire the ultimate blow to the *pax deorum*; or perhaps he feared the office would have fallen into the hands of a rival if he relinquished it. He did not persecute pagans or desecrate their holy sites, although his successors would do both; although he sponsored and supported the building of many churches, he deliberately avoided putting any of them in the political core of the city of Rome (Fig. 12.12). His artistic symbols generally combined Christian and pagan motifs, if and when he used traditional Christian symbolism. His triumphal arch in Rome, for example, contains no explicitly Christian imagery. It is the only public monument that proclaims the cause of his victory, and it does so in remarkably innocuous language. He won at Milvian Bridge *instinctu divinitatis*, "by the prompting of *a* deity." Such vague language could easily accommodate

Christians and pagans – there was nothing particularly revolutionary about being inspired by a god in battle.

His major economic innovation was a clear improvement on Diocletian's. He issued the *solidus*, a new high-quality gold coin that helped stabilize the economy at the highest level. It became, in fact, the world's longest-lasting monetary standard, maintaining its weight and purity into the eleventh century. With this coin, he standardized as well an old practice of the donative (*donativum*), in which a monetary gift was given to soldiers usually by an ascending emperor – in effect, a "thank-you" for the office. Constantine mandated that a *solidus* be awarded on a regular basis – every five years – as a way to encourage and maintain army loyalty. The problem with the silver coinage and inflation continued, but the *solidus* gave much-needed stability at the highest economic level.

Finally, to complete the IEMP analysis, Constantine formalized and standardized Diocletian's twofold division in the army as well as proposed an influential innovation. He deliberately recruited non-Roman Germans to help fill the ranks of the army, beginning a trend in which non-Romans came to dominate Roman armies. Germans were cheaper and, frankly, easier to recruit than Roman citizens. Recruiting at or beyond the peripheries of empire would remain standard, as we will see in the next chapter; Germans came to dominate the western army, and Arabs and Armenians came to dominate the Roman army in the East.

In sum, the Roman world had been saved once again by a conservative revolution. In the process, it was transformed into a new type of empire. Christian rhetoric from the fourth century onward can mask the fact that Constantine was as conservative as Diocletian, albeit in the same knee-jerk and reactive sort of way. When such conservatives attempt to restore a world to the Good Old Days, they invariably end up creating something new. Christianity was the most obvious novelty, but it was far from the only innovation at work.

Christianity brought a new way of viewing past and present that challenged traditional patterns of Roman nostalgia. Christians of Constantine's day were not looking back wistfully, to any era – not to the Augustan Principate, not even to the republic at its high noon. Their days were the best of all days, their times the best of times:

> Men had now lost all fear of their former oppressors; day after day they kept dazzling festival; light was everywhere, and men who once dared not look up greeted each other with smiling faces and shining eyes. They danced and sang in city and country alike, giving honour

first of all to God our Sovereign Lord, as they had been instructed, and then to the pious emperor with his sons, so dear to God. Old troubles were forgotten, and all irreligion passed into oblivion; good things present were enjoyed, those yet to come eagerly awaited. In every city the victorious emperor published decrees full of humanity and laws gave proof of munificence and true piety. Thus all tyranny had been purged away, and the kingdom that was theirs was preserved securely and without question for Constantine and his sons alone.[17]

Christians could indeed live with, indeed thrive in, this kind of earthly kingdom. No earlier stage of Roman history could hold a candle to this new age, this veritable Kingdom of God on earth. For pagans, on the other hand, there were endless reasons to long for a bygone era, as we will see in the next chapter.

Perhaps the Dominate actually brought an even more ancient world to light. A comparatively distant ruler with a heavy hand brandishing a strong religious ideology – Diocletian and Constantine did not have to look far for this imperial model. The later Roman empire surely crafted its own innovations, but the continuities within the Age of Ancient Empires are clear. The later Roman Empire bears striking resemblance to older Near Eastern and Hellenistic Empires, even more so than the earlier Roman Empire.

When the Roman Empire is remembered today, it is usually the Augustan Principate that commands center stage. Often it is portrayed as a classical age and a pivotal moment in Western civilization. It is worth noting, however, that the form of empire shaped by Diocletian and Constantine was what was actually passed on to subsequent ages – to Europe, Byzantium, and Islam. It is to the formation of these worlds that we now turn.

CHAPTER THIRTEEN

UNIVERSAL EMPIRES AND THEIR PERIPHERIES IN LATE ANTIQUITY

Valiant king, the gods have given you your empire and success. They have no need of human honor; but if you convert to one religion all the nations and races in your empire, then the land of the Greeks [i.e., Byzantines] will also obediently submit to your rule.[1]

– Zoroastrian priestly address to Sasanid Persian King Yazdegird
II (r. 439–457)

* How did universalism shape the Late Antique world across political boundaries?
* How did religion interact with politics throughout Late Antiquity?
* What roles did religious diversity and heterodoxy play in empire resistance?

THE SHIFTS OF THE THIRD AND FOURTH CENTURIES signaled the beginning of an era of far-reaching transformation. Late Antiquity, as that era is known, stretched into the seventh and eighth centuries and included areas ranging from Gibraltar to Afghanistan and from the Danube to Ethiopia. The twilight of the Age of Ancient Empires was one of its most all-embracing moments.

This chapter explores Late Antiquity up to the sixth century, and the next chapter continues the story to the end of the ancient world with the establishment of the first Islamic empire. At Late Antiquity's core was a revived universalism, an ideology that had lain dormant for several centuries in both East and West. Neither the Romans of the early empire nor the Arsacid Parthians were expansive or universalist in any consistent or meaningful sense. However, the Roman and Persian (Sasanid) Empires of Late Antiquity were both driven to universalism by a potent and unprecedented combination of strongly centralized political systems and zealous religious ideologies.

Behind the strong political and religious claims of both Romans and Sasanid Persians were expansive "state churches," a phenomenon new to the ancient world. These were global in scope, and they insisted on uniform belief, rejecting alternatives and variations in ways unknown in prior ages. Neo-Assyrian rulers and priests were confident that Ashur ruled the cosmos as his hunting ground; Achaemenid Persian leaders knew that Ahura-Mazda gave justice, truth, and light; Roman emperors of the Principate believed that proper rituals of the Imperial Cult maintained *pax deorum*. None of these leaders, however, had insisted that their subjects or citizens actually *believe* in rigorous systems of doctrine or dogma. Nor were their conquests aimed at gaining new worshippers or converts per se. Leaders of Late Antiquity, such as the Persian priests and emperor above, saw conversion itself as a means of unification and expansion, as is clear in the opening quotation of this chapter.

A superpower struggle between the Roman and the Sasanid Persian Empires took center stage for much of Late Antiquity. Memories of past empires served as models of conquest – Achaemenids likely inspired the Sasanid Persians, and Alexander, the great Achaemenid nemesis, spurred on

into this power struggle vortex. Both their cooperation with and resistance to the powers at the center – in part via religious orthodoxies and heterodoxies – would shape the subsequent histories of western Europe, eastern Europe, Armenia, Ethiopia, and the Arabian Peninsula, among others.

Geographically, the era saw a shift back toward the birthplace of the Age of Ancient Empires. The final three empires of the ancient world, all creatures of Late Antiquity, were decidedly eastern: the Eastern Roman or Byzantine, the Sasanid Persian, and the first Islamic or Umayyad. Age-old divisions between East and West reemerged, even if two of the Late Antique empires held sections of the western Mediterranean for a time. In the larger scheme of things, it is worth noting that the approximately 1,500-year-old Age of Ancient Empires had only one decidedly western installment – the Roman Empire – albeit a significant and remarkably long-lived one. After the demise of the western Roman Empire, our story ends in the East, ultimately back in Mesopotamia once again. Subsequent ages would see a shift even farther to the east and to the north toward central Asia. The great empires to follow – Turkic and Mongolian – heralded a new center of geopolitics and a decidedly new era.

ROMAN POLITICAL AND RELIGIOUS UNIVERSALISM

Imperium sine fine was a fond memory by the dawn of Late Antiquity. Romans still read the phrase in Vergil, but by the second century, they spoke less emphatically of their empire as an organic entity with a divine destiny to expand throughout the whole world. The dominant image of the empire was becoming instead a fortress or army camp encircled by a figurative wall. Although in some places he retained language of *imperium sine fine*, the second-century orator Aelius Aristides praised Rome because

> beyond the outermost ring of the civilized world, you drew a second
> line, quite as one does in walling a town. . . . An encamped army like a
> rampart encloses the civilized world in a ring.[2]

The third-century historian Herodian likewise referred to Rome as an army camp surrounded by "the wall of the Roman empire,"[3] and the anonymous third-century author of the *13th Sibylline Oracle* invoked images of "disorderly races" coming up against the "walls" of the Roman Empire.[4] By the fourth century, the notion was fairly common among historians and orators. Such images reveal a subtle shift in *mentalité*; they would have had no place in Vergil's Rome.

In Late Antiquity, however, the Roman Empire (and the Sasanid Persian) began to look once more like a typical ancient empire – universalism returned with force, in theory and practice. Rome began to look more like its former self, in some ways. The motivating factors were new, however, inspired now by a shift in religion. Regardless of whatever prompted Constantine to convert to Christianity, the One God, One Faith, One Empire model was a powerful and much-needed political and ideological boost to the empire. In short, it helped revive and justify the dream of empire and world expansion.[5] Christian emperors could now be hailed not for keeping "the wall" intact but for "extend[ing] the realms of the East beyond the limits of things and the boundaries of Nature."[6] The focus of universalism was now a fused image of empire and Christ, rather than just the emperor himself.

Christianity, as a global faith, held that those outside the fold should be inside; this had strong political ramifications for a Christian empire. The churchman Tertullian, self-proclaimed "citizen of the cosmos" and enemy of the Roman order, could exult in the early third century, before Christianization at the top, that there were places outside of the empire, "inaccessible to the Romans but subject to Christ."[7] Christians would certainly not see things this way once their faith fused together with imperial ideology. Missionary efforts among peoples outside of the empire would now be sponsored by the central government. Peoples and places outside should now be inside the Christian Roman Empire. As the bishop Eusebius proclaimed at the dedication of a basilica in Jerusalem in 335:

> The Roman Empire, . . . in order to merge the entire race into one unity
> and concord has already united most of the various peoples, and it is

further destined to obtain all those not yet united, right up to the very limits of the inhabited world.[8]

Constantine might have been cautious about parading Christianity before Rome's aristocracy, but he was significantly less restrained with peoples outside of the empire. He and his successors strove either to win or influence Goths, Armenians, Aksumites (Ethiopians), Iberians, Persians, and others.

The fourth-century mission to the Goths, a Germanic people on the outskirts of the empire, was likely conceived in Constantine's reign. Ulfila, a Christian Goth, was commissioned by imperial power as "bishop of the Christians in Getic [Gothic] lands." Ulfila was instrumental in diplomatic relations between the Goths and the Romans in the mid-fourth century. It is difficult to see this move separately from Constantine's and later emperors' desire to co-opt the Goths, as we will see subsequently. To make them coreligionists and brothers would pull them more directly and cleanly into the Roman sphere.

Constantine also sought to influence Christians abroad, such as those Constantine converted; Persian bishops were among those at the Council of Nicaea, held in what is now Iznik, Turkey. Constantine reached out to Persian Christians, even calling himself "bishop of the Christians of Persia." His overtures to them coincided with his conflicts with the Sasanid *shahinshah* Shapur II (r. 310–379), and were perceived, probably correctly, as a political threat. These Christians paid the price with four decades of persecution by the Sasanids, ending only with Shapur II's death in 379. The Christians of Persia would learn quickly to distinguish themselves from their Roman/Byzantine coreligionists.

If Constantine saw Christianity as a great unifier, he was quickly frustrated – "although universalist by inner logic, it ends up generating pluralism."[9] Monotheistic religions in general tend toward rigid dogmatism and exclusive orthodoxy and provoke controversy and division, inherent impediments to a universal empire. Challenges to that orthodoxy – that is, heterodoxies – were made very public when Christianity became the favored Roman faith. Constantine, "the thirteenth Apostle," as he was effectively declared, immediately set out to solve these divisions. The very year after the Edict of Toleration, he called a council at Arles to solve a schism over the nature of the Christian Church. A breakaway Christian movement in North Africa known as Donatism was claiming to be the one true Church, strongly provoking those who were convinced that they, in fact, were actually the one true Church. About a decade later, Constantine convoked and presided at the Council of Nicaea (325), to solve a deep division over Christ: was Christ actually eternal

13.1. Aureus with bust of Carus. MFA
Images; gift of Michael C. Ruettgers.

God or a being created by God in time and thus subordinate to God? Those
who taught that Christ was a created being were known as Arians. Their
opponents, who prevailed at the Council of Nicaea, taught the Trinity – one
God in three persons: Father, Son, and Holy Spirit – and that Jesus was thus
God. Arianism was politically significant in the fourth and fifth centuries,
both in the imperial court itself and among barbarian peoples who converted
to this form of Christianity.

Of the many other controversies of the next few centuries, two were
intrinsic to the power politics of Late Antiquity. After the Council of Nicaea
had affirmed that Jesus was God, the next round of debates addressed how
the person and nature of Christ related to each other. Ultimately, the answer
that prevailed (i.e., the orthodox one) was that Christ was *one* person with *two*
natures – human and divine. Two major and influential alternate views stood
in opposition to the orthodox formulation, both of which became vital to
the identities of peoples surrounding the eastern Roman Empire in particular.
The Nestorians (or Church of the East, as they call themselves), who were
condemned at the Council of Ephesus in 431, held that in the incarnate Christ
there are *two* separate persons, one human and one divine. Nestorianism came
to define Persian Christianity as well as much of the Christianity that spread
throughout the Near East, Central Asia, and even to China. The Miaphysites,
condemned at the Council of Chalcedon in 451, taught that there was in
the person of the incarnate Christ but a single nature, a divine one. Egyptian
Coptic, Ethiopian Coptic, Syrian, and Armenian Christians all adopted Miaphysitism (Monophysites), at least for a time. Such distinctions were real and
important to the identities of Late Antique people, and significant historical
changes flowed from them.

13.2. Tetradrachm of Lysimachus with Alexander wearing the ram's horn of Amon. Erich Lessing/Art Resource, NY.

Late Roman universalism had additional inspirations, going back to earlier

world empires. Memories of Alexander the Great had long inspired would-be world conquerors. Several Roman emperors over time had aspired to an Alexandrine model in their own campaigns against Persians. Constantine intentionally invoked the image of the world conqueror. For example, one of his coin issues broke directly with Roman coin styles to present himself as an Alexander (Figs. 13.1–13.3). Wearing an Alexander-style diadem instead

13.3. Gold medallion of Constantine. British Museum/Art Resource, NY.

of the traditional laurels of his Roman predecessors, Constantine was clearly associating himself with world conquest. The bishop Eusebius noted Constantine's "heavenly gaze" on this coin, demonstrating the close connection between ideological universalism and conquest:

> How deeply his soul was impressed by the power of divine faith may be understood from the circumstance that he directed his likeness to be stamped on the golden coin of the empire with eyes uplifted as in the posture of prayer to God: and this money became current throughout the Roman world.[10]

The emperor Julian (r. 361–363), the son of Constantine's half-brother, likewise directly invoked Alexander in his ultimately fatal conquests deep in Persian territory. The image of Alexander as a symbol of universalism was potent and long-lived, passing on to subsequent empires. Several centuries later, stories of Alexander – the "Alexander Romance," as they are called – would even appear in the Qur'an as a symbol of Islamic universalism as realized at the end of time.

Third and fourth century henotheistic sun worship also provided a precedent for Late Antique universalism. One of the few successful Roman conquerors of the third century before Diocletian was Aurelian (r. 270–275), who not only defeated both the Palmyrene and Gallic Empires (see Chapter Twelve) but also began expansion against Persia before he was murdered in 275. He ruled and conquered in the name of Sol Invictus, the unconquered sun, the images of which he seized from Palmyra and set up in a state sun-worshipping cult. Constantine continued long after his Christian conversion to include solar imagery within his official visual program. The emperor Julian, who was the only Roman emperor after Constantine to reject Christianity, found in sun worship a respectable alternative. In strongly henotheistic language, he praised the sun god in his *Hymn to King Helios*, "the most mighty god."

Universal empire and the sun often have been connected together, sometimes for an obvious reason: the sun looks over all and is thus the perfect symbol for universalism. The British and Spanish Empires of the modern world each claimed status as an "empire on which the sun never sets." A Sasanid ambassador once referred to a theoretical universal empire as "that over which the sun watches."[11] More than a millennium earlier, the Greek historian Herodotus put in the mouth of Xerxes I of Achaemenid Persia: "We shall extend the Persian territory as far as God's heaven reaches. The sun will then shine on no land beyond our borders."[12] The ideological connections also ran deep, however, as in one Babylonian text that praises King

13.4. Theodosius and court, Istanbul. Slide by Mark W. Graham.

Nebuchadnezzar, "who like the sun-god oversees the totality of the lands, who determines right and justice, who destroys evildoers and criminals."[13]

RENOVATIO: BYZANTIUM, THE NEW ROME

For more than 500 years, Roman imperialism managed to unite the western and eastern Mediterranean and lands attached to them. This was a notable and rare accomplishment, carried out only a few times before, and on a comparatively limited basis, by colonizing Phoenicians and Greeks. The political and cultural divide between East and West ran deep, even if not always wide. The western Roman Empire always retained a primarily Latin character and the eastern Roman Empire a dominant Greek character, which had various philosophical and worldview ramifications.

As the empire fragmented in the third century, Diocletian realized that the key to political recovery was recognizing the East–West division while uniting the halves via the Tetrarchy (see Chapter Twelve). Constantine likewise recognized the division, but he significantly favored the East, a wise and pivotal move in the long run. By the reigns of the eastern emperor Arcadius (r. 395–408) and the western emperor Honorius (r. 395–423), the division between an eastern and western empire was permanent. The eastern Roman Empire (Byzantine), unlike the western, would have a long history ahead; more than a millennium, in fact. How long into that period it could still be considered "ancient" is a matter we pick up in the next chapter.

Between 324 and 330, Constantine built his eastern capitol of Constantinople on the ancient site of Byzantium, adorning it with Christian symbols at its very core. Defeating his fellow Augustus-turned-rival, Licinius, in 324, he became sole leader of the Roman Empire. He was then free to fashion an imperial city to his liking, and he began immediately. At the crossroads between Europe and Asia, Constantinople clearly proclaimed a shift in the center of the empire's gravity, decidedly eastward. Constantinople would have its own Senate, its own consuls; it was nothing short of a new Rome.

Being a conservative Roman, Constantine did not presume to found a new empire. To his mind, this was a *renovatio romani imperii*, a renovation of the Roman Empire. Yet he did, in fact, create something new. Over a millennium later, scholars would call it the Byzantine Empire, although it would continue to call itself simply the Roman Empire. Here, as the bishop Eusebius proclaimed, would be replicated on earth God's eternal rule in heaven: "As in heaven, so on earth." This was a profound and deeply motivating mandate for the emperors. Byzantines later reimagined the history of the Roman Empire to make this ideology look traditional. One early sixth-century Byzantine writer, Cosmas Indicopleustes, clearly articulated the universalist vision while assuming that the empire, in fact, had always been the Kingdom of God:

> For while Christ was yet in the womb, the Roman empire received its power from God as the servant of the dispensation which Christ introduced, since at that very time the accession was proclaimed of the unending line of the Augusti by whose command a census was made which embraced the whole world. . . . The empire of the Romans thus participates in the dignity of the Kingdom of the Lord Christ, seeing that it transcends, as far as can be in this state of existence, every other power, and will remain unconquered until the final consummation.[14]

Constantine proclaimed his faith by adorning the center of Constantinople with churches. He had deliberately avoided putting churches in the political center of the old Rome, but a Christian eastern empire demanded a thoroughly Christian capital. The city proclaimed – through its gold-glittering art and its architecture as well as the forty-day dedication celebration – eternal and universal imperial victory. The relatively undisputed prominence of the city of Rome was forever lost.

13.5. Reconstructed Theodosian walls, fifth century A.D. DeA Picture Library/Art Resource, NY.

The city of Rome continued to be struck by bad fortune. In 410, it was sacked by Goths under the command of a German and former officer in the Roman army. The city recovered afterward, but the blow to its prestige was irreparable – it had, after all, been nearly eight hundred years since the "eternal city" had fallen to an external invading force. Three days of public mourning were declared at Constantinople, but nothing was done to help. To keep something similar from happening to the New Rome, the eastern emperor, Theodosius II (r. 408–450), built a set of walls around Constantinople (Fig. 13.5). The eastern empire more or less let the West take care of its own problems – some were there well before 410, and they would only continue to increase thereafter. Britain was abandoned in 410, North Africa fell to invading Germanic Vandals a few decades later, Visigoths took Spain and Gaul, and so on.

The barbarian settlements and invasions, which continued to shape the western Roman Empire decisively, had much less impact on the eastern empire. A major factor was simply geography. Constantinople was better secured against attacks owing to its position on the Bosphorus, which was

13.6. Vandal baptistery, Sbeitla, Tunisia. Slide by Mark W. Graham.

easily backed up by sea power. Its frontiers were generally easier to defend, not being as open as those of the western empire. The relative infrequency of successful invasions kept its tax base – and thus economic vitality – intact. The bulk of its revenue, as with most ancient empires, had always come from agricultural land tax, and peace helped secure this.

With the loss of Rome, however, the eastern Romans could experience, from time to time, a traditional sense of Roman nostalgia. Could theirs really be a *Roman* Empire if it did not even hold Rome or any western provinces? To complicate matters further, these areas were now held by barbarian Arian heretics. In 468, even while the western Roman Empire still had an emperor, the eastern emperor Leo (r. 457–474) tried to regain some lost portions of the western empire, but his attempts to take North Africa were thwarted by the Vandals.

The next major attempt to recover parts of the West met with more success. In 533, the Byzantine emperor Justinian (r. 527–565) and his coemperor and wife Theodora, sent an army westward under general Belisarius, a veteran of the wars with Sasanid Persia. Reconquest aimed to restore the empire as well as restore orthodox Christianity in these regions now held by Arian heretics – to Justinian, two sides of the same coin. The Byzantines were able to take North Africa from the Vandals, sections of Italy from the Ostrogoths, and even a coastal strip of southern Spain from the Visigoths. It was enough

13.7. Empress Theodora and attendants, Ravenna. Cameraphot Arte, Venice/Art Resource, NY.

to give some substance to Justinian's claim that he had restored the Roman Empire. The Byzantines held North Africa for over a century until the Muslim conquest, and parts of Spain for about seventy years. However, they lost key holdings in Italy fairly quickly as the Lombards, another Germanic invading group, moved into Italy beginning in 568.

Justinian, like Diocletian, had risen to the throne from military roots. His military and defense measures brought the early Byzantine Empire to its height. He strengthened the natural defenses of the Byzantine Empire and commissioned fortifications along its eastern and northern frontiers, and all across North Africa to Morocco. These would help deter groups of Bulgars, Gepids, Avars, and Slavs. To the south, he courted the Ghassanid Arabs as military clients, a move with clear ramifications in later centuries. Warfare with the Sasanids continued intermittently on the eastern frontier throughout the sixth century. Hopes were high when, in 532, he and the Sasanids agreed to the Endless Peace. Unfortunately, this optimistically named treaty lasted for only eight years before decades of warfare broke out once again.

Justinian's greatest legacy is probably the Codex Iustinianus, a civil law collection that aimed to restate the entirety of Roman law. The opening lines of the Codex speak volumes about his dynamic combination of religious ideology and politics:

> It is Our will that all peoples who are ruled by the administration of Our Clemency shall practice that religion which the divine Peter the apostle transmitted to the Romans. . . . We shall believe in the single Deity of the Father, the Son and the Holy Spirit under the guise of equal majesty and of the Holy Trinity. We command that those persons who follow this law shall embrace the name of Catholic Christians. The rest, however, whom we adjudge demented and insane, shall sustain the infamy attached to heretical dogmas. Their meeting places shall not receive the name of churches, and they shall be smitten first by divine vengeance and secondly by the retribution of Our own initiative which we shall dispense in accordance with the divine judgment.[15]

Carrying on a long tradition in which the success of the empire depended on divine favor, he sought to restore and purify the Christian Empire. Pagans, heretics, and homosexuals would taste divine Roman wrath.

Justinian's heavy hand also attacked tax evasion, which had a long and established tradition among the Byzantine nobility. This, along with his reconquest of grain-rich North Africa, helped strengthen the economy for a time. A significant challenge to his reforms, however, came with a devastating plague – perhaps bubonic – which first hit in 540, killing as much as a third of the population, and wreaking economic, ideological, and political disasters. Nevertheless, the Byzantine Empire itself would outlive the ancient world by many centuries.

THE RISE OF THE SASANID PERSIAN EMPIRE

Sasanid Persians had a convenient way of dividing the world – "Shapur, *shahinshah Eran ud Aneran*," that is, "king of kings of Iran and non-Iran." There was Iran/Persia, their heartland, and then the rest of the world, simply non-Iran, which they were also divinely destined to rule. The Sasanids were just discovering a dynamic Late Antique fusion of ideology and politics as the Roman Empire in the West was struggling to find its way in the early third century. They brought a strong and centralized empire back to the Near East – a real-world empire that would meet late Rome's universalist claims solidly with their own.

13.8. Hagia Sophia, Istanbul; at the center of the Byzantine Empire. Slide by Mark W. Graham.

Unlike the more than 450-year-old Arsacid Parthian state they overthrew, itself a decentralized state made up of semi-independent principalities,[16] the Sasanids emerged with strong centralization and became increasingly more so, focusing on the *shahinshah*. *Shahinshah* Khusrau I (r. 531–579) gave a tidy summation of what kept the whole system together:

> The monarchy depends on the army, the army on money; money comes from the land-tax; the land-tax comes from agriculture. Agriculture depends on justice, justice on the integrity of officials, and integrity and reliability on the ever-watchfulness of the King.[17]

Details of the Sasanid rise remain obscure, but it can be defensibly dated to 224. The loose feudal structure of the Parthian state was ultimately its undoing. Over a decade or so, a local leader named Ardashīr (r. 220–241) began consolidating power over surrounding rulers until he was able to challenge and defeat the Arsacids at the center. He continued typical ancient patterns of elite replacement, putting his own family members in place as local rulers (satraps) and replacing the Arsacid-placed ones.

Ardashīr began Sasanid expansion on several fronts: to the East against the Kushans of India and to the West against the Romans. The third-century

Roman historian Herodian records that Ardashīr was driven to recover the Achaemenid Empire of old: "It was his right to restore and reunite the whole empire as the Persians had once held it."[18] Shapur II (r. 310–379) purportedly asserted the same a little over a hundred years later in 358, in a letter to the Roman emperor Constantius (r. 337–361): "That my forefathers' empire reached as far as the river Strymon and the boundaries of Macedonia even your own ancient records bear witness; these lands it is fitting that I should demand."[19] Debate continues among recent historians over how seriously to take Roman accounts of Persian motivations, but most at least give some credence to the Roman sources here.

The Sasanid expansion hit Rome in the middle of the Third-Century Crisis. Under Ardashīr's son and successor Shapur I (r. 241–272), the Sasanids enjoyed much success on their western frontier with Rome, seizing key Roman frontier defense cities. It was in one of Shapur's campaigns that the Sasanids captured the Roman emperor Valerian and made him a footstool for the *shahinshah*. In the aftermath of this Sasanid victory, Odaenathus of Palmyra began the expanse of Palmyra against the Sasanids. This was also the moment when Zenobia took advantage of Roman weakness (see Chapter Twelve). The frontier between the Romans and Sasanids remained tense, with each side alternately scoring ambiguous victories over the course of the reigns of the next few emperors on either side. *Shahinshah* Narses (r. 293–302), after a massive Sasanid defeat, made a treaty with Diocletian that brought four decades of peace between the two powers.

Sasanid political and religious ideology was clear from the start. Ardashīr is reported to have said:

> Religion and kingship are two brothers, and neither can dispense with
> the other. Religion is the foundation of kingship and kingship protects
> religion. For whatever lacks a foundation must perish, and whatever lacks
> a protector disappears."[20]

His first official act was lighting a sacred fire at Ctesiphon that at once signaled his rise as shah (all his successors would take the title *shahinshah*) and proclaimed Zoroastrianism as the official imperial religion (Fig. 13.9). Like any religion, Zoroastrianism evolved over time. It remained an essentially dualist faith as under the Achaemenids, but it had become firmer and more rigid. It became, in effect "the 'state church' of the Sassanian empire with a hierarchy parallel to the court hierarchy of the crown."[21]

The Zoroastrian religion was a means of expansion under Ahura-Mazda, the god of justice, light, and truth. Before Late Antiquity, it was rather rare for a political power to force belief onto its subjects and conquered peoples

13.9. Investiture of Ardashīr I. SEF/Art Resource, NY.

or to use conversion as a vehicle for imperialism. However, henotheism and monotheism tend to demand conformity as a way to guarantee their rule. An Armenian writer records an address by Zoroastrian priests/magi to the *shahinshah* Yazdegird II (r. 439–457):

> Valiant king, the gods have given you your empire and success. They have no need of human honor; but if you convert to one religion all the nations and races in your empire, then the land of the Greeks will also obediently submit to your rule.[22]

Zoroastrian Persians were less likely to persecute than their Roman counterparts, but they were known to victimize Christians, Jews, and Manichees. Some came to insist on "orthodox" beliefs of Zoroastrianism, even among conquered peoples such as Armenians. Orthodox religion was the basis of a universal empire in Sasanid Persia as much as in Constantinian Rome and Byzantium.

Zoroastrianism also helped maintain a rigid social structure, which was seen as reflecting the cosmic and divine order ("as in heaven, so on earth"). The *shahinshah* presided over four social groups, strictly and hierarchically arranged: priests (magi), military, cultivators, and artisans. Sasanid law was religious law, administered by Zoroastrian priests in a way similar to the

Roman bishops of Late Antiquity, who served as major local social and political figures. At the head of the state church was a chief magus, an official in the royal court.

The transition to Sasanid rule had not removed overnight the Parthians' more local, feudal control of the army, but by the sixth century, the Sasanid army was a unified fighting force. Prompting such change was a late fifth-century invasion by the Huns. Under *shahinshah* Peroz (r. 457–484), the Huns momentarily turned the Sasanids into tribute-paying vassals. Once the Sasanids recovered from this temporary setback, they responded with increased expansion and centralization. They moved against Byzantium in 540, sacked Antioch, and took Armenia. To the south, they expanded their empire into Yemen in southern Arabia.

The supreme military commander was the *shahinshah*, who personally led his army into battle. As Ammianus Marcellinus records of the Persian ruler:

> And when the first gleam of dawn appeared, everything so far as the eye could reach shone with glittering arms, and mail-clad cavalry filled hill and dale. The king himself, mounted upon a charger and overtopping the others, rode before the whole army, wearing in place of a diadem a golden image of a ram's head set with precious stones, distinguished too by a great retinue of men of the highest rank and of various nations.[23]

Although he made the tactical decisions, he almost never took part in the actual fighting. Warfare with the Romans and Huns prompted innovation in armaments on both sides of the Roman–Persian frontier. Heavily armed mailed cavalry, for example, appeared within both Roman and Sasanid armies. A military man himself, the Roman historian Ammianus Marcellinus was clearly impressed by Sasanid ironclad warriors:

> The Persians opposed to us serried bands of mail-clad horsemen in such close order that the gleam of moving bodies covered with closely fitting plates of iron dazzled the eyes of those who looked upon them, while the whole throng of horses was protected by coverings of leather. The cavalry was backed up by companies of infantry, who, protected by oblong, curved shields covered with wickerwork and raw hides, advanced in very close order.[24]

Ammianus is here describing the *cataphracti*, the heavily armed cavalry made up of Sasanian nobility. The army also fielded infantry, who were peasants recruited by the king whenever the need arose, and mounted archers.

The Sasanid economy was strongly and centrally controlled, as well as a source of stability. Whereas Roman silver coinage was annually being debased in the third century, the Sasanid silver coinage maintained its purity and would continue to do so for centuries. After their defeat by the Huns, the Sasanids tightened up their tax structure under Khusro I (r. 531–579). A series of agrarian reforms brought much taxable productivity as well. As with the Byzantines, the chief source of imperial revenue was agricultural land tax. The Sasanids maintained a vibrant international trade, especially after Khusro I's reforms. Their trading circuit linked India, China, Byzantines, and Arabs.

POLITICS, RESISTANCE, AND HETERODOXIES AT THE PERIPHERIES OF THE EMPIRES

Late Antique political power and religious ideologies necessarily projected well beyond imperial frontiers. The responses by peripheral groups also helped define the era. Ranging from solid, long-term kingdoms to wandering groups, peripheral peoples were shaped by interactions with the universalist empires. In some cases, peripheral groups underwent a sort of secondary state formation, forming coherent polities in imitation of or resistance to

nia, Ethiopia, and the Arabian Peninsula bear clear marks of their interactions with Late Antique empires.

Religious ideologies permeated imperial relations with peripheries. Adopting Christianity, for example, connected a group, for better or for worse, directly to the Roman/Byzantine sphere of influence. Many of the peripheral states adopted Christianity in the time of Constantine or soon thereafter. Most, however, would adopt a variety other than Byzantine imperial orthodoxy, and so heterodoxy shaped international relations. There were several reasons for this. The heterodox (often simply called "heretics") frequently were forced to peripheral areas by simply being excluded from the Christian Empire. Thus, peripheral peoples often encountered heterodoxies first.

More often, heterodoxies served an intentional role. Conversion to any form of Christianity connected a group to the Roman/Byzantine political and cultural sphere. Roman emperors defined themselves as the defenders of Christianity and acted as the patron. Adopting a heterodox form actually allowed peripheral groups a certain measure of distance. Heterodox groups, then, could have it both ways – rest within Rome's protective sphere as Christians yet remain somewhat independent. Heterodoxy thus became a major means of resisting or at least softening the hold of imperial hegemony.

Ethiopia's conversion and creation of a Christian monarchy demonstrates the nuance of this ideological and political connection. Sometime in the early

fourth century, so the story goes, two shipwrecked Roman merchants in the
Red Sea introduced Christianity to the Ethiopian (Aksumite) court. At the
time, Ethiopia (Aksum), a major power in the Red Sea region, was being
openly courted by both Constantine and Shapur II for a political alliance.
The king, Ezana (r. 333–356), converted to Christianity and then requested
that the Roman emperor send a bishop to help establish the faith. Constantius
(r. 337–361) responded with the following letter:

> It is altogether a matter of the greatest care and concern to us, to extend
> the knowledge of the supreme God; and I think that the whole race of
> mankind claims from us equal regard in this respect, in order that they
> may pass their lives in hope, being brought to a proper knowledge of
> God, and having no differences with each other in their enquiries con-
> cerning justice and truth. Wherefore considering that you are deserving
> of the same provident care as the Romans, and desiring to show equal
> regard for your welfare, we command that the same doctrine be professed
> in your churches as in theirs.[25]

The point is clear. Accepting Christianity assumed Constantinople's spiritual
authority, which gave the Roman emperor the right of reprimand (even if not
outright political authority). As might be expected, proud kings of smaller
independent kingdoms could find such "concern," as any form of patronage, a
mixed blessing at best. They often found themselves in the difficult position
of wanting to enjoy imperial friendship on one hand, and having to resist
interference on the other. Adopting a form of Christianity other than imperial
Roman orthodoxy was one solution to this dilemma, whether intentional or
not. Ethiopia would later adopt Miaphysitism soon after it became an official
option. Just after the Council of Chalcedon, Miaphysite missionaries from
Egypt and Syria, the most famous of whom were known as the "Nine Saints,"
fled the Byzantine Empire, bringing Miaphysite Christianity with them (Fig.
13.10).

Miaphysitism helped Ethiopia articulate a self-confident Christian identity that was not beholden to Byzantine (orthodox) patronage. Ethiopia's
national epic, the *Kebra Nagast* (*Glory of the Kings*), traced in its original form to
the sixth century, shows how an alternate form of Christianity melded with
politics in Late Antiquity. *Negus* (king) Kaleb (r. c. 520) is a righteous Christian
king who divides the inhabited world between himself and the Byzantines.
His kingdom is an eternal one, because his Miaphysitism is actually the correct form and Byzantine orthodoxy the heterodox. The connection of religion
and politics was a vital one for the Ethiopians, and the *Kebra Nagast* often was

13.10. The Nine Saints. Photo by Ondřej Žváček, public domain image.

actually included within Ethiopian biblical manuscripts. To this day, Mia-

Christianity was a multifaceted aspect of resistance to both the Roman and Sasanid Empires in the case of Armenia. Armenia had a long history on the fringes of empires, going back to Urartu, the secondary state formed as the Neo-Assyrian Empire arose. During the Roman Empire, it vacillated between client-state status and province; with the rise of the Sasanids and for the next few centuries, it essentially served as a buffer state between the two major empires. The Armenians gravitated toward the Roman/Byzantine sphere and would come to play a significant role in the Byzantine army in the centuries ahead. In the third century, Armenia was seized by the Sasanids, and Zoroastrian clergy then began forcing their beliefs on the Armenians. The Armenians resisted Sasanids and Zoroastrianism, and it is precisely (coincidentally?) at this moment that Christianity first appeared among the Armenians. Their king, Tiridates IV (r. 298–330), converted to Christianity (either in 301 or 314), and was brought firmly into the sphere of the Christian Roman Empire. Constantine and his successor continued to court Armenia as a fellow Christian state, already having much cultural affinity with them (Greek, for example, remained a major administrative language in Armenia). Christianity became a central aspect of the Armenian "national" spirit and a vital element of their resistance, first against the Sasanids and later against Islamic empires.

Armenians, like the Ethiopians, also adopted Miaphysitism, probably as resistance to Byzantine imperial control as well. The Armenians felt betrayed

when, in 451, the Byzantine emperor Marcian (450–457) refused to aid them
in a struggle with the Sasanids. As one sixth-century Armenian put it, "this
ignoble man [Marcian] thought it better to preserve the pact with the hea-
then [Sasanids] for the sake of terrestrial peace, than to join in war for the
Christian covenant."[26] Within a half century, Miaphysite Christianity, now an
official option following the Council of Chalcedon (451), came to dominate
in Armenia. Miaphysitism was officially adopted at the Armenian Council
of Dvin in 506. Armenians probably had further incentive to adopt Miaphysitism; many Persian Christians adopted the Christology of the Church
of the East (Nestorianism). Armenian Miaphysitism thus probably helped
them keep some distance from hated Persians, even Christian ones.

The Christians of Persia came to embrace Nestorianism, partially to distinguish themselves from the Byzantine Christians in the eyes of their Sasanid
overlords. Because of Constantine's and later emperors' overtures to and claims
over Persian Christians, they were suspected as a fifth column within the
empire, much as Japanese Americans were viewed during World War II.
Constantine's contemporary Shapur II launched forty years of persecution
against them, which stopped only after his death. By 424, Persian Christians
had declared their independence from the see of Antioch. Later, their adoption of Nestorianism worked to allay Sasanid fears and helped differentiate
these Persian Christians from their Byzantine counterparts. Sasanid emperors
came to understand quite well what the theological differences meant politically. When Khusrau II (r. 590–628) conquered a section of the Byzantine
Empire, he offered its Christian inhabitants the option of Nestorianism or
Miaphysitism; orthodoxy was off limits because it was inextricably linked to
Byzantium.

Groups of Arabic-speaking peoples also converted to Christianity while
caught in between the Byzantine and Sasanid superpowers. By the third
century, small tribal groups were forming larger confederations that fought
in the border skirmishes and warfare across both frontiers. They often fought
alongside the armies of both empires. In time, Arabic-speaking peoples came
to make up significant portions of the imperial fighting forces, at least for
specific campaigns, when friendly Arabs might even "easily match or double
or triple," the number of regular Byzantine forces in Syria, Mesopotamia, and
Palestine, for example.[27]

Two major confederations began to emerge in the north of the peninsula
in a form of secondary state formation, under control of leaders known as
phylarchs. The Lakhmids, on the Sasanid western flank, tended to gravitate
toward Persia, and the Ghassanids, on the Byzantine eastern flank, generally
went with the Byzantines (Fig. 13.11). The Arabs knew the terrain of the

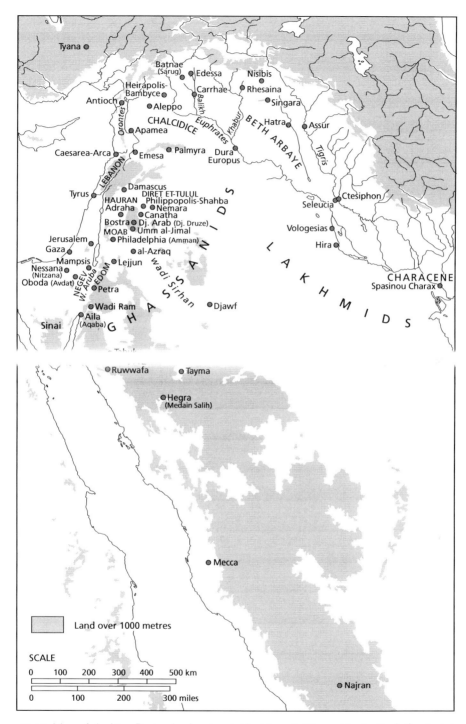

13.11. Map of Arabian Peninsula showing Lakhmids and Ghassanids. In *Cambridge Ancient History*, vol. 12, 2nd ed., p. 499.

frontier regions, the climate, and the military methods used by both sides. By the end of the fourth century, Christianity was well established among the Arabs of northern Arabia on both sides – they had their own episcopate, monasteries, saints, and liturgy. By the fifth and sixth centuries, Nestorian Christianity dominated among the Lakhmids, and Miaphysitism among the Ghassanids. Heterodox Christianity was, again, an identity marker distinguishing one group from the other. We explore in the next chapter the longer-term impact of Christianity among the Arabic speakers of the northern Arabian Peninsula, as well as the effect of the larger tribal groupings on the wars between the empires.

A final set of peripheral groups came to dominate the western Roman Empire. The third century saw Germanic peoples settle in unprecedented numbers within the Roman Empire. Almost all of the barbarian peoples converted to heterodox Arian Christianity either before or just after they settled within Roman frontiers. Like most of the other groups we have discussed, they converted during or soon after the reign of Constantine.

The barbarian settlements must be understood as part of structural-level demographic shifts along the frontiers of the Roman Empire. Economic ties and political relationships had long bound these peoples to the Romans (as seen in Chapter Ten). These connections shaped the barbarians, even those far from Roman frontiers. The Roman sources often present barbarian identity as fixed and timeless, but new barbarian identities were constantly being negotiated and new groups established. These patterns and processes continued into the fifth century and beyond.

As seen throughout this study, however, structural changes must be balanced with the events. A critical turning point came in the late fourth and early fifth centuries, when the Huns, originally a Mongolic warrior groups from the Central Asian steppes, suddenly entered the Mediterranean arena. The Huns depended on a regular flow of treasure and booty as well as local recruits as they went, and thus they spread far and wide, moving against wealthy kingdoms. When they arrived near Roman frontiers in 376, the Huns were a completely new people to the Romans, not shaped by long-term correspondence across the frontier.

Their swift appearance forced many barbarian peoples settled just outside Rome's frontiers to make a choice: join the Huns or move into Roman territory for protection. Germanic peoples took both options. The Romans initially welcomed some refuges onto Roman soil and settled them as *foederati* – federated peoples or federates – as a buffer against the Huns and other potential invaders. The Romans recruited heavily among *foederati* for their army. By the middle of the fifth century, the bulk of the western Roman army consisted of barbarian federates. Many a high-ranking officer in the Roman army was of barbarian descent. Just a few years after this initial settlement began in 376, a group of Gothic federates, badly mistreated by their new Roman overlords, rose up against them in one of the worst military disasters in Roman history. The Battle of Adrianople (378) is said to have wiped out two-thirds of the emperor's field army, including the emperor, Valens, himself. More problems followed. In 406, large groups of barbarian Vandals, Suevi, and Alans crossed an unusually frozen Rhine River to move into the empire. The western Roman frontier armies were getting less and less able to hold such groups out. In 410, under the command of Alaric, who had once fought under Theodosius I, Goths sacked the city of Rome itself.

Over the course of the fifth century, various barbarian groups territorialized the western Roman Empire. That is, they began carving out their own kingdoms within the limits of the western empire. The Vandals took over North Africa, Sardinia, and Corsica, declaring in 439 a kingdom that would last for just short of a century before the Byzantines ended it. In 455, they even sacked the city of Rome. In Spain and parts of Gaul, the Visigoths set up a

eighth century. The Franks established a kingdom that encompassed much of modern-day France and Germany. The Ostrogoths would form a kingdom in Italy in 489, which lasted until challenged by the Byzantines in 536. In 476, Romulus Augustulus, the last of the Roman emperors, was replaced by Odoacer, a barbarian *rex*, or king. The western Roman Empire was no more.

With few exceptions, the barbarians were continuators of the Roman world, rather than its destroyers. "An able Goth wants to be like a Roman, only a poor Roman would want to be a Goth," or so said Theodoric, the Ostrogothic king of Italy. Through a process known as *imitatio romani*, they shaped their kingdoms with essentially Roman ideology, economics, military, and politics. Barbarians wrote law codes in Latin and used Roman symbols of power. They even continued Roman offices and political structures as much as possible.

A major difference was the form of Christianity espoused by the new masters of western Europe. It is risky to generalize about why many very different peoples converted to Arianism, but there are some patterns. Missionaries among them, in the fourth century, tended toward Arianism, partially because several fourth-century emperors themselves had Arian leanings. Barbarians, however, retained their heterodox connections after Arianism was no longer in vogue in the Roman court and probably did so for similar reasons to Ethiopians, Armenians, and Arabs. It is worth noting that the only major barbarian group to convert to orthodox Christianity, the Franks, received immediate favor and support from the Byzantine Empire as well as the Catholic Church. Their success as the founders of the Frankish kingdoms and then empire several centuries later, the veritable foundation of western Europe, gives solid testimony to the continued important role of religious ideology in the politics of the age.

Outmoded versions of the barbarian story usually feature myriads of hairy, stinky barbarians pouring over the frontiers en masse and destroying the high civilization of the Romans. This view is challenged on all sides today, but much fruitful debate continues on the fall of the western Roman Empire and the rise of the barbarian kingdoms. Although in ancient as well as some modern sources, a few moments of destruction usually make the headlines, the settlements of the barbarians were largely peaceful as they carved the western Roman Empire into separate kingdoms. A few ancient empires still survived in the East, however, and one more would emerge before the curtain fell on the Age of Ancient Empires.

CHAPTER FOURTEEN

THE FORMATION OF THE ISLAMIC WORLD EMPIRE

His is whatever is in the heavens, and whatever is on the earth.

– Qur'an section from the Dome of the Rock Inscription[1]

* How did the inhabitants of the Arabian Peninsula become empire

* In what ways did Islam show continuity with the Age of Ancient Empires?
* In what ways did Islam break with the ancient past?
* What marked the end of the Age of Ancient Empires?

IN 691/692, a leader of Islam's first dynasty, the Umayyads, constructed the Dome of the Rock in Jerusalem (Fig. 14.1). "Built this cupola the servant of God Abd al-Malik, Commander of the Faithful: May God accept this work from him and be satisfied with him," proclaims the dedicatory inscription. The monument, among the first and most famous works of early Islamic architecture, effectively proclaimed the emergence of the last ancient empire. Like all its predecessors, this new empire needed high-status architecture to assert its identity, respectability, and strength in a remarkable age of empires now more than fifteen hundred years old.

To accomplish this, the monument looked both to the past and to the future. Through imitation of antique monuments, it asserted the Islamic Empire's place within the pantheon of ancient empires. It was modeled after a Byzantine baptistery and pilgrimage center, and its interior decoration clearly echoed Byzantine and Sasanid royal imperial imagery and style. It was located on an ancient and broadly recognized holy site, the Temple Mount, where Judaism's First and Second Temples had once stood. Christians and Jews had long revered the site of Jerusalem, and Muhammad and his early followers

14.1. The Dome of the Rock. Picture by Lee Wishing IV.

originally prayed toward this holy city before he officially shifted the direction
of prayer to Mecca.

The new empire also declared its superiority in this old world via the
Dome of the Rock. It was located exactly opposite, and rising above, the dome
of the Christian Church of the Holy Sepulcher, sending a distinct message to
the Christian majority (Fig. 14.2). More explicitly, perhaps, unambiguously
antitrinitarian passages from the Qur'an encircle the interior arcades under
the dome – this was a new and better empire under a superior revelation. Late
Antiquity's distinct fusion of a centralized political system with a zealous and
narrow religious ideology was clear in this monument, as in the final ancient
empire that constructed it.

The Dome of the Rock thus provides a valuable window onto the major
themes of this final chapter. Like the Dome, the Islamic world empire blended
old and new, marking a significant transition in the history of the Near East
and the ancient world in general. With Islam's rise, the Byzantine Empire –
which, counting its Roman phase, was now approximately eight hundred
years old – ceased to be universalist in ideology and became one kingdom

14.2. The Dome of the Rock and the Church of the Holy Sepulchre. Picture by George Klaeren.

among others. The Sasanid Empire suddenly disappeared altogether. Both empires continued to serve as models for the new Islamic Empire in myriad ways, however, and Islam inherited a central quality of the Age of Ancient Empires in general: an imperial ideology in which a ruler dispenses justice on behalf of God or gods in order to maintain an orderly universe/cosmos: "His is whatever is in the heavens and whatever is on earth," as a Qur'anic line inscribed at the Dome of the Rock reads.

The Umayyad dynasty pulled together an impressive military and economic system to support their cosmic universalist claims. They would rule the Islamic community, the *umma*, for a little more than a century, never seeing themselves as one realm among others. They were divinely appointed to expand their empire throughout the whole world, bringing the righteous reign of God over all. Such universalism, familiar to ancient empires since the rise of the Neo-Assyrians, effectively ceased with the demise of the Umayyads in 750.

A new age then emerged as the Islamic Empire, like the Byzantine before it, settled down to an existence as one kingdom – or rather several kingdoms – among others. The Age of Ancient Empires had ended in Europe in the fifth century and among the Byzantines and the Sasanids in the seventh century. The long age would finally close, in the Near East, in the eighth century somewhere between the fall of the Umayyads and the early years of their successors, the Abbasids.

THE CLASH OF EMPIRES AND THE END
OF THE (ANCIENT) WORLD

With only a few brief respites, Byzantine and Sasanid warfare raged on during the latter half of the sixth and first third of the seventh century, defining the immediate context of Islam's rise. The superpower contest drained valuable human and material resources from both empires, one of many factors contributing to the early Muslim victories. These wars also broadly shaped Late Antique mentalities both within and beyond the two great empires. Directed by their respective religious teachings, many Christian, Jewish, and Zoroastrian observers made sense of the military and political crises in apocalyptic terms. The strife and catastrophe surely marked the end of the world, they reckoned, even if each group defined that moment in their own way – the coming of the Davidic Messiah, the triumphal return of Christ, or the ultimate showdown between forces of cosmos and chaos, light and darkness, truth and falsehood. At one desperate moment, a Byzantine emperor focused apocalyptic fervor by widely proclaiming a Holy War against the Persian infidels. He did this at precisely the time that Muhammad's movement was emerging. Islam was thus shaped by the general Late Antique apocalyptic mood and this Holy War ideology. This would be yet another example of how peripheral resistance to an empire can incorporate a central imperial ideology, as we saw with Urartu in Chapter Three – that is, fighting fire with fire.

In the last decade of the sixth century, a rare moment of peace came to the empires. Khusro II, a rival to the reigning Sasanid emperor, asked the Byzantine emperor Maurice to help him secure the Sasanid throne. This was not the first time that something like this had happened, but the tone of this negotiation reveals some larger shifts under way. Khusro's emissary to the Byzantines presented his plea for intervention along with an unprecedented formula for lasting peace between the two empires. Peace could be maintained, he declared, if both empires would simply drop their respective claims to the world, that is, universalism:

It is impossible for a single monarchy to embrace the innumerable cares
of the organization of the universe, and with one's mind's rudder to direct

a creation as great as that over which the sun watches. For it is never possible for the earth to resemble a unity of the divine and primary rule, and to obtain a disposition corresponding to that of the upper order.[2]

Khusro II's plea for Byzantine intervention worked, as did his bid for the throne, and the *shahinshah* awarded the Byzantines with important territorial concessions along their eastern frontier. Such explicit and high-level questioning of universalism, however, foreshadowed some fundamental changes. Even if universalism was subdued, for example, in third-century Rome, ancient empires had never officially conceded that world domination was ultimately impossible. That had been a guiding principle from the very dawn of the Age of Ancient Empires. When the Byzantines finally abandoned this ancient quest, a new Islamic world empire would more closely resemble an ancient empire than did the Byzantine.

The Byzantines did not intervene in Sasanid affairs from a position of comparative strength, however. Political, military, and economic problems were plaguing them at center and periphery alike. Assassination and usurpation were not unknown in their make at this same time. Worse, the government was having some serious problems paying soldiers, especially the Armenian and Arabic-speaking mercenaries who were important federates for the Byzantine army, even if on a campaign-by-campaign basis.[3] The Byzantine chronicler Theophanes recorded a telling interchange between a Byzantine bureaucrat and some Arabic-speaking bedouins around this time:

> Some of the nearby Arabs received a small subsidy from the Emperor for guarding the mouths of the desert. At that time a eunuch came to distribute the soldiers' wages. The Arabs came to get their pay, as was customary, but the eunuch drove them away, saying, "The Emperor pays his soldiers with difficulty; with how much more to such dogs as you?"[4]

Meanwhile, renewed invasions simply exacerbated these internal problems. In the late sixth century, two new invaders appeared from the East, the Slavs and the Avars, significantly overstretching Byzantium's already-strained resources. To make matters worse, the emperor Maurice was overthrown and murdered in a coup by Phocas, one of his generals. Partly to avenge the death of Maurice, his former patron, Khusro II broke his truce in the first few years of the seventh century and invaded Byzantine territory, claiming that he was avenging a recently usurped Byzantine emperor. He also likely had dreams of restoring a Persian empire to its Achaemenid limits and glory. Over the next two decades, the Sasanids enjoyed much success, seizing and apparently spreading destruction in Antioch, Jerusalem, and Alexandria.

They even joined together with Avars for a crippling, if not ultimately successful, siege of Constantinople. Although most of these areas were restored briefly to Byzantine rule, as we will see, Syria, Palestine, Egypt, and parts of Anatolia never fully recovered from these destructive conquests before the completely unexpected arrival of conquering Arabian armies from the south.

The Byzantine emperor during the most successful of the Sasanid campaigns, Heraclius (r. 610–641), slowly figured out how to deal with the Sasanid threat. He would be the last emperor of early (ancient) Byzantium. The Sasanid capture of the "True Cross" from Jerusalem, which seemed to signal the end of Byzantium (if not the world itself), caused him to nearly abandon Constantinople and move the Byzantine capital to Carthage, North Africa (where he had grown up), held by the Byzantines from the time of Justinian's conquests. The True Cross, widely believed to be the one on which Christ had died and that was built, it was said, from wood from the Tree of Life in the Garden of Eden, was Late Antiquity's most renowned holy relic. Dissuaded from the drastic plan to abandon Constantinople, he then proposed a series of desperate measures to save the empire. He significantly reduced military pay and even seized gold and silver from church décor to meet army pay, revamped the army, allied with the powerful Turkic Khazars, heavily recruited Armenian cavalry, and put forth a strong image of Holy War against Persian infidels. The desire to reconquer Jerusalem and recover the True Cross from Ctesiphon lent a strong religious aura to his campaigns. Ideology of a Holy War was thus widely disseminated, particularly among those, like the Arabians, needed in the war effort. Through these efforts, Heraclius was able to turn the campaign around.

By 630, after winning several crucial victories and taking advantage of internal problems that were now plaguing the Sasanids – *shahinshah* Khusro II himself had been betrayed and killed by members of the Sasanid nobility in 628 – Heraclius reclaimed Jerusalem and returned the True Cross (Fig. 14.5). His coins immediately and proudly showcased the relic. He styled himself as a "new Constantine," and Church writers of his time and after presented him as a Christian Alexander the Great and an apocalyptic crusading king. For the moment anyway, the Byzantines were riding high, and the Sasanids were clearly on the defensive.

In just three years, however, the new balance of power was utterly upended as attacks by Arabic-speaking warriors came against both empires. The Sasanid Empire collapsed entirely in less than two decades. The Byzantine Empire survived, but immediately lost significant territorial holding; the Roman Mediterranean Empire was now gone for good. Reversing centuries

14.3. Combat between Emperor Heraclius and Khusraw (Chosroe/Khusrau) II. Réunion des
Musées Nationaux/Art Resource, NY.

14.4. Walls of Diyarbakir, near the Byzantine–Sassanid frontier. Slide by Mark W. Graham.

of universalism, the Byzantines aimed merely to survive, encircled by hostile peoples.

The Byzantines had long lacked the human and material resources to support their universalist claims; the invasions by Arabic-speaking nomads made that all too clear. The Byzantine Empire had a new mood, one often described, for lack of a better term, as "medieval"; it was no longer an ancient empire. The Age of Ancient Empires had one more shining example left, however, one that owed much to these two prostrate empires.

THE ARABS AND THE RISE OF ISLAM

To understand the rise of Islam, we must consider, once more, different levels of historical time. Both the top layer, that of events, and the middle layer, of longer-term sociological patterns, worked together to produce one of history's pivotal moments. The immediate conquests, as often, dominate in the sources, but they were just a part of the story.

As seen in Chapter Thirteen, Arabic speakers had long played a part in the back-and-forth struggles between the Byzantine and Sasanid Empires. "To the Arabs on both sides this war was a source of much profit, and they wrought their will upon both kingdoms," according to one late-fifth/early-sixth-century Christian writer from Edessa.[5] Their participation was itself connected to several demographic shifts going on in the Near East over a few centuries.

Centuries of migrations by Arabic speakers into southern Mesopotamia and the Levant moved parallel to larger demographic shifts going on along the frontier between the Byzantines and the Sasanids as well as the southern frontiers of both empires. Recent archaeological studies, for example, have revealed changing settlement patterns in the Byzantine Near East in general between the fifth and seventh centuries. In the fifth and sixth centuries, it appears that Byzantine settlements became more concentrated, populations grew, and agriculture expanded. The earlier seventh century (a bit earlier in some estimations), however, saw the beginning of a definite period of decline in population, concentration of towns, and agriculture. Along the frontier with Arabia, the Byzantine population was drastically reduced, and the frontier settlements and defenses in the area were largely abandoned. When the conquering Arab armies arrived here in the seventh century, they found a significantly weakened Byzantine population. Demographic shifts and military conquests together help explain their victories in this region.

By the early seventh century, areas of the Near East had significant and socially diverse Arabic-speaking populations, which settled in different

14.5. Emperor Heraclius barefoot and wearing a shirt carrying the Holy Cross to Jerusalem. Réunion des Musées Nationaux/Art Resource, NY.

patterns. As they moved out of their original homeland, they brought traditional lifestyles with them from the Arabian Peninsula. Many Arabic speakers were settled cultivators, tending grain or palm trees in oases. Many others were traders or craftsmen in small market towns throughout the Arabian Peninsula and beyond. A small but influential minority were nomads or bedouins, pasturing camels, goats, and sheep.

The Arabic speakers did not have an overarching identity as Arabs per se, politically, socially, or religiously. They tended to identify with large tribal groupings known as *qabilah*, and with smaller clan and family units within them. Although *qabilah* identity was not necessarily exclusive or fixed, the tribal units inspired great loyalty and pride. Strong competition, contention, and even deep animosity and blood feuds played out among the tribes and families. Larger polities such as the Ghassanid and the Lakhimid kingdoms, as we saw in Chapter Thirteen, were themselves of fairly recent vintage, arguably forged as secondary states amid an early phase of the Byzantine–Sasanid conflicts. Collectively, they spoke essentially mutually unintelligible dialects of Aramaic and Arabic. By Muhammad's day, a common poetic dialect of Arabic was just beginning to gain wide acceptance as a sort of lingua franca or *koiné*. It would in turn become the language of the Qur'an, the revelation to Muhammad and Islam's holy book. Various religions proliferated and competed among the Arabians, ranging from pantheism to Jewish and Christian monotheism, the latter mostly in Miaphysite or Nestorian forms, as we saw in the previous chapter.

Muhammad was born into the powerful Quraysh *qabilah* in the central Arabian city of Mecca around 570. Unlike regions to its north, Mecca itself had managed to stay out of the Byzantine–Sasanid conflict, but only with conscious effort. In Muhammad's youth, Quraysh leaders thwarted Byzantine efforts to forge an alliance with Mecca. Mecca was by no means isolated from the old world, however. It held a position on two major trade arteries: a North–South route ultimately connecting the Mediterranean Sea and Indian Ocean and a West–East route that linked Mesopotamia with Ethiopia and East Africa. Inhabitants of Arabia had long carried on trade – as far back as the Neo-Babylonian Empire (see Chapter Four). Mecca also was a pilgrimage center, focused heavily on a building known as the Ka'aba that housed, among a plethora of gods, a divine relic, the Black Stone. The Ka'aba attracted a wide variety of religious pilgrims, even Christians who came to honor God the Creator.

Very little is known of Muhammad's early life. Almost every claim about him, even his year of birth, is hotly disputed. By general consensus, sometime in the first decade of the seventh century, following a career as a moderately successful merchant, he began a life of local wandering, asking the large "meaning of life" type of questions. After a decade of such wandering, he received a vision in which an angel called him to be a messenger of the one and only God. He donned the mantle of a prophet and began unfolding a basic message, which one leading scholar succinctly summarizes:

> The world would end; God the all-powerful, who had created human
> beings, would judge them all; the delights of Heaven and the pains of
> Hell were depicted in vivid colours. If in their lives they submitted to
> God's Will, they could rely on His mercy when they came to judgement;
> and it was God's will that they should show their gratitude by regular
> prayer and other observances, and by benevolence and sexual restraint.[6]

A Believer's Movement slowly came together around this message.[7] The title Muslim literally means "submitter" – that is, to the will of the one and only God. The movement initially included all those who shared Muhammad's vision of establishing a righteous community on earth in preparation for the coming of God. Monotheists like Jews and Christians numbered among

Muhammad's initial followers; devout adherents of either faith would have no serious qualms with his basic message. When Muhammad began demanding that all of Mecca submit to the one and only God or face divine wrath, he ran afoul of local polytheist leaders and had to flee for his life in 622; the flight was known as the Hijra, and the year of it became Year One in the Muslim calendar, which was proclaimed about a decade after his death (before, it might be noted, the idea of a Christian calendar had caught on anywhere).

He landed in Yathrib (later called Medina), a trade depot due north of Mecca that had once been a part of the Neo-Babylonian Empire (see Chapter Four). While in Yathrib, his movement armed and began interfering with traders going to and from Mecca. Not long before he died in 632, Muhammad and his armed followers made their way back to Mecca; his movement by this time had grown to an impressive size and, although there was some stiff resistance to his return, many Meccans welcomed them back. Only later, perhaps even several decades after Muhammad's death, did Muslim identity became hardened enough to necessarily exclude Christians and Jews from the new Believer's Movement. Meanwhile, many Christian Arabic speakers

What drove Muhammad and his armies to conquer is a subject of deepest controversy. If the Qur'an can be taken as an accurate indication of his message (another topic of serious debate), it is clear that the common Late Antique themes of universalism and apocalypticism shaped both his message and his method. A significant portion of the Qur'an addresses the Apocalypse (the Last Day, the Overwhelming Event) when God the righteous judge would return and set the whole world to right. Believers were enjoined to a Holy War to prepare themselves and the world for the impending day of reckoning: Muhammad's last recorded speech admonished that "Muslims should fight all men until they say 'There is no god but God.'"[8] The goal seems to have been to build a universal righteous community – a melding of Late Antique monotheism with dynamics drawn from deep in the Age of Ancient Empires.

With Muhammad's death in 632, the big question was whether the movement could hold together without him. He had been the religious and political head of the *umma*, the community of Believers. As with some other great innovators we have encountered throughout the Age of Ancient Empires, he left no clear succession plan. Two of Muhammad's senior companions, Umar and Abu Bakr, his father-in-law, called for unity. When Umar pledged loyalty to Abu Bakr, the entire Quraysh tribe followed suit, and Abu Bakr was declared the leader of the community, with the title of *khalifa*. A few Believers tried to claim the prophetic mantle for themselves; at this point, Muhammad was proclaimed the *last* prophet, a claim he probably did not make during his lifetime, but one with powerful focusing and unifying effects for his movement thereafter. Within two years of Muhammad's death, the *umma* was more powerful than ever before, and conquests pushed to the north, the west, and the east.

Initial expansion against the Arabian kingdoms and regions of the north was quick and fairly easy. The Lakhmid and Ghassanid coalitions dissolved almost immediately, and the Byzantines and Persians did not assist their erstwhile allies. The great empires had long looked down on the Arab-speaking peoples, and thus there was little love lost. One Arab ambassador proclaimed to the Sasanid *shahinshah*: "Once the Arabs were a wretched race, whom you could tread underfoot with impunity. We were reduced to eating dogs and lizards. But, for our glory, God has raised up a prophet among us."[9] Such treatment, along with unpredictable and often infrequent pay, made the move to a growing and successful army a fairly easy choice for many. This created immediate and serious problems for the Byzantine and Sasanid Empires for whom the only realistic defense against an offensive was the Arabic speakers themselves. The empires had both ignored the Arabian frontier while concentrating much-needed resources elsewhere. The demographic shifts within the Byzantine Near East had left key areas sparsely populated and unable to stand against the invasions. Again, two levels of historical time were well meshed together here.

Abu Bakr was succeeded as the political, military, and religious head of the *umma* by Umar (r. 634–644), who put the community directly on the path toward world empire. Through a combination of diplomacy, negotiation, and outright conquest, the expansion under Umar was remarkably swift. Principal cities such as Damascus and Alexandria, a granary of the Byzantine Empire and only recently retaken by the Byzantines from the Sasanids, were acquired through negotiation. Most areas were won through conquest. The Arabic armies, well trained in the fighting techniques of the great empires, bested the Byzantine and Sasanid armies in armored cavalry warfare.

It is important to note that the Arabic armies were not simply copies of the Byzantine and Sasanid. They were led by a well-organized and highly effective Arabic-speaking warrior aristocracy, and they augmented the cavalry warfare with camels, more effective in the desert terrain. The armies first routed the Byzantines at Yarmuk in 636, only four years after Muhammad's death; in the following year, they took Antioch as well as delivered the Sasanid Empire a blow from which it never recovered at the Battle of Qadisiya. By 641, the Sasanid realm had largely descended into anarchy, and a decade later, the

14.6. Ahwal-i Qiyamat – Muhammed [sic] and the first three caliphs (*khalifas*), Abu Bakr, Umar,
Uthman. BildarchivPreussischerKulturbesitz/Art Resource, NY.

final *shahinshah*, Yazdegird III (r. 632–651), grandson of Khusro II, was killed
while fleeing from the armies.

Further weakening Byzantine power in Syria and other vital regions were
heterodox Christian clergy who did not explicitly encourage resistance or
revolt against the invading armies. An older generation of scholars believed
that active Miaphysite and Nestorian betrayal of Byzantine orthodox overlords was the major reason for Islamic victories; although this did happen in a
few instances such as when Nestorians handed over Takrit and Mosul, most
recent scholars believe that this was not the norm. The reticence of such leaders to encourage significant resistance to the invading armies clearly played
into the invaders' hands, however; this was one of many factors contributing
to their victories.

As the armies expanded, they generally did not settle down in antique
cities among the Christians, Jews, and Zoroastrians. Rather, they founded
garrison towns where they lived as a separate conquering class, supported by

lucrative tribute. Kufah, Basrah, and Fustat were some of these garrison towns that later would grow into important cities in their own right. In each garrison town, the successful armies promptly built a simple mosque where the local military commander led the faithful in daily prayers – military and religious power were fused tightly together. Under Umar's successor, Uthman (r. 644–656), the Muslims took to the sea, winning Cyprus, largely with the help of Phoenician sailors. At this stage, conversion to Islam as such was not really an issue – many Christians fought alongside Muslims in these conquests, and many Christians lived in Muslim-ruled territories free from harassment so long as they did not revolt.

As the armies expanded in multiple directions, trouble was brewing at the political center. Uthman and Ali ibn Abi Talib (r. 656–661), the next two *khalifas* after Umar, were assassinated by political opponents. Ali was the cousin and son-in-law of Muhammad, and his supporters would much later remember his assassination as a key moment in the formation of Shi'ite (from *Shia Ali*, or Party of Ali) identity. Stability returned to the *umma* rather quickly, however, as Ali's son, Hasan, worked out a deal to pass leadership on to Muawiyah (r. 661–680), a prominent member of the powerful Umayya family, who founded the first Islamic dynasty, the Umayyads.

THE UMAYYADS: THE FIRST ISLAMIC (AND THE LAST ANCIENT) EMPIRE

The Umayyad period (661–750) was the only time in history that the entire Islamic *umma* was united around a single political center. During this period, strong and influential Islamic institutions came together to create and support the first Islamic Empire – with an organized army, fairly standardized taxation, consistent coinage, and politico-religious public works such as the Dome of the Rock and the Great Mosque of Damascus. With its capital in Damascus, Syria, the realm remained a Mediterranean empire under the Umayyad *khalifas*. The interplay between clear continuities with the ancient past and creative innovations defined this period, especially in its politics and religion.

For the first generation of their rule, the Umayyads borrowed much directly from their Sasanid and Byzantine predecessors. In the western portions of the realm, especially at Damascus, Greek continued as an official administrative language of the realm in matters of taxation, as it had for several decades. In the eastern portions of the realm, the Persian language of Pahlavi, or Middle Persian, retained a special administrative role. Early Umayyad coinage was struck in barely modified Byzantine and Sasanid styles. The fronts of many coins were essentially unchanged from Byzantine models,

14.7. Byzantine solidus, from Carthage, 610–613. British Museum/Art Resource, NY.

but on the reverse a vertical bar simply replaced the cross on a pedestal, as on
Heraclius' coinage (Figs. 14.7–14.8).

The Umayyads also at first followed older Roman patterns of elite cooperation, leaving Christian or Zoroastrian governors often left in their official

positions after their homelands were folded into the growing Islamic world
empire. St. John of Damascus, to give just one famous example, was from an
Arabic-speaking Christian family of that city who had formerly worked in the
Byzantine (and maybe Sasanian) administration and then later served in the
same capacity under the Umayyads.

By the second generation of the Umayyads, beginning with the reign
of Abd al-Malik (r. 685–705), some clear signs of differentiation signaled a

14.8. Gold dinar with a standing caliph, Umayyad dynasty, 695–696. British Museum/Art
Resource, NY.

14.9. Gold dinar of Caliph (*khalifa*) Abd al-Malik. British Museum/Art Resource, NY.

stronger and more self-confident Islamic identity. In the last decade of the
seventh century, Arabic replaced Greek and Pahlavi as the administrative
language of the entire realm. At almost exactly the same time, a distinctively
Islamic coinage began to appear (Fig. 14.9). The new coins featured Arabic
religious quotations such as the *shahada*: "There is no god but God, and
Muhammad is his prophet." By this time as well, prestigious administrative
positions were going almost exclusively to Arabic-speaking Muslims, and
patterns of elite replacement became the norm in newly acquired regions.

Also by this time, the confessional lines around a distinctive Islam were
more firmly set, and Christians and Jews were increasingly excluded from the
Believer's Movement, a change with clear religious and political implications.
The Dome of the Rock, built in the late seventh century, provides interesting
evidence of this change (Fig. 14.10). Circling the interior arcade under the
dome runs a long inscription:

> O ye People of the Book, overstep not bounds in your religion; and
> of God speak only truth. The Messiah, Jesus, son of Mary, is only an
> apostle of God, and His Word which he conveyed into Mary, and a Spirit
> proceeding from Him. Believe therefore in God and His apostles, and say
> not "Three." It will be better for you. God is only one God. Far be it from
> His glory that He should have a son. His is whatever is in the heavens,
> and whatever is on the earth. . . . God witnesses that there is no God
> but He; and the angels, and men endued with knowledge, established in
> righteousness, proclaim there is no God but He, the Mighty, the Wise.[10]

14.10. Interior view of cupola of the Dome of the Rock. Scala/Art Resource, NY.

On the whole, the Qur'an is rarely so explicitly antitrinitarian; in fact, this is one of only a few such passages – by far the strongest one – from the Qur'an. The choice of this particular inscription made a strong political/religious statement of Islamic identity, and its inclusion on the Dome's interior complements many other indicators of a hardening Islamic identity.

Christians (and Jews) maintained special status, however, as "People of the Book" (Ahl al-Kitab) and *dhimmis*, "protected people"; Zoroastrians held the latter status as well. There was little if any forced conversion among peoples of these faiths. This represented something of a break from general Late Antique tendencies to insist that all subjects embrace a narrow orthodoxy. Part of this was simply pragmatic, no doubt – for a few centuries after the initial conquests, Muslims remained a minority among Christians in former Byzantine holdings and among Zoroastrians within Persia. It was actually not until the ninth century – a century or so after the Umayyad collapse – that Muslims made up a majority in most areas of the *umma*. All non-Muslims, however, were required to pay a special tax, the *jizya*. Never before in the ancient world had tax assessment depended on confessional identity. Some modern scholars point to the *jizya* itself as an unintended incentive to conversion.

Such differentiation, however, moved alongside many traditional Near Eastern and Byzantine patterns of rulership that the Umayyads fostered, primarily those that combined religious and political authority. An aura of divine power had long hung over ancient rulers, and the Umayyad *khalifas* carried on the tradition. Their new subjects throughout the Mediterranean and Near East had long expected and relied on rulers who established and maintained justice on behalf of God or gods. The succession to the office of *khalifa* was standardized through traditional and divinely sanctioned ceremonies. Umayyad *khalifas* ascended to the throne at the city of Jerusalem, regarded by Jews, Christians, and Muslims alike as the *omphalos*, the primordial navel of the world.

Umayyad architecture tells an interesting story of the competitive borrowing and adaptation that characterized the Umayyad period. Much about the Dome of the Rock was clearly recognizable to those from an old world: the styles of its thin walls, classical columns, symmetrically patterned marble paneling, mosaics, and the dome itself were all borrowed directly and indirectly from Byzantine structures. To Christians and others, it called to mind a baptistery and pilgrimage center. The interior of the building, still remarkably intact since its original construction, is decorated with a variety of Byzantine- and Sasanid-inspired royal motifs. Pictured trumpets signaled Judgment Day; these, along with much else about the monument, proclaim the Apocalypse or the coming consummation of the age in familiar Late Antique terms.

Built during a critical turning point in Muslim identity and self-expression under *khalifa* Abd al-Malik, the monument features unprecedented elements as well. Like the conquering armies, this was not a simple copy of a past model. Conspicuously missing from the interior décor were any human or animal figures, extremely common in Byzantine and Sasanid art, religious or otherwise. By the time of the Umayyads, Islam had come to frown on such representations in religious art – only plants and vegetation appear; this was a new and better empire under a final revelation, after all.

Even the most distinctive piece of Islamic architecture, the mosque, shows both continuities with and differences from the ancient past. The most famous Umayyad mosque further nuances the story. The Great Mosque of Damascus was built by *khalifa* al-Walid (r. 705–715), the son and successor of Abd al-Malik, who had built the Dome of the Rock (Fig. 14.11). Damascus was an exception to conquering settlement patterns; here, many Muslims did settle among the city's population rather than in the garrison towns. Thus,

14.11. Ilwan, hall of worship, Great Umayyad Mosque of Damascus. DeA Picture Library/Art Resource, NY.

an important mosque was needed in Damascus, and it had the opportunity to make a bold and public statement.

The Great Mosque that was built in Damascus was constructed on the site of the Christian Cathedral of St. John (which, in turn, stood within the sacred precinct of the ancient temple of Haddad/Jupiter) and was designed in part to upstage the imperial Byzantine churches of the conquered Levant. It was a large mosque, and had a variety of important functions beyond the most obvious one of congregational prayers and worship. The *khalifas* and governors addressed the Muslim faithful here. It also housed the court of the Muslim judge, the *qadi*, and served as a center of Muslim education.

The actual style of the mosque looked back to Islam's origins: it was designed as an Arabic community center modeled after Muhammad's own house, which had a large courtyard where the Believers could gather. Some architectural elements recall the open court and three-aisled hall and the Roman forum and basilica, however. The courtyard mosaics of the Great Mosque call to mind floor mosaics of Roman and Byzantine villas, but without human or animal figures. The Great Mosque presented a stunning combination of new and old, strongly asserting the presence and identity of an ancient Islamic empire.

A later and more remote Umayyad building likewise makes a strong imperial and universalist statement that blends new and old in a lively way. At Qusayr Amra, a retreat palace and bathhouse in modern-day Jordan, six past and present world leaders were painted on a wall and labeled in both Arabic and Greek; four of their titles are still legible – a Byzantine leader, simply labeled Caesar; Khusro, former *shahinshah* of the Sasanids; Roderick, erstwhile king of the Visigoths of Spain; the Negus of Ethiopia; and two others, variously identified as the emperor of China, a Khan of a Central Asian Turkic group such as the powerful Khazars, and an Indian prince.

In the words of the foremost scholar of this complex, "The six kings are symbolic figures who stand for the whole political and cultural heritage of the world the Arabs had now inherited."[11] The Umayyad nobleman who built and decorated it could now gaze on the rulers of the world, of the immediate past and present, as if they were coming to him, in a remote semidesert region, for an audience. His Arab empire had surpassed all empires in greatness. The complex also has an audience hall, a bathhouse, mosaic floors, hunting scenes, and figures of scantily clad women and men – all clear incorporations of Roman bath culture into even remote sections of the Umayyad realm.

The Umayyad rulers continued age-old patterns of world conquest as well. Their conquests brought the *umma* to its early height, drawing roughly the frontiers it would hold for centuries. In the West, Byzantine North Africa and Visigothic Spain fell to Muslim armies by the early eighth century; they seriously threatened the Frankish kingdom, but it survived. In the East, armies moved into northwest India (today's Pakistan) and central Asia, where they met and bested the expanding Tang Chinese at Samarqand. Islam would continue to spread unevenly and sporadically after the fall of the Umayyads, but the heyday of Islamic conquest was by then in the past.

Immense wealth flowed into the Umayyad treasuries from these conquests. Ironically, the wealth that helped proclaim the empire and adorn it on par with previous world empires significantly contributed to the dynasty's fall. Late Antiquity's general tendency toward narrow and unyielding religious rigor would ultimately inspire some to sever the hand that fed them. Some Muslims were not much impressed with the new levels of opulence and luxuriousness that seemed to come with military success, as had long been the case in the Age of Ancient Empires. These remembered or imagined (or longed for) a rigorous period of Islamic history in which ascetic piety and apocalyptic fervor guided the life of the Muslim community.

Opposition came from several other quarters as well. A descendant of Muhammad's uncle, Abbas, helped pull together various strands of opposition "in the name of a member of the Prophet's family." One of these strands

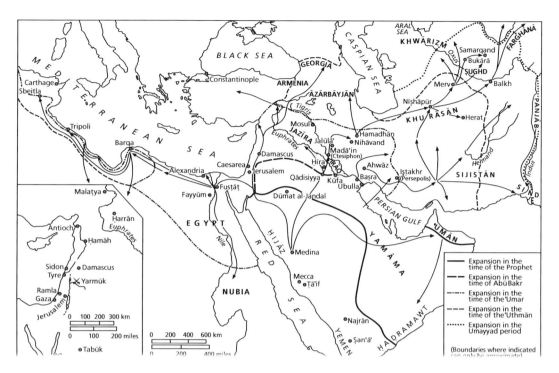

14.12. The Muslim world up to c. 750. In *Cambridge History of Islam*, vol. 1 (1970), p. 59.

was partisanship for Ali, Muhammad's cousin and son-in-law, whose memory inspired a small but dedicated movement that would eventually crystallize as the Shi'ites. The "Party of Ali" looked back to the assassination of Ali as a critical point at which the Muslim community began to lose its way. The Umayyads had only exacerbated the central problems thereafter, these critics claimed. In addition, a Muslim army from Khurasan, supported by a hetero-geneous matrix of anti-Umayyad factions, moved westward and overthrew the Umayyads in 750.

The new dynasty, the Abbasids (named after Muhammad's uncle), was centered in Baghdad, close to Ctesiphon, the old Sasanid capital. The Abbasids carved out a specifically Middle Eastern kingdom, as opposed to the Mediterranean empire, which ended with the Umayyads. Although they arose with assistance from ascetic purists – which they promptly disavowed and betrayed once they came into power – the Abbasids quickly outshone all contemporary and many past rivals in splendor. Baghdad soon became a world-renowned city of wonders heralded by visitors from far and wide.

Modern scholars have noted many powerful allusions to past empires in the very structure of Baghdad. The city was built on a strictly circular plan, reminiscent of Sasanid cities, and the *khalifas* were elevated to office in Baghdad in Sasanid-style court ceremonial. By this time, however, the ancient world had become a memory, a distinct historical period from the past to be emulated. Much like their contemporary far to the West, the Frankish Empire of Charlemagne, the Abbasids would look back to the ancient world as a distinct period to copy, but the very effort of trying to resurrect a past era presumed that it was by now gone.

Unlike the Umayyads, the Abbasids were not militarily expansive. With their rise, the period of early Islamic conquest came to an end, and a period of uneasy and ultimately unsuccessful consolidation of the *umma* began. The Abbasids never, in fact, ruled over the entire *umma*, nor would any other Islamic rulers after them. They arose through a coalition united only by opposition to the Umayyads; they desperately struggled to maintain unity once they removed that dynasty from power.

The establishment of a breakaway Umayyad state in Spain just after 750 was a sign of things to come, and throughout the Abbasid period (750–1258), especially after 950, the Abbasids often found themselves hardly in control of areas outside the immediate environs of Baghdad. Egypt and North Africa quickly learned to function apart from the Abbasid rulers, with their own independent or quasi-independent kingdoms, as did many parts of Iran. Like the Byzantine and Frankish Empires to their west, the Abbasids necessarily came to define themselves as one realm among others, and a new period began in the Near East, often known, for better or for worse, as "medieval." The original Mesopotamian heartland of the Age of Ancient Empires had become its resting place.

NOTES

INTRODUCTION

1. Vol. 1 (Cambridge: Cambridge University Press, 1986), vii.
2. "The Pastophorus of the Vatican (XXVIth Dynasty)," in *Records of the Past*, trans. Peter Le Page Renouf, in ed. S. Birch, Series I, vol. X (London: Samuel Bagster
3. Keith Hancock, *Survey of British Commonwealth Affairs*, vol. 2 (London: Oxford University Press, 1940), 1.
4. M. I. Finley, "The Fifth-Century Athenian Empire: A Balance Sheet," in *Imperialism in the Ancient World*, ed. P. D. A. Garnsey and C. R. Whittaker (Cambridge: Cambridge University Press, 1978), 103–4.
5. *Empires* (Ithaca, NY: Cornell University Press, 1986), 12.
6. *Sources of Social Power*, vol. 1, 19.
7. *Sources of Social Power*, vol. 1, 19.
8. Livy, *Books from the Foundation of the City* 8.13.16.
9. Joseph Schumpeter, *Imperialism and Social Classes*, trans. Heinz Norden (New York: Augustus M. Kelley, 1951), 6–7.
10. Thucydides, *History of the Peloponnesian War* 5.89.

CHAPTER 1

1. E. E. Evans-Pritchard, *Social Anthropology and Other Essays* (Glencoe: Free Press, 1962), 210.
2. James B. Pritchard, ed. *The Ancient Near East. Volume 1: Anthology of Texts and Pictures* (Princeton, NJ: Princeton University Press, 1958), 51; hereafter "Pritchard ANE."
3. "Vase Inscription of Lugal-Zagesi," cited from J. Nicholas Postgate, *Early Mesopotamia: Society and Economy at the Dawn of History* (London: Routledge, 1992), Text 2:3.
4. E. Sollberger, *Corpus des inscriptions "royales" présargoniques de Lagash*: Ukg. 16 (Geneva 1956), cited

from Amélie Kuhrt, *The Ancient Near East c. 3000–330 B.C.*, vol. 1 (London: Routledge, 1994), 43.
5. Walter Farber, "Die Vergöttlichung Naram Sîns," *Orientalia* 52 (1983), 67–72, cited from Marc Van de Mieroop, *A History of the Ancient Near East ca. 3000–323 B.C.* (Malden, MA: Blackwell, 2004), 64.
6. Pritchard, ANE, 175–76
7. Pritchard, ANE, 262–63
8. William L. Moran, *The Amarna Letters* (Baltimore: Johns Hopkins University Press, 1992), 61–62.
9. Pritchard, ANE, 185.
10. Pritchard, ANE, 186.

CHAPTER 2

1. A. Livingstone, *Court Poetry and Literary Miscellanea*, State Archives of Assyria 3 (Helsinki: Helsinki University Press, 1989), 26–27.
2. "Ashurnasirpal II (883–859): Expedition to the Lebanon," cited from Pritchard, ANE, 188.
3. A. K. Grayson, *Assyrian Rulers of the Early First Millennium. B.C. I (1114–859 B.C.)*, The Royal Inscriptions of Mesopotamia, vol. 2 (Toronto: University of Toronto Press, 1991), 275.
4. Grayson, 293.
5. Amelie Kuhrt, *The Ancient Near East c. 3000–330 B.C.*, vol. 2 (London: Routledge, 1994), 511.
6. Kuhrt, vol. 2, 509.
7. Steven Garfinkle, "The Assyrians: A New Look at an Ancient Power," in *Current Issues and the Study of the Ancient Near East*, ed. Mark W. Chavalas (Claremont, CA: Regina Books, 2007), 53–96, at 82.
8. Garfinkle, 83.
9. *Nations and Nationalism* (Ithaca, NY: Cornell University Press, 1983), 9–10.
10. Kuhrt, vol. 2, 534.
11. Gershon Galil, *The Lower Stratum Families in the Neo-Assyrian Period* (Leiden: Brill, 2007).

12. Francis Joannés, *The Age of Empires: Mesopotamia in the First Millennium B.C.*, trans. Antonia Nevill (Edinburgh: Edinburgh University Press, 2005), 59.

13. Daniel David Luckenbill, *Ancient Records, Assyria and Babylon*, vol. 2 (Chicago: University of Chicago Press, 1927), 162.

14. Garfinkle, 95.

15. Paul-Alain Beaulieu, "World Hegemony, 900–300 BCE," in *The Companion to the Ancient Near East*, ed. Daniel C. Snell (Malden, MA: Blackwell, 2005), 48–61, at 49.

CHAPTER 3

1. Kuhrt, vol. 2, 554.

2. P. Hulin, "New Urartian Inscribed Stones at Anzaf," in *Anatolian Studies* 10 (1960), 207.

3. Cited from Kuhrt, vol. 2, 556.

4. W. C. Benedict, "The Urartian-Assyrian Inscriptions of Kelishin," *Journal of the American Oriental Society* 81 (1961), 383.

5. Steven Holloway, *Aššur Is King! Aššur Is King! Religion in the Exercise of Power in the Neo-Assyrian Empire* (Leiden: Brill, 2002), 172 and 135–36.

6. "La formation de l'état urartéen," *Acta Anatolica* 37 (1987), 393–411.

7. Kuhrt, vol. 2, 393–94.

8. Pritchard, ANE, 191.

9. V. Scheil, *Recueil des travaux* 22 (1900), 157.

10. Pritchard, ANE, 19–20.

11. II Chronicles 2:7, 13, 14; cf. I Kings 7:13–51, NRSV.

12. Maria E. Aubet, *The Phoenicians and the West: Politics, Colonies, and Trade* (New York: Cambridge University Press, 1993), 217.

13. Pritchard, ANE, 231.

14. I Kings 4:21, NRSV.

15. I Kings 10:26–29, NRSV.

16. I Kings 3:9, NRSV.

17. I Kings 11:6, NRSV.

18. Isaiah 1:15–17, NRSV.

19. Amos 2:6–7, NRSV.

20. Amos 3:6, NRSV.

21. II Kings 23:3, NRSV.

22. Kuhrt, vol. 2, 469, 436.

CHAPTER 4

1. R. G. Kent, *Old Persian: Grammar, Text, Lexicon*, 2nd ed. (New Haven, CT: American Oriental Society, 1953), DNb.

2. A. K. Grayson, *Babylonian Historical-Literary Texts* (Toronto: University of Toronto Press, 1975), 84–85.

3. E. Weidner, "Hochverrat gegen Nebuchadnezzar II," *Archiv für Orientforschung* 17 (1954), 1–3.

4. Paul-Alain Beaulieu, "World Hegemony, 900–300 BCE," in *A Companion to the Ancient Near East*, ed. Daniel C. Snell (Malden, MA: Blackwell, 2005), 48–61, at 56.

5. Beaulieu, 57.

6. Mark Chavalas, ed., *The Ancient Near East: Historical Sources in Translation* (Malden, MA: Blackwell, 2006), 385.

7. Chavalas, ed., 394–95.

8. Chavalas, ed., 385.

9. Amos 9:14–15, NRSV.

10. Kuhrt, vol. 2, 598.

11. Chavalas, 428–29.

12. Kent, DNa.

13. "Behistun Inscription" 4.55, in *The Sculptures and Inscription of Darius the Great on the Rock of Behistûn in Persia*, trans. L. W. King and R. C. Thompson (London: British Museum, 1907).

14. Kuhrt, vol. 2, 669.

15. "The Passover Papyrus," in Pritchard, ANE, 278.

CHAPTER 5

1. Robin Waterfield, trans. (Oxford: Oxford University Press, 1998).

2. 9.114–115, Richmond Lattimore, trans.

3. 9.128, Richmond Lattimore, trans.

4. See Jean M. Davidson, "The Oikoumene in Ferment: A Cross-Cultural Study of the Sixth Century," in *Scripture in Context: Essays on the Comparative Method*, ed. Carl D. Evans et al. (Pittsburgh: Pickwick Press, 1980), 197–219, and Robert Bellah, "What Is Axial about the Axial Age?" in *Archives Européennses de Sociologie* 46 (2005), 69–87.

5. Kent, Plate 1.

6. Herodotus, *The Histories*, Preface; Waterfield trans.

7. *Histories*, Preface; Waterfield trans.

8. F. Jacoby, *Fragmente der griechischen Historiker* (Leiden: Brill, 1940), 1F1a; Marincola trans.

9. 7.8; Waterfield trans.

10. 7.135; Waterfield trans.

11. 7.139; Waterfield trans.

CHAPTER 6

1. Rex Warner, trans. (London: Penguin Books), 1954.

2. R. Potter, trans., in *The Complete Greek Drama*, vol. 1, ed. Whitney J. Oates and Eugene O'Neill (New York: Random House, 1938), lines 531–46.

3. Lines 401–5.

4. Lines 420–25, 429–36.

5. Lines 800–805.

6. *The Peloponnesian War* 1.23, Steven Lattimore, trans. (Indianapolis: Hackett Publishing Group, 1998).

7. 2.40–41, Rex Warner, trans.

8. 3.37–47, Rex Warner, trans. slightly modified.

9. 5.89, Rex Warner, trans.

10. 5.105, Rex Warner, trans.

11. 489, Walter Hamilton, trans. (London: Penguin, 1960).

12. *Alexander's Fortune and Virtue* I.329, in *The Hellenistic World from Alexander to the Roman Conquest*, ed. M. M. Austin (Cambridge: Cambridge University Press, 1981), selection #19, 36–37.

CHAPTER 7

1. Diodorus of Sicily 19.105.3–4; *The Hellenistic World from Alexander to the Roman Conquest: A Selection of Ancient Sources in Translation*, ed. M. M. Austin (Cambridge: Cambridge University Press, 1981), 56–57, slightly modified.

2. Arrian, *The Campaigns of Alexander*, trans. J. R. Hamilton (London: Penguin Books, 1971), 7.27.

3. Diodorus 19.61–62.2; cited from Austin, *Hellenistic World*, 55–56.

4. David Braund, "After Alexander: The Emergence of

World, ed. Andrew Erskine (Malden, MA: Blackwell, 2003), 19–34, at 26.

5. Diodorus 19.105.3–4.

6. Athenaeus, *Deipnosophistae* 6.253; cited from Austin, *Hellenistic World*, 64–65.

7. *The Greeks and the Irrational* (Berkeley: University of California Press, 1951), 242.

8. P. Lévêque, "La guerre à l'époque hellénistique," in *Problèmes de la guerre en Grèce ancienne*, ed. J.-P. Vernant (Paris: La Haye, 1968), 261–87, at 279.

9. Patrick Baker, "Warfare," in *Companion to the Hellenistic World*, ed. Erskine, 373–88, at 376.

10. See Erskine, *Companion to the Hellenistic World*, throughout.

11. See Peter Green, *Alexander to Actium: The Historical Evolution of the Hellenistic Age* (Berkeley: University of California Press, 1990), and Peter Green, *The Hellenistic Age: A Short History* (New York: Modern Library, 2007).

12. *Stoicorum veterum fragmenta* I, ed. H. von Arnim (Leipzig: B. G. Teubner, 1905), lines 15–25.

13. Carphyllides, *Anthologia Palatina* 7.260; cited from Green, *Alexander to Actium*, 388.

14. Nilakanta Sastri, *Age of the Nandas and Mauryas*, 2nd ed. (Delhi: Motilal Banarsidass, 1967), 79.

15. *Alexander the Great: A Reader*, ed. Ian Worthington (New York: Routledge, 2003), 166.

16. Diodorus 40.3, from Hecataeus, *Fragmente der griechischen Historiker* 264 F6; in *The Hellenistic World from Alexander to the Roman Conquest: A Selection of Ancient*

Sources in Translation, 2nd ed., ed. M. M. Austin (Cambridge: Cambridge University Press, 2006), 380.

17. I Maccabees 2:27, 49, NRSV.

18. See Erich Gruen, "Jews and Greeks," in *Companion to the Hellenistic World*, ed. Erskine, 264–279.

CHAPTER 8

1. "From the Tomb of the Scipios," in *Roman Civilization: Selected Readings* vol. 1., 3rd ed., ed. Naphtali Lewis and Meyer Reinhold (New York: Columbia University Press, 1990), 523.

2. 1.9, *The Early History of Rome*, trans. Aubrey de Sélincourt (Baltimore: Penguin, 1960).

3. 1.13, Sélincourt trans.

4. 1.13, Sélincourt trans.

5. 1.30, Sélincourt trans.

6. 6.18; *The Rise of the Roman Empire*, trans. Ian Scott-Kilvert (London: Penguin, 1979).

7. 1.3; Scott-Kilvert trans.

8. "From the Tomb of the Scipios," in Lewis and Reinhold, 523.

10. 1.32; Sélincourt trans.

CHAPTER 9

1. 1.278–79.

2. T. J. Cornell, *The Beginnings of Rome: Italy and Rome from the Bronze Age to the Punic Wars (c. 1000–264 B.C.)* (London: Routledge, 1995), 396.

3. Polybius, *The Rise of the Roman Empire* 1.1; trans. Ian Scott-Kilvert (London: Penguin Classics, 1979).

4. Erich S. Gruen, *The Hellenistic World and the Coming of Rome* (Berkeley: University of California Press, 1984). The review of the various arguments to follow here is based on his pages 5–7.

5. Polybius 18.46, Scott-Kilvert trans.

6. Polybius 29.27, Scott-Kilvert trans.

7. Zonoras, *Epitome* 9.30, cited from Lewis and Reinhold, 209.

8. Appian, *Roman History* 12.9, cited from Lewis and Reinhold, 215.

9. Plutarch, *Life of Cato the Elder* 23.23, from *Makers of Rome*, trans. Ian Scott-Kilvert (London: Penguin Books, 1965), 119–51.

10. Plutarch, *Life of Cato the Elder* 4, Scott-Kilvert trans.

CHAPTER 10

1. *Res Gestae Divi Augusti: The Achievements of the Divine Augustus*, trans. and ed. P. A. Brunt and J. M. Moore (London: Oxford University Press, 1967), section 34.

2. Lewis and Reinhold, vol. 1, 556.

3. Karl Galinsky, *Augustan Culture* (Princeton, NJ: Princeton University Press, 1996), 316.

4. Brunt and Moore, section 8.

5. Brunt and Moore, section 34.

6. Brunt and Moore, section 6.

7. *The History of the Decline and Fall of the Roman Empire*, vol. 1 (London: Penguin, 1994), 31.

8. G. Baker, ed., *Farming the Desert: The UNESCO Libyan Valley Survey* (Tripoli: Society for Libyan Studies/UNESCO, 1996).

9. *Satire* 10.78–81.

10. "A Discourse of Claudius in the Senate," in *Readings in Ancient History: Illustrative Excerpts from the Sources* vol. 2, ed. W. S. Davis (Boston: Allyn and Bacon 1912–1913), 187.

11. *The Origins and Deeds of the Goths* 1.25, trans. Charles C. Mierow (Princeton, NJ: Princeton University Press, 1908), 7.

12. H. Mattingly, trans., *Tacitus: The Agricola and the Germania* (London: Penguin Books, 1948), section 4.

CHAPTER 11

1. *To Rome* 104; cited from James H. Oliver, "The Ruling Power: A Study of the Roman Empire in the Second Century after Christ through the Roman Oration of Aelius Aristides," *Transactions of the American Philosophical Society* n.s. 43 (1953), pt. 4, 895–907.

2. Tacitus, *Agricola* 30 in *Tacitus: Agricola and Germany*, trans. A. R. Birley (Oxford: Oxford University Press, 1999).

3. *To Rome* 97–99.

4. 30; Mattingly trans.

5. 32; Mattingly trans.

6. 21; A. R. Birley trans.

7. Clifford Ando, *Imperial Ideology and Provincial Loyalty in the Roman Empire* (Berkeley: University of California Press, 2000).

8. *To Rome* 59–60.

9. *To Rome* 33.

10. 10.24, 10.34, 10.38, 10.40; cited from *Readings in Western Civilization 2: Rome: The Late Republic and Principate*, ed. Walter E. Kaegi and Peter White (Chicago: University of Chicago Press, 1986), 178–82.

11. Peter Garnsey and Richard Saller, *The Roman Empire: Economy, Society, and Culture* (Berkeley: University of California Press, 1987), 102.

12. *Agricola* 21; Birley trans.

13. Garnsey and Saller, 164.

14. Menander 377.19–28, in *Menander Rhetor*, trans. and ed. D. A. Russell and N. G. Wilson (Oxford: Clarendon, 1981).

15. *To Rome* 103.

16. *Natural History* 2.3; cited from John Bostock, trans. (London: Taylor and Francis, 1855).

17. *To Rome* 32.

18. 14.31.

19. *The Jewish War* 5.369, trans. G. A. Williamson (London: Penguin Books, 1981).

20. 6.230.

21. 7.315.

22. 18:12–13, NRSV.

23. 2, 21, 14.

24. Ando, *Imperial Ideology*.

25. *Histories* 4.74; in *As the Romans Did: A Sourcebook in Roman Social History*, ed. Jo-Ann Shelton (New York: Oxford University Press, 1988), 289.

CHAPTER 12

1. 103; in *Rome and Its Empire, A.D. 193–284*, ed. Oliver Hekster (Edinburgh: Edinburgh University Press, 2008), 110–12.

2. Cassius Dio, *Roman History* 77.15.2.

3. *Constitutio Antoniniana*, cited from David Potter, *The Roman Empire at Bay, A.D. 180–395* (London: Routledge, 2004), 138–39.

4. David S. Potter, *The Roman Empire at Bay, A.D. 180–395* (London: Routledge), 137.

5. A. H. M. Jones, *The Later Roman Empire, 284–602: A Social, Economic, and Administrative Survey*, vol. 1 (Norman: University of Oklahoma Press, 1964), 31.

6. *Paganism and Christianity, 100–425 C.E.: A Sourcebook*, eds. Ramsay MacMullen and Eugene Lane (Minneapolis, MN: Fortress Press, 1992), 225.

7. Acts 11:26.

8. Apuleius, *The Golden Ass*, trans. E. J. Kenney (London: Penguin Books, 1998), 11.12.

9. Pliny the Younger, *Letter* 10.97; cited from *As the Romans Did*, trans. Jo-Ann Shelton, 399–416.

10. "The Passion of Perpetua," from *The Acts of Christian Martyrs*, ed. Herbert Musurillo (Oxford: Oxford University Press, 1972).

11. *Apology* 38; cited from *A Source Book of Roman History*, ed. Dana C. Munro (Boston: D. C. Heath, 1904), 170.

12. *On the Crown* 13; cited from *The Ante-Nicene Fathers Vol. 3: Latin Christianity: Its Founder, Tertullian*, ed. Alexander Roberts and James Donaldson (New York, Scribner's, 1903), 101.

13. Eusebius, *Ecclesiastical History* 4.26.7ff; trans. Kirsopp Lake (Cambridge, MA: Harvard University Press, 1926).

14. *Epistle* 80.1.

15. *Fontes Iuris Romani Anteiustiniani*, ed. S. Riccobono et al., vol. 2, 2nd ed. (Florence: Barbera, 1940–1943), 544–89; translation cited from Stephen Williams, *Diocletian and the Roman Recovery* (New York: Methuen, 1985), 153.

16. *Codex Iustinianus* V, 5, 2; translation cited from Williams, *Diocletian*, 162.

17. Eusebius, *Ecclesiastical History* 10.9; cited from Eusebius, *The History of the Church from Christ to Constantine*, trans. G. A. Williamson (London: Penguin Books, 1965).

CHAPTER 13

1. Elishē, *History of Vardan and the Armenian War*, trans. Robert W. Thomson (Cambridge, MA: Harvard University Press, 1982), 63.

2. *To Rome* 81–82.

3. 2.11.5.

4. 105.

5. See Garth Fowden, *Empire to Commonwealth: The Consequences of Monotheism in Late Antiquity* (Princeton, NJ: Princeton University Press, 1993).

Introduction, Translation, and Historical Commentary with the Latin Texts of R. A. B. Mynors, ed. C. E. V. Nixon and B. S. Rodgers (Berkeley: University of California Press, 1994), 2.23.1.

7. *Against the Jews* 7.

8. *In Praise of Constantine* 120; cited from *In Praise of Constantine*, ed. H. A. Drake (Berkeley: University of California Press, 1977).

9. Fowden, *Empire*, 156.

10. *Life of Constantine* 4.15; cited from *A Select Library of Nicene and Post-Nicene Fathers. Volume 1: Eusebius*, ed. Henry Wace and Philip Schaff (Oxford: Parker and Company, 1890).

11. Theophylact Simocatta 4.13.7–8; from *History of Theophylact Simocatta: An English Translation with Introduction*, trans. and ed. Michael Whitby and Mary Whitby (Oxford: Oxford University Press, 1986).

12. *Histories* 7.8.3; cited from George Rawlinson, trans. (Hertfordshire: Wordsworth, 1999).

13. Kuhrt, vol. 2, 595.

14. *Christian Topography* 70–71; from *The Christian Topography of Cosmas, an Egyptian Monk*, ed. and trans. J. W. Crindle (London: Hakluyt Society, 1897).

15. 1.1.1; cited from Cyril Mango, *Byzantium: The Empire of the New Rome* (London: Weidenfeld and Nicolson, 1980), 88.

16. Richard N. Frye, "The Sassanians," in *The Cambridge Ancient History*, 2nd ed., vol. 12, ed. Alan K. Bowman,

Peter Garnsey, and Averil Cameron (Cambridge: Cambridge University Press, 2005), 461–480, at 463.

17. Cited from Peter Brown, *The World of Late Antiquity, A.D. 150–750* (London: Thames and Hudson, 1971), 166.

18. 6.2.1–2.

19. Ammianus Marcellinus 17.5.5; from *Ammianus Marcellinus with an English Translation* vol. 1, ed. and trans. John C. Rolfe (Cambridge, MA: Harvard University Press, 1982).

20. Muruj al-Dhabab; cited from R. C. Zaehner, *The Teachings of the Magi* (London: Allen, Unwin, and Macmillan, 1956), 85.

21. Frye, "The Sassanians," 474.

22. Elishē, *History of Vardan and the Armenian War*, 63.

23. 19.1.2; cited from Rolfe, trans., vol. 1.

24. 24.6.8; cited from Rolfe, trans., vol. 2.

25. "Letter of Constantius to the Ethiopians against Frumentius," in "In Defense of Constantius" 31, in *Nicene and Post-Nicene Fathers. Volume 4: St. Athanasius: Select Works and Letters*, ed. Philip Schaff and Henry Wace (Oxford: Parker and Company, 1892), 250.

26. Elishē, *History of Vardan and the Armenian War*, 124.

27. See Walter Kaegi, *Byzantium and the Early Islamic*

1992), 39–41.

CHAPTER 14

1. Oleg Grabar, *The Formation of Islamic Art* (New Haven, CT: Yale University Press, 1973), 60.

2. Theophylact Simocatta, in *History of Theophylact Simocatta: An English Translation with Introduction*, trans. and ed. Michael Whitby and Mary Whitby (Oxford: Oxford University Press, 1986), 4.13.7–8.

3. Kaegi, *Byzantium and the Early Islamic Conquests*, 39–40.

4. Theophanes, *Chronicle, The Chronicle of Theophanes Anni Mundi 6095–6305 (A.D. 602–813)*, trans. and ed. Harry Turtledove (Philadelphia: University of Pennsylvania Press, 1982), section 335–36.

5. Joshua the Stylite, *Chronicle* 64; in Irfan Shahîd, *Byzantium and the Arabs in the Sixth Century*, vol. 1 (Washington, DC: Dumbarton Oaks Research Library and Collection, 1995), 16.

6. Albert Hourani, *A History of the Arab Peoples* (Cambridge, MA: Harvard University Press, 1991), 16.

7. See Fred M. Donner, *Muhammad and the Believers* (Cambridge, MA: Harvard University Press, 2010).

8. Hourani, *History* 19.

9. Cited from Brown, *World of Late Antiquity*, 193.

10. Translation in Grabar, *Formation of Islamic Art*, 59–60.

11. Garth Fowden, *Qusayr Amra* (Berkeley: University of California Press, 2004), 198.

FURTHER READING

Some books have been useful throughout this study or in multiple chapters. Michael Mann's *Sources of Social Power*, Volume 1 (Cambridge: Cambridge University Press, 1986), provides the theoretical model for the whole text, even if much of the historical material is, naturally, dated by this point. The many volumes of *The Cambridge Ancient History* (Cambridge: Cambridge

edition of each volume. Specialist essays in M. T. Larsen (ed.), *Power and Propaganda: A Symposium on Ancient Empires* (Copenhagen: Akademisk, 1979), remain valuable for all periods of ancient history.

For the Near East specifically, Amélie Kuhrt's *The Ancient Near East c. 3000–330*, 2 vols. (London: Routledge, 1995), is an impressively detailed and engaging narrative that interweaves close analysis of primary sources. J. Sasson (ed.), *Civilizations of the Ancient Near East*, 4 vols. (New York: Scribner's, 1995), consists of detailed and well-regarded essays. The essays in Mark W. Chavalas (ed.), *Current Issues and the Study of the Ancient Near East*, Publications of the Association of Ancient Historians 8 (Claremont, CA: Regina Books, 2007), address many important questions and ongoing controversies with up-to-date information. Daniel C. Snell's (ed.) *A Companion to the Ancient Near East* (Malden, MA: Blackwell, 2005) contains a series of excellent overviews and focused chapters by specialists. Marc Van de Mieroop's *History of the Ancient Near East, ca. 3000–323 B.C.* (Malden, MA: Blackwell, 2004) is an impressively readable and remarkably detailed survey.

For the Greek and the Hellenistic period, see Sarah B. Pomeroy, Stanley M. Burstein, Walter Donlan, and Jennifer Tolbert Roberts, *Ancient Greece: A Political, Social, and Cultural History* (New York: Oxford University Press, 1999).

For the Roman period in general, J. Rich and G. Shipley (eds.), *War and Society in the Roman World* (London: Routledge, 1993) contains specialist articles for all periods of Roman history. The essays in G. W. Bowersock,

Peter Brown, and Oleg Grabar (eds.), *Late Antiquity: A Guide to the Postclassical World* (Cambridge, MA: Belknap, 1999), span the final three chapters here.

INTRODUCTION

Doyle, Michael W. *Empires.* Ithaca: Cornell University Press, 1986.

Eisenstadt, S. *The Political Systems of Empires.* New York: Free Press, 1963.

Ferguson, Niall. *Empire: The Rise and Demise of the British World Order and the Lessons for Global Power.* New York: Basic Books, 2003.

Garnsey, P. D. A., and C. R. Whittaker, eds. *Imperialism in the Ancient World.* Cambridge: Cambridge University Press, 1978.

Hall, John A., and Ralph Schroeder. *An Anatomy of Power: The Social Theory of Michael Mann.* Cambridge: Cambridge University Press, 2006.

Hardt, Michael, and Antonio Negri. *Empire.* Cambridge, MA: Harvard University Press, 2000.

Mann, Michael. *Incoherent Empire.* London: Verso, 2005.

Morris, Ian, and Walter Scheidel. *The Dynamics of Ancient Empires: State Power from Assyria to Byzantium.* Oxford: Oxford University Press, 2009.

Schumpeter, Joseph. *Imperialism and Social Classes.* Translated by Heinz Norden. New York: Augustus M. Kelly, 1951.

CHAPTER 1

Algaze, G. *The Uruk World System: The Dynamics of Expansion of Early Mesopotamian Civilization.* Chicago: University of Chicago Press, 1993.

Bryce, T. R. *The Kingdom of the Hittites.* Oxford: Clarendon, 1998.

Drews, Robert. *The End of the Bronze Age: Changes in Warfare and the Catastrophe ca.* 1200 B.C. Princeton, NJ: Princeton University Press, 1995.

Horden, Peregrine, and Nicholas Purcell. *The Corrupting Sea: A Study of Mediterranean History.* Malden, MA: Blackwell, 2000.

Horst, Klengel. *Syria:* 3000 *to* 300 B.C. Berlin: Akademie Verlag, 1992.

Moran, William L. *The Amarna Letters.* Baltimore: Johns Hopkins University Press, 1992.

Oppenheim, A. L. *Ancient Mesopotamia.* Rev. ed. Chicago: University of Chicago Press, 1968.

Postgate, Nichol. *Early Mesopotamia: Society and Economy at the Dawn of History.* London: Routledge, 1992.

Potts, D. T. *The Archaeology of Elam: Formation and Transformation of an Ancient Iranian State.* Cambridge: Cambridge University Press, 1999.

Rowlands, Michael J., Mogens Larsen, and Kristian Kristiansen. *Centre and Periphery in the Ancient World.* Cambridge: Cambridge University Press, 1987.

Ward, W. A., M. S. Joukowsky, and P. Astrom, eds. *The Crisis Year: The 12th Century* B.C. Dubuque, IA: Kendall Hunt, 1992.

CHAPTER 2

Boardman, J., et al., eds. *The Assyrian and Babylonian Empires and Other States of the Near East, from the Eighth to the Sixth Centuries* B.C. New York: Cambridge University Press, 1991.

Braudel, Fernand. *The Mediterranean and the Mediterranean World in the Age of Phillip II.* Translated by Siân Reynolds. 3 vols. Berkeley: University of California Press, 1976.

Carter, Elizabeth, and Matthew W. Stolper. *Elam: Surveys of Political History and Archaeology.* Berkeley: University of California Press, 1984.

Galil, Gershon. *The Lower Stratum Families in the Neo-Assyrian Period*. Leiden: Brill, 2007.

Holloway, Steven W. *Aššur Is King! Aššur Is King! Religion in the Exercise of Power in the Neo-Assyrian Empire*. Leiden: Brill, 2002.

Joannès, Francis. *The Age of Empires: Mesopotamia in the First Millennium* B.C. Translated by Antonia Nevill. Edinburgh: Edinburgh University Press, 2005.

Oded, B. *Mass Deportation and Deportees in the Neo-Assyrian Empire*. Wiesbaden: Reichert, 1979.

Parker, B. *The Mechanics of Empire*. Helsinki: Assyrian Text Corpus Project, 1998.

Saggs, H. *The Might That Was Assyria*. London: Sidgwick and Jackson, 1984.

Van Driel, G. *The Cult of Aššur*. Assen: Van Gorcum, 1969.

CHAPTER 3

Akkermans, Peter M. M. G., and Glenn Martin Schwartz. *The Archaeology of Syria: From Complex Hunter-Gatherers to Early Urban Societies (c. 16,000–300 BC)*. Cambridge: Cambridge University Press, 2003.

Aubet, M. E. *The Phoenicians and the West: Politics, Colonies and Trade*. Translated by Mary Turton. New York: Cambridge University Press, 1993.

Cline, Eric H. *From Eden to Exile: Unraveling Mysteries of the Bible*. Washington DC: National Geographic, 2007.

Cogan, M. *Imperialism and Religion: Assyria, Judah and Israel in the Eighth and Seventh Centuries* B.C.E. Society of Biblical Literature Monograph Series 19. Missoula, MT: Scholar's Press, 1971.

Joannès, Francis. *The Age of Empires: Mesopotamia in the First Millennium* B.C. Translated by Antonia Nevill. Edinburgh: Edinburgh University Press, 2005.

Liverani, Mario. *Neo-Assyrian Geography*. Rome: Herder, 1995.

Pitard, Wayne T. *Ancient Damascus: A Historical Study of the Syrian City-State from Earliest Times Until Its Fall to the Assyrians in 732* B.C.E. Winona Lake, IN: Eisenbrauns, 1984.

Zimansky, Paul E. *Ecology and Empire: The Structure of the Urartian State*. Studies in Ancient Oriental Civilization 41. Chicago: Oriental Institute of the University of Chicago, 1985.

CHAPTER 4

Barstad, Hans M. *The Myth of the Empty Land: A Study of the History and Archaeology of Judah during the "Exilic" Period*. Oslo: Scandinavian University Press, 1996.

Beaulieu, Paul-Alain. *The Reign of Nabonidus, King of Babylon 556–539* B.C. New Haven, CT: Yale University Press, 1985.

Boyce, Mary. *Zoroastrians, Their Religious Beliefs and Practices*. Boston: Routledge & Kegan Paul, 1979.

Briant, Pierre. *From Cyrus to Alexander: A History of the Persian Empire*. Translated by Peter T. Daniels. Winona Lake, IN: Eisenbrauns, 2002.

Brinkman, J. A. *Prelude to Empire: Babylonian Society and Politics, 747–626* B.C. Philadelphia: University of Pennsylvania Museum, 1984.

Choksy, J. K. *Triumph over Evil: Purity and Pollution in Zoroastrianism*. Austin: University of Texas Press, 1989.

Cook, J. M. *The Persian Empire*. New York: Schocken Brooks, 1983.

Dandamaev, M. A. *The Culture and Social Institutions of Ancient Iran*. Cambridge: Cambridge University Press, 1988.

Vanderhooft, David Stephen. *The Neo-Babylonian Empire and Babylon in the Latter Prophets*. Atlanta: Scholar's Press, 1999.

Vogelsang, W. J. *The Rise and Organisation of the Achaemenid Empire: The Eastern Iranian Evidence*. Leiden: Brill, 1992.

Wiesehöfer, Josef. *Ancient Persia from 550 BC to 650 AD* Translated by Azizeh Azodi. London: Tauris, 1996.

CHAPTER 5

Asheri, David, Alan Lloyd, and Aldo Corcella. *A Commentary on Herodotus Books I–IV.* Edited by Oswyn Murray and Alfonso Moreno. Oxford: Oxford University Press, 2007.

Briant, Pierre. *From Cyrus to Alexander: A History of the Persian Empire.* Translated by Peter T. Daniels. Winona Lake, IN: Eisenbrauns, 2002.

Emlyn-Jones, C. J. *The Ionians and Hellenism. A Study of the Cultural Achievements of the Early Greek Inhabitants of Asia Minor.* London: Routledge, 1980.

Evans, J. A. S. *Herodotus, Explorer of the Past. Three Essays.* Princeton, NJ: Princeton University Press, 1991.

Gorman, Vanessa B. *Miletos. The Ornament of Ionia: A History of the City to 400 B.C.E.* Ann Arbor: University of Michigan Press, 2001.

Green, Peter. *The Greco-Persian Wars.* Berkeley: University of California Press, 1996.

Hignett, Charles. *Xerxes' Invasion of Greece.* Oxford: Clarendon Press, 1963.

Hoglund, K. G. *Achaemenid Imperial Administration in Syria-Palestine and the Missions of Ezra and Nehemiah.* Atlanta: Scholars Press, 1989.

Lazenby, J. F. *The Defence of Greece, 490–479 B.C.* Warminster, United Kingdom: Aris and Phillips, 1993.

Miller, M. C. *Athens and Persia in the Fifth Century B.C.: A Study in Cultural Receptivity.* Cambridge: Cambridge University Press, 1997.

Morgan, Kathryn A. *Myth and Philosophy from the Presocratics to Plato.* Cambridge: Cambridge University Press, 2000.

O'Grady, Patricia F. *Thales of Miletus: The Beginnings of Western Science and Philosophy.* Aldershot, England: Ashgate, 2002.

Pritchett, W. K. *The Greek State at War.* 5 vols. Berkeley: University of California Press, 1975–91.

CHAPTER 6

Boedeker, D., and Kurt A. Raaflaub. *Democracy, Empire, and the Arts in Fifth-Century Athens.* Cambridge, MA: Harvard University Press, 1998.

Bosworth, A. B. *Conquest and Empire: The Reign of Alexander the Great.* Cambridge: Cambridge University Press, 1988.

Bosworth, A. B. *Alexander and the East: The Tragedy of Triumph.* Oxford: Oxford University Press, 1996.

Cohen, Edward E. *Athenian Economy and Society.* Princeton, NJ: Princeton University Press, 1992.

Hamel, D. *Athenian Generals: Military Authority in the Classical Period.* Leiden: Brill, 1998.

Hammond, N. G. L. *The Genius of Alexander the Great.* London: Routledge, 1997.

Hansen, Mogens H. *The Athenian Democracy in the Age of Demosthenes.* Oxford: Blackwell, 1991.

Heckel, Waldemar. *The Conquests of Alexander the Great.* New York: Cambridge University Press, 2008.

Kagan, Donald. *The Outbreak of the Peloponnesian War.* Ithaca, NY: Cornell University Press, 1969.

Kagan, Donald. *The Archidamian War.* Ithaca, NY: Cornell University Press, 1974.

Kagan, Donald. *The Peace of Nicias and the Sicilian Expedition.* Ithaca, NY: Cornell University Press, 1981.

Kagan, Donald. *The Fall of the Athenian Empire.* Ithaca, NY: Cornell University Press, 1987.

Meiggs, Russell. *The Athenian Empire.* Oxford: Clarendon Press, 1972.

Miller, M. C. *Athens and Persia in the Fifth Century* B.C.: *A Study in Cultural Receptivity*. Cambridge: Cambridge University Press, 1997.

Worthington, Ian. *Alexander the Great: Man and God*. Harlow, United Kingdom: Longman, 2004.

CHAPTER 7

Bar-Kochva, B. *Judas Maccabeus: The Jewish Struggle against the Seleucids*. Cambridge: Cambridge University Press, 1989.

Baumgarten, A. I. *The Flourishing of Jewish Sects in the Maccabean Era: An Interpretation*. Leiden: Brill, 1997.

Bongard-Levin, G. M. *Mauryan India*. London: Stosius/Advent Books, 1986.

Burkert, Walter. *Ancient Mystery Cults*. Cambridge, MA: Harvard University Press, 1987.

Erskine, Andrew, ed. *Companion to the Hellenistic World*. Malden, MA: Blackwell, 2003.

Gera, Dov. *Judaea and Mediterranean Politics, 219 to 161 B.C.E.* Leiden: Brill, 1998.

Green, Peter. *Alexander to Actium: The Historical Evolution of the Hellenistic Age*. Berkeley: University of California Press, 1990.

Green, Peter. *The Hellenistic Age: A Short History*. New York: Random House, 2007.

Gruen, E. S. *Heritage and Hellenism: The Reinvention of Jewish Tradition*. Berkeley: University of California Press, 1998.

Karttunen, K. *India and the Hellenistic World*. Helsinki: Finnish Oriental Society, 1997.

Kuhrt, Amélie, and Susan Sherwin-White. *Hellenism in the East: The Interaction of Greek and*

California Press, 1987.

Levine, Lee. *Judaism and Hellenism in Antiquity: Conflict or Confluence?* Seattle: University of Washington Press, 1998.

Martin, Luther. *Hellenistic Religion: An Introduction*. New York: Oxford University Press, 1987.

Sherwin-White, Susan, and Amélie Kuhrt. *From Samarkhand to Sardis: A New Approach to the Seleucid Empire*. Berkeley: University of California Press, 1993.

Sievers, J. *The Hasmoneans and Their Supporters: From Mattathias to the Death of John Hyrcanus I*. Atlanta: Scholars Press, 1990.

Tritle, Lawrence A., ed. *The Greek World in the Fourth Century: From the Fall of the Athenian Empire to the Successors of Alexander*. London: Routledge, 1997.

Walbank, F. W. *The Hellenistic World*. Cambridge, MA: Harvard University Press, 1981.

Wallace, R. W., and E. M. Harris. *Transitions to Empire: Essays in Greco-Roman History, 360–146 B.C. in Honor of E. Badian*. Norman: University of Oklahoma Press, 1996.

CHAPTER 8

Beard, M., J. North, and S. Price. *Religions of Rome*. Cambridge: Cambridge University Press, 1998.

Cornell, T. J. *The Beginnings of Rome: Italy and Rome from the Bronze Age to the Punic Wars (c. 1000–264 B.C.)*. London: Routledge, 1995.

David, Jean-Michel. *The Roman Conquest of Italy*. Translated by Antonia Nevill. Malden, MA: Blackwell, 1997.

Gruen, E. S. *Culture and Public Identity in Republican Rome*. Ithaca, NY: Cornell University Press, 1992.

Harris, W. V. *War and Imperialism in Republican Rome 327–70 B.C.* Oxford: Oxford University Press, 1979.

Keppie, L. *The Making of the Roman Army: From Republic to Empire*. Totowa, NJ: Barnes and Noble, 1984.

Lancel, Serge. *A History of Carthage.* Translated by Antonia Nevill. Oxford: Blackwell, 1995.

Lintott, A. *The Constitution of the Roman Republic.* Oxford: Clarendon, 1999.

Lomas, K. *Rome and the Western Greeks, 350 B.C.–A.D. 200: Conquest and Acculturation in Southern Italy.* London: Routledge, 1993.

MacNamara, E. *The Etruscans.* London: British Museum Publications, 1990.

Nicolet, Claude. *The World of the Citizen in Republican Rome.* Translated by P. S. Fall. Berkeley: University of California Press, 1980.

Rosenstein, Nathan, and Robert Morstein-Marx. *A Companion to the Roman Republic.* Malden, MA: Blackwell, 2006.

Smith, C. J. *Early Rome and Latium. Economy and Society c. 1000–500 B.C.* Oxford: Oxford University Press, 1996.

CHAPTER 9

Badian, E. *Publicans and Sinners: Private Enterprise in the Service of the Roman Republic.* Ithaca: Cornell University Press, 1972.

Beard, Mary, and Michael Crawford. *Rome in the Late Republic: Problems and Interpretations.* London: Duckworth, 1999.

Dyson, Stephen L. *Creation of the Roman Frontier.* Princeton, NJ: Princeton University Press, 1987.

Gruen, E. S. *The Hellenistic World and the Coming of Rome.* Berkeley: University of California Press, 1984.

Gruen, E. S. *Studies in Greek Culture and Roman Policy.* Leiden: Brill, 1990.

Harris, W. V. *War and Imperialism in Republican Rome 327–70 B.C.* Oxford: Oxford University Press, 1979.

Kallet-Marx, R. M. *Hegemony to Empire: The Development of the Roman Imperium in the East from 148 to 62 B.C.* Berkeley: University of California Press, 1995.

Lintott, A. *The Constitution of the Roman Republic.* Oxford: Clarendon, 1999.

Mouritsen, H. *Plebs and Politics in the Late Roman Republic.* Cambridge: Cambridge University Press, 2001.

Nippel, W. *Public Order in Ancient Rome.* Cambridge: Cambridge University Press, 1995.

Rosenstein, Nathan. *Rome at War.* Chapel Hill: University of North Carolina Press, 2003.

Syme, Ronald. *The Roman Revolution.* Oxford: Clarendon, 1939.

Taylor, Lily Ross. *Party Politics in the Age of Caesar.* Berkeley: University of California Press, 1949.

Wallace, R. W., and E. M. Harris. *Transitions to Empire: Essays in Greco-Roman History, 360–146 B.C. in Honor of E. Badian.* Norman: University of Oklahoma Press, 1996.

CHAPTER 10

Ando, Clifford. *Imperial Ideology and Provincial Loyalty in the Roman Empire.* Berkeley: University of California Press, 2000.

Brunt, P. A. *Roman Imperial Themes.* Oxford: Clarendon, 1990.

Burns, Thomas S. *Rome and the Barbarians, 100 B.C.–A.D. 400.* Baltimore: Johns Hopkins University Press, 2003.

Cunliffe, B. *Greeks, Romans, and Barbarians: Spheres of Interaction.* New York: Methuen, 1988.

Duncan-Jones, R. *Structure and Scale in the Roman Economy.* Cambridge: Cambridge University Press, 1990.

Erdkamp, Paul. *The Grain Market in the Roman Empire.* Cambridge: Cambridge University Press, 2009.

Galinsky, Karl. *Augustan Culture: An Interpretive Introduction*. Princeton, NJ: Princeton University Press, 1996.

Galinsky, Karl. *The Cambridge Companion to the Age of Augustus*. Cambridge: Cambridge University Press, 2005.

Garnsey, P., and R. Saller. *The Roman Empire: Economy, Society, and Culture*. London: Duckworth, 1987.

Isaac, B. *The Limits of Empire: The Roman Army in the East*. Oxford: Clarendon, 1990.

Laurence, R., and J. Berry. *Cultural Identity in the Roman Empire*. London: Routledge, 1998.

Lintott, A. *Imperium Romanum: Politics and Administration*. London: Routledge, 1993.

Luttwak, E. N. *The Grand Strategy of the Roman Empire from the First Century A.D. to the Third*. Baltimore: Johns Hopkins University Press, 1976.

Mackay, Christopher S. *Ancient Rome: A Military and Political History*. Cambridge: Cambridge University Press, 2004.

Mattern-Parkes, Susan. *Rome and the Enemy: Imperial Strategy in the Principate*. Berkeley: University of California Press, 1999.

Nicolet, Claude. *Space, Geography, and Politics in the Early Roman Empire*. Ann Arbor: University of Michigan Press, 1991.

Osgood, Josiah. *Caesar's Legacy: Civil War and the Emergence of the Roman Empire*. Cambridge: Cambridge University Press, 2006.

Wells, Peter. *The Barbarians Speak: How the Conquered Peoples Shaped the Roman World*. Princeton, NJ: Princeton University Press, 1999.

Whittaker, C. R. *Frontiers of the Roman Empire. A Social and Economic Study*. Baltimore: The Johns Hopkins University Press, 1994.

CHAPTER 11

Ando, Clifford. *Imperial Ideology and Provincial Loyalty in the Roman Empire*. Berkeley: University of California Press, 2000.

MacMullen, Ramsay. *Paganism in the Roman Empire*. New Haven, CT: Yale University Press, 1981.

Overman, J. Andrew, and Andrea Berlin. *The First Jewish Revolt: Archaeology, History, and Ideology*. London: Routledge, 2002.

Price, J. P. *Jerusalem under Siege: The Collapse of the Jewish State 66–70 CE* Leiden: Brill, 1992.

Richardson, P. *Herod: King of the Jews and Friend of the Romans*. Columbia: University of South Carolina Press, 1996.

Rives, James B. *Religion in the Roman Empire*. Malden, MA: Blackwell, 2007.

Saller, R. P. *Personal Patronage under the Early Empire*. Cambridge: Cambridge University Press, 1982.

Turcan, R. *The Cults of the Roman Empire*. Oxford: Blackwell, 1996.

Webster, G. *Boudica: The British Revolt against Rome A.D. 60*. Totowa, NJ: Rowman and Littlefield, 1978.

CHAPTER 12

Ando, Clifford, and Jörg Rüpke, eds. *Religion and Law in Classical and Christian Rome*. Stuttgart: Steiner, 2006.

Barnes, T. D. *Constantine and Eusebius*. Cambridge, MA: Harvard University Press, 1981.

Barnes, T. D. *The New Empire of Diocletian and Constantine*. Cambridge, MA: Harvard University Press, 1982.

Cameron, Averil. *The Later Roman Empire, A.D. 284–430*. Cambridge, MA: Harvard University Press, 1993.

Corcoran, Simon. *The Empire of the Tetrarchs: Imperial Pronouncements and Government A.D. 284–324*. New York: Clarendon, 1996.

Ferguson, E. *Backgrounds of Early Christianity*. Grand Rapids, MI: William B. Eerdmans, 1987.

Hekster, Oliver, ed. *Rome and Its Empire*, A.D. *193–284*. Edinburgh: Edinburgh University Press, 2008.

Lenski, Noel, ed. *The Cambridge Companion to the Age of Constantine*. Cambridge: Cambridge University Press, 2006.

Lieu, S. N. C., and D. Montserrat. *Constantine. History, Historiography and Legend*. London: Routledge, 1998.

MacMullen, Ramsay. *Christianizing the Roman Empire*. New Haven, CT: Yale University Press, 1984.

Millar, Fergus. *The Roman Near East*, 31 B.C.–A.D. 337. Cambridge, MA: Harvard University Press, 1993.

Potter, D. S. *The Roman Empire at Bay*. London: Routledge, 2004.

Stark, Rodney, *The Rise of Christianity: How the Obscure, Marginal Jesus Movement Became the Dominant Religious Force in the Western World in a Few Centuries*. San Francisco: HarperCollins, 1997.

Wilken, R. L. *The Christians as the Romans Saw Them*. New Haven, CT: Yale University Press, 1984.

Williams, Stephen. *Diocletian and the Roman Recovery*. New York: Methuen, 1985.

CHAPTER 13

Blockley, R. C. *East Roman Foreign Policy: Formation and Conduct from Diocletian to Anastasius*. Leeds: Cairns, 1992.

Brown, Peter. *The World of Late Antiquity*. London: Thames and Hudson, 1971.

Burns, Thomas S. *Barbarians within the Gates of Rome: A Study of Roman Military Policy and the Barbarians, ca. 375–425 A.D.* Bloomington: Indiana University Press, 1994.

Cameron, Averil. *The Mediterranean World in Late Antiquity*, A.D. *395–600*. London: Routledge, 1993.

Clark, Gillian. *Christianity and Roman Society*. Cambridge: Cambridge University Press, 2004.

Dignas, Beate. *Rome and Persia in Late Antiquity: Neighbors and Rivals*. Cambridge: Cambridge University Press, 2007.

Drake, Hal. *Constantine and the Bishops: The Politics of Intolerance*. Baltimore: Johns Hopkins University Press, 2000.

Evans, J. A. S. *The Age of Justinian: The Circumstances of Imperial Power*. London: Routledge, 1996.

Fowden, Garth. *Empire to Commonwealth: Consequences of Monotheism in Late Antiquity*. Princeton, NJ: Princeton University Press, 1993.

Goffart, Walter. *Barbarian Tides: The Migration Age and the Later Roman Empire*. Philadelphia: University of Pennsylvania Press, 2006.

Graham, Mark W. *News and Frontier Consciousness in the Late Roman Empire*. Ann Arbor: University of Michigan Press, 2006.

Greatrex, Geoffrey. *Rome and Persia at War*, 502–532. Leeds: Francis Cairns, 1998.

Halsall, Guy. *Barbarian Migrations and the Roman West*, 376–568. Cambridge, MA: Cambridge University Press, 2007.

Heather, Peter. *The Fall of the Roman Empire: A New History of Rome and the Barbarians*. Oxford: Oxford University Press, 2006.

Lee, A. D. *Information and Frontiers: Roman Foreign Relations in Late Antiquity*. New York: Cambridge University Press, 1993.

Odahl, Charles. *Constantine and the Christian Empire*. 2nd ed. London: Routledge, 2010.

Mitchell, Stephen. *A History of the Later Roman Empire*, A.D. *284–641: The Transformation of the Ancient World*. Malden, MA: Blackwell, 2007.

Walker, Joel. *The Legend of Mar Qardagh: Narrative and Christian Heroism in Late Antique Iraq*. Berkeley: University of California Press, 2006.

Ward-Perkins, B. *The Fall of Rome and the End of Civilization*. Oxford: Oxford University Press, 2005.

Whittow, M. *The Making of Byzantium, 600–1025*. Berkeley: University of California Press, 1996.

CHAPTER 14

Berkey, Jonathan. *The Formation of Islam: Religion and Society in the Near East, 600–1800*. Cambridge: Cambridge University Press, 2003.

Bonner, Michael. *Aristocratic Violence and Holy War: Studies in the Jihad and the Arab-Byzantine Frontier*. New Haven, CT: American Oriental Society, 1996.

Cameron, Averil. *The Byzantine and Early Islamic Near East: States, Resources and Armies*. Princeton, NJ: Darwin Press, 1995.

Cook, Michael. *Commanding Right and Forbidding Wrong in Islamic Thought*. Cambridge: Cambridge University Press, 2000.

Crone, Patricia. *Meccan Trade and the Rise of Islam*. Princeton, NJ: Princeton University Press, 1987.

Donner, Fred M. *The Early Islamic Conquests*. Princeton, NJ: Princeton University Press, 1981.

Donner, Fred M. *Muhammad and the Believers*. Cambridge, MA: Harvard University Press, 2010.

Grabar, Oleg. *The Formation of Islamic Art*. New Haven, CT: Yale University Press, 1973.

Hawting, G. R. *The Idea of Idolatry and the Emergence of Islam: From Polemic to History*. Cambridge: Cambridge University Press, 1999.

Hodgson, M. *The Venture of Islam: Conscience and History in a World Civilization. Volume 1: The Classical Age of Islam*. Chicago: University of Chicago Press, 1974.

Kaegi, Walter. *Byzantium and the Early Islamic Conquests*. Cambridge: Cambridge University Press, 1992.

Kennedy, Hugh. *The Prophet and the Age of the Caliphates: The Islamic Near East from the Sixth to the Eleventh Century*. 2nd ed. London: Longman, 2004.

Madelung, Wilfred. *The Succession to Muhammad: A Study of the Early Caliphate*. Cambridge: Cambridge University Press, 1998.

Shahid, Irfan. *Rome and the Arabs*. Washington, DC: Dumbarton Oaks, 1984.

Shahid, Irfan. *Byzantium and the Arabs in the Sixth Century*. Washington, DC: Dumbarton Oaks, 1995.

INDEX

96475822R00216

Made in the USA
Middletown, DE
30 October 2018